Taking My Country Back

Taking My Country Back

Volume 2 of 2 Volumes

*By Treason from Within,
Liberals have stolen our Heritage. . . .
Now we have a Plan to take our Country Back!*

R. Dean Chrisco

Total Fusion Press
Strasburg, Ohio

Taking My Country Back
Published by Total Fusion Press
PO Box 123, Strasburg, OH 44680
www.totalfusionpress.com

Copyright © 2014 by Vineyard Way, LLC

All rights reserved. No part of this book may be reproduced or transmitted in any form or by any means, electronic or mechanical, including photocopying and recording, or by any information storage and retrieval system, without permission in writing from the publisher.

ISBN (paperback): 978-0-9903100-7-5
ISBN (hardcover): 978-0-9903100-5-1

Library of Congress Control Number: 2014956402

Cover Design by Sarah Kuehn
Interior Design by Kara Starcher
Edited by Linnette Hayden

Published in Association with Total Fusion Ministries, Strasburg, OH.
www.totalfusionministries.org

24 23 22 21 20 19 18 17 16   2 3 4 5

Dedication

To Kristi

To Beth

Praise for this book – Volume 2

In these scholarly and informative books, Dean presents a thought-provoking recipe for reclaiming America's heritage of liberty and self-governance. I may not agree with all the solutions proposed here, but our author definitely nails the problems he identifies from our history as well as our Framer's dreams for America. This is a must read for any Conservative.

Senator Brian D. Nieves

26th District Missouri State Senator, 2010 – Present;
Former Majority Whip in the Missouri House of Representatives, 2002 - 2010

Praise . . .

America needs a medical desk reference help book to fix government and our sick culture. This is it! Within these pages, our author provides insight for the healing of America. In today's America, freedom seems cheap and is taken for granted; the gift of liberty granted by our Framers is traded for bobbles and empty promises. People in American don't even know what being American really means anymore. Trading self-reliance for reliance on government, we have people who rely on the same government for cradle to grave provisions. Kennedy's quote of "Ask not what the country can do for you but what you can do for the country" has fallen on deaf ears. It is time that we give of ourselves to save our country. It is time to give until it hurts or if we continue down our path we will hurt until we give in. And it is time to read this must read provided by an author for any citizen who loves freedom. And it's in language you will understand.

Representative Bryan E. Spencer,

63rd District, Missouri House of Representatives, 2012-Present;
Public School Teacher, Grades 7-12, Certified in
Social Science, Behavior Disorder, Learning Disabilities,
Taught Government and U. S. History 1990-Present.

Praise . . .

This is the most important book to come across my desk in the last twenty-five years — it tells the story of America. This work warns us that unless we make a drastic course correction, America as the Founding Fathers established it, will be lost forever. Dean's impeccable research and dazzling combination of biography and detailed history reminds us in an inspirational way about who we are, what has happened to us along the way, and who we can be once again. In my mind, this is the biggest literary contribution in decades that displays American history with our true heritage. Every conservative, Christian, child, or person who loves America should consider this a "must read" on their bookshelf for handy reference.

Rev. Joseph R. Finnell

*California business owner; Senior Pastor;
Past President, Southern California Ministerial Association*

Praise . . .

Scholastic aptitude test scores are on the decline. U.S. History is being rewritten. Abortion is the litmus test for all things Congressional. What was right is now wrong. What was wrong is now right. Situational ethics has replaced moral absolutes. Everything is relative. No one is culpable. With the abundance of lawyers, society is more litigious than ever.

A transformation from within is attempting to remove the Bible, and Constitution from the American culture. The needle on the moral compass is spinning "right" and "left", rather than "up" toward God. A noticeable decline is obvious, as America continues to make God insignificant. With a pen as a substitute for a surgeon's scalpel, Dean diagnoses the "disease" that threatens our nation. He exposes the symptoms of this "cancer." He prescribes a course of action that produces a healthy outcome. This is a must read if our country is to avoid a post mortem.

Fred Zimmermann
Retired school administrator with 34 years' experience in education

Praise ...

In his seminal work, Dean charts the way to the beginning of a turnaround in the direction our country is headed. *"Where Did My Country Go?"* provides a comprehensive, articulate and thoughtful account of our country's history and the events and influences that have impacted its evolution. Against this backdrop, our author correctly analyzes how we arrived at our current state, addresses the fundamental issues facing our country today and points the way to positive change for our nation and our way of life. This is essential reading for anyone concerned about the future of our country.

Charles "Chuck" MacNab

Past Vice President and President, American Airline Pilots Association (All airlines); Vice Chairman of the International Council of Airline Pilots Association (All airlines); Past Member of the New York City Aviation Development Council; Editor and Publisher, Riteon.org

Praise . . .

FINALLY! A writer who writes the TRUE history of America! If you have read any other book, on the history and degradation of this American civilization, you wasted your time — You should have read this one first. The treatise contained in this book, volumes 1 & 2, should be in every classroom in America. Our author serves as a guide, to help move the American people away from the precipice where nationally, we now stand. If we follow Dean's roadmap, we can still find that America can be saved, with our best days ahead.

Nicholas Watts
Entrepreneur, business owner, and community leader

Table of Contents

Foreword		xv
Author's Note		xvii
Introduction		xix
Chapter 1	Our American History Is Being Rewritten for Us	1
Chapter 2	When Governments Become Evil and Destructive	57
Chapter 3	Destruction by Betrayal of the Free Press	117
Chapter 4	Destruction by Bad Barristers and Bad Court Verdicts	143
Chapter 5	The Trouble with the "Great Pretender"	159
Chapter 6	The Truth about: Discrimination, Prejudice, the New and Old Racists, Slavery and Reparation	229
Chapter 7	The History of Labor Unions Is Their Trouble	265
Chapter 8	The Trouble with the Church	291
Chapter 9	Where Do We Start?	311
Chapter 10	Listen to the Past Speak to the Future	323
Chapter 11	Find the Servant-Driven Leaders	339
Chapter 12	Reforming and Starting Over	353
Chapter 13	Defending Our "Shining City on the Hill"	367
Appendices		381
Notes		386

Foreword

RECENTLY I READ IN *THE WASHINGTON Times* — the Friday, August 8, 2014 edition reporting: "Americans' trust in government has plummeted to an all-time low . . . " A 2014 CNN poll similarly delivered more critical and sad news: **just 13 percent of Americans say the government can be trusted** to do what is right always or most of the time. A slightly larger percent say the government can be trusted "some of the time," and about 10 percent say they "never" trust the government for anything, according to the same poll. "The number who trust the government all or most of the time has sunk so low that it is hard to remember that there was ever a time when Americans routinely trusted the government," CNN Polling Director Keating Holland said.

If you are one of those Americans asking yourself where has my country gone, what is happening here? Then you must read this book to understand how we have drifted from our core principals which are still a beacon to the rest of the world even as we let them slip away. This is the biography of America. It is a must read for every citizen to understand where we came from, the causes of our current problems, and how we the people can reverse the dangerous path we are on. Like a biography, as you walk through the pages of this book, your soul will feel the joy of mountain top experiences long forgotten; the pain from the dark valleys our nation has traversed. You will become reacquainted with an old friend whom you haven't seen for decades, a friend who will reveal to you stories no longer told, stories forgotten, a true antiquity of our heritage. You will learn about our ancestor's forbearing and enduring patience; it took 163 years from the Jamestown Settlement in 1607 to the Incident on King Street in 1770 (Boston massacre) to become angry enough for colonists to revolt and become Americans. There were other important and forgotten secrets of our lineage, struggles of our birth, searching of our youth, indiscretions of our adolescence, the rise to a beacon on a hill. As the overwhelming success Alex Haley's Roots demonstrated, people yearn and need to know their heritage, so today Americans have a yearning to know their roots as a Nation. Not understanding of our heritage has left a deep emptiness in the collective soul of our country, allowing us to drift ever closer to the precipice of destruction from within, deviating from the sure path of a harmonious journey set forth by our founding fathers.

We are still on that journey as Americans. We must know where we began and understand the course laid out by the Forefathers. As an American over the age of 60 who travels the U.S. frequently I can feel the palpable concern of our citizens. We feel lost as a people, disoriented as a nation. This much discontent is a symptom of a serious problem with many causes we must understand. This book will help us to see in depth through the haze and the shadows to see clearly the detailed causes and rediscover our restorative course for the nation.

A "dream" of America is still alive within the breasts of our countrymen we need to revisit the dream as our Forefathers envisioned it so that we may rise to live the dream again. The dream and ideology which has become clouded in our own country still inspires peoples around the world, it is sometimes more vibrant and strong in peoples of other countries which have never experienced our freedom. They dream the dream of our Forefathers that we seem to have lost along the way. As I write this forward in August 2014, I have just returned from a two week business trip to China. I was there to meet people who were interested in applying for EB-5 visas offered by the US to foreign nationals who are willing to invest $1 Million dollars which will create 10 American jobs. The program was created by congress in the 1990's to help create jobs in America through foreign investment I found that all of the citizens I met still see America as a "shining beacon on the hill", the American dream still intact. Of the 13,000 or so EB-5 visas granted every year to foreign nationals almost 8,000 are to Chinese. Why do so many want to immigrate to America? Because the ideology and government devised within our constitution has remained a beacon to the rest of the world.

The author of this book has been gifted with a life of sound Christian morality, the finest university education, tremendous business experience, people skills and management in some of the largest corporations in America. Dean has also been employed in other countries by these businesses to use his skills in attracting top talent to the team. These combined experiences along with his wonderful clear writing skills give him an objective view of the extraordinary gift our founding fathers have given us. His passion seen through his words are given to reawaken that spark within us, fanning the oxygen of "these truths we hold to be self-evident" on the tinder of our present understanding to refuel the fire of liberty and justice for all.

"With the ancient is wisdom; and in length of days understanding." (Job 12-12)

Paul Lambi

US Nuclear Submarine Veteran; Four-Term Mayor of Wentzville, Missouri;
Co –Founder of Graduate America Priority One

Author's Note

NO SINGLE PERSON IS A SELF-MADE man; that is especially true of me. The 17th Century poet and cleric, John Donne, knew that too and the connection we all have with others. He wrote, "No man is an island, entire of itself; everyman is a piece of the Continent . . . " in Meditation 17 of his "Devotions upon Emergent Occasions" published in 1624. While he wrote within the context of his extreme illness, I write from a framework of the great debt of gratitude I owe to more than a few. Each has been an incredible encouragement to me along my pathway and in the penning of the book I privately refer to as "Country."

From the days of contemplation, preparation, and the eventual writing, I became only more aware of my unworthiness, how little I know, and my need for the One Who sustains me — Jesus of Nazareth. To Him, this work is dedicated.

My conscience and teacher through life has been my Mom. Though illness took her from this life over four decades ago, her loving, and at times, very stern words have lasted a lifetime in my ears and mind; they still help me remember where my "out-of-bounds" lines are, as I call them. To each who knew her in life, their independent narrative seemed always phrased with the same, identical words; "My, she was an angel." That description falls short, but does come close.

Second, a great encourager to me was a friend nicknamed "Doc", who prodded and pushed me for years to write again. I am thankful for his importunity. A myriad of others, both friends and family, have encouraged me. . . . Neighbors Nancy, Joel, and Rob as well as Jim, Charlie, Derek, Gary, Gary Dean, Paul, Patty, Gloria, Dave, and Etcyl . . . they have provided support in unique ways encouraging me to stay the course.

A mammoth encourager has been Nick. He deserves more than honorable mention, as early on he became so excited when reading an early draft of the message of this treatise. In many ways, he has become the son that I never had. A many-talented business leader, he is best known for what a few call his "Midnight Gun Emporium."

My high school English teacher's lessons on grammar and syntax haunted me during this writing. Editors, Fred and Elaine worked hard to alleviate my nightmares that this book would exit its printing looking similar to Lord Timothy Dexter's work of the 19th Century. His book contained only 8,847 words; many of them misspelled, and there were no punctuation marks of any kind. In spite of the fact he was forced to give away his book for free at first because of its bad grammar, it still became so popular that eight editions were printed and all were sold out. He did print a separate edition having a page containing 13 lines of nothing but punctuation marks with the instruction, "Distribute them as you please."

My hope is this writing will help in restoring the America I remember. My family, and friends should inherit an America that is freer, healthier, and more responsible than the one my generation is leaving behind. Here's hoping for the restoration and safeguarding of this magnificent gift, America, which they will receive.

— Dean

Introduction

THOUGH WE AMERICANS HAVE THE NOTORIOUS habit of looking back in time, we often fail to see the proverbial forest because of the trees. We tend to forget both who we are and much of the arduous trek our ancestors have made. We tend to hide those national events, scars, and memories which seemed evil or brought pain. We have elevated other memories, those historical moments which spoke of our genius, our fortitude, our nobility. Framed carefully in what we define as the "good ol' days," we tend to recall life when it seemed like a stroll in the park, a Broadway play without any villain or evil drama. The truth is, when we look at ourselves in the historical mirror, we must face the reality of many villains, the toll that they and their drama have taken, the wars, the killing, the senseless attacks upon our freedom, and even now, the treason against our national heritage and even the scenery for quite some time.

In my first volume, I offered for your consideration what should be the nation's retrospective affection for childhood heroes such as George Washington — his extraordinary life and achievements — revitalizing a demoralized group of colonies into a young vibrant nation. He and the other Framers were intelligent and daring folks, having built something marvelous for each of us. It is called America. Many great men and women followed building enterprises and institutions upon that liberty; thankfully many of them have in their dying moments passed along their legacies so we could all experience even more freedom. Witness however in that volume, through the last 150 years, the many attacks that have chiseled away at the foundation of this marvelous experiment and mighty nation called The United States of America. We witnessed our failures that were manifold and manifest. We saw and experienced the sway which Humanism, Marxism, and other treasonous acts have taken from our integrity. Yet many who do not understand historical events fail to see them within their proper context. Thus they miss both the appropriate lessons and the associated "danger signs" which come with taking particular actions. We definitely suffer from what some may call "presentism" — the delusion of portraying, explaining, or interpreting historical events from only the perception of current-day experiences and attitudes. What we face is the need for a triumphant campaign to rescue us from this lazy entrapment.

In this volume, we will face more of our intellectual errors. Especially we will come in contact with those voices from the present and the past that will call us back to a proper perspective to help in the restoration of this nation to rise from the ashes like the fabled Phoenix.

Witness Abraham Lincoln, Winston Churchill, and Ronald Reagan gentlemen all, and each snubbed by their parties at critical junctures during their decades; yet observe their diplomacy, their concessions, and their retreats into solitude. Thankfully they did not remain in their own isolationism, but arose to become remarkable leaders. And what follows I am convinced is not a people to succumb to treachery or any loss on the battlefield. I surmise that our people long now for strong leadership, ones whose positive outlook, inner drive, and amiability conceals a rugged toughness and individualism that few can recognize or properly analyze. We hunger to listen and follow these individuals who have iron in their words and especially in their souls to help lead us out of our "wilderness years" of wandering aimlessly, foolishly, and recklessly under Barack Obama. It is a rocky and uphill climb since traditional American virtues seem to no longer inspire or animate a majority of the electorate. Virtues such as liberty, hard work to earn what you take home, free enterprise, personal initiative and aspirations to moral greatness, should be entrenched in our behaviors and culture. In spite of those flaws, we must save "our shining city on a hill."

This book is intended to be a primer and a guide to real-world conservative choices, as well as a meditation on the underpinnings and foundation which made America so great. It speaks to the joys and practicality of faith in a Divine Healer, the idealism we should all hold in our hearts, and the knowledge that Christian beliefs, democracy, as well as free enterprise are the best hope for America. Hopefully, the book is arriving, fortuitously, at a moment in time when Conservatives and Christians are in much need of an inspiriting examination of what can yet turn out to be our finest hour.

"The time has come to turn to God and reassert
our trust in Him for the healing of America...
our country is in need of and ready
for a spiritual renewal..."

— Ronald Reagan

40th President of the United States of America

Chapter One

Our American History Is Being Rewritten for Us

PRIOR TO THE BIRTH OF MY first daughter, the full tour of emotions starting with excitement, then anxiety, some fear, the fatigue, and ultimately the joy that came over the family and me through the hours of my wife's hard labor in the hospital, as I waited for and finally welcomed my little girl's arrival. As a first-time expectant father — young and still myself wet behind the ears — so many thoughts swirled in my head. When there was the fatigue I felt while regularly looking at a clock that seemed to run more slowly each hour. Would she be born okay? Would her mother be okay? Why is this taking so long? Is something wrong? Where is the doctor? Why don't they tell me something? In those days expectant fathers weren't in the birthing room with mom as they are now, rather we were made to wait "alone" in what seemed to be a far-removed and tiny waiting room in an out of the way place. It was never visited by hospital staff at any time that I could tell, but it was equipped with magazines; the most recent ones were about three-years old. My thought was that if I die here, it may be a year or so before they find the body, when they bring another load of magazines to the room. When my second daughter was born, the emotions were exactly the same, but I was a little more assured that time, having been through this process 16 months before. Though a different hospital, the waiting room seemed the same with the same three year old magazines.

I loved holding my little girls in my arms when they were born. What a tender time to speak softly to them and express my love that would only grow. With my first it was the fear of breaking her; she seemed so tiny, though she weighed nearly nine pounds at birth. And the million or so questions that were going through my mind as I held her, praying she would be well and grow up having a childhood filled with fun, learning, and lots of carefree days. It was when she was approximately two months old that we were alerted there was a problem. It was her left hip, and it turned out to be something that happened in her breech birth. It had to be remedied quickly so as to avert more problems later. The result was fourteen surgeries before she was three-years old. A different challenge or problem with each operation it seemed, ranging from something very minor to one occasion when we almost lost her in surgery.

At age ten, she was accepted at Shriner's Hospital. Recalling our first trip to Shriner's when she was admitted as a patient to be there for eight weeks. My naïveté led me down a road of thoughts dwelling on the sins that must be in my life, pushing God I was certain on a trek to punish me and my daughter. Wrapped in self-pity, I helped in getting her checked into her room. Later I planned on going to a local restaurant to sit and reflect on all that was happening. Opening the door, preparing to go into the hall, there was no way I could have been prepared for what awaited me there.

In the blink of an eye, I was standing in what seemed to have become a warzone hospital. It was full of all these adorable, laughing, and obviously resilient little children of various ages who were in need of various levels of medical help. Some seemed to be in desperate need of surgery, and in what seemed like a personal flashback, I thought for a moment they were survivors of a bomb blast. One little girl, very gaunt, could not walk at all; her bones had a strange disease. I was told she had never taken a step before. She was 13 years old. Another boy stood at a pinball machine gently fingering the buttons. He wore a half-body cast; extending down his arms to his wrists; his shoulders had been deformed and he was in the middle of a number of surgeries to repair them. Another boy was in a standing motorized cart, leaning back but in a slightly upright position; but his bones were too weak to hold his weight. There were many others with hands, feet, forearms or legs that needed obvious surgery. Some were missing parts of limbs and were in various stages of casts and bandages. Then zipping by me in full laughter came was a little boy lying belly down in a cobbled-together flatbed wagon. I learned later his backbone could not hold him up, so he was forever captive to a wagon or cart if he wanted to be mobile, since his spine was actually on the outside of his body. And he was playing and laughing as he sped down the hall and around me. A nurse noticed my ghostly pale tint and asked if I was okay. I know my bottom lip was quivering with emotion as I told her that I had never seen a sight like these children before. I was in shock and simply stunned. I remember clearly telling her, "I thought we had huge medical problems, but they are nothing compared to many of the other childrens' problems." She told me that was a common observance of parents and she tried to reassure me that the children were going to receive the best care possible. My thoughts went quickly from "God, why is this happening to us," to "Oh my God, we have no problems compared to many of these sweet, and innocent little kids."

I remember once back in our room trying to compose myself, excusing myself to drive to the drug store, only to use the time to drive a few blocks away, park the car out of sight, and cry my eyes out for all those children. I remember praying that day for God to heal every child in the world. I even expressed the desire to do nothing with my entire life but to go and touch these children and have God restore their bodies through my touch. If He would only use me in that manner, I promised to go very quietly and secretly go and help these kids. That would be enough for me to do with my life. My heart seemed to heave within my chest in seeing all the innocents in such torturous pain as their little lives were being rewritten by serious illnesses. My mind hauntingly held the memory of seeing their little eyes and the eyes of their parents telling the story of their pain. Their history was being rewritten into a different story from what they had all once hoped for each of them.

Flashbacks into that world still hit me unannounced and well up tremendous emotion in me as I am sure others feel, who have witnessed similar scenes.

Today, similar emotions, fear, and anger are in my heart and mind; this time for witnessing a revisionist history being rewritten for our country. Like those children and their parents back in that hospital so many years ago, the scenes from our nation are not so different, yet so opposite of what I and others had ever imagined they could be. Our younger generations lives are being used as scrolls upon which is being rewritten the scaring illnesses of Liberal Progressivism, Fascism, the Marxism that is shredding what was once a great nation.

The Leftist minds have schemed for a century to change this country, to transform it away from any set moral codes. The avenue they chose to accomplish their mission: rid the land of the Christian message and the Bible. They literally became the devil's own. Once that rule book was gone, the moral codes would be shut down, but so would our integrity and voices of reason. Their scheme included a game plan of bullying people to eventually shut up, surrender and accept their idiom. And they have taken some pathological and hypocritical paths to do this. One was a national town hall meeting they called with the agenda to discuss bullies.

Leftists have made it a regular practice of bullying people who disagree with them for at least the last 150 years. That makes it certainly ironic that on March 10, 2011, President Barack Hussein Obama led a White House conference on what was packaged as the biggest plague to hit America since the Great Depression — that of bullies taking over our streets. If it were not so sad, it would be humorous to witness the biggest bully, amongst the biggest gang of bullies to hit America since sliced bread, standing before America lecturing citizens about bullies. Of course their own bullying technique has taken on actions such as editing, attacking certain structural cores of our country, and rewriting them. All the while they lecture us on bullying; a harangue that sounds like fingernails on a chalkboard.

The "Anti-Religious" Bullies

Most progressive historians [as an example] have wanted for decades to secularize our founders. Take this quote from W.E. Woodward. He wrote that "The name of Jesus Christ is not mentioned even once in the vast collection of Washington's published letters."[1]

Unless someone "calls their bluff," Progressives will continue to speak such tripe unabated. They want a fight. We need to give them one. Anybody who has read some of George Washington's writing knows he mentions God and divine providence. If interested, it is not too difficult to do just a little more research finding there were also times in which he mentions Jesus Christ. For example, when George Washington wrote to the Delaware Indian Chiefs (June 12, 1779) he said: "You do well to wish to learn our arts and ways of life, and above all, the religion of Jesus Christ. These will make you a greater and happier people than you are. Congress will do everything they can to assist you in this wise intention."[2]

There are many other samples among Washington's written materials from which to choose. For example, a well-worn, handwritten prayer book found among Washington's personal writings after his death had the name "Jesus Christ" appearing sixteen times.[3]

Some of the best documented cases of historical revision were provided by the work of Paul Vitz and funded by the U.S. Department of Education. He notes that "One social studies book has thirty pages on the Pilgrims, including the first Thanksgiving. But there is not one word (or image) that referred to religion as even a part of the Pilgrims' life."[4]

Another textbook said that "Pilgrims are people who take long trips." They were described entirely without reference to religion. One reference said the Pilgrims "wanted to give thanks for all they had" but never mentioned that it was God to whom they wanted to give thanks.[5]

Historical revisionism is a sad attribute of American public education today. The revisionist work has grown exponentially through the years and frankly has become unacceptable to the point that it has taken on a posture of "religious bullying" that is commonplace today. And this bullying type of revisionist activity is being led by Liberal or so-called "Progressive" leadership within the school system. The designed results of this that students are not getting the true story of America; nothing close to the truth. Often, references of important persons who were critical to our nation's' founding, freedom, and success as a leader in the world, are left out of teaching, especially when Christianity was a central part of that person's declarations in life. To deny students the truth is not only shameless, it is a form of treason. Whenever a teacher is not a Christian, or does not have warm feelings toward those with religious views, or when the same teacher does not like free enterprise, it is not up to them or their leaders to withhold these facts when teaching. Children deserve to be taught the truth, rather than have lies presented to them about the glories of socialism simply because the teacher is a socialist.

While this is previously plowed ground from a portion of Volume 1, one should be aware that in today's American public education experience, there have been so many continuous Leftist revisions of our history that any conservative ideal or event from the past has been literally blotted out by Liberal Progressives. They have revised or completely removed from history textbooks these truths, so students will never be able to read or study them under their biased tutelage. For those conservatives who grew up in the 50s and 60s, it is more than disquieting to learn these facts about modern education and see the direction toward which our country is being hauled or dragged, especially for the past 30 years. The agenda of these "Liberal Progressives" which has been in recent years led by the Clintons, Barack Obama, George Bush to some extent have taken their toll. It is easily seen in the millennial generation. The moral, ethical, and political footing in our society has been purposely dragged to the Left, away from the foundation of truth, away from fixed moral codes, and away from our Constitution. I am prepared to call it treason. It is a treason of transforming our nation into a third-world banana republic. It is a treason that erodes the very sovereignty of U.S. Citizens through lies, fake agendas, bad laws, and massive debt. It certainly is a treason that has eroded the morality that has been a foundation of our society.

The new revised history of our nation, even now continuing to be rewritten, denies our true legacy establishing Socialist Marxist rule as a substitute for our Constitution. Our country is changing into something we do not like; an evil and ugly trademark. It carries a sad story showing how amiable Americans have acquiesced to the Progressive movement. Over time, our strength and abilities have diminished. We have become a nation willing to settle for citizens who are losing their possessions, now huddled in poverty, depending on the government for virtually everything. This abandons the bright hope once given us, and what was once the common American experience of days gone by.

A true Liberal, Progressive, Marxist, Leninist, Communist, or whatever title they choose for identification has one powerful attribute. They never give up on their plans. NEVER! They may postpone them for a time, but reviewing what has transpired over the last century, proves they never give up. They are ever so patient in reaching their goals. Some of their goals already reached are:

Anti-First Amendment Freedom — Freedom of the Press

To call ourselves "the Land of the Free," now we must use a mask to hide the new American identity. Or we have to negate the past 25 years and operate totally on the reputation from distant times past. That reputation has certainly tanked over the past few years. At one time, possibly during the time of Reagan, we were touted as being Number 1, Numero Uno, the "Big Cheese, or Head Honcho" perched atop the heap of all nations, for providing freedom to its citizens, including members of the press. By 2012, the US had dropped to 20th place on this world-wide list. Last year, in 2013, we dropped another 27 places; that is in only one year, and is now ranked as 47th in the world as a country for allowing that same measured freedom of the press and to citizens. That means there are now 46 other nations that stand above us in supplying the writers, editors and members of press corps freedom to report what they see, without fear of reprisal.

One reason cited for this "arresting drop" is that now our government is actually arresting certain members of the press corps for truthful but unkind coverage of certain regime activities. How about them apples?! To put it in the vernacular of a Fascist, or the current regime, "Crackdown was the word of the year in 2011. Never has freedom of information been so closely associated with democracy. Never have journalists, through their reporting, vexed the enemies of freedom so much. Never have acts of censorship and physical attacks on journalists seemed so numerous. The equation is simple: the absence or suppression of civil liberties leads necessarily to the suppression of media freedom. Dictatorships fear and ban information, especially when it may undermine them."[6] They are quietly arresting them when they do report on the links with the Obama Administration to some organized chaos. "The United States (47th) also owed its fall of 27 places to the many arrests of journalists... more than 25 were subjected to arrests and beatings at the hands of police who were quick to issue indictments... "[7]

The arrests came with stealth and strong-armed threats. Reminiscent of Hitler's brown shirts, the only thing that seemed missing were the letters "SD." You may not have heard the statistic. Either that or possibly you may be in denial thinking it impossible. However, the data is there, it's known globally, and it is undeniable. Not much press has been offered about it, since fear of retribution is felt among the press corps. So far the arrests have served their purpose of frightening the major media outlets from even reporting on them. To date, the only ones that have mentioned the arrests, to my knowledge thankfully are, Glenn Beck on the Blaze Network, also Dana Loesch, and Rush Limbaugh with his EIB Network.

Government Bullying, Monitor-Style

Going hand in hand with the Fascist or Marxist move of curtailing the freedom of Americans was an announcement made by the Obama Administration in February 2014. They stated as a "matter of fact" they were going to put a monitor in the various newsrooms around the country. This is a direct violation of the First Amendment, which the administration knows, but is doing regardless. Members of the Federal Communications Commission (FCC) are to be placed in every major news media source to monitor those outlets, all "to ensure fairness of what news is presented." This move should be worth another 47 point drop to the bottom of all nations, joining those regimes of the past: Stalin, Hitler, Mussolini, and Mao as last in freedom of the press. Of course on the same scale in today's world, the Muslim Brotherhood sits in the basement, or last in freedom of the press. It was also announced the FCC will target print news, radio news, and television news. The Marxist, Leninist, Hitleresque type of regime cannot stand for there to be any negative reporting of their activities and failures. The inferiority complex of our leadership should be visible. The progressive desire to be in control of everything including the printed word and even the thoughts of its subjects is too surreal. It also speaks of the horrible nature of those who claim to love this country, and what they really feel about it. While some have been speculating about the intent of an extensive FCC survey of U.S. newsrooms, regulating and collecting data on the

CHAPTER ONE — OUR AMERICAN HISTORY IS BEING REWRITTEN FOR US

news media goes entirely unreported as the former "diversity czar" has spelled out.

Details of this plan have been made known because an FCC commissioner has come forward with the story. Ajit Pai, this commissioner at the FCC revealed what he called "a brand new Obama Administration program that he fears could be used in 'pressuring media organizations into covering certain stories." The strategy under which this will be operated involves a rouse by the government in pretending to investigate why more black minorities are not in an equity position with more of the news organizations. The threat of discrimination or a charge of racism is enough to get the media to submit. Nobody will oppose that for fear of being branded in the public square. We should force the government to tell the truth which is this: money is the reason why many minorities are not in ownership positions in broadcasting. That has nothing to do with racism or discrimination. The biggest barrier to anybody owning anything is money! The claim they make is a rouse. Our current leadership will invent a victim if possible — they did it here in claiming racism, hiding the real problem and taking over what is being said.

The FCC, at the behest of the Obama Administration, proposed an initiative to thrust the Obama Administration into newsrooms across the country. With its 'Multi-Market Study of Critical Information Needs,' or CIN, the agency plans to send researchers to grill reporters, editors and station owners about how they decide which stories to run. A field test in Columbia, S.C., was scheduled to start the ball (or in this case, the effort) rolling. "The purpose of the CIN, according to the FCC, is to ferret out information from television and radio broadcasters about 'the process by which stories are selected' and how often stations cover 'critical information needs,' along with 'perceived station bias' and 'perceived responsiveness to underserved populations.'" Said differently, Obama and the Leftists have developed a formula for what they believe 'the free press' should be covering. Government is therefore sending monitors into newsrooms across America to peer over the backs of press personnel as they make editorial decisions. History shows that every major repressive regime of the modern era began with an attempt to intimidate and control the press. An interesting note — that move was almost always preceded by government takeover of health care.

Over-reaching even farther, the same governing Liberals say the FCC will now have regulatory authority over newspapers. There is no Constitutional authority for this. The explanation given is the government wants to ensure newspapers are not biased in serving "minority populations." What an announcement! There is not much to do with the newspaper business to bring it in line with Obama regs. Most of the newspapers in this country are so far left leaning they will support any ideas that wear the Marxist brand. History shows of course that when the First Amendment was written there was no radio and TV. In those days, there was only printed mass communication which was done through the newspapers, pamphlets, etc. The Framers did not want to regulate newspapers. They wanted "freedom of the press." The federal government issues licenses because the airwaves are considered public; broadcasters are granted permission to use them for several types of programs. A typical station will do music, news, ballgames, infomercials, political events, auctions, talk, etc. But still, in the news division of those broadcast outlets, the First Amendment applies.

And the First Amendment applies with newspapers; they are totally off-limits, and yet the commissioner the FCC says they are "now expanding the bounds of regulatory powers to include newspapers, which it has absolutely no authority over, in its new government monitoring program." (Source: The Rush Limbaugh Radio Program, February 19, 2014)

Every dictator and regime that has been tyrannical in the modern era has begun by taking over health care and control of the media. That was first on Hitler's priority list; Stalin too. The Marxist dictatorships always follow the same script. They want to control what is said. Dictators always are insecure enough that they want no competition and they sure do not want a story covered in a way that shows their deceit. In health care, insurance was the same; dictators always want total control over everybody in the country.

Bullying through the Fairness Doctrine

These two words are favorites of Progressive Liberals today: Fairness Doctrine. To them it simply means whatever is reported on TV or radio as opinion must be in agreement with Leftist opinion on any subject. It is really designed to rid the radio waves of conservative talk shows.[8]

In 1987, Ronald Reagan was able to get rid of this Fairness Doctrine. Obama is leading a huge resurgence in reenacting it. To do so he masks the real purpose under what he called "encouraging minority ownership of media centers." Anyone opposing the Fairness Doctrine today would be viewed through the lens of this new moniker and immediately and called a racist. Southside Chicago politics in its new personage of Obama will gag or persecute anyone who questions what he is doing. According to National Review, the monitor in stations will have greater responsibility that is far more sinister than first thought, more than just looking at minority ownership. A portion of the story shows National Review has uncovered,

> "...the existence of the FCC's new 'Multi-Market Study of Critical Information Needs,' a study that would send FCC researchers (monitors?) into newsrooms across the nation to determine, among other things, whether news organizations are meeting citizens 'actual' as opposed to 'perceived' information needs. As designed, the study empowers researchers to not only ask a series of questions of news staff, it also provides (in pages 10 and 11) advice for gaining access to employees even when broadcasters and their Human Resources refuse to provide confidential employee information. The Obama administration FCC is abusing its regulatory authority by attempting to discern the inner work-

ings of American newsrooms. And what will these FCC monitors ask [both management and staff] when they do get access?... 'What is the news philosophy of your station? Who is your target audience? How do you define critical information that the community needs? How do you ensure that community gets this critical information? Have you ever suggested coverage of what you consider a story with critical information for your customers (viewers, listeners, readers) that was rejected by management?'" [9]

Placing a monitor inside a local TV or radio station or within a network newsroom or newspaper editorial office asking these questions, could retrieve loads of information which can be turned around and used as ammunition on the respective media outlet. In days long gone by, the terminology used for this information was termed "public ascertainment in local stations." Quick interviews and just simple question of the neighborhood gas station owner, or his mechanic, even the local restaurant manager would reveal what community leaders think important because the airwaves are public. "How does community input influence news-coverage decisions?" [10]

Questions which station owners and managers will be asked range from, "What are the demographics of the news management staff? What are the demographics of the on-air staff? What are the demographics of the news-production staff?" Here is just a sample of the questions for corporate general managers, news directors, and editors: "What is the news philosophy of your station? Who else in your market provides news? Who are your main competitors? How and why are you restricted in what you try to say?"

There is a First Amendment clause devoted solely to freedom of the press. The government has no business asking any of these questions.... "How much does your station air every day? Is the news produced in house, or is it provided by an outside source, as in a syndicated radio show? Do you employ news people? How many reporters and editors do you employ? Do you have any reporters or editors assigned to topic beats? If so, how many, and what are the beats?" [11]

Old fashioned journalism does not exist in this country any longer, thanks to Leftists such as Nancy Pelosi, Harry Reid, Barack Obama, and many of the editorial staffs at major newspapers and news stations. It is long gone. The Leftist agenda has replaced the real news with a mixture of lies, half-truths, and campaigning for the Socialist goals. Their attempts at news actually resemble some of the soap operas from the 1970s. The only thing missing is the organ music. Bottom line, the media purpose of the shows in New York, Washington, and Los Angeles is to advance the Democrat Party agenda.

Just as our freedom is being threatened by the manic soap opera, freedom of communication is now being threatened by the announcement of this FCC survey. There are few news outlets which were not already in Obama's hip pocket before his announcement. But thankfully when the news broke through those few independent and conservative sources, there was a huge uproar over the campaign by Obama and his team. Mr. Obama responded by announcing a pull back, stating they would not do it. However, this is most likely a patient stall tactic. It is clear his regime thought they could get away with doing this. To have pulled it off, Hugo Chavez would have been proud; he made a habit of doing such things regularly.

"The government has no place pressuring media organizations into covering certain stories," FCC Commissioner Ajit Pai wrote. But staying true to their reputation, Democrats, Socialists, and Communists will not give up on their idea of bringing the misery of collectivism into this country. They are relentless, they will cheat, steal, and lie to get control of what news is broadcast. Good conservative people must awaken, smell the proverbial coffee, see the details of the treasonous activity, and then respond to these Leftists. As Edmond Burke once said, "For evil to triumph, good men must do nothing."

Liberal Bullying Intends to End Democracy

With the release of his 2014 budget for review, Obama delivered a speech saying it represented "the end of austerity." Whatever else might be said, it is enough to say that no person who believes in capitalism would make such a statement. And yet, there he was; the supposed leader of the free world. Upon review of the statement, it should be no shock for an analytical thinker. Obama has for years been speaking of reparation, of punishing those who worked hard and were able to get ahead. Some conveniently forgot that he said, "You didn't build that; you didn't make that happen." Following that and other similar statements in following speeches, he then proceeded as the president who "led" in unprecedented spending; enough to compile more national debt than all past presidents combined. That's right; he piled up more debt than 240 years' worth of presidents! And while he did that on his liberal "high horse" he has been confusing terms; the word "austerity" with the term "private industry," but his intentions are clear. By the time he is finished, there will be less than a handful of commodities to which he has not destroyed the availability. That will include petrochemical energy, money and freedom itself.

The rest of the world has been trying to get their hands around the idea of austerity. The term is misunderstood and yet bandied about to support many causes. One Socialist group considers it worse than any venomous evil stating it causes recessions and economic inequality. Others claim it is the tonic to solve the puzzles of tough economic times. Most of those from the millennial generation for example have no benchmark against which to examine such a term as austerity. That generation in Greece and other countries used the word as their reason to demonstrate and riot. Some are using the word to shield their true intentions. Obama is one of those. He loves the Keynesian approach to any economic challenges; his borrow, spend, borrow, spend mentality demonstrates his rejection of austerity. Obama, a

CHAPTER ONE — OUR AMERICAN HISTORY IS BEING REWRITTEN FOR US

classic Socialist, and his Keynesian approach become a propellant launching us further toward economic calamity. Obama rejects cutbacks in taxes and spending, the best saviors for economic woes. (See Figure 1)

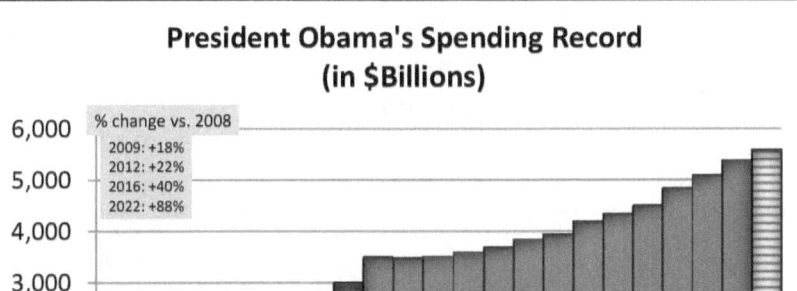

Figure 1

Source: Budget of the U.S. Government FY2013, Historical Tables, Table 1.1.
Analysis of the President's 2013 Budget. Congressional Budget Office.

There are different opinions offered for the excessive government spending which we will explore below. Mr. Obama and the Liberal politicians say borrow and spend, borrow and spend while exponentially growing the central government. An alternate approach says we should run government on a cash basis. It says if income falls short of expenses, cut salaries, lay some government workers off, and if needed sell off government assets such land holdings. There are other opinions or approaches that offer combinations of the two. With all these approaches floating around, we should have a reality check on what works and what does not.

Obama said in his 2008 campaign and early in his first term he would cut the deficit in half. He said that because George W. Bush was a spender like none the country had seen up to that point. However, each of the budgets Obama presented for 2009, 2010, 2011, and 2012 were guilty of being an unprecedented 75 percent higher than those budgets of 2000-2007. The budget of 2011 had the notoriety of being voted down by the Senate 99-0. Further, Obama's spending was unprecedented in that he presided over trillion-dollar deficits for four consecutive years of his first term. This four year leap in spending was financed with a $5 trillion increase in the national debt. Stacked on top were stimulus plans. 2009 stimulus was pledged by Obama for those "shovel-ready" jobs. Actually, the stimulus was a payoff for Obama support. Of the money spent in Wisconsin for example, a swing state, 80 percent of that money went to public-sector unions. Those jobs were already locked in. Right-to-work states received $265 less per person than states which were unionized. States with the preponderance of representatives being Democrats received nearly $475 more per person. (See Figure 2)

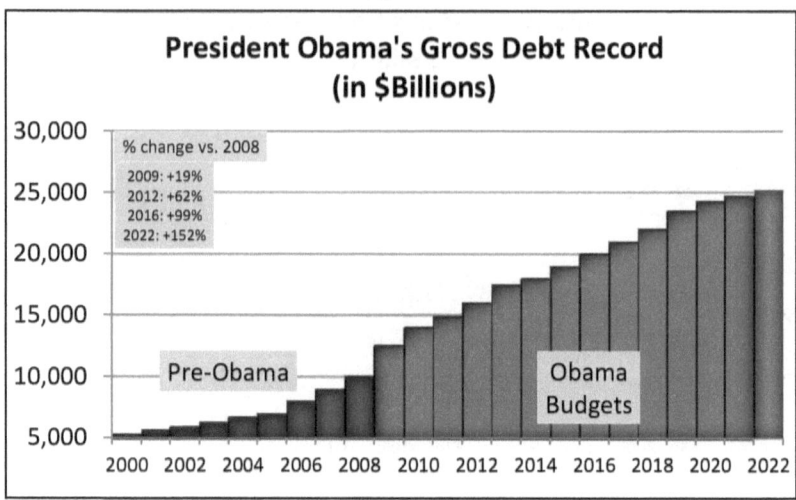

Source: Budget of the U.S Government FY2013, Historical Tables, Table 7.1
Analysis of the President's 2013 Budget. Congressional Budget Office.

Rich Democrat donors also received payback grants. Some of the top recipients: George Kaiser a $535 million and largest stakeholder in Solyndra — that company ended in bankruptcy! Google's founders Larry Page and Sergey Brin, also large stakeholders in Tesla Motors — they received a half-billion to help keep the startup company alive. Though teetering near default, they do hold a little promise of the future. Then there is NRG Solar owners Steve Cohen and Warren Buffet — they received big bucks from Obama. Both were supporters. The list goes on. . . . Fisker Automotive, guaranteed $529 million by Obama. They manufacture only in Finland. There was Enerl, supposedly creating 1,400 jobs with the $118.5 in stimulus — bankrupt in 2012. Beacon Power received $43 million — bankrupt. Energy Conversion Devices received $13.3 million in stimulus — bankrupt. Abound Solar — $400 million in stimulus — bankrupt. Amonix Solar — $15.4 million in stimulus — lasted 14 months before going bankrupt. Cogentrix — $90.6 million in stimulus — it took them 3 years to get their project off the ground — No bankruptcy yet. Bright Source Energy — received $1.9 Billion in stimulus when they were $1.8 billion in debt. Each job they created cost $1 million. Evergreen Solar — received $125 million and — filed for bankruptcy in 2011. The list goes on. For sake of space, let us just say all this stinks because they all failed. It is a great mistake to judge policies and programs by their stated intentions; rather we should judge them by their results. And now, the 2013 and 2014 budgets have established debt levels that go off the chart. No austerity here; just wild spending!

Most every family has to make serious and painful budget decisions at some point. This may require slashing, cutting, or delaying certain expenditures. Life gets tough; when you get old, it gets tougher. What is required is a truthful look at circumstances, money that is being brought in or not brought it, and then re-budgeting based upon revenue. When a family member loses a job, budgets must be recalculated with many potential cuts. But inside our government, the only thing they seem to discuss is the end of austerity, or facing life seriously. Since Progressive liberals came into control of government, there is a mutated version of austerity that gets global press on a daily basis. It is promoted by professors of economy at Ivy League Universities, the International Monetary Fund (IMF), and most of all by the current occupant of the White House. The "brand of austerity" they teach is a cutback in government services, while hiring more government personnel and simultaneously raising taxes. This only hamstrings taxpayers and workers already stressed out as government has become so addictive and terribly top-heavy due to corruption. Obama having joined forces with questionable banks has generated profiteering by corrupt bankers but also some very violent demonstrations. Together he wishes to build a corporate government which will never cut budgets but will always grow even in severe downturns in the economy.

Thankfully, there is an old, reliable philosophy of economics which stands in contradiction to the Obama and Keynesian stimulus approach. It is the Austrian School which teaches true "austerity." That consists of cutting "government" budgets, "government" spending, laying off "government" employees, reducing "government" salaries and "government" benefits, and if necessary selling "government" assets; all to pay debt or to cut expenses. Never should private citizens pay the cost of poor management by politicians, no matter what the IMF dictates.

Cutting costs of and reducing the size of the centralized government represents not the terror and horror of madmen as reported by Socialists, but simple common sense; it is called austerity. Ironically, it is exactly what the same Socialists expect of an individual or family when they have their income sliced. A perfect example is a single wage earner who, when he loses his job, will drastically cut his budget — the thermostat is turned down in winter and up in summer, no more movies, expensive restaurants, no more big vacations until a new revenue stream is established by a new job. This is exactly what should be happening in government when money is tight. It is called living within their means. That is austerity at its finest.

None of the Democrats and only a percentage of the Republicans in government have a clue on how to cut budgets, trim expenses, or cut back to basic services. In their vocabulary, cutting back to essential services means they will remove security guards from the border, close national parks, and cut back on veteran services at the V.A. Our federal government has grown up over the past few decades like a spoiled child; it knows only how to spend money, not make any. If they were to accept a "Libertarian" style of legislating, they would focus on their main tasks for which they were hired; keep the borders secure and melt the national debt.

But liberals, especially Barack Obama, love to point to Europe as the model for the U.S. to follow. While Europe has had deadly financial problems, in fact, most politicians in Washington and popular media commentators authoritatively claim that the cause of those problem is austerity, i.e., they claim the government is not spending enough.

To clear the air, a simpler and thorough explanation of what is really happening needs to be aired. The simplest manner through which to understand these complicated national and international issues is to put them on a more personal level. For example, a neighbor man who wisely saved part of his income each month would surely be considered austere. Or, said differently he would not spend more than he makes. Looking at Europe, touted by Leftists as examples of financial responsibility, a quick review shows not one nation in the "Eurozone" spends less than they collect in revenue. Personalizing this again for deeper understanding, let us suppose another neighbor spent 6 percent more in 2010 than his income that year, he spent 17 percent more than his income in 2011, spent 38 percent more than his income in 2012, and in 2013 he spent another 30 percent more than he made that year. We would not call this neighbor's spending habits sustainable; he certainly would not be considered austere. This is a precise example of Spain, spent more each year than they made. Yet they and the world claim that austerity has caused their problems. Their only remedy now is austerity; that is to reduce costs in government, salaries in government, and lay off some government employees.

An interesting side note: demonstrations and riots have been on-going in Greece where austerity is discussed publicly. The only place in Europe where austerity exists is ironically in Eastern Europe, where Marxism is the rule of the day. Latvia, for example, appears to be Europe's most austere nation. They have adopted this plan because the unlimited borrowing against the future has not worked at all. That they have become one of the fastest growing economies is proof of austerity's positive impacts. It would grow faster if they dumped the Marxist regime. Estonia is fast growing also. It adopted what I call a partial austerity plan: the primary change was in cutting government salaries. Western Europe, where one would think austerity would be buckled into place, hardly has any austerity at all. In contrast to Eastern Europe there simply is no significant austerity in most of Western Europe or the U.S.

In contrast, the typical federal government policy on austerity in America cannot be viewed as being credible. In any serious plan, to balance the budget, government employees would be given cuts in wages, benefits, and retirement. The biggest cuts would fall on politicians, appointees, and senior bureaucrats. Instead, what we see in America today is government employees receiving larger salaries and bigger pay increases while workers in the private sector, expected to support the government salaries, have their pay packages scaled back. It is an upside down world. Government thinks it creates wealth. It creates nothing except stress. Only the private sector produces anything which can be marketed and sold to the consumer. In a rational world, government employees and programs should bear most of the burden of any austerity policy.

The America of the future must insist on cutbacks in government regulation. Most of these outrageous regulations have been destroying our democracy by overburdening taxpayers, discouraging small business entrepreneurs, adding unnecessary costs to manufactured goods, while simultaneously doing the opposite of what they promised; not keeping us safe. One empirical study found that regulation was so costly to business that "eliminating the job of a single regulator grows the American economy by $6.2 million and nearly 100 private sector jobs annually."[12]

Tax cuts should be the heartbeat of any serious economic plan in a free society. That is real austerity. History shows that overburdening taxes will discourage production. The key to allowing austerity to reign in business is simply knowing that some taxes are over burdening and discouraging to production of most any product. He was right in saying tax cuts on investment and capital will stimulate economic activity and production.

Tax increases such as Obama continually touts and his mentor Karl Marx always preached in his time, make no sense for the nation. Liberals point to the IMF which long ago adopted the same notion of taxes; they did so because the fund is managed by socialists. While they pretend to stand for "the working man" none of them step toward any policy that is guided by the idea of increasing production and especially profits. Instead the legislation is always about the limiting of production and the burdening of successful individuals and companies with higher taxes. A truly "representative" government would create policies limiting its own growth and making life more inspirational for the citizens it supposedly represents. Translation: always in hard times, tax increases would be out; tax cuts in.

In spite of credible evidence, the Campaigner in Chief, Mr. Obama, continues to campaign for higher taxes. He has proven this in the last two years, this time pushing for the removal of "tax breaks" for the retired rich. This would be the first step toward robbing our IRAs. Some have even suggested that "austerity" should involve extending existing taxes onto charities and nonprofits, which is nothing but a backdoor tax increase. These are some of the dumbest suggestions, especially in economic crises. Only a fake austerity here.

Austerity does not mean, for example, budget cuts that would eliminate garbage collection, laying off police officers, or shutting down the fire department while leaving the military, education, and the spy state untouched. This is just a form of extortion offered by Leftists that does not solve the problem. Ideas like these only reveal the true nature and intent of those who are in government.

The Keynesian stimulus approach does not work. Also the IMF-inspired socialist approach, which is calls "austerity," does not work. Only real austerity works. This means cutting government employee incomes, benefits, and retirement benefits. This alone would encourage them to run a taut ship in the future. Obama, the government he represents and those on the public trough should not become wealthy themselves; the private sector must be reserved for that activity. To properly and completely recover from economic hard times, eradicate regulations and their regulators, sell off government assets, and cut those taxes.

A New Foreign Policy Is Revised in a Rewritten History

We are now writing a new history with regard to our position taken on human rights in other nations. In the past our leadership has always forcefully denounced and applied pressure to those leaders who have chosen to violate human rights of their own citizens. Go back and look at what Dwight Eisenhower, or John Kennedy, or Richard Nixon, even Jimmy Carter, or Ronald Reagan had to say about despots who tried to reign over their citizens with an iron hand. They took a stand and politically intervened over time. However, since Obama has been present in the Oval Office, we have left that cherished and higher position. We hear about red lines being drawn in the sand within various countries by our president. It reminds me of the bully on the playground who says while drawing a line with his shoe in the dirt, "Go ahead, just step over this line." And then we hear a speech offering the following, "We will be monitoring the human rights of those citizens in this nation to ensure they comply with . . . " The only people who do not know this announcement has no teeth are those in the Democrat Party. The leaders in foreign nations certainly know the words are empty. But the words are offered, and then all goes quickly back to destroying our own citizen's freedoms.

A Shot of Marxism Followed by a Muslim Chaser

History will show however that we now rush to be at the side of the Muslim Brotherhood wherever they may be striving to infiltrate another nation, and supporting their stated goal of taking the nation for Islam. And whether you hear it reported or not, with that stated goal, comes an accompanying set of goals, to subjugate women in that society. Strange that the Democrat controlled N.O.W. would support that position, or is it strange? Not really, since their goal all along had very little to do with women's rights. It was all about supporting fascism. So with our support, comes the mistreatment of, jailing of, and even murder of the country's citizens, especially those with an opposing faith to Islam, such as Christianity. In particular there has been the burning of buildings used for worship by Christians. And about this our illustrious leader has been nothing but silent. In Venezuela, citizens are being beaten, thrown in prison, and having their possessions taken from them for speaking out against the Communist regime, the US cannot even offer words of discouragement to this regime, and since it appears

Obama has been in concert with Hugo Chavez. By the way the FCC dictate in this country to have all news be level, is a banana republic trick, something that Chavez always did when he was leading Venezuela. The media stays silent on this issue.

If a Conservative or Republican President would conduct business in this manner, Leftists would stand up, scream into TV cameras, oppose it, and storm the White House. They would do this with the aid of an instrument they despise; the Constitution. Because it is Obama leading this activity, the Democrats following him are nothing more than a booster club; interested only in his political success.

New History in Public School

The headline reads, "Obama Administration Takes Groupthink to Absurd Lengths: School Discipline Rates Must Be 'Proportionate.'" That headline is from *Forbes Magazine*, issued February 20, 2014. Translated, what it means is Obama wants discipline to be proportionate, not based on any particular wrong actions of students, but based on race. Example: if a black student is sent to the office for misbehavior, there must also be several white students sent to the office to keep the punishment racially proportionate. The administration would call this equality.

"Top of Form; The reason that they use the word "equality", it is just about a magic word for young people. They think everybody should be equal, except of course for them. There should be no inequality. There should not be any unfairness, and everybody should be happy, and everybody should be treated the same. I have heard a relative using these words. She was taught that in school. So Obama uses code words. It is almost as if you could legalize murder or bank robbery, or stealing gas at the pump if you just called it getting equal; if it were a part of a civil rights act."[13]

Over time, many students and inexperienced citizens, the politically underweight, in our country have heard the words "equality" and "inequality" on a daily basis. Repetition of hearing has made the words sound good; especially in school. This model is how Progressives launched their revolution to create a Socialistic Marxist state nearly a century ago. Where the Progressives launched it is interesting; it was in school with the young, innocent, and impressionable minds sitting and listening in the classroom.

With that knowledge, the fog lifts so that one can see discipline in school is not the real Obama agenda. To proportionate it out on racial lines and establish the "equality" of which he speaks is a sick, cynical model. But that is his agenda. The end result will be something as described by America's talk show host who has the largest national audience, "Soon school officials under threat of the federal government will either start disciplining students who should not be or, more likely, will not discipline some students who should be, and that is what is on the agenda. It is going to be totally illegal, but this is going to be done under the auspices of equality and fairness. Here's a pull quote from the story: "[I]n January, [the Obama] administration -- specifically the Departments of Justice and Education -- went even further with a 'guidance' letter that demands a group equality approach to student discipline in America's public schools.'"[14]

Obama said in the Fall of 2013 that income equality is the 'defining challenge of our time.' While that is horribly laughable, he has raced forward with keystones of his transformation process for our nation. Specifically his moves have started within the Departments of Justice and Education. A prophetic picture, yet horrible to imagine, can be seen in the school of tomorrow, given what Obama has said. Imagine an Obama hall monitor placed there to regulate equal punishment along racial lines for behaviors in school. That will be their version of fair justice. What a crippling challenge for the educators of tomorrow. Language and math are secondary to ethnicity. And the ever present DOJ will be standing by with a legal paddle to take swift action against teachers and administration.

Bureaucrats and especially Obama in his thinking, start with a swirly picture of everything in America is unfair. The school system must be transformed into fairness. No more punishing a group of black students on a bus attacking a white student unless ten other white students are jerked out of their seats and punished first. Why? Because it is only fair in the liberal mind. The end result — there will be no students changing conduct. The pressure will be all on the faculty and administration in the form of grabbing other innocent students and punishing them and in reports they file. That will be in keeping score, and keeping records to prove with Excel spreadsheets and PowerPoint® presentations that there is no unfairness. This will only make the jungle to get worse than it already is. Children are not learning much as it is now, so if discipline totally is eradicated, it will only get worse.

The Problem with Common Core in Schools

You can sex up your fourth grader: that appears to be the message coming from the new curriculum in school.

If Common Core survives the challenges to stay in schools, it will be the new 800-pound gorilla in the classroom. That and its government union approved materials. On the approved list of Common Core reading materials and teaching materials is a book called *It's Perfectly Normal*. It is reported to be on the 4th grade reading list in Tennessee. However, I cannot verify that. The photos and diagrams in this book tell the story of what this is all about; naked bodies all in various stages of weight graphically showing the difference between the male and female body. Until recently, most parents were not aware that this book was on a "suggested reading list" in any school let alone the 4th grade classrooms. School Board elections will be held on the platform of whether Common Core materials should survive in the various schools. One thing is for sure. Progressives love the free sex morality both for straight sex and gay sex; even with elementary school children, such as fourth graders. That a liberal should facilitate a classroom of children with this material is questionable.

Chapter One — Our American History Is Being Rewritten for Us

Some educators indicate the material in this and other books within the Common Core curriculum is appropriate. If so, schools should not exempt the parents providing their input. It is interesting to note that Facebook blocks pictures on its site from the book, *It's Perfectly Normal*. While someone may not classify this as true porn, grade school children do not need to see this. If individuals viewed these images on their computer screen at work in a corporate setting, it would be called pornography. If it is porn in the work place, it is porn in school.

Parents are a part of the problem. They range from very afraid to less afraid or embarrassed to speak with their children about sex. When I was a teenager, my Mom was not afraid to answer questions. She always detoured final jeopardy and made her point clear by saying that I had to be home from a date by 9:00 PM when I first started dating. Sometimes feeling persecuted or just shopping for another answer, I asked my grandfather why I was supposed to be home so early. He told me that it normally took a boy until at least 9 PM to work up enough courage to start doing things a boy should not be doing. Point made! As I got older, the time to arrive home got later and later.

Two things should be remembered regarding the school and sex education. First for parents; find out what is really being taught. Second, discover who is really teaching. The book used in Common Core attempts to teach that certain sexual behaviors such as masturbation, premarital sex and the use of birth control are "normal". That is "what" is being taught. Whether these sexual behaviors are normal is not the issue. The very expression that they are normal by this book is teaching a certain moral perspective about sexual behavior. That should not be taught under the authority of the government school. The secular humanists have wanted to have control of sex education for the last 100 years. For 240 years America was known as a place that allowed parents to teach their children sexuality in the manner they wanted; both the morality and the science. All parents were nervous in broaching the subject, but it was handled. Besides, why would anyone want the government to teach such a thing if they cannot get it right themselves?

This is an incredibly important distinction. Common Core and in particular this book is not teaching children about the science of sexuality, it is teaching a **moral perspective** about sexuality. That is the issue, the distinction between teaching our children the science of sexuality versus the morality of sexuality, which leads to the second question; Is the school responsible for teaching our children morality? So let's turn this around. To those of you who believe that this book is appropriate for fourth graders, if the school presented a book that taught that these sexual activities were abnormal, and encouraged self-discipline and self-control and abstinence from sexual activity until marriage, would you feel that your personal values and morals were being undermined by the school? Abstinence and self-control are an alternative moral value to sexual expression and sexual freedom and sexual license. The only reason the schools are not teaching that is because those who set the curriculum happen to share a more liberal view of sexual morality. If school officials held traditional views of sexual morality, those of you who are more liberal may very well feel that those school officials are infringing on your right to teach your children your values. The answer is NO! This is not appropriate to be taught in school at any age, because public schools do not have the right to teach any moral perspective on sexuality. If schools are going to teach on human sexuality, then schools should stick to the science of sexuality, and leave the moral element to the family. Bottom line the government is amoral. Those who are amoral cannot teach morality. They do not know how.

A Cannabis Club Economy

On your next trip to Colorado, drive through a local shopping strip center. Look for the sign that reads, "Cannabis for Sale Here!" Or you might see one with a newsprint background, "Extra! Extra! Get your Pot Here." Either way, it is a sign that the world is changing rapidly. My maternal Grandpa would not have liked this economy. He came from the old school, remarking to me once that he feared the day when "illegal" drugs, as he called them, such as cocaine, crack cocaine and heroin would be sold on the street corner. My Grandpa does not have to turn over in his grave because at least a portion of what he feared has become legal.

The message is simple. We are sinking lower and lower on the food chain of morality. Whatever may be legal in one or two states does not make the activity right. It can be legal and also wrong at the same time. Every society has its challenges I know. Ours is having a life-threatening challenge on morality, on right and wrong. Only a simpleton would insist that situational morals are suitable for neighborhood or society. Remember as ISIS members move to your neighborhood, their flexible morality teaches it is appropriate to behead anyone not agreeing with them.

Legal solutions to a problem cannot stand apart from ethics and strict morality that is if a society is going to continue to exist. With the recent legalization of recreational cannabis use in both Washington state and Colorado, we're able to see a similar experiment in action. And with all the new tax revenue being raised from the sale of "pot" other states are moving quickly to pass legislation to get in on the act. Whether it is right or not, they want to make it legal.

While the 18th Amendment prohibiting alcohol production and sales precluded state-level legalization, federal drug laws enjoy no such constitutional backing. On November 6, 2012, Amendment 64 to the Colorado State Constitution was approved by Colorado voters in the form of a popular ballot initiative. The amendment mandated that "the use of marijuana should be legal for persons twenty-one years of age or older and taxed in a manner similar to alcohol."

What's more, the amendment mandated that industrial hemp be legal and that "all parts of the plant" plus seeds, oils, extracts, and other forms of cannabis be legal as well. They also legalized were "marijuana accessories" including "any equipment, products or materials of any kind which are used, intended for use, or designed for use in planting, propagating, cultivating, growing, harvesting, composting, manufacturing, compounding, converting, producing, processing, preparing, testing, analyzing, packaging, repackaging, storing, vaporizing, or containing marijuana, or for the ingesting, inhaling, or otherwise introducing marijuana into the human body."

The amendment was certified by the governor of Colorado on December 10, 2012, and the recreational use of cannabis has been legal under Colorado law ever since.

Amendment 64, with all its language covering "equipment, products, [and] materials," hints at the economic complexity that has always existed behind recreational drugs, but which now, in a limited case in a limited jurisdiction, has emerged from the black market and underground operations into the light of the larger marketplace. The cannabis market is not simply a matter of putting some leaves in small bags. The new legal market, instead, is a market with far better quality control and accountability on the part of merchants. And much higher prices I can only imagine. And it means economic growth for many industries that have never traditionally been connected with recreational drugs.

Supporting the cannabis merchants are a wide variety of enterprises from distribution warehouses to financial institutions, attorneys, short-haul truckers, and more. The new demand for commercial real estate to serve the needs of both producers and retail outlets has created a need for real estate brokers who can specialize in the cannabis industry, while attorneys assist with the drafting of legal documents, and accountants must be hired to keep track of the money. Unfortunately, many of these industries must continue to be wary of federal law, even when state law is clear on the matter. Banks, specifically, which are regulated at the federal level, only recently were given the green light by federal regulators to open accounts for cannabis-related businesses. The legality of this sort of banking remains on shaky ground, however, and many banks remain loath to participate, thus crippling the financial and banking opportunities for the cannabis industry in Colorado and Washington.

Cannabis has become a modern day "gold rush" with an ever burgeoning revenue stream for many private-sector business men and women across the many segments of business in Colorado. They range from restaurant workers to retail clerks to insurance brokers, all making mega bucks from the "pot" industry. A large portion of business leaders and politicians mock this industry thinking their participation would require a willing suspension of beliefs and morals. The Denver Metro Chamber of Commerce is one of those boycotting the fast cash approach. The chamber works for the ever-expanding base of business in Colorado, but they just will not submit to the pressure from those businesses who are selling. Rather, they have decided to support the prohibition of cannabis since according to them "to profit from the legalization of marijuana at the expense of . . . children." (Source: See Ryan McMaken, "Colorado's New Cannabis Economy," LewRockwell.com, February 21, 2014)

One might say that some of the merchants and anti-cannabis politicians lack a sense of reciprocity. No give and take just an unwillingness to bend even when there is a pot of gold at the end of a burning cigarette. Those who want to see more people on board with the idea of standing down and allowing the industry grow. But data as it is gathered, and has been gathered over the decades shows some disturbing trends about cannabis being a gateway drug. Nevertheless, those who want the drug to be legal will dismiss any data that is counter to their position. Of course, for chamber of commerce management who believe the drug to be dangerous, no amount of evidence or data would change their minds either.

It is not easy to challenge an industry in a region or state because that pendulum can swing both directions. For example, any industry can be both popular and unpopular to different people in the same region. For example, a manufacturing plant can create traffic problems, but also create many new jobs. The scenery might include representatives and other business leaders arguing two sides of an issue in the 21st Century economy; about cannabis for example and its harm to the public. Some argue for the continued sales of the product since it represents a new cash crop which business can exploit. And the state makes extra tax revenue to boot.

This is one of the arguments during our moment in time, where money is the chief motive of about everything under the sun. But there are other products where data shows them to be more dangerous than the "pot." Even so, they are not challenged for the most part, especially in Colorado and Washington. Case in point — Officials and residents in Tennessee, Missouri, and Texas are thrilled to have Jack Daniels, Anheuser-Busch InBev, and Frito Lay as giant business interests in their respective states. Politicians in particular joyfully croon the platitudes of these giants of commerce, both for the huge tax revenue generated as well as the tens of thousands of jobs for residents. However, a few people argue that these industries are more injurious to shoppers' health than cannabis has ever been. Drunk driving and obesity-related issues kill nearly twenty percent of Americans; cannabis rarely kills anyone. While I am certainly not arguing for cannabis, the point of the argument should be clear. Healthcare costs are high in a large part due to diet, and diets filled with snack foods, saturated fats, Trans fats, alcohol, and sugared soft drinks have all contributed to diseases such as diabetes, osteonecrosis, to name two, plus car crashes that end lives and drive up costs enormously. Some estimates indicate that nearly 20 percent of Americans die early from the use or misuse of such products.

Entire industries have arisen to warn, teach, and attack problems associated with the risks of using such products; MADD, AA, NA, etc. Very seldom are the same whistle blowing techniques used with other products as are used with cannabis; seems so inconsistently applied.

Some very interesting support businesses have sprung up to support each of these industries. For example, think of the whiskey barrels that are manufactured that when sawn in half that make great planter for flowers. Of course there are also the industrial hemp products too. Hemp is used to make some of the strongest ropes available. There are so many benefits for these products, and one need not even order a drink or smoke any pot to indulge in that market place. The real cure for all the associated problems is not more attorneys, but rather a platform of morality by which one can make proper decisions on how to treat the human body.

The Obama New Normal in Unemployment

Unemployment has different outlooks depending on who is speaking and what statistics are used. Obama crows that the number of those out of work has dropped to an 8 ½ year low, or 6.4 percent. One should be cautious; he celebrates a rosy but phony picture he is trying to sell. He touts the Bureau of Labor Statistics (the BLS); it is the official civilian unemployment rate. In February 2013 that rate was 8.9 percent. This figure (called U-3) is extremely misleading in our time. It does not account for:

- The potential workers who are discouraged in not being able to find work any longer;
- Anyone who no longer receives unemployment insurance;
- Cooking of the books, e.g., 25 million jobs have been removed from the baseline of jobs used in the calculation, thus artificially reducing their official unemployment number even further.

Nearly 100 million Americans are no longer in the work force. Government figures which are shared with the public fail to explain the rationale for bureaucrats having removed many types of jobs from their periodic reports. The calculation used to show official unemployment is not reflective of what is true or accurate, just lifting people from the page as if they simply did not exist, thus reducing their number by another sizable percentage. That is not an accurate report.

Everyone knows that the unemployment situation is very bad, and the official figures (not surprisingly) understate the problem. The White House numbers resemble some scientific and astronomer's report stating there are no asteroids in our solar system. There is a more serious problem than most are willing to recognize. Every week it seems that official reports state that unemployment has dropped another portion of a percent. However, the report is immediately followed by the rather grim news that the number within the workforce has dropped to another record low.

John Williams at Shadowstats.com estimated in November 2011 that if we include the short and long-term discouraged workers, then the actual unemployment rate is currently closer to 22 percent. Using the same approach in 2014, while Obama touted that the unemployment rate is a ridiculous 6.4 percent, in truth it was actually above 20 percent.

To see just how unusual our current predicament is, it is actually more instructive to look at the level of employment numbers within private industry, the actual headcount within the various industries, because it is harder to disguise these numbers. (See Figure 3)

The chart in Figure 3 displays the total employees among private sector industries from the late 1930s through to the current day. Notice that during every recession, shown is shaded areas, jobs were lost, as shown by the dips in the line graph. But jobs would usually bounce back during the recovery phases also shown by the progressing line, so that, from a distance, it generally rises in a steady fashion. But that pattern of behavior all changed following 9/11 in the new century. Arguably, there have been two or three recessions since the 2001 attack on American soil. Many economists argue that we continue to be in the 2009 recession, having never come out of it. Here is an example:

In February 2011, the level of private-sector jobs sat at 108.3 million. That number was lower than it was back in June 1999 when there were actually 108.6 million jobs. Fifteen years had come and gone. The U.S. had increased its population by some 31 million, by immigration and natural birth rates. Yet during the same time period there were 300,000 fewer jobs in the private sector. "Just a cursory inspection of the chart above shows that there hasn't been a comparable period of stagnant job creation since the late 1930s. The conclusion is this: the unemployment numbers and percentages this administration has been providing are bogus, political in every way."[15]

Figure 3

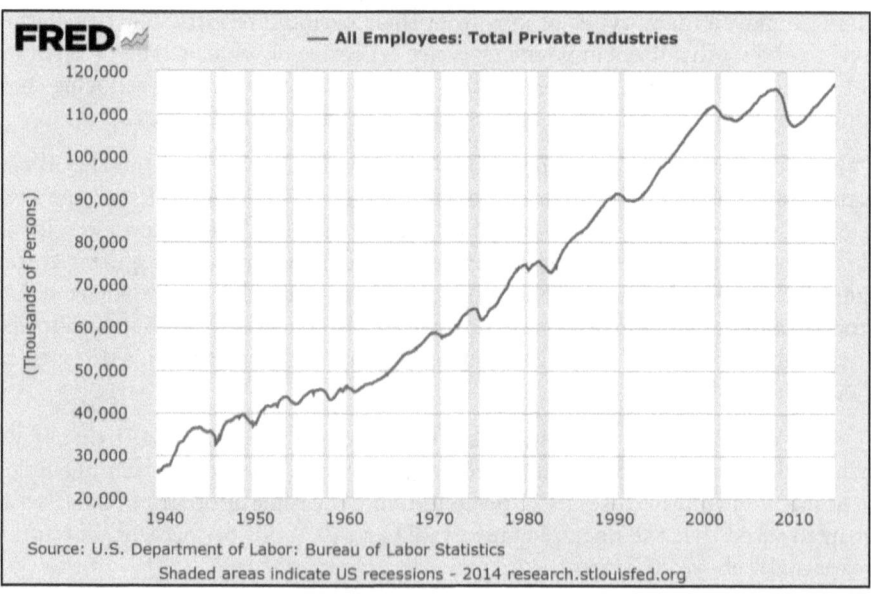

Chapter One — Our American History Is Being Rewritten for Us

Understanding Unemployment

Unemployment, as it is reported today by the American Government, is at best confusing; at worst it is deliberately misleading. During difficult times, it can be extremely frustrating since few understand the numbers anyway. To best understand the truth behind the unemployment numbers offered out of the fog the government reports, we should clarify what employment is. Different terms of definition and methods of defining those out of work have been manufactured over time in classifying a worker as "unemployed." They classify a worker as unemployed when an individual (a) is willing to work at a competitive wage or salary for some categories of jobs, but (b) can't find any employer willing to make an offer to this particular worker, even though (c) the employer views the worker as similar in job fit with other workers already on the payroll.

Figure 4

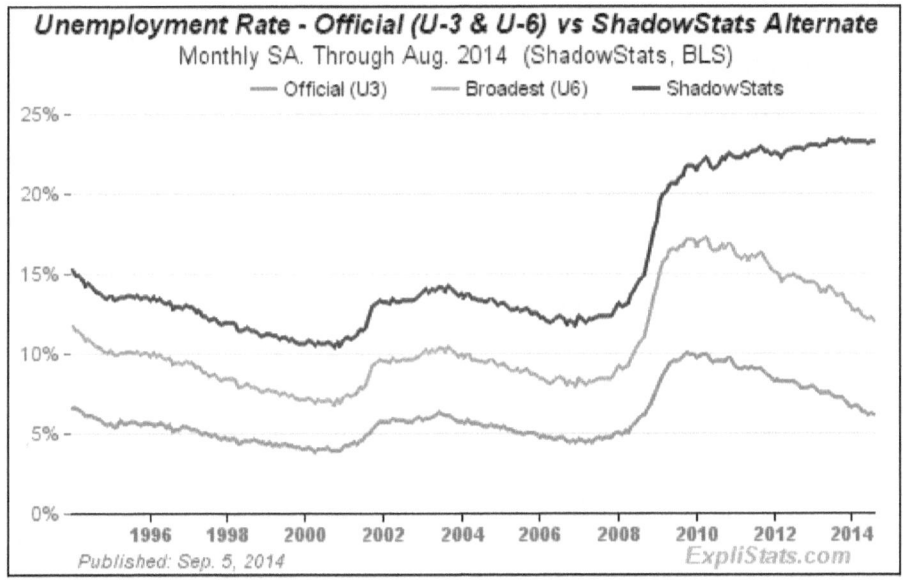

There is another factor involved in the employer view of a worker. It is (c) viewing the "supply chain curve of labor" and how it fits or does not fit as an example of unemployment. For example, just to show why this is an important point of consideration, think about the "market" for starting centers in the National Basketball Association. It's a limited market, and extremely limited when hiring seven footers who are agile and can move quickly. But imagine for a moment that I could play for a team that was not even competitive and in last place in their division, I would play for much less than what the average center gets paid these days, say 30 percent less just to prove myself. The problem is that no pro scouts would even look at me, because they would not see me as being a part of an appropriate "supply curve of labor" in this highly specialized market, because the players, minor league scouts, and even team owners wouldn't see me as an asset or even a commodity for one of the teams. I would be out of shape, weaker, slower, older, fatter, and therefore not even a candidate for any position, except for water boy. Therefore my inability to play and get a job is not a good example of unemployment, because I have not worked in that market, nor do I currently have the skills for any of the jobs.

The first point (a) is also relevant. When we say that someone "can't find a job," there is a presumption that the person has a willingness to get up and go to work, and is willing to work at the pay range or rate of the jobs for which he is qualified. But if a person is insisting on having a starting base salary of $250,000 per year, and is saying that "I can't even get a job as a dishwasher in this town." In one sense he's not unemployed. In fact, he is probably what could be called voluntarily unemployed. When a person is listed as unemployed if not willing to work at the going rate for jobs he has the qualification, he is not really unemployed.

Unemployment and Time

Employers can hire for either temporary or full-time employment, the latter meaning they are willing to make a commitment to view the job on a longer-term basis. Depending on the job description, employers can spend vast resources in training a new hire, during which time the employee is not really "earning their keep" for the pay or salary he or she is receiving. The worker is "locked in" in getting up to speed as quickly as possible too, and would like to only take a job where he or she thinks "things will work out" at least for a few years or longer. Typically it's tough to explain why a résumé shows a worker changing jobs every few months.

Because of the long-term view most employers have traditionally taken in putting an employee into an employment agreement, those same employers will recruit diligently, taking a great deal of time to screen out and then qualify in those potential workers, making an offer and filling the position. Interviewing for jobs vary; for some positions employers may require up to three or even four sessions over an expanse of time to get many looks at a candidate using a variety of interviewers in varied settings. It is important to qualify a candidate as to skill sets of the position, the motivation to do the job, and the cultural fit within the company.

Within these parameters, it helps to think of the labor market analogous to the housing market as opposed to commodities such as groceries or gasoline. On a moment's notice, the market price may not "clear" the housing market because there always seems to be sellers who have their houses "on the market" waiting for a bite from a serious buyer.

The labor market is similar in many ways. Even during boom periods, the unemployment rate never reaches zero. At any given time, there are always several million workers in the United States who are in between jobs. They either quit their previous position; they were terminated, or laid off from a job. Today it is not uncommon for companies to go out of business leaving workers in between jobs.

At the height of our last recession, which I maintain has not only continued but gotten much worse; many workers are transitioning to other activities. When in October 2009, the official unemployment rate hit 10.1 percent there were 3.4 million hires in the private sector. That sounded exciting. The problem, of which most people are unaware, was that there were simultaneously 3.7 million job "losses" (layoffs, terminations, furloughs, etc.) in the private sector. No matter what an administration reports as the unemployment rate, the job-turnover rate should be a reminder how complex the market is with a flow of workers back and forth.

What makes the current economy so awful, then, is NOT that there is unemployment, or that there are unsold houses. Rather, things are bleak because it is so unusually difficult for workers to find buyers of their labor services at a reasonable rate, for home owners to find buyers of their houses, all because of so many unknowns in legislation coming from the administration.

Persistent and High Unemployment

There are a few reasons why unemployment is high today and the future looks fairly bleak for the next several years. Unemployment is certainly much higher than the administration claims and the future less rosy than promised. Here are a few of the problems. These are all contributing factors to the problem, but not necessarily listed in order of their measurable importance:

- Boom times often lead to misallocation of resources, both in finance and people. Boom cycles cause "feeding frenzies" by employers which start too many long-term projects. When the bubble pops, recessions start. Costs during downturns range, but usually spell a minimum of smaller profits on projects. Downturns also negatively impact the completion of projects. Layoffs occur; the remaining workers get jumpy trying to wait it out until the next upswing.

- When many businesses and consumers believe business activity is unsustainable; the brakes are applied seemingly everywhere. Growth vanishes; most activity comes to a halt. The Keynesian disciples within an economy try to spend their way out of the recession or the downturn. The problem only become much worse by the incurring the huge amounts of debt, thus extending the downturn for a longer period of time. The Austrian methodology believes in paying for things as you go, not going into debt. Those disciples also understand that some booms are unsustainable in the first place.

- Politicians in government will raise minimum wages, artificially making low-skilled workers more expensive: in 2009 the minimum wage rose from $6.55 to $7.25 per hour. And the minimum wage is being increased again in 2014. In the 2009 example, anyone with productivity worth more than the $6.55 but less than $7.25 per hour, turned production into a losing proposition financially for their employer. In turn, the employer reduces man hours. In some cases there are layoffs, making unemployment worse.

- Unemployment became more attractive to workers when the government extended unemployment benefits. Extension of the benefits to 99 weeks and even further, made it easy for those seeking work to continue unreasonable salary expectations as they try to find a new job. In many cases, the extension kept them unemployed.

- Obamacare combined with the unilateral law changes Obama made while skirting Congress has convinced many that government should not be in control of health care. Even the most liberal of the liberals are taken aback by the train wreck. Being a planned curse on the American people by Mr. Obama, the "Affordable Care Act" is radicalizing America as never before, making employee health benefits many times more expensive. The biggest problem: every Marxist regime has started by taking control of national healthcare to control the population. Many employers simply froze hiring during the Obama management hopscotch back and forth in granting and denying waivers as political favors. They want some good consistent news.

- Long-term business planning becomes difficult by the Federal Reserve pumping money into the stock market, by manipulating interest rates, keeping unemployment high. Some analysts argue the Fed reduces unemployment; others with whom I agree contend the opposite, by having policies that threaten to bring high inflation, even hyper-inflation to America. The Fed Chairman's actions have also kept thousands of business owners up in the air undecided about what to do. Some owners stockpile commodities like silver, gold, and other commodities thinking the dollar may crash in the short-term. That actually makes the unemployment calamity worse.

- The plight of American workers is made bleaker by these hurdles and roadblocks the government puts in their way, making unemployment much worse than "official" statistics indicate. Once we begin understanding the nature of unemployment, we can begin to see some of the "true" solutions.[16]

The chart in Figure 5 demonstrates the problem of having a huge percentage of the working population that is now unemployed which contributes to the problems described above.

Figure 5

The Marks of New Communism

There is a new American history being written for us. It is not the American dream of yesteryear, thanks to Mr. Obama and his Progressive peons doing the transformative writing. The socialist transformation of this society is being brought to us on a covered wagon of sorts, sold to citizens in a disinformation campaign. It renames or hides what is really going on. It is intended to fool people, labeling campaigns one way with names that seem to present good ideas. However they are misleading in every way.

Leftists have made a science out of masking the ugly face of Marxism over the years. The foundation actually comes from Lenin's phrase "useful idiots" to describe those in the West who naively promoted Marxism without knowing what it really was. That is visible today with people saying they will always vote a straight Democrat ballot because they think it is the party that "cares about the little guy." They have no clue for which they are voting. It was Stalin who perfected this Marxist science. At his request, all East European countries "liberated" by the Red Army at the end of World War II began their march toward Marxism by donning socialist masks. Just months after the Red Army "liberated" the Kingdom of Romania, Stalin merged that country's Communist Party with the Social Democratic Party, producing the Workers' Party. East Germany went the same way. Overnight, the old Communist Party, which had become infamous after being accused of setting the Reichstag on fire in 1933, was renamed the Socialist Unity Party of Germany. The Hungarian Communist Party, which had created the short-lived Hungarian Soviet

Republic in 1919, was quietly re-christened the Hungarian Working People's Party. Most East European governments similarly concealed their road to Marxism by posting innocuous nameplates at the door, such as People's Republic or Popular Republic. Renaming often puts a new mask on an old activity. This is a part of our current American history that is being written for us by people who do not understand what is happening.

For example, the terms Socialism or Marxism have been common words over the years. Each being a scarecrow, liberals renamed the term to seem friendlier, calling the philosophy "Progressivism" and, of course, its adherents — the "Progressives." Americans need their eyes opened that progressivism and progressives are code words for Marxism or Marxists, or Communism or Communists. Using a benign term makes them seem friendlier as well as new and improved.

Due partially at least to this "renaming project," there is a war that is ongoing in which the transformation project is also being renamed and framed as democracy but it is really underground Marxism or underground socialism. In every country that became Marxist, the transformation process began with undercover Marxism, disguised as various kinds of free lunches. If the Democratic Party has its way, it will use undercover Marxism to transform the United States into a socialist country in all but name.

This new history is being written for us at break neck speed as we slide deeper into Marxism, faster than most thought even possible. A quote from a Pravda article just a few years ago really carries the message most of us should sit up and hear, "American capitalism gone with a whimper" It really says all that needs to be said to communicate the message. Like the breaking of a great dam, the American descent into Marxism is happening with breakneck speed, against the backdrop of a passive, hapless people, that some call "sheeple," because they seem to be willing to follow Progressives anywhere. Very few times will you hear the Republican Party even mention the danger of Marxism in America. True Conservatives seem the only ones saying so.

There is a new generation of Americans who have just reached voting age and who have no longer been taught real history in schools, like is in this book, along with most of the people belonging to the 47 percent of households paying no taxes that Mitt Romney mentioned, became fascinated by Marx's utopia — 'to each according to his need.' Millions of Americans cheered. Some electoral gatherings looked like Ceausescu's revival meetings.... "They were galvanized by the prospect that a new administration would force rich Americans to pay a part of their own health care, mortgages, loans and school tuition." The Republican Party and the Tea Party movement have not engaged these 47 percent; they have not seriously tried to affect their thinking. Apparently they thought that they had 53 percent solidly on their side last November.

This is exciting many people because most love free lunches, and undercover

Marxism is threatening to become a U.S. national policy. People who love free lunches will certainly vote for them again, unless our conservative movement will explain to them with stunning clarity and power that the redistribution of wealth is *stealing*, and that the sudden economic collapse of the Marxist Soviet Union dramatically proved that stealing does not pay, even when committed by the government of a superpower.

Unsustainable Health Care Act

Healthcare history has come to the shores of America. For the first time in history our nation is said to have mandated healthcare for everyone. The problem is that with the daily failures of Obamacare, more people are currently outside of coverage as opposed to those who were out of coverage before this ridiculous law went into effect. By the way, those who did not have insurance before 2011 were 15 million. With Obamacare, it appears approximately 50 million are thrown out of coverage. But of course, coverage does not appear to be the purpose of this law. Any Marxist regime starts in the early stages by taking control of the health care and insurance business. Too, this is a TAX, intended to tax higher income persons so as to redistribute that money to poor families, another Marxist doctrine.

Legal Experts with No J.D.

Those "legal" experts testifying before Congress are also making history. Hollywood has become more of a representative in Congress than first through, with actors in mass testifying about an assortment of world issues, none of which is their expertise. Celebrities testifying on Capitol Hill are a staple. Congress is enamored with the celebrity psyche; the Hollywood Actors Guild is enamored with moving legislation their way. Both parties win: lawmakers attract attention they typically would not for their issues, and the VIPs, from Bono to Elmo, get to soak up some of that special gravitas that only a congressional microphone can provide.

A New Economy Is Here: Welfare Pays Better Than Work

It is really old news, but the value of the full package of welfare benefits for a typical recipient in each of the 50 states and the District of Columbia exceeds the poverty level. Because welfare benefits are tax-free, their dollar value is often greater than the amount of take-home income a worker would have remaining after paying taxes on an equivalent pretax income.

In 40 states welfare pays more than an $8.00 an hour job. In 17 states the welfare package is more generous than a $10.00 an hour job. In Hawaii, Alaska, Massachusetts, Connecticut, the District of Columbia, New York, and Rhode Island welfare pays more than a $12.00 an hour job — or nearly two times the minimum wage. In nine states welfare pays more than the average first-year salary for a teacher. In 29 states it pays more than the average starting salary for a secretary. And in the six most generous states it pays more than the entry-level salary for a computer programmer. Most welfare recipients, particularly long-term recipients, lack the skills necessary to obtain the types of jobs that pay top or even average wages.[17]

The individuals who do leave welfare for work most often start employment in service or retail trade industries, generally as clerks, secretaries, cleaning persons, sales help, and restaurant workers and servers.

Although it would be nice to increase the wages of entry-level workers to the point where work paid better than welfare, government has no ability to do so. (Attempts to mandate wage increases, such as minimum wage legislation, result chiefly in increased unemployment.) There is a wide disparity among the states regarding the attractiveness of welfare. The value of the total package of benefits relative to a job providing the same after-tax income ranges from a high of $36,400 in Hawaii to a low of $11,500 in Mississippi. In eight jurisdictions: Hawaii, Alaska, Massachusetts, Connecticut, the District of Columbia, New York, New Jersey, and Rhode Island welfare pays at least the equivalent of a $25,000 a year job.[18]

The pretax value of welfare benefits substantially exceeds the amount a recipient could earn in an entry-level job in virtually every state. The numbers suggest that recipients of aid are likely to choose welfare over work, thus increasing their long-term dependence. Although the evidence shows that, in the long term, an individual is better off in the labor force than on welfare, moving from welfare to work is likely to lead to at least a short-term decline in income and, for some, perhaps a permanent reduction of income. That may be why 68.6 percent of welfare recipients report that they are not actively seeking work.

Figure 6

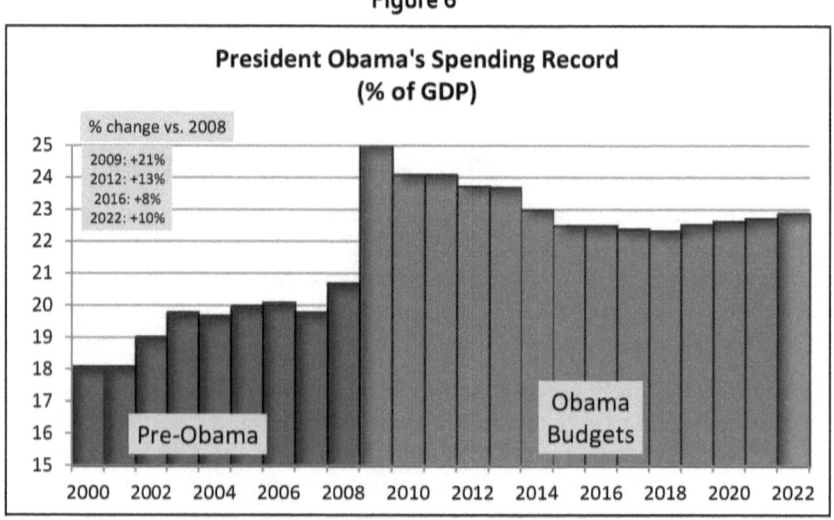

Source: Budget of U.S. Government FY2013, Historical Tables, Table 1.2.
Analysis of the President's 2013 Budget. Congressional Budget Office.

Welfare benefits are especially generous in large cities. Welfare provides the equivalent of an hourly pretax wage of $14.75 in New York City, $12.45 in Philadelphia, $11.35 in Baltimore, and $10.90 in Detroit. For the hard-core welfare recipient, the value of the full range of welfare benefits substantially exceeds the amount the recipient could earn in an entry-level job. As a result, recipients are likely to choose welfare over work, thus increasing long-term dependence.[19] It should also be noted that for the years 2009-2012, there were sharp increases to the rates of welfare checks paid.

The New Normal in Spending

Measuring Mr. Obama's record relative to the economy shows he has sharply increased spending well above historic norms and into record territory. Dating back to 1960, federal spending has averaged approximately 20 percent of economy or GDP. See Figure 6 on previous page.

The New Environmental Movement

We are being told in today's society that we as a nation or a world cannot survive another twenty years unless we cut out all uses of petrochemical and oil products, cut the use of paper products by at least 50 percent (this includes the use of toilet paper), shut down most of the coal-fired power plants in the country, stop driving SUVs, and stop using pesticides of all kinds. This is the new American history which the liberals and progressives are writing for our country. In response, it is really clear to me that in order to survive as a nation, one of the most challenging and imperative tasks confronting America today is to do a deep and lasting cleanup of the environmental movement. Without it, our civilization simply will not survive. It will be killed off by this poison that is being passed around in the name of environmentalism.

The environmentalist tree-huggers, and fear mongers of our day, a sizeable percentage of the Progressive movement, are worse than any smog which used to hang over Los Angeles. The new future of our world consists of blitz campaigns warning of major hurricanes and global warming, which according to them are all caused by human activities. They have been working their rallies long enough that they believe most Americans are willing to adopt the mentality of primitive tribal villagers, who would hopefully make human sacrifices of conservatives to the local volcano to avoid the wrath of Mother Nature.

Past news coverage for any one of the local Al Gore global warming conferences with his SUV sitting outside idling while he speaks, or a Green Peace Rally trying to save the snail darter fish, in my moments of weakness, I feel like Elijah off in the wilderness, thinking, "Am I the only one who has not bowed the knee to this fake religion?" However, it is my hope that there is a sufficient portion of the American thinking public that will be rational. Hopefully, they can connect the dots in these government studies and deservedly reject most of what is reported using an intellectual outrage. We can truly save our nation and our world from these tree hugging terrorists who want to take the nation back to the Stone Age. The truth is we have need of dealing with these environmental "revisionists" as can be seen in a twenty-five year old work by George Reisman, in his essay entitled "The Toxicity of Environmentalism."

While it is not necessary to question the good intentions and sincerity of the overwhelming majority of the members of the environmental or ecology movement, it is vital that the public realize that *"in this seemingly lofty and noble movement itself can be found more than a little evidence of the most profound toxicity."* [20] Another representative showing direct evidence of willful dishonesty within the environmental movement has pushed the topic of global warming to get disciples even at the cost of honesty saying, " . . . to do this, we need to get some broad-based support, to capture the public's imagination. That, of course, entails getting loads of media coverage. So we have to offer up scary scenarios, make simplified, dramatic statements, and make little mention of any doubts we may have. This "double ethical bind" we frequently find ourselves in cannot be solved by any formula. Each of us has to decide what the right balance is between being effective and being honest."[21]

While environmentalists do much of their work through the EPA, which they most assuredly control now just as if it were the thermostat in their own home, or a roadster parked in their garage. They will adjust the temp on their attacks up or down or drive slower or faster based on their whims at the time. Whether a spotted owl in Oregon, a snail darter in the Little Tennessee River, or a tsetse fly on a construction site in Los Angeles, the environmentalists will close down both work and entire industries in logging, farming or construction respectively, saying they are working to save these species. I remember years ago, a major construction project in Los Angeles was shut down indefinitely because an EPA Inspector found 5 flies, which were on the endangered list on the site. The best bet for the construction manager should have been simply to hire two drivers to haul cow manure a block away from the construction site and dump it. That would take care of the flies on the building site. Most homemakers I know want to have flies on the endangered species list because of the frustration of dealing with them in their home.

Week to week the threatened products list changes. One week it can be a highly-advertised imported bottled water product, as it was in the 90s that was removed from the market shelves because a laboratory test showed that samples contained up to thirty-five parts per billion of benzene. Environmentalists "assumed" this was a threat to public health that required pulling the water off the shelves. Actions like these don't even grab headlines anymore since they have become a common practice in the everyday life of America now. Whether it is a pesticide, a fertilizer, some additive, some preservative, or an alleged bearer of pollution, all are proposed as threats that must be removed when the number of "projected" deaths hit the threshold of one in a million deaths. That projected death rate per million is less than one-third of the same chance of death from an airplane flying overhead dropping an object on a house.

The religious fervor of these environmental militants is seen through the words of Bill McKibben who published a book called *The End of Nature*:

"In some ways the most dismal development of the last seventeen years — even more than the ever darkening science — is the inability of the American political system to take seriously our peril. Nothing fundamental has shifted in our scientific understanding since 1988 — as this book makes clear but its mere existence, we knew enough long ago to get to work, and if we had, our peril would be smaller. But we didn't. A bipartisan effort to do nothing has been wildly successful. The Clinton-Gore administration oversaw the conversion of the American vehicle fleet, from cars to semi military vehicles, and a resulting 15 percent increase in carbon emissions. George W. Bush renounced the Kyoto Treaty within a few weeks of taking office, beginning the downfall of our public image around the world that has continued unabated. His administration's energy plan foresees a plan where we will drill, mine, refine and combust our way to 30 percent more carbon emissions within a generation."[22]

He went on to say, "Hurricane Katrina created a million refugees. Scientists using various computer models have calculated there may be 150 million such refugees by mid-century — that is, 150 simultaneous Katrinas . . . And the computer models hint at surprises lurking ahead . . . the cycles of the Earth now move more quickly — spring on average comes a week earlier across the Northern Hemisphere than it did two decades ago . . . "[23]

Incomes around the world vary based on continent, nation, and locale. At times local economies do not demand an extravagant income to survive such as is the case in places like La Jolla, Ca., San Francisco, the French Riviera, or Bali. "I've spent time in the Indian state of Karala, where, on the annual income of $300 and hence with minimal environmental impact on the globe, people have life expectancies, birthrates, and literacy rates that rival our own."[24]

What most environmentalists do not want to admit, including McKibben, is that the environmental models have been using inaccurate data. In fact, some of the data to build the famous "hockey stick" which Al Gore used in his Inconvenient Truth was deliberated massaged to make the temperatures appear to be higher than they really were, at least according to the scientist who "crunched" the data. This puts a question mark behind everything they say or present. It becomes rather obvious there is a conspiracy in the global warming or climate change groups, all driven by an agenda, which is to collect revenue. It could be likened to an environmental speed trap, which has the obvious, very heavy fines associated with them.

Environmentalists want to push back the clock to colonial days; no electricity, no automobiles, no airline industry for the world. Except for them of course. They do not seem to be willing to sacrifice themselves, but want the rest of the world to cut itself off from technology which they stay comfortable in the U.S. making speeches.

Environmental concerns are not evil. They are good. My friends used to call me an environmentalist years ago in the 1970s, because I was careful with nature; having great respect for all living things, the soil, the air, and most of all people. That last point is what is missing with the modern attack from the environmental left. They talk of caring for people but it is just talk. They are more interested in their radical movement. Possibly if they did not drive SUVs while lecturing us on the evils of an SUV or if they walked to work instead of driving while they speak of the evils of oil, then just possibly more thinking people would at least give them some credence. But their "shtick" is so obvious in its political clothing; they are in a money grab. For such a great nation as we have had, it is terrible to see our new American history being written in this way.

Regulating an Out of Balance Life

Modern environmentalists today, who we see on TV and supporting their rallies, can be overbearing. Some even talk as if they are opposed to human life, except for their own of course. The premise of nature's intrinsic value being at or above that of humans actually existed and goes back, in the Western world, as far as St. Francis of Assisi, "who believed in the equality of all living creatures: man, cattle, birds, fish, and reptiles. Indeed, precisely on the basis of this philosophical affinity, and at the wish of the mainstream of the ecology movement, St. Francis of Assisi has been officially declared the patron saint of ecology by the Roman Catholic Church."[25]

The idea many of the leftist environmentalists have is wrong for a couple of reasons. First they quote a Saint in the Catholic Church erroneously. Second, they attempt to put mankind into some sort of a "penalty box" — all through environmental regulations. There are even a few within the environmentalist movement that appear to have the desire to destroy man and his works because they see mankind's progress in industrialization as being the systematic destroyer of the good, and thus evil.

Therefore, environmental regulations are necessary to keep people in check. I am told by a plumber on the West Coast, that increasing the water pressure within an entire single family dwelling is against environmental code — regulation prohibits it. "Government environmental regulations have made a mess of our daily lives. Whether it is the banning of effective products like DDT, or mandating inferior functionality in our appliances and fixtures, government's role here is indisputably to degrade our quality of life . . . was stunned to hear President Obama claim exactly the opposite in a speech to the U.S. Chamber of Commerce. He ridiculed those who predicted disaster from government regulations as far back as 1848. "It didn't happen," he said. "None of the things came to pass." Then he went further to say that government regulations "enhanced" industry and "made our lives better." Regulations often spark competition and innovation."[26]

Back to the animals; there are predators which on a regular basis destroy sources of clothing, shelter, and food for people; sources such as fruits, vegetables, cotton, trees, cattle, sheep, and goats. These are all hunted by a variety of "animals," including varieties of insects, such as beetles, grasshoppers, termites, some bees, as well as larger animals such as coyotes, wolves, and snakes. Just as these animals are viewed as predators which destroy valued sources of shelter, clothing, and food, on a basis of what they call intrinsic value, some purist environmentalists view mankind as a predator. Man systematically plows up areas of earth and destroys some wildlife, forests, jungles, and natural scenery. Environmentalists hold these scenes of nature to be intrinsically valuable, which by their doctrine is used mostly to attack man. In the end, environmentalists can become predators themselves.

Of course, the environmental movement as spoken of by the Left is not an absolute evil. Not all the words or messages of are made out of pure poison. Very few are. No one would listen to their messages if they were full of nothing but poisonous words. Around a kernel of truth, they mix loads of poison that is then coated with a sweet sugary coating. But as all con-men are inclined to do, eventually the mixture has much more fakery or poison to it than the good stuff. If you swallow environmentalism as preached by the leftist today, you inevitably swallow poisonous doctrines.

Human happiness is important and certainly so is human fecundity. Keeping the environment healthy is equally important. Most Americans favor "environmentalism" and do not associate it with a desire for a virus to wipe out humanity, instead associating it with "the desire for a healthier environment."[27]

It is cosmically unlikely that the developed world will choose to end its orgy of fossil-energy consumption, and the Third World its suicidal consumption of landscape. Until such time as Homo sapiens should decide to rejoin nature, some of us can only hope for the right virus to come along.[28]

One huge problem is that so-called modern environmentalists have long ago joined forces with Liberal and Progressive politics. Their statements filled with poison can no longer be considered as coming from some kook fringe. Rather they make statements which coincide with the mainstream of Liberal Progressive thought. Their significance is twofold. First, their far out statements do not represent just a small percentage of the Leftist movement. Second, they speak as if every event is a potential disaster to the world, speaking in parts per hundred, rather than parts per million. Everything suddenly contains an enormously higher level of toxicity than is deemed to constitute a danger to human life in virtually every other case in which deadly poison is present.

But the toxicity level of the environmental movement as a whole is substantially greater even than parts per hundred. It is certainly at least at the level of several parts per ten. This is obvious from the fact that the mainstream of the environmental movement makes no fundamental or significant criticisms of the likes of Messrs. Graber and McKibben. John Muir, for example, had a spoken wish for alligators to "be blessed now and then with a mouthful of terror-stricken man by way of dainty." Members of the Sierra Club or Green Peace, must have applauded when first hearing those words. It is interesting to see a poisonous hatred for people, those outside the Democrat Party I would presume. What is extremely interesting is the lack of attention these environmentalists pay to birds that are killed flying over the solar panel farms in the Western U.S. If they had been killed by some conservative driving a bulldozer digging a basement for his new house, there would have been all hell to pay in front of TV cameras. It goes to show where their true interest lies; not with the animals, but with the monetary paybacks from Liberal politicians in Washington.

There is something much more important than the Sierra Club's genealogy however; something which provides an explanation in terms of basic principle of why the mainstream of the ecology movement does not attack what might be thought to be merely its fringe. This is a fundamental philosophical premise which the mainstream of the movement shares with the alleged fringe and which logically implies hatred for man and his achievements. The Sierra Club's premise is that nature possesses intrinsic value on its own. They claim the value is important in spite of the presence of human life. In other words, humans should move off Planet Earth so as to not disturb plants and animals. I support that idea only if applied in the following manner: all the environmentalist liberals and Marxists are to leave first. Once they are all gone, we will renegotiate with the plants and animals.

Given the underlying moral bankruptcy and emptiness of the movement, it is certainly not possible to accept at face value any of the claims it makes of seeking to improve human life and well-being. The most tragic and absurd of scenes would be to take advice on how to improve your life from those who wish you were dead. That is precisely what is "wished" in the modern environmental movement regardless of whatever scientific analysis is used to give it credibility. The scenario can be horrifying if an alleged scientific expert or doctor believes in the "intrinsic value of nature" as pumped out by the environmental movement of the 20th and 21st Centuries. Imagine going to your physician to be treated for a virus, being unaware that all along he the doctor, is fighting on the side of the germs, rather than being on your side.

Over the years, it is not surprising that virtually every sound of the alarm by environmentalists has actually been a false alarm. Take for example the "great Alar scare" of 1989. Alar, was a chemical spray used for many years since the 1960s on apples in order to preserve their color and freshness. It was discovered in 1980 by none other than EPA research that Alar breaks down over time into a byproduct called "unsymmetrical dimethyl hydrazine" or UDMH. An initial study showing that UDMH can cause cancer was published in 1973. Subsequent studies published in 1977 and 1978 confirmed that Alar and UDMH caused tumors in laboratory animals. The EPA investigated what it termed "the hazards of Alar" starting in 1980; with an on and off emphasis they arrived at a conclusion in 1985 that Alar and UDMH were a carcinogen that caused cancer. The environmentalists went ballistic with public scares about Alar. While it might be said that Alar could cause cancer, so can many consumables if taken in heavy doses. If the claims of environmentalists had actually been true, and the use of Alar would result in 4.2 deaths per million over a seventy-year lifetime, there is an interesting twist to the analysis. What that means is that eating apples sprayed with Alar over a 70-year lifetime would be less dangerous than driving to the market to buy them. At the time of the scare there were approximately 250 million people in the U.S. (Consider: 4.2 deaths per million over a seventy year period means that in any one year in the United States, with its population of roughly two hundred and fifty million people, approximately fifteen deaths would be attributable to Alar! This is the result obtained by multiplying 4.2 per million times 250 million and then dividing by 70. In the same one-year period of time, approximately fifty thousand deaths occur in motor vehicle accidents in the United States, most of them within a few miles of the victims' homes, and undoubtedly far more than fifteen of them were most likely on trips to the supermarket to buy apples.) Nevertheless, a panic ensued, followed by a plunge in the sale of apples, the financial ruin of an untold number of apple growers, and the virtual disappearance of Alar.

Before the panic over Alar, there was the panic over asbestos. According to *Forbes* magazine, it turns out that in the forms in which it is normally used in the United States, asbestos is one-third as likely to be the cause of death as being struck by lightning.[29]

Then there is the alleged damage to lakes caused by acid rain. According to *Policy Review*, it turns out that the acidification of the lakes has not been the result of acid rain, but of the cessation of logging operations in the affected areas and thus the absence of the alkaline run-off produced by such operations. This run-off had made naturally acidic lakes non-acidic for a few generations.[30]

Besides these cases, there were the hysterias over dioxin in the ground at Times Beach, Missouri, TCE in the drinking water of Woburn, Massachusetts, the chemicals in Love Canal, and radiation at Three Mile Island. According to Prof. Bruce Ames, one of the world's leading experts on cancer, it turned out that the amount of dioxin that anyone would have absorbed in Times Beach was far less than the amount required to do any harm and that, indeed, the actual harm to Times Beach residents from dioxin was less than that of drinking a glass of beer. (The Environmental Protection Agency itself subsequently reduced its estimate of the danger from dioxin by a factor of fifteen-sixteenths.) In the case of Woburn, according to Ames, it turned out the cluster of leukemia cases which occurred there was statistically random and that the drinking water there was actually above the national average in safety, and not, as had been claimed, the cause of the leukemia cases. In the case of Love Canal, Ames reports, it turned out upon investigation that the cancer rate among the former residents has been no higher than average. (It is necessary to use the phrase "former residents" because the town lost most of its population in the panic and forced evacuation caused by the environmentalists' claims.) In the case of Three Mile Island, not a single resident has died, nor even received an additional exposure to radiation, as the result of the accident there. In addition, according to studies reported in *The New York Times*, the cancer rate among residents there is no higher than normal and has not risen.[31]

Before these hysterias, there were claims alleging the death of Lake Erie and mercury poisoning in tuna fish. All along, Lake Erie has been very much alive and was even producing near record quantities of fish at the very time the claims of its death were being made. The mercury in the tuna fish was the result of the natural presence of mercury in sea water; and evidence provided by museums showed that similar levels of mercury had been present in tuna fish since prehistoric times.[32]

And now, in yet another overthrow of the environmentalists' claims, a noted climatologist, Prof. Robert Pease, has shown that it is impossible for chlorofluorocarbons (CFCs) to destroy large quantities of ozone in the stratosphere because relatively few of them are even capable of reaching the stratosphere in the first place. He also shows that the celebrated ozone "hole" over Antarctica every Fall is a phenomenon of nature, in existence since long before CFCs were invented, and results largely from the fact that during the long Antarctic night ultraviolet sunlight is not present to create fresh ozone.[33]

Environmentalists' claims turn out to be proven wrong in the vast majority of times, because their data is sloppy and not valued; only the emotional message to frighten people is valued. Over the years, there have been enough fraudulent scares that a loss of confidence in true science has resulted. The claims rest on unsupported conjectures and wild leaps of imagination from scintilla of fact to arbitrary conclusions, by means of evasion and the drawing of invalid inferences. It is out and out evasion and invalid inference to leap from findings about the effects of feeding rats or mice dosages the equivalent of a hundred or more times what any human being would ever ingest, and then draw inferences about the effects on people of consuming normal quantities. Fears of parts per billion of this or that chemical causing single-digit deaths per million, or the ozone is disappearing or man is artificially warming the planet; none of these claims rest on science, but on imagination.

A rational thinking person can come to the following conclusion very quickly. It is for all intents and purposes impossible for an individual to observe two groups of people, a million in each group, over a 70-year time period. It cannot be done. But just imagine for a moment in trying to do this. Though they are not identical people in each group, they are as close to identical as possible. One group eats apples daily coated with Alar. The other group does not. At the end of 70 years, 4.2 members of

Group A die. Stating that the 4.2 deaths came from the Alar coated apples is closely attune to attending a some breakfast meeting at a local restaurant where twelve locals are gathered to discuss and solve the world's problems. The breakfast talk at this table of knowledge, while touted by some in attendance as earth shattering, is in reality random assumptions, amateur manipulation of data, wild guesses as to cause, etc. In such a session, one might start with the known consequences of a quarter-ton safe falling ten stories onto the head of an unfortunate passerby below, and from there go on to speculate about the conceivable effects in a million cases of other passersby happening to drop from their hand or mouth an M&M or a peanut on their shoe, and come to the conclusion that 4.2 of them will die.[34]

Further, the claims of environmentalists willfully ignore many important facts. The truth is that of at least half of the natural chemicals found on earth will cause cancer in lab rats when force-fed to them in massive quantities. Also, many carcinogens, poisons, and radiation exist in nature. The same principle applies to man-made chemicals when fed in massive doses. Professor Bruce N. Ames of the University of California, Berkeley, and an expert in the study of cancer caused from radiation has stepped forth with a valuable message in this arena. According to the good doctor, the cause of cancer in rats being fed chemicals, natural and man-made, is not the chemicals themselves, but the destruction of body tissue caused by the massive and excessive doses. An example is rats have commonly been fed saccharin in doses comparable to humans drinking 800 cans of diet soda a day. Many natural poisons exist on Planet Earth. Arsenic is one of the deadliest poisons, but it is natural. Apple seeds have cyanide in them. Cherry pits do too. Raspberries contain glycosides. Oleander, one of the most beautiful plants, is also a deadly poison, as are many other plants and herbs. Radium and uranium, with all their radioactivity, are not rare in nature.

Environmentalists have the horrible habit of not opening their eyes and seeing what exists in nature. They also associate every evil not with nature but with mankind. If they had the same safety standards for nature as they do for man, they would shriek and run for cover. Most likely, they would destroy half of the world building force-fields, barricades, and air-tight shelters against nature with its carcinogens, toxins, and radioactive material that constitute the other half of the world.

The false claims of environmentalists over the years have created a modern day fairy tale similar to the little boy who cried wolf, yet turned 180°. The cries range in number and size: radiation poisoning, food irradiation, the Greenhouse Effect, DDT, asbestos, potato arsenic, ozone layer destruction, and on it goes. But in the modern-day fairy tale it is really the story of the wolf crying loudly about the dangers of the little boy. When you analyze the messages, the real danger is that of listening to the wolf.

A tyrannosaurus rex sized predator today is the willful dishonesty of the environmental movement. There have been and are many of them. Stephen Schneider was one who deciphered data that was eventually homogenized into a hockey stick, where though dishonesty inappropriate data was used to build it. Predicting a global catastrophe like he did is not wrong in and of itself. Willful dishonesty within the environmental movement is the serious predator. Given the misinformation of the data that went into building the "Hockey Stick" that Al Gore so proudly promoted "inconveniently", there should be sources totally independent of the environmental movement to verify claims before we accept their data again.

Environmentalism as it is defined by Progressive Liberalism is a manufactured lie. It is also a weird sickness. One of them will mutter the term "intrinsic value," followed quickly by a statement that the environment is being destroyed by free enterprise. In their sickness, the only savior of the planet will be socialism. They exclude themselves from their eventual judgment that of saying that the forests, jungles, rock formations, oceans, plant life and animals are more important than human beings. Their reasoning goes like this; assets such as the fish, plant life, birds, etc., should be valued while the "commodities" of human beings should be viewed as expendable.

This becomes obvious when watching them work as they announce that a species is being threatened. A good example is the snail darter fish in Northern California, which environmentalists say are "endangered." Water rights have been curtailed for several years in the bread basket of America by EPA rule. No vegetables grow there now, just weeds. It turns out that saving only a few fish was more important than allowing humans to feed themselves with good vegetables that will be lacking at the right prices in the local market.

If one realizes that the entire world physically consists of nothing but chemical elements. These elements are never destroyed. They simply reappear in different combinations, in different proportions, in different places. Apart from what has been lost in a few rockets, the quantity of every chemical element in the world today is the same as it was before the Industrial Revolution. The only difference is that, because of the Industrial Revolution, instead of lying dormant, out of man's control, the chemical elements have been moved about as never before; in such a way as to improve human life and well-being. For instance, some part of the world's iron and copper has been moved from the interior of the earth, where it was useless to now constitute buildings, bridges, automobiles, and a million and one other things of benefit to human life. Some part of the world's carbon, oxygen, and hydrogen has been separated from certain compounds and recombined in others, in the process releasing energy to heat and light homes, power industrial machinery, automobiles, airplanes, ships, and railroad trains, and in countless other ways serve human life. It follows that insofar as man's environment consists of the chemical elements iron, copper, carbon, oxygen, and hydrogen, and his productive activity makes them useful to himself in these ways, his environment is correspondingly improved.

All of the earth moving, all of the building of houses and all the other business adds up to only moving elements from one place to another. Like shuffling a deck of cards to properly play a game; cards like elements are rearranged to make the earth's elements in an order to improve his life and environment.

As trucks which run on oil and gas, both natural elements, are necessary to bring products from a manufacturer or grower to where they can be used, all such economic activity has the purpose of making life better and even improving the environment. In this example, roads were built using chemical elements and products such as trucks were built using carbon elements of steel, iron, and copper. Trees were cut down and used in building bridges. The net result is that the environment, though rearranged has become more suitable for economic activity and better living.

Environmentalists make many claims about man's destruction of the environment; most of them are bogus and built around the doctrine of intrinsic value. Global warming, climate change, ozone depletion, snail darter fish dying; all these claims are based on their intrinsic value doctrine as well. Environmentalists have fears, not of the earth decaying to the point it can no longer support humans, but that mankind will refine the earth so that farms will replace some jungles. They cannot bear to think of the earth becoming a garden for mankind. In the words of McKibben, "The problem is that nature, the independent force that has surrounded us since our earliest days, cannot coexist with our numbers and our habits. We may well be able to create a world that can support our numbers and our habits, but it will be an artificial world."

The banner of the environmental movement as it exists in the modern day is one of toxicity. Nothing in the movement should be confused as having anything to be done in promoting better human health or extending human life. It is done to protect plants and animals; such as the reduction of smog, cleaning up the beaches, dump sites, and parks. In the land of the environmentalists, their concern even with such genuine problems as dirty air and polluted water turns into only a weapon to attack industrial civilization.

Americans should resist cooperating with the radical environmental movement as the same thing will most likely happen in the U.S. as happened in Russia and Germany years ago. While there was a pretense of innocence in the beginning of such a movement in those nations, it was not long until it had joined itself with Nazism and Communism, all in the name of defeating poverty, and leveling the playing field. Even though the actual goals and programs of the Communists and Nazis were no secret, many people did not realize that such pronouncements and their underlying philosophy must be taken seriously. But working side by side with the likes of Lenin and Stalin or Hitler and Himmler, did not achieve the kind of life these people had hoped to achieve. It did, however, serve to achieve the bloody goals of those monsters. And along the way, those who may have started out innocently enough very quickly lost their innocence and to varying degrees ended up simply as accomplices of the monsters.

Viewing any dictatorial regime, evil needs to team with some good in order to be in full disguise of its nature and to gain the obedience of faithful followers. The doctrine of intrinsic values will be baked into the regime cake, to make the poison of the recipe go unnoticed for as long as possible. When one views the Obama administration with this historical lens, suddenly the desire for gun control, universal government health care, environmental control, equalizing of all pay packages, one can almost make out the ghost of a treacherous individual standing behind the scenes pulling the levers and turning the knobs. The end result is the destruction of freedom, which so many of the good people who followed had no intention of seeing happen. There is much need to be alert and cautious as one is being read the recipe of what appears to be honest, faithful, and true concern for citizens. Beware of the lesser known ingredients of intrinsic values, mixed together with level playing fields. The recipe sounds good, but makes a bitter, bitter cake.

It is alarming in America today to see the number of young people, who have been enlisted in the environmentalists' campaign to throttle the production of those commodities to make life so fulfilling and enjoyable; those of fossil energy. Sadly, it is succeeding with them. It is obvious they do not even understand the ramifications of what they do, since their position will do nothing less than the destruction of the Industrial Revolution. While they think they do well, they are chiseling away at the support systems which keep their Play Stations operational, their recreational vehicles motoring along the roads. It will bring certain poverty, misery, and third-world filth to the door of every American if it is not stopped.

The essential feature of the Industrial Revolution was to replace the use of man-made power. To the relatively feeble muscles of draft animals and the still more feeble muscles of human beings, and to the relatively small amounts of useable power available from nature in the form of wind and falling water, the Industrial Revolution added man-made power. It did so first in the form of steam generated from the combustion of coal, and later in the form of internal combustion based on petroleum, and electric power based on the burning of any fossil fuel or on atomic energy.

This man-made power is the essential basis of all of the economic improvements achieved over the last two hundred years. Its application is what enables us human beings to accomplish with our arms and hands the amazing productive results we do accomplish. To the feeble powers of our arms and hands is added the enormously greater power released by these sources of energy. Energy use, the productivity of labor, and the standard of living are frankly inseparable.

For example, it is not surprising that the United States enjoys the world's highest standard of living. This is a direct result of the fact that the United States has the world's highest energy consumption per capita. The United States, more than any other country, is the country where intelligent human beings have arranged for motor-driven machinery to accomplish results for them. All further substantial increases in the productivity of labor and standard of living, both here in the

United States and across the world, will be equally dependent on man-made power and the growing consumption of energy it makes possible. Our ability to accomplish more and more with the same limited muscular powers of our limbs will depend entirely on our ability to augment them further and further with the aid of still more such energy.

In total opposition to the Industrial Revolution and all the marvelous results it has accomplished, the essential goal of environmentalism is to block the increase in one source of man-made power after another and ultimately to roll back the production of man-made power to the point of virtual nonexistence, thereby undoing the Industrial Revolution and returning the world to the economic Dark Ages. There is to be no atomic power. According to the environmentalists, it represents the death ray. There is also to be no power based on fossil fuels. According to the environmentalists, it causes "pollution," and now global warming, and must therefore be given up. There is not even to be significant hydro-power. According to the environmentalists, the building of the necessary dams destroys intrinsically valuable wildlife habitat.

Only three things are to be permitted as sources of energy, according to the environmentalists. Two of them, "solar power" and power from windmills, are, as far as can be seen, utterly impracticable as significant sources of energy. If somehow, they became practicable, the environmentalists would undoubtedly find grounds for attacking them. The third allowable source of energy, "conservation," is a contradiction in terms. "Conservation" is *not* a source of energy. The actual meaning is simply using less. Conservation is a source of energy for one use only at the price of deprivation of energy use somewhere else.

The environmentalists' campaign against energy calls to mind the image of a boa constrictor entwining itself about the body of its victim and slowly squeezing the life out of him. There can be no other result for the economic system of the industrialized world but enfeeblement and ultimately death if its supplies of energy are progressively choked off.

Large numbers of people have been enlisted in the campaign against energy out of fear that the average mean temperature of the world may rise a few degrees in the next century, mainly as the result of the burning of fossil fuels. If this were really to be so, the only appropriate response would be to be sure that more and better air conditioners were available. (Similarly, if there were in fact to be some reduction in the ozone layer, the appropriate response, to avoid the additional cases of skin cancer that would allegedly occur from exposure to more intense sunlight, would be to be sure that there were more sunglasses, hats, and sun-tan lotion available.) It would *not* be to seek to throttle and destroy industrial civilization.

If one did not understand its underlying motivation, the environmental movement's resort to the fear of global warming might appear astonishing in view of all the previous fears the movement has professed. These fears, in case anyone has forgotten, have concerned the alleged onset of *a new ice age* as the result of the same industrial development that is now supposed to result in global warming, and the alleged creation of a "nuclear winter" as the result of man's use of atomic explosives.

The words of Paul Ehrlich and his incredible claims in connection with the "greenhouse effect" should be recalled. In the first wave of ecological hysteria, this "scientist" declared:

"At the moment we cannot predict what the overall climatic results will be of our using the atmosphere as a garbage dump. We do know that very small changes in either direction in the average temperature of the Earth could be very serious. With a few degrees of cooling, a new ice age might be upon us, with rapid and drastic effects on the agricultural productivity of the temperate regions. With a few degrees of heating, the polar ice caps would melt, perhaps raising ocean levels 250 feet."[35]

The 250-foot rise in the sea level projected by Ehrlich as the result of global warming has been scaled back somewhat. McKibben gave what he called, the "worst case scenario" which is eleven feet, by the year 2100. Others have estimates at approximately seven feet. According to a United Nations panel of alleged scientists, it is supposed to be 25.6 inches. (Even this still more limited projected rise did not stop the UN panel from calling for an immediate 60 percent reduction in carbon-dioxide emissions to try to prevent it.) The temperatures since the 1990s have been getting colder.

Chris Turney, professor of climate in Australia and his team discovered that in December 2013 when on a mission to Antarctica with scientists and journalists aboard a ship that got stranded, being frozen in record high levels of summer sea ice. It was "not what Turney and his fellow alarmists had in mind." However, it should not have been entirely surprising. Despite hysterical fear-mongering by the United Nations and self-styled "climate experts," sea-ice cover in the Southern Hemisphere hit a new record in September of 2013 for the second year in a row, according to the National Snow and Ice Data Center. The latest data show Antarctic sea ice is more than two standard deviations above normal, climate researchers reported. That is bad news for Turney and the 73 self-styled "scientists," "journalists," and crew members participating in the global-warming expedition. According to the Australian Maritime Safety Authority (AMSA), their ship, the *MV Akademik Shokalskiy*, has been trapped in 10-feet thick ice slabs since December 24. Three vessels with ice-breaking capabilities have attempted to reach the alarmists so far. All of them failed. "A helicopter rescue attempt on December 30, meanwhile, was reportedly aborted due to strong winds. . . . In the real world, despite hysterical warnings of climate doom . . . even premier alarmist institutions and the UN have admitted that the data show "global warming" actually stopped some 17 years ago. Alarmists, somewhat humorously, perhaps, try to explain away the inconvenient facts by citing what critics refer to as "The Theory of The Ocean Ate My

CHAPTER ONE — OUR AMERICAN HISTORY IS BEING REWRITTEN FOR US

Global Warming." Few independent scientists have bought into the controversial theory, which the Obama administration pressured the UN to include in its latest "global-warming" report. The "science" behind UN global-warming theories, meanwhile, has imploded. Many experts are now forecasting global cooling."[36]

Over time while the population has witnessed similar incidents, there has been a significant and growing distrust of the science and technology environmentalists use to sustain their claims. The irony is so thick; to cut it, a knife is required. Sad, yet almost humorous is the environmental movement's argument that the only solutions to climate change can be offered by the same science and technology. Interestingly, this movement claims science is untrustworthy in engineering a safe atomic power plant, or producing a pesticide that is safe. They are viewed as having so little ability; they cannot even be trusted to bake a loaf of bread with chemical preservatives. Now here is the irony — mention global warming and suddenly this science and technology have a breathtaking trust and confidence of the environmentalists. With no questions asked, they voice total reliability for solving problems in an area in which, until recently, no one, not even the staunchest supporters of science and technology, had ever thought to assert very much confidence at all. Science, so bumbling and untrustworthy throughout society, suddenly is treated in treated as a deity, when forecasting the weather for the next one hundred years. And the environmental movement demands that we bow before their god who now has the answer.

America and the remainder of the western civilization are being told by the environmental movement that we must abandon the Industrial Revolution; the demand is all based on this extended weather forecast of environmental science. Said differently, environmentalism is all about the destruction of the western way of life.

Two of the engines developed by this same science, which has driven western civilization into premier position in the world, amazingly are being attacked by the environmentalists. The first is power plants. Environmentalists hate coal-fired power plants, but they hate nuclear power even more. The second is the internal combustion engine, requiring the use of petrochemical products which environmentalists hate also. Now here is the key; these environmentalists base their distrust of these engines on "caution" and "prudence." No matter what assurances are given by scientists and engineers using math and physics to develop fail-safe backup systems, air scrubbers, low-lead fuels, better miles per gallon, etc., environmentalists are unwilling to trust the future, gambling on unborn leaders to make solid decisions. However, they are willing to destroy the economy of the modern world, and throw away the industrialized civilization onto an ash heap, all based on a one hundred year weather forecast.

The meaning of this insanity is that industrial civilization is to be abandoned because this is what must be done to avoid bad weather and very bad weather. If we destroy the energy base needed to produce and operate the construction equipment required to build strong, well-made, comfortable houses for hundreds of millions of people, we shall be safer from the wind and rain, the environmental movement alleges, than if we retain and enlarge that energy base. If we destroy our capacity to produce and operate refrigerators and air conditioners, we shall be better protected from hot weather than if we retain and enlarge that capacity, the environmental movement claims. If we destroy our capacity to produce and operate tractors and harvesters, to can and freeze food, to build and operate hospitals and produce medicines, we shall secure our food supply and our health better than if we retain and enlarge that capacity, the environmental movement asserts.

The insanity of the environmental movement becomes frighteningly clear when one suddenly realizes that its purpose is not to save anything; it is to destroy western civilization. To think that in our drive to cope with our environment, there are actually people who will claim intelligence in following a movement which says that man should not take action upon nature; rather we will control nature by our inaction. That is the inaction of drilling for energy not conducting business. In so doing, there is a belief that nature will be kind and send no threatening forces our way. This is part of a demented faith system which states that threatening forces of nature are not the product of nature, but of us! Thus speaks the environmental movement.

All of the insanities of the environmental movement become intelligible when one grasps the nature of the destructive motivation behind them. They are not uttered in the interest of man's life and well-being, but for the purpose of leading him to self-destruction.

It must be stressed that even if global warming turned out to be a fact, the free citizens of an industrial civilization would have no great difficulty in coping with it. That is, of course, if their ability to use energy and to produce is not crippled by the environmental movement and by government controls otherwise inspired. The seeming difficulties of coping with global warming, or any other large-scale change, arise only when the problem is viewed from the perspective of government central planners.

Whether global warming comes or not, it is certain that nature itself will sooner or later produce major changes in the climate. To deal with those changes and virtually all other changes arising from whatever cause, man absolutely requires individual freedom, science, and technology. In a word, he requires the industrial civilization constituted by capitalism.

There is a truly good side represented in true environmentalism. Achieving a foundation of greater cleanliness, better health, and longer life for all living plants, animals, and mankind is a wonderful goal. But that goal is aided by the technological advances which modern environmentalists oppose. In the last two centuries, loyalty to these values has enabled man in the Western world to accomplish much, but not to put an end to famines and plagues, and to eliminate the once dread diseases of cholera, diphtheria, smallpox, tuberculosis, and typhoid fever, among others. Famine in much of the world has been ended, because the industrial civilization so hated by the environmentalists has produced the greatest abundance and variety of food in the history of the world, and created the transportation system required to bring it to everyone. This same hated civilization has produced the iron and steel pipe, and the chemical purification and pumping systems which enable everyone to have instant access to safe drinking water, hot or cold, every minute of the day. It has produced the sewage systems and the automobiles that have removed the filth of human and animal waste from the streets of cities and towns.

While the Industrial Revolution has become the target or environmentalists, it should be remembered even by them that the average life span of the adult American was increased from fifty to sixty-five years. While it is true in the early days of coal-powered trains, particularly in the mining areas, coal dust became a part of the necessity to do extra home cleanings. People were okay with the extra little mess so they could have the extra conveniences of electricity and natural gas. This industrial revolution helped in taming the entire continent. It also has enabled us to prepare to build a communication system that is truly global.

In the 1980s under Ronald Reagan, while socialism in this country collapsed for a time, Leftists sent in their "B Team," the environmental alarmists. They raised the convention of global warming to new heights. The now popular "green" movement that has arisen is being promoted heavily in failed green energy startups by our current president. While the advertising of the movement sounds so promising of a new world, it is in many ways just a repackaging of the old Red movement of the Communist party. While stopping just short of calling the environmentalists Communists, the similarities are jaw dropping. Notice the similarities:

- No difference in desired results — both want to strip personal liberty and enjoyment from life.

- The Reds always claimed individuals could not be left alone because they would create a monopoly or exploit others. The Greens claim the individual must never be left alone because it will result in production that destroys the ozone causing climate change.

- A big centralized government is required to both control and mandate economic activity. The Reds require it to allegedly achieve equal human prosperity for all. The Greens require it for the alleged sake of avoiding environmental damage.

- Environmentalism is a backdoor attempt for economic control where the straight forward Communist attempt for control failed earlier. The Red movement wanted to paralyze individualism through social engineering. The Green movement wants to paralyze individualism by prohibiting engineering of any kind.

Environmentalism is the frontrunner of the rising tide of irrationalism that has engulfed our culture. The last two centuries have witnessed a relentless attack on reason and logic as being the base of knowledge. This attack has been led most recently by the Democrat Party as led by their philosophical leaders; from Immanuel Kant Over to Bertrand Russell. An expanding loss of confidence in reason and critical thinking is taking place as a result. It has been a slippery slope, followed by mankind gradually losing that one philosophical mark which distinguishes him different from the animal world. This has progressed so rapidly and thoroughly throughout the general public that we have arrived at this juncture in culture: in daily thought, there is now no difference in man, animals, or plant life. This explains why the doctrine of St. Francis of Assisi is constantly used by the environmentalists concerning their equality. Also it explains what is now accepted with virtually no opposition.

Environmentalists are often guilty of confusing terminology. They have brought forth a prominent statement of their 'faith' which they term "doctrine of intrinsic values." Their definition of the term intrinsic value simply means that we accept their definition of what it means without question. In other words, they expect people to do as they say, rather than learn on their own. Actually, they are confusing two different value systems. The term they should have used, but did not, is instrumental or rational value. Allow me to illustrate briefly. The sun rising in the morning provides beauty, warmth, it supports life on earth; therefore it has an intrinsic value in and of itself. When the sun beating down on my skin, endangers my health (health is intrinsic) my response is to put on sunblock, a medicine, which has instrumental or rational value. Whether I respond or not to the sun does not change its intrinsic value. For example, health is intrinsically valuable; medicine is instrumentally valuable. A $1 bill has no intrinsic value; what it may buy is instrumentally valuable. It has a value which it is assigned and is accepted. Any 'rational value' is instrumental value based on its assignment: it helps you get what you want based on assigned value.

As a society or culture abandons reason, several events start to occur,

- A void is created that begins to fill with the visible growing hatred and fears, that we see now;
- Environmentalism feeds upon hatred and fear; Leaders of the movement use those emotions to attack the public;
- The only successful way to deal with reality is reason. To the degree that people abandon reason, they must feel terror before reality, because they have no way of dealing with it, other than reason.
- By the same token, their frustrations mount, since reason is their only means of solving problems and achieving the results they want to achieve.
- In addition, the abandonment of reason leads to more and more suffer-

ing as the result of others' irrationality, including their use of physical force.

- Thus, in the conditions of a collapse of rationality, frustrations and feelings of hatred and hostility rapidly multiply, while cool judgment, rational standards, and civilized behavior vanish.
- In this new irrational environment, monstrous ideologies appear. Monsters in human form emerge alongside them, ready to put them into practice. The environmental movement, of course, is such a movement.

If critical thinkers are absent after these processes have evolved, there is no one left to fight for true, conservative human values. Any critical rational thinker becomes a warrior in essence, to protect the value of the intellect, to protect man the rational being, and to protect the industrial civilization he created and requires. Any such rational thinker today is to be praised, first for the courage to stand up for values, secondly to stand in the face of intense attack and ridicule. Third and most importantly he is due acclaim for standing up for truth.

It is time for the American people to awaken and be made aware of how the evil of this environmentalism run by Leftists. Americans need to understand these things about environmentalists:

- They have been rewriting our history by writing new rule books for society;
- What they and this environmentalism actually stands for;
- What Americans stand to lose;
- What they already have lost, as the result of its growing influence;
- The environmental movement's responsibility for the energy crisis and the accompanying high price of oil and oil products, which is the result of its systematic and highly successful campaign against additional energy supplies;
- Its consequent responsibility for the enrichment of Arab sheiks at the expense of impoverishing hundreds of millions of people around the world, including many millions in the U.S.;
- Its responsibility for the vastly increased wealth, power, and influence of terrorist governments in the Middle East, stemming from the high price of oil it has caused, and for the resulting wars in the region.

Additionally, the American people must be made aware of how the environmental movement has progressively made life more difficult for them. They must be shown how, as the result of its existence, people have been prevented from taking one necessary and relatively simple action after another, such as building power plants and roads, extending airport runways, and even establishing new garbage dumps. They must be shown how the history of the environmental movement is a history of destruction: of the atomic power industry, of the Johns Manville Company, of cranberry growers and apple growers, of sawmills and logging companies, of paper mills, of metal smelters, of coal mines, of steel mills, of tuna fishermen, of oil fields and oil refineries. And these are only the tip of the iceberg. They must be shown how the environmental movement has been the cause of the wanton violation of private property rights and thereby of untold thousands of acres of land not being developed for the benefit of human beings, and thus of countless homes and factories not being built. They must be shown how this has negatively impacted the economy. They must be shown how as the result of all the necessary actions it prohibits or makes more expensive. The environmental movement has been a major cause of the marked deterioration in the conditions in which many people now must live their lives in the United States. That it is the cause of families earning less and having to pay more, and, as a result, being deprived of the ability to own their own home or even to get by at all without having to work a good deal harder than used to be necessary.

In summation, Americans need to see that the environmental movement, by its very nature, is an army of swarming pests, going between man and the work he must do to sustain and improve his life.

A remedy successful enough to tame this movement will come only when the American people understand these issues. The remedy must include the repealing of every law, regulation, and executive order that is tainted by the doctrine of intrinsic value. This needs to include the repeal of all legislation requiring the banning of man-made chemicals merely because a statistical correlation with cancer in laboratory animals can be established when the chemicals are fed to the animals in massive, inherently destructive doses. The overriding purpose and nature of the remedy would be to break the constricting grip of environmentalism and make it possible for man to resume the increase in his productive powers in the United States in the remaining years of this new century.

Rational critical thinkers must do heavy lifting in cleaning up a second area of the environment; the philosophical, intellectual, and cultural environment, so critical to the preservation of fixed moral standards in America.

At the core of Leftist environmentalism is what they call the "toxic pollution" meaning the philosophical pollution of the industrialized world. However, the real poisonous toxin which needs to be cleaned up is in the heads of the Leftist "intellectual" mainstream. The intellectual toxins seem to always gather where reason is kicked out. They are highly contagious, foul the cultural air, and are death to freedom; Among them are collectivism in its various forms of Marxism, racism, nationalism, and feminism; and cultural relativism, determinism, logical positivism, existentialism, linguistic analysis, behaviorism, Freudianism, Keynesianism, the environmentalism mentioned before, and more.

Chapter One — Our American History Is Being Rewritten for Us

The results of these intellectual toxins, their doctrines, and their attacks on civilization and reduction of the human spirit being seen as the "huddled masses" are highly visible. Just look around. Marxism results in the kind of disastrous conditions now prevailing in Eastern Europe and Russia. Every variety of collectivism denies the individual's free will, his ideas, character, and vital interests. Because they view ideas as determined by group membership in a class structure, their doctrines deny the very possibility of reason. Their effect is the creation of conflict between members of different groups: for example, between businessmen and wage earners, blacks and whites, English speakers and French speakers, men and women.

It is common to see people who being controlled by three toxins within this intellectual pollution: determinism, existentialism and relativism. Determinism is the doctrine that says a man's actions are controlled by forces beyond his power of choice. Existentialism is the philosophy that man is trapped in a "human condition" of inescapable misery, leading people not to make choices they could have to improve their lives. Relativism denies the value of modern life in the industrial world, undervaluing civilization and deterring their willingness to work hard within it. These doctrines blind people in various ways; for example to the real value of inventions such as automobiles, light bulbs, and automatic clothes washers. They only focus on natural conditions such as unpolluted air.

Logical positivism denies the possibility of knowing anything with certainty about the real world. Linguistic analysis regards the search for truth as a trivial word game. Behaviorism denies the existence of consciousness. Freudianism regards the conscious mind (the "Ego") as surrounded by the warring forces of the unconscious mind in the form of the "Id" and the "Superego," and thus as being incapable of exercising substantial influence on the individual's behavior. Keynesianism regards wars, earthquakes, and pyramid building as sources of prosperity. It looks to peacetime government budget deficits and inflation of the money supply as a good substitute for these allegedly beneficial phenomena. Its effects, as the present-day economy of the United States bears witness, are the erosion of the buying power of money, of credit, of saving and capital accumulation, and of the general standard of living.

These intellectual toxins can be seen bobbing up and down in the "intellectual mainstream," just as raw sewage can be seen floating in a dirty river. They fill the intellectual mainstream. Virtually, every college and university in the Western world is a philosophical cesspool of these doctrines, in which intellectually helpless students are baptized into several times over several years until they are made believers. Then they are turned loose to contaminate the rest of society. The contemporary liberal arts education, which was at one time a wonderful education, is now substantively contaminated with these irrational doctrines and others like them.

With the project to clean up the intellectual arena, only the most powerful, industrial-strength, philosophical and intellectual cleansing agents will do. These cleansing agents are, above all, the writings of Ayn Rand, and Ludwig von Mises.

These two towering intellects are, respectively, the leading advocates of reason and capitalism in the twentieth and twenty-first centuries. A philosophical-intellectual cleanup requires that all or most of their writings be introduced into colleges and universities as an essential part of the core curriculum, and that what is not included in the core curriculum be included in the more advanced programs. To incorporate these authors into a prominent place in the educational curriculum is a central goal. Reaching this goal will positively impact that everyone should work for who is concerned about his cultural environment and the impact of that environment on his life and well-being. Only after this goal is accomplished, will there be any possibility that colleges and universities will cease to be centers of civilization-destroying intellectual disease. Only after it is accomplished on a large scale, at the leading colleges and universities, can there be any possibility of the intellectual mainstream someday being clean enough for rational people to drink from its waters. Remember the adage, "if you put garbage in, you will get garbage out." The same is true in building a curriculum worthy of real education.

The 21st Century should be the century when man begins the colonization both the solar system, and the earth with rational civilization, not a return to the Dark Ages. Which it will be, will depend on the extent to which new rational thinkers can succeed in restoring to the cultural environment the values of reason and capitalism.

However, a minority seems to be thinking rationally today. As the author and poet John Milton wrote, loneliness was the first thing that God's eye named "not good."

"We are living in a time when sensitivities are at the surface, often vented with cutting words. Philosophically, you can believe anything so as you do not claim it a better way. Religiously, you can hold to anything, so long as you do not bring Jesus Christ into it. If a spiritual idea is eastern, it is granted critical immunity; if western, it is thoroughly criticized. Thus, a journalist can walk into a church and mock its carryings on, but he or she dare not do the same if the ceremony is from eastern fold. Such is the mood at the end of the twentieth century. A mood can be a dangerous state of mind, because it can crush reason under the weight of feeling. But that is precisely what I believe postmodernism best represents - a mood."

— Ravi Zacharias

Author of "Jesus Among other gods"

Chapter Two

When Government Becomes Evil and Destructive

"Whenever any form of government becomes destructive of these ends life, liberty, and the pursuit of happiness it is the right of the people to alter or abolish it, and to institute new government…" — Thomas Jefferson

"I predict future happiness for Americans if they can prevent the government from wasting the labors of the people under the pretense of taking care of them." — Thomas Jefferson

"THE BUDGET SHOULD BE BALANCED, THE Treasury should be refilled, public debt should be reduced, the arrogance of officialdom should be tempered and controlled, and the assistance to foreign lands should be curtailed lest Rome become bankrupt. People must again learn to work, instead of living on public assistance." — Cicero, 55 BC

It doesn't appear that we have learned this lesson in the past 2000 years…

Abraham Lincoln's encouraging vision of "government of the people, by the people, and for the people" raised hopes that have never been realized. But his name can no longer be used to justify the error that he could not have foreseen in 1863. He could not have envisioned that, a century after he was assassinated, government in the United States, and even more in Great Britain in Europe, would dominate economic life. If he had survived, he would not now have approved of the dominant government that democracy has produced. For it is no longer "of" the people, "by" the people, "for" the people.

The application of economics favoring special interest groups bring forth the form of government today that Lincoln would not have commended in any year, let alone 2014. The federal government is now very different from the one based on the common people that Lincoln thought would prevail. Although his vision is still the most common encyclopedia definition of "democracy" Lincoln cannot now be claimed as the father of our 20th-21st century form of democracy.

Lincoln would now see government not of, by and for all the people, but of, by, and for some kinds of people. He would see it not as of all the people but as of the political activists. He would see government not as by the people but as managed by the politicians and their officials. And he would see government not for the ordinary people, but as for the organized, in well-run, well-financed, and influential business organizations, professional associations, and trade unions. It is government "of the Busy (political activists), by the Bossy (government managers), and for the Bully (lobbying activists)."[1] He would see the myriads of government regulations and taxes that smother individuals and businesses of the private sector.

In New York City, a new mayor with strong teacher union connections wants to extend pre-school public school programs by assessing a higher tax on those making $500,000 or more a year. At the national level, President Obama has stressed that those making $250,000 or more a year should pay higher taxes. The argument is also based on the idea that the government should step in and cure the problem of "income equality."

Using this kind of logic, one might bar certain teams from winning more championships (the New York Yankees, the Green Bay Packers, the Boston Celtics) because they have won many more championships than most other teams; and that is so unfair by liberal logic. The logic saying government must correct inequalities is dense and not common sense. But inequalities among humans are many and are impossible to define since every individual is unique. Yet these kinds of policies not only do not work, they hurt our economy. They have been discussed and in some cases tried. In effect, they tell the successful: "You're doing too well. We must do something about you."

People's God-Given Rights Must Limit Government

Because an individual has God-given or "natural" rights long before either the formation of a state or its fundamental political, is therefore an irrefutable axiom that the state cannot take from that individual that which they have not given. At least that is the irrefutable conclusion drawn in *The Law*, Frenchman Frédéric Bastiat's work from the mid-eighteenth century. Bastiat also makes the case that a man can only delegate to this state those powers that he possessed prior to the state; therefore a man has not the right to coerce another man to give to a given charity. **Given that I cannot force you or you cannot force me to give to a charity of my choice, neither can a government (state) force you to give to a charity of its choice. But the state does precisely that, they require you give to their charity whether you like it or not.** If you try and argue, they will force you to comply. If you still resist, they will take your assets and possessions. If you try to protect yourself legally, or "lawyer up" as some say, the state has shown they have the wherewithal to wipe you out. Too bad the government does not realize they do not have the right to force you to pay a charity to which you would not voluntarily make a donation. The state makes any resistance an empty argument since they will bully you to support their favorite two charities: welfare and the state.

An "Uncompromising Imperative" from the State (Thus Sayeth the State)

The state has placed a couple of unwritten rules (like laws) in place which state — Rule 1: Don't ever question the state; Rule 2: If confused, see Rule 1. Some will observe that because it is the state, it must be given more elbow room and more privilege in performing its will to accomplish its stated goal of making everybody's life better, even if we must surrender some rights to achieve the ultimate goal of social justice. Others have stressed that perhaps there is a higher rationale for allowing the state to violate our natural rights by confiscating our property coercively, or raising taxes to exurbanite rates for the supposed betterment of others. However, just the exact opposite is the reality. The state spreads misery to all, spreading it around like drinks at a Christmas party. The more their plan fails to produce "utopia" results, the more they double down and raise the stakes by doing more of the same.

The state's coercion coupled with their stated explanation of rationale and their subsequent collectivistic activities are troubling and therefore a topic of discussion by many academics. While the philosophies vary in explanation of what is happening, two philosophers stand above others especially when connecting their theorems, and looking at them in tandem: Immanuel Kant and T. Patrick Burke. Kant says the state sees itself as placing on citizens a "categorical imperative," meaning, the state tells us what to do unconditionally, without questions, in everyplace, in every time, and to all people. In other words we have an unconditional obligation to follow this imperative or directive. The state offers little explanation for their power other than to explain it comes from one place, simple reason. (It is interesting to note in this "reason" the state exempts its representatives from following many of the same unconditional obligation it encroaches upon the citizenry; i.e., edicts providing themselves a pass on participating in the Affordable Care Act, Social Security, uniformly paying their taxes and subsequent support of the welfare state.) This "reason" carries with it purpose for only those who are affected. For instance, Kant distinguishes between the categorical imperative and what he calls a hypothetical imperative, always subjective, certainly not objective, which might in print read as follows: "poor people would live better if they were on welfare." That provides "reason" to those who are poor, but no one else; and therefore cannot be an unconditional action applying to all persons, at all times, in all places.

Author Roger Scruton, in his introductory book on Kant, suggests there are various forms of "the categorical imperative" used by the state to maneuver people. One variant sounds innocent and friendly, it is the Golden Rule from the Bible; Matthew 7:12 — "In everything do to others what you would have them do to you, for this sums up the Law and the Prophets." Historical figures have used the Golden Rule. Abraham Lincoln did in his statement, "As I would not be a slave, so I would not be a master." And this variant is based on "reason only." A second variant states that men should be treated as ends and not as means. The same imperative in corporate speak might be, "Treat people as assets — not commodities." Through this natural law even if 99 people out of 100 in a community voted that they should donate clothes to a particular charity, Kant's categorical imperative would deny the community the right to coerce this one man. He argues the community of men would be using this one man as a means and not as an end, a rational being with human dignity.

An important addendum is added by Professor T. Patrick Burke to the unwarranted nature of state coercion for the purpose of charitable giving, or welfare. His persuasion is that the act of refusing to help someone in need in not necessarily unjust, as the state contends, because after all the charitable giving, the needy person is left in the same position as before they received welfare. A variant form of what Burke says might be the program to help people learn to eat fish, as they also learn to catch fish themselves, as opposed to always having to fish for them. In earlier days, this was called workfare or on-the-job-training. So refusing to help according to what the state calls "help," is not the so called criminal act it is portrayed to be. It is simply not obliging to follow the state in their formula of operation, which never solves problems with their actions. They usually make them only worse. The non-Christian may look at this scenario and only come away with the thought that we must never become bound by some higher concept of justice as to help all who come to us in need, since they believe we will become nothing less than slaves to all of mankind who chooses not to work. The fearful reality is that if we continue growing the welfare state, we all become commodities of the state rather than assets. Besides, the largest purpose of government charities seems to grow the overhead portion larger, helping people becomes a bi-product.

"The State" Can't Level the Playing Field Even If It Wanted To

The real issue is that the state (Federal government) presents us with a zero-sum game, all based on their intoxicating mix of power, plutocratic prestige and boast of self-importance. To say there is no good news in the emerging socialist movement which has taken hold in America, would be an understatement. Their desire to absent people from their private property and their rights makes an economic calculation for success absolutely impossible. Socialists either refuse to learn from history or they have no interest in history, thinking themselves to be wiser than other generations before them. Not only does collectivism lead to the death and destruction of millions of lives wherever it is tried, one of the subsequent problems the "oh so wise state" has is they have no idea what to produce or what resources to use in its production whatever the desired good may be; the historical record is clear that government intervention makes us all poorer. In his 1920 work, *Economic Calculation in the Socialist Commonwealth*, Ludwig von Mises presented the crux of the problem, saying: Think of two worlds, the world of the mind containing preferences and the world of markets and prices. One's preferences are ordered in the mind according to greatest need. These preferences are different for different people and change within the same person constantly. These internally held preferences meet in the market with all other preferences to produce money prices, which allows us to make economic and economical decisions about what to produce, and how to produce it, and what to buy. Mises pointed out that without market prices, the economic czar is blind as to what to produce and how to produce it. Market prices are determined only by people expressing preferences for what they actually own; i.e., private property. The economic czar is not spending his own money or taking his own product to market to sell. So, how can he rationally decide what to do? Mises's answer was that he cannot.

Since the government is composed of individuals who are not spending their own money or taking their own product to market, there is no way that they can decide rationally which charities, if any, should be state supported. They fall back upon what can only be called corrupt relationships; i.e., helping friends, choosing organizations that may hire them in the future, buying off organizations that are particularly persistent and annoying, etc. This behavior is best described by "public choice theory," which explains that actions of individuals in government are guided by the same self-interest as they are in all other areas of life, ridiculing the idea that those in government have higher ethical considerations.

In the end we observe that state welfare is imposed coercively; it has no justification other than that of pure force. No one has a natural right to our labor or our property; there is no categorical imperative to demand the help of others and none to shame us for refusing to "help" others through state coercion; and there is no possibility of rational economic calculation to determine which charities for the state to support and to what extent.[2]

This all sounds like an FDR tax policy that remained in place after World War II. This was a time in our history when the Liberal Progressive tax policy dominated the coercion of the state system prior to the Kennedy administration tax cuts in the early 1960s. People not versed in history are shocked to discover that in the 1940s and 1950s the United States had marginal tax rates of 94 percent. Just imagine living then; when you reached a point of income that you were only allowed to keep six pennies out of every dollar you earned. A rational person would be tempted to ask, "Why should I keep working?" Well, that is exactly what transpired during those two decades. Higher income people would stop working late in the year as they started bumping up against the threshold of a 94 percent tax rate on further income. Unlike liberals, I do not see where that is helpful to an economy. It is detrimental in every way to a scientific and growing society. Allow me to introduce you to a lady named Ayn Rand and a novel she wrote called *Atlas Shrugged*.

When Ayn Rand was writing the draft of her novel, her working title was "The Strike." I will not destroy the story line of that book, one of the greatest books outside of the Bible, but suffice to say that in her novel when business people are pressed hard by the Fascist State for more and more taxes to support the non-producers, many of them decide to not work any longer, go out of business or otherwise quit. What is the reason? People who are not working are making as much as those who are. So what is the sense of that? You see where this is going, since the same story is true when workers of the 1940s and 1950s hit a 94 percent tax bracket, they decided to take the rest of the year off, at a minimum. They were being hit with what J. S. Mill called "a success tax." What it took Liberals to realize and most of them did not even realize it then, was that to have the brainpower of America sitting on the bench not producing anything, and was not helping the nation. The Kennedy administration saw it and cut taxes, which is one of the reasons I say that if he were alive now, there is no way he could be a part of the Democrat Party as it exists. Today as the state has become so intrusive in taxes, these business owners may decide to just be consumers rather than helping to build production by starting companies, or even leaving their companies open. Liberals try to tax companies out of existence on one hand, while on the other hand they cry for financial help during high unemployment and underemployment and extremely weak job growth. So bureaucrats do not get it; they never will. Liberals do not get it; they never will. When you get offensive with your taxes with wealthy people, who build all the employment opportunities by the way, they will pick up their gloves and go home. No need for them to work. Why do it for only 6 cents on a dollar earned?

So the wealthy people have their story of government gone wrong; the business owners, job creators, etc. But what about the rest of us? What about those of us not making $500,000? Raising taxes on wealthy job creators is not going to make up the deficit spending. That is the truth of this situation, but the so-called wisdom of Liberalism presses on saying it will. Just look at the various socialist governments around Europe or any other place in the West and you will find huge deficit spending in the hundreds of billions of dollars every year. When these governments try to tax the job creators in their country past the point of sense, the job creators stop production. That is why you see that *Atlas Shrugged* is printed in several languages. Unlike the rest of us, the rich do not have to work for taxable wages. They already have substantial wealth. About the rest of us; only the least-informed among our tax brackets believe the state will give us a break on our taxes after they tax the big money guys. They cannot because of the overhead costs. The millions of individuals who have "positions" in the government now, outweigh workers in the private sector and are very expensive to "carry." Therefore, all tax increases are eaten up in these overhead costs.

These bureaucracies are so very expensive to maintain, like with Social Security for example. The way it is treated by the state, it turns out to be not much more than just another tax, since they dip into it whenever they so choose. Over all, the state reminds me of a drug addict: their addiction is too fierce; they will go to great lengths to grab another revenue stream and keep spending at an exponentially greater rate each year. If Social Security has a big surplus one quarter, they just dip in a little deeper for a favorite spending habit. Then they levy more new taxes. In the 1980s I watched as the government developed a hazardous waste superfund through a new tax. All the toxic waste sites were supposed to be cleaned up across the country. It turns out, they spent the money on other things, and very, very few of the sites were ever cleaned up. Now, in need of more infusions of cash, global warming, or "Climate Change" as Liberals want to call it now since nothing is warming. This is planned to be just another superfund where huge taxes are collected that will all just go to support their drug habit; money to spend, spend, and spend. It is a beautiful fleecing as fleecings go, "you send it and we'll spend it" is their philosophy that dominates their attention as they wait and nearly panic in between cash infusions. You take all the risks, they want to share in the reward.

Someone may ask, "What happened to all the money; where did it go?" Most of the money was spent in administrative costs: more interns, bigger offices, more political junkets, more drones to watch over the public they do not trust, etc. If the government had a brain in their collective head, they would not raise taxes on anyone. They would give everyone a huge tax break. Turns out tax breaks, especially to businesses produce jobs and raise more tax revenue than tax increases. Tell a liberal that, they will call you nuts. Conservatives had a great plan to let wage earners control their own investment of Social Security. The Liberals screamed that the Conservatives were trying to steal the money, a trick the liberals actually pulled off themselves. The growing welfare state will not stop growing until we break the cycle of people depending on the other guy to feed them. Everyone should build their own assets and take control of their own lives through a remarkable system of private property ownership, and stop the coercion of the government.

Regulations That Attack Free Enterprise

To push for their proposed leveling of the playing field, the government and its regulations exert onerous influence over everyone, including business to shackle them in every decision that is made: from hiring, promoting workers, compensation, and benefits such as healthcare. There are literally tens of thousands of Securities and Exchange Commission regulations in the U.S. The Federal Trade Commission claims "self-imposed authority" to regulate virtually every business practice: how grapefruit juice is labeled to the types of revenue streams a company may establish, and the types of contracts a company may have. Law firms that practice labor law, must be able to access millions of pages of laws and regulations that impact employment, an employment contract or relationship, how employment may legally end between entities. Both law firms and companies must spend tens of thousands of dollars each year just to keep up with the new employment laws coming out of Washington, all supposedly to level the playing field.

Then Myriads of Agencies Wield Authority

George Washington would not recognize the government of today. Mountains of paperwork and bookkeeping are demanded by the IRS for even the tiniest businesses. For any merger or acquisition, the so-called Justice Department must be consulted for its opinion. They pick the winners and the losers. The Occupational Safety and Health Administration (OSHA) becomes just another taxing authority as they supervise job safety programs for every company. They have over 4,000 regulations which the agency enforces every year by fines. These regulations include such things as the size of toilets, the permissible shape of toilet seats, the height of ladders, the size of extension cords, etc. Generally, any program or product, such as a toilet, is made worse and more burdensome under their "guidance." Or as one man told me in a hardware store on day, "Toilets used to work, until the government got into the toilet business."

State and local regulations are many times more invasive and onerous than their federal cousins. All of us can remember the days when the types of mufflers and tail pipes on a car were regulated by the state and county with particular attention paid to those that might be louder than normal. Fines usually accompanied those, but the regulations get worse. In Montgomery County, Maryland, for example, inappropriate hand gestures are outlawed there; probably because some bureaucrat was fingered one day for cutting off another driver.

What most people do not know is that all these regulations existed back in 1978, when Jensen and Meckling first made their apocalyptic warnings about what was coming. Orson Wells saw it many years earlier with his novel, *1984*. Just turns out *1984* came later than anyone thought it would. In 1980 the budgets for federal regulatory agencies in the U.S. totaled about $6.2 billion, but had tripled to $18.5 billion by 1999. In 1982 constant dollars, that is a 57 percent increase, which was accompanied by more and more regulators on the payroll. In 2014 there are 10,000 more regulators than there were in 1980, all to effectively tax business with fines.

Regulation has affected the stock market also. Back before Obama, the market could have gone even higher than it is now, were it not for the large degree of governmental control over production that is exercised through regulation. While the market was more volatile because of many uncertainties created by the myriad of regulatory sneak attacks on companies, it is very possible that the 1987 U.S. market crash was caused by proposed regulation and taxation of corporate takeovers. Today with the Obama economy in the tank, the Dow Jones average is being propped up by the Federal Reserve which is infusing large amounts of printed dollars to support it. This action gives the impression that the economy is doing much better than what it actually is.

Beware of Government Wars

Government wars create suffering rather than relief and answers.

Regulations are killing America rapidly in every segment of society; socially, economically, and psychologically. Politicians are the sole instigators of the death nil legislation since they are the ones who voted them in. To pass the buck, some politicians often blame individual regulators or agencies of regulation for being high-handed when they simply enforce the regulatory law that Congress passed. I give you two prime examples. First, Congress passed the Immigration Reform and Control Act of 1986 (IRCA), but it is the U.S. Department of Labor (DOL) that is charged with enforcing or "regulating" it. Second, the Americans with Disabilities Act, which Congress also passed, is also enforced by two agencies within the DOL; the Equal Employment Opportunity Commission (EEOC) and the Office of Federal Contract Compliance Programs (OFCCP). "By law" through these regulatory agencies, companies are often forced to make accommodations for the potential hiring of a 425 pound mechanic who cannot fit under the vehicle, in case one applies for the job. This same accommodation applies for the hiring of half-blind school bus drivers, little league coaches who are paraplegic in wheelchairs, and to top all this off, the building of wheelchair ramps on strip club stages, just in case a disabled stripper applies for employment. Liberal politicians caused this suffering; no one else who did.

Regulation in many of these situations is nothing short of a tax which politicians dispense upon corporations and some individuals because they are not pandering to the political interests of those in control. It becomes an easy tax since corporate ownership is relatively invisible, widely dispersed and often politically in cohesive. To raise attention to this would be too volatile for corporate owners, shareholders, since their interests would most likely face declines in value on the market due to the press. Standing in contrast to this group are the special-interest groups which are, by their very definition very focused and politically organized; therefore they are usually immune from attack by the regulations.

American politicians can be bellwether leaders, active in planning large amounts of regulations upon the public; most are not passive in approaching their positions. Take Hillary Clinton, who goes on one of her "listening tours" where constituents press upon her and others like her what they want to see, she then comes back to Washington and focuses on passing legislation that will please the ones who are putting cash in her pockets. These political animals are true entrepreneurs in every sense of the word. They will create social and economic crises, or gorilla dust which is a perception of crises, then come forward offering their remedies to resolve the stated crises. This will involve their services, usually involving many loud speeches, rallying political favors. One of the favorite remedies a politician will offer as a means of resolution is war. War allows politicians to move the "out of bounds" markers from the scene, making an avenue for their myriad rationales to control and regulate society and economic activities even further. Once the war is over, the regulations are hardly ever abandoned. Here one can see the reason why basically all domestic policies are labeled as wars: war on drugs, on poverty, on fast food, on drunk driving, on unemployment, on global warming, etc. So presidents and other politicians are always proclaiming a crisis which must be answered by a war. Jimmy Carter once declared that there was a "crisis of confidence" after he had exhausted all other reasonable sounding crises to speak about. With Obama, we have a crisis of too many taxes, to which he proposes the typical solution of more taxes which should solve the original problem. One of the things many do not perceive is that politicians actually do better when their wars on poverty, drugs, and unemployment are not going well; the better it is for the politicians. For such a case they just propose fixes for their failed policies that always involve more new taxes, more government intervention, more government regulation; all to "solve" the problems they created with their previous activities.

Getting a politician like Obama, Feinstein, or Pelosi to admit there are a source of the problem is like trying to create rain on Mars. They will only blame other individuals or corporations as the villains, or capitalism in general. So we move from one crisis to another. Capitalism is blamed. New taxes are adopted with accompanying regulation and more government employees of course. Take the farming and agriculture industry, the government has had the policy ever since the Hoover administration to simultaneously pay farmers to grow more (with price supports) and less (with acreage allotments), and then to subsidize the thousands of failing farms with low-interest loans and grants where were a form of welfare. The result: the farm industry overall was made much weaker and volatile through regulation, reflected in the farm commodities prices on public markets as well as the stock prices of publicly-traded agri-business corporations. Once again, government regulation and intrusion is the culprit for these glitches, but the farm industry and agriculture business always was blamed.

In today's socialistic-charged atmosphere there are many professors, teachers, and writers who continuously present the need for government intervention into everyday economic systems of exchange between the private individuals or companies, because as they will say, the system is prejudicial, not perfect, or in need of repair. And the common chorus among these is that the government needs to do something to stop it.

The economists and political commentators with rare exceptions have been mistaken and misleading. Economic systems based on exchange between individuals and on selling and buying between firms usually correct themselves in time if they are free to adapt themselves to changing conditions of supply and demand. Government "cures" usually do more harm than good in the long run because of three stubborn and too-long neglected excesses of government: their "cures" are begun too soon, they do too much, and they are continued too long. Once a government cure is introduced, it stays for years or decades. Antitrust law to prevent or end monopoly, is continued long after the monopoly has been ended by technical invention or other cures.[3]

The simple truth today in the 21st century is that what remains of our democracy, which is in fact a representative republic, has had its character changed. It resembles an addict whose habit is growing so fast, that not even the amount of substance is able to satisfy new demands. It has spent everything in the bank accounts,

Chapter Two — When Government Becomes Evil and Destructive

savings account, and now is making demands for more with the increasing appetite. Whether we like it or not, it rules the greater portion of our lives, making greater and greater demands from us for more money each year. It should be very clear by now to anyone that the representative republic is no longer representing we the people, but has in fact become a plutocracy which seems to hold only a self-interest in survival. No longer does it focus, nor even give a glancing thought, to "representing" and "serving" the choices of the people who placed them there. Because of the inefficiencies of all branches of our government (the legislative, the judicial, and the executive); none will stand on the principle of the Constitution. Through this void we have become a socialist democracy with a fascist dictator at the top. The result is: it is a dictatorship. There was true genius in the form of government which our Framers gave us: the representative republic. Within it State's rights ruled, the central government was not powerful, resulting in the true feel of a freedom with most of the control being held at the state and local level.

Today, conservatives in legislative positions seem to lack courage. In this void, the Progressives have done a power grab. States' rights are fading. Everyone seems to be working for a boss in Washington, D. C. In reality then, two of the three divisions of government have been neutralized, resembling a group of people who are under the effects of Captain Kirk's "stun gun" from the TV Show *Star Trek*. The result is a dictatorship from the remaining branch of government, the presidency. What is seen then are 500 "representatives" walking in lock step speaking together but in the wrong voice; the voice of Marxism or Socialism. How could voices of reasonable conservative people be silenced? Where is the representation for the people? We need to examine the path for these actions. How did all this current mess get set up?

The 1920s, 1930s, and 1940s Set This Up

History will show that the two world wars combined with the twenty-year interwar period, has impacted events directly in ways most people could never imagine. Movements started, matured and exploded in every possible direction. While appearing to be unrelated, they were critically linked to the tensions created by the wars, with the interwar period becoming a social incubator for the initial movements feeding tensions in the world. "See you in 20 years," the diplomats said to each other as they left the Paris Peace Conference. The message was prophetic since war did indeed break out just over 20 years after the signing of that Versailles Treaty in 1919. The world was changing drastically during that interwar period.

Other significant and deadly historical trends, many of them indirectly related to the First World War itself, were starting. European imperialism, admittedly influenced by the strains of global war, was developing its first real fissures. British socialism was begun during these days. When Churchill later retired in the 1950s, socialism consumed England with a vicious appetite. The intellectual movement associated with Modernism accelerated during the 1920s. The electronic media emerged rapidly. The BBC started radio broadcasts in 1921. Einstein got the Nobel Prize for Physics in 1921. The great Max Weber died in 1920. Freudian terminology: "Oedipus Complex" or "displacement activity", were becoming household terms, at least in educated circles. Dress hemlines shot upward. Jazz altered popular music radically. Movies got sound and color.[4]

Immediately following World War I, a few democracies peeked out from under the rubble in postwar Europe, but as in the case of Germany, totalitarian regimes and makeshift dictatorships started the wave of the future. As George Gershwin wrote into the lyrics of "Slap that Bass" in 1937,

> Dictators would be better off
> If they'd zoom zoom now and then.
> Today, you can see that the happiest men
>
> All got rhythm.
> With politics and taxes
> And people grinding axes
> There's no happiness

Unfortunately, though many basses were slapped during the interwar period, from Los Angeles to St. Louis to Paris to Vienna, the world was still in a mess.[5]

The French and their historians called this time the *Entre-deux-guerres*, a time which proved to have seriously altered the direction of events in world history. If any history student wishes to grasp the true foundations of the world today, then he or she will need to grasp the events of the 1920s and 1930s; they were fateful. Most history classes facilitated in our government schools do only a surface scan of American and world history. Most start with a mention of World War II, and then quickly move into the 1960s; then quickly to the modern day. Any prior history for today's student is in effect a dark hole; the "teacher" can make it into whatever they want it to be at the moment.

For one thing, the *Entre-deux-guerres* practically created totalitarianism. The Bolsheviks captured the Russian government in 1917-1918. Shortly thereafter, Mussolini's Fascism took control in Italy, and later Hitler's Nazism in Germany. All three cases featured movements that gave life to the words "terrible simplifiers," a phrase coined by historian Jacob Burckhardt during the late nineteenth century. Burckhardt meant the kind of mass movements guided by violent demagogues to which European civilization had become susceptible. The interwar years delivered in spades, under the guidance of Hitler, Mussolini, and Stalin; and lesser simplifiers too. The first socialist governments ruled for various lengths of time in Western and Central Europe. And East-Central Europe was likewise guided by socialist policies, for most of the time after the mid-twenties by nationalist dictators. And where nominal socialists were not in power, the welfare/warfare state came to be the norm. The forces of collectivism found fulfillment in many, many ways throughout the world.[6]

During the same time, there was another awakening of sorts out of which true champions of liberty and democracy came forth to properly frame the events. The framing was a contrast that was visible between true liberty against the backdrop of socialism; seeing that contrast gives proper understanding of the movements. The Libertarian movement came of age as did the socialist calculation debate, as well as totalitarianism, the Great Depression, the ultimate promotion of Hitler and Nazism, and the New Deal in the U.S.

From a number of perspectives, the First World War was the death knell of the century of what at that time of the world was called "bourgeois liberalism."[7] There is confusion surrounding that term today, since by the latter half of the twentieth century, the word "liberal" no longer carried the meaning it once had. The bourgeois liberalism or classical liberalism of earlier generations was a belief in free markets, decentralized government or a weaker federal government, civil liberties, free trade, and toleration, especially of others. It is the true context from which we got our word, humane. But liberals define term "liberalism" in a completely different manner. It has come to mean big government controlling all social and economic life. It translates into centralized processes, and the welfare state we see today. Today's statists and news broadcaster such as Chris Matthews co-op words of the free-market for their own use; thus giving them totally new meanings. For example, when a statist uses the word business, he really means unions. They are not interested in what the business does, but rather what the business can give them in power and control. The word business in their world has a whole new definition.

World War I certainly paved the way for totalitarianism, statism, and the resulting mass violence that distorts modern life. So few understood what was really happening early on. Fewer still recognized the war as the facilitator of the future for what it was, and fought back. Understanding what this crucial period of time meant both for society and as a piece of the history of individualism, we must investigate ideas, culture, politics, economics, and more.

Some periods of history produce more intensity upon the human experience, and impact the future more than others. The 20 years between the wars was one of those intense periods, producing both good and evil. The period certainly produced a design for the world to come.[8]

The Two Camps of Government

Generally, all social theory can be "boiled down" or condensed into two camps: one is those purposing that society is here to bring peace, and two; those for which the ingredient and purpose is violence and conquest. The governments for each will take on the features of one of two similar overarching groups. This is the fundamental distinction between capitalism, known as social liberalism to the older generations, and fascism.

Capitalism, in its truest form as seen in America many years ago, represented a movement of the theory of society in which human cooperation emerged spontaneously and without coercion, by means of the natural processes of the market economy. In other words, it did not rely heavily on government. It recognized that society seemed to manage itself without the involvement of extraneous forces like kings, aristocracies, or parliaments, and that the intervention of those forces was more likely aimed at the enrichment of a favored group or of the state itself than of at the well-being of society at large.[9]

Free-enterprise with its associated competition to produce was itself a spontaneous product of capitalism. It can operate without government directing it since it has from the outset encouraged entrepreneurs to focus on producing the outputs which are valued at varying degrees by society, and then to produce them in the most cost efficient, quality-driven, and quick to market, so as not to miss the market window for the product. Using their skill sets, appropriate education, passion, and field of desire, individuals focus on producing services or the consumer goods for everyone to enjoy. None of this required at that time, nor does it require now the intervention and regulation of "the state." The market when allowed to operate freely will work out problems and appropriate solutions for the consumer, the product, and the workers.

For the classical liberal [or the current conservative], the state was almost an afterthought, never the center of business. Some would have it provide a few basic services, while others conceived of it as nothing more than a night watchman. Beginning with Gustave de Molinari, the classical-liberal tradition even groped toward the possibility that the state was a dangerous, parasitical, and ultimately unnecessary monopoly. And, of course, it was against a backdrop of peace that the classical liberal described the progress of mankind.[10]

A fascist views society and the state through a totally different lens. The simple conventional virtues of commerce, that of producing, trading, and earning profit, working smart and hard, and moving on to the next day to repeat the process, are viewed with hatred and contempt when stacked next to the code of the warrior, which is what the fascist considers himself. To the fascist, greatness comes not through these ordinary daily pursuits of the market, nor the conviction to perform the duties of a position description, or in the obedience to the duties of one's state in life. No, it comes only through the struggle against other performers, who are viewed as ruthless and greedy, for which the fascist needs the watchful eye and discipline of the government "to level the playground." And therein the cry for social justice is born and raised.

It is Benito Mussolini's famous remark, "Everything for the state, nothing outside the state; nothing above the state", that truly sums up the essence of fascism. The good of the Nation, as defined by the fascist leader, surpasses all other concerns and allegiances. When a fascist speaks there is a tenor of religious reverence for the Nation. Illustrating that was a 1920s Italian fascist youth movement which composed the following creed:

"I believe in Rome the Eternal, the mother of my country, and in Italy her eldest Daughter, who was born in her virginal bosom by the grace of God; who suffered through the barbarian invasions, was crucified and buried; who descended to the grave and was raised from the dead in the nineteenth century; who ascended into Heaven in her glory in 1918 and 1922; who is seated on the right hand of her mother Rome; and who for this reason shall come to judge the living and the dead. I believe in the genius of Mussolini, in our Holy Father Fascism, in the communion of its martyrs, in the conversion of Italians, and in the resurrection of the Empire."[11]

For this type of worshipful devotion to be captured by the Nation, as viewed through the text of 1920s fascist youth, there must be an even greater allegiance and unaltered devotion to the nation's charismatic leader. The leader's absolute will must be unimpeded as he moves through his own edicts, orders, and orchestrated blather. The crucial ingredient for the Fascist nation's successful destiny is that the leader must be obeyed by the masses. Ultimately, the leaders will and desire must trump all business activities on Main Street and the array of accomplishments that comprise the free market. The various companies, professions, unions, and government departments must work together with a conscious plan to ensure the best outcome for the leader, which feeds down then to the Nation. When you preview the current scene in America, hearing current-day liberals and progressives loudly calling conservatives and libertarians "fascists," it would almost be humorous except for knowing the true meaning. No one could be more anti-fascist than a libertarian or conservative.

Political centralization is essential to fascism, for if the Nation is the embodiment of the people and if it is through the Nation that every individual realizes his destiny, there can be no toleration for resistance by lesser jurisdictions within the Nation. The Nation takes on the character of the charismatic leader, demanding not just respect but total devotion as States lose their rights, and become nothing more than vassal districts. Everything must be done for the good of the central state.

One does not have to look very hard or far to see the tendencies and features of fascism in America today. We have not totally arrived yet, but are well on the way. But It would be foolish to pretend that America is the very opposite of the fascist dystopias like Hitler's Germany or Mussolini's Italy. Whether it is the emphasis on centralization, the glorification of the leader as he speaks of what he is doing for the nation, the yearning for a "third way" between capitalism and socialism, the elevation of "state service" above the same areas of service we freely provide one another on the market, the creepy and incessant references to "my president," "our president," or "the One," or the depiction of the state as the newly arrived instrument of divinity, the commonalities are neither trivial nor few.

Americans no doubt recoil from or laugh at that passage from the Italian Fascists I shared with you a few moments ago. But few Americans are in a position to render such a judgment. Most have absorbed the idea that their government, far from a merely utilitarian contrivance established to provide them with some basic services, as many early Americans doubtless conceived of it, is a redemptive force in the world.[12]

Fascism becomes a quasi-religion of the state, having many of the liturgical trappings of a faith system. Today, you can hear the "You will never see another leader like this who has so much charisma," or "If you question the president, you're a racist." These statements seem almost churchy and eerily familiar to the "Hail Mary" for Catholics or the "Don't ever question the pastor," which Baptists commonly hear as one of the three points in a sermon. The result is that many Americans, and perhaps many nominal American Christians, are for that reason not scandalized at politicians' appropriation of religious language to describe their government. It bothers them not at all to learn that the iconic Abraham Lincoln said "the gates of hell shall not prevail against" American government ideals, or that when George W. Bush said "the light shined in darkness and the darkness did not overcome it," and by "light" it seems he must have meant American government ideals.

In U.S. history, historians have been unkind to U.S. Presidents who avoided these messianic overtones, or war, or who seemed modest in office. They rarely even received honorable mention. In fact, since these historians usually favor form over substance. Presidents who lacked the qualities mentioned above were denounced as dull and boring, or were totally neglected in their pages of record; and sometimes they were named only to shackle them with the horrid historical rumors of their day, possibly giving only one sentence in posterity. All this in spite of how good they might have been. You can guess at the views and activities of the presidents favored by the opinion molders. The paradox in a supposedly educated nation is to view near total failures in office. Some possessing bankrupt personalities or pathologies that would put the average citizen sentenced to a lengthy prison term; receiving praise and honor as if being divinity and having healed the world. You can almost smell the apocalyptic ink the writers use on them. We must heed the prophetic message of historian Ralph Raico as he once warned, "Beware of the politician who is 'beloved.'"

The cult of personality surrounding the U.S. president has waxed and waned over the past century, waxing in concert with the heightened amount of National Socialism or Fascism involved in the character filling the Oval Office. Gradually it has reached greater and greater heights until now culminating in the creepy crescendo of disgusting videos of schoolchildren being led by union teachers in pledging their allegiance to Barack Obama with their "Mmmm, Mmmm, Mmmm!" of adoration. Then appearing was the YouTube videos of Hollywood actors promising their eternal loyalty. While other presidents, Bill Clinton and Woodrow Wilson were looked upon with some adoration of the progressives, none of them ever reached the level by their fans that Obama has; being hailed by his apostles with titles ranging from "The One," "The Divine Pharaoh," all the way to the "Black Jesus."

Chapter Two — When Government Becomes Evil and Destructive

The Progressive propaganda has worked, to some extent at least. The mainstream progressive media has circled the wagons to protect their vanguard as when Edward Snowden revealed the extent to which this their leader and government was spying on and lying to them. The comments from many listeners of network news and even those on Capitol Hill brought back scenes of the Old West, as they were concerned about how their ruler would react, when they demanded not that these spying activities cease, but that the leaker himself be captured by a global posse and silenced through a public lynching. The man who had embarrassed their czar should be tried for treason and executed according to most of the frightened progressive Democrats and Republicans. I have heard this phenomenon described as a case of society-wide Stockholm Syndrome and I do not think that is far from the mark.

If some of the superstitions of fascism have made their way into American life, it could be because both fascism and whatever it is that America has become, share in a common and maniacal superstition: namely, the state itself. The state has been cloaked in an element of mystique with all manner of flattering terms but confusing rhetoric. The state looks after the general welfare, provides economic stability, protects us from the bad guys, prevents inequality, and binds us together in a common cause greater than ourselves.[13] At least that is what the statist will claim to their protégé, while that same state strips many citizens of their freedoms, money and worldly goods.

A microcosm of this trend is the current situation in America, compounded by Republicans; currently they are doing everything they can to avoid any kind of disagreement with the czar. They have caved on everything piece of legislation such as the debt ceiling, and appear to not be willing to have confrontation even on Obama's brazen lawlessness in any matter. It is time we viewed the 2014 central state for what it really is: a mechanism that has devolved into "authoritarianism" by which president rules with an iron fist, while legislators cower in the corner from that fist. However, they all perform these roles only to enrich themselves at the expense of the ruled. Everything else including the feigned love and concern for the American public is nothing but "gorilla dust."

Presenting the New and Improved Americano Fascism

When the typical person thinks of Fascism, he probably identifies it with the cult of some foreign leader, framed in the nationalistic style and picture-form of Hitler and Mussolini. "Fascism" has become a term of general disparagement and rebuke, except of course for the fascist. At times it is tossed casually in the direction of anything a critic happens to dislike. Unfortunately, fascism is a real form of government, and basically has become a stick with which to beat opponents arbitrarily. The misappropriated abuse of this important word undermines its true value as a term referring to a very real phenomenon. Therefore the spirit of fascism that lives on now in America is not easily identifiable due to confusion of terminology.

What, then, is fascism? For the fascist, the following summation is true,

- It is an aggressive nationalism and imperialism;
- It is a supreme leader who brings a domination of the economy, the business and social life of citizens, and even the state or regional governments by the central or federal government.
- For a fascist, the state, the emperor, or the federal government is the apparatus by which the people's common destiny is realized, and in which the potential for social justice and social greatness are to be found.
- To accomplish this, individual rights, and the individual himself, are strictly subordinate to the state's great and glorious goals for the nation.
- In foreign affairs, the fascist attitude is reflected in a belligerent chauvinism, in contempt for other peoples, and a society-wide reverence social justice and the martial virtues.

This sounds like the modern America. Surely we are being punished for our past sins.

We have at a minimum, a limited form of dictatorship. Evidence is seen when the president can say, "I have a pen and I have a phone." In effect he is saying, "I will do what I want if Congress won't agree with me." That is a dictator imposes his will over the entire country. We are reaping the results of what has happened over the past century, for the executive branch has spread so dramatically that it has become a joke to speak of checks and balances. What the kids used to learn in civics class has nothing to do with reality. As for the leadership principle, there is no greater lie in American public life than the propaganda we hear every four years about how the new president/messiah is going to usher in the great dispensation of peace, equality, liberty, and global human happiness. The idea here is that the whole of society is really shaped and controlled by a single will; a point that requires a leap of faith so vast that you have to disregard everything you know about reality to believe it. It brings to mind more totally, the revolutions of yesteryear in Latin America, with the El Presidente campaign of the challenger promising land reform, more rights, and social reform. Once elected the new emperor, he or she tossed out the earlier promises, especially that of land reform, did the usual power grab, and things continued the downward spiral for the subjects under the caudillo. Given that against the backdrop of the last six years, allow me to be the first to welcome you to the American version of Fascism and Marxism.

At the core of fascism beats the heart of madness for imperial control of the economy. As some long ago realized and pointed out, socialism can come about while the form of capitalism remains. In this type of socialism, the government dictates economic decisions and the ostensible business owners must obey its orders. Hitler called his version "National Socialism," which was in reality fascism. But whether name you hang around the neck of this creature, it is precisely this pattern found in the Nazi regime, and, unfortunately, it has become increasingly prevalent in America today. This pattern is seen daily, the latest example being the "unlawful" edict of the current president regarding Obamacare. It is suddenly illegal for a company to reduce its workforce in order to cut taxes by refusing to provide the new health care for an employee. I mean he said so. Thus he has spoken and thus it shall be written. And the teeth of the law: the company must prove to the IRS that their actions were "lawful" according to the new edict. Not to be confusing, but this action shows a rapid growing fascism which has quickly become "Stalinism," which is total autocratic rule and total forced suppression of dissent.

The reality of the bureaucratic administration has been with us in America to greater or lesser degrees at least since the New Deal; that is when FDR modeled the planning bureaucracy that lived in World War I. The planned economy, whether in Mussolini's time or ours, requires a ton of bloated bureaucracy. With FDR, it had to be run through one of the 250 some odd newly created departments or agencies. Bureaucracy is the heart, lungs, and veins of the planning state. And yet to regulate an economy as thoroughly as this one is today is to kill prosperity with a billion tiny cuts.[14]

Of course, those who are patriots and those devoted to freedom will in jettison an identified fascism, with its blind power worship of a neo-god figure on the throne and its dangerous economics, as well as "the welfare lotto" as I call it which seems to have new winners every hour. Set against those who reject fascism, are those who find the fascist dream, as wonderful, appealing, and possessing an emotional ecstasy which brings shortness of breath and weakness in the knees. The good and bad news is that a fascist state cannot sustain itself long as nations go. The underpinnings cannot hold up financially, morally, or ethically.

The fascist style emphasized inspiration, magnificence, industrial progress, grandeur, all headed by a valiant leader making smart decisions about all things. At least the propaganda machine said they were smart decisions. This style of American rule was present during the New Deal and has raised its ugly head a few times through the Cold War; and is in full bloom now.

Fascism lives in Never, Never Land. Meaning it can never achieve its aims. So there is a way in which it makes sense to speak of it as a stage of history: we are in what appears to be a late stage of fascism. The opulence has faded from the bloom, and we are being left with is a gun pointed at our heads. There is a huge and growing debt and morality which is in the sub-basement of humanity. And the system was created so it could be sold as being great, but it is reduced in our time to being crude. It is like a star that once appeared brilliant, used up its resources, exploded into a supernova or neutron star, and then collapsed into a black hole. Such seems to be the lifecycle of our home: America. Valor is now violence. Majesty is now malice.[15] And so we are left with the propaganda machine telling us how brilliant the president is, with all his programs. Like the Left says about Obamacare; or Obama's green jobs policy; or his foreign policy; or his home remortgage policy; or his Keynesian deficit spending plan. All are totally bankrupt, but the media continues to talk of their wisdom.

Over the years we seem to have built a box around us. Will we be able to pass GO, let alone collect the $200? The answer is to find leaders who are willing to say and do things which are unpopular, socially and politically, all for the good of the Constitution. They must say things that others wish not to hear.

The Destruction by Unchecked Liberal or Fascist Government Is Producing Poverty

The U.S. Department of Commerce by direct orders from their chief publishes duplicitous poverty statistics in order to make poverty appear worse than it actually is and to "justify" such economically disparaging policies as increases minimum wage increases and tax increases for the alleged purpose of redistributing income to the "poor." Take for example, in its published poverty statistics the Commerce Department does not deduct taxes from the reported income of the more affluent Americans, thereby artificially inflating their income; while at the same time not counting any welfare benefits as income of the "poor," which artificially deflates their income. This shows a more radically larger and fraudulent gap between wealthy and poor. This statistic is then used to promote a war on poverty and the "crisis" in America claims that also there is also an obesity crisis; especially among the less affluent.

The huge challenge today is to get a wider slice or segment of the public involved in the cause for liberty in America. People seem to be asleep, moving through the motions of ritual life, seemingly unaware of the freedoms which are being robbed from them by the state. As such, some have called them 'sheeple'. So how do we get sheeple awakened and alert to the cause of liberty? I think it is by continuing to teach both the historical and philosophical elements of liberty as are found in the Constitution. We can turn to people who have exemplified liberty in their own lives. The career of Ron Paul stands out as a fair example. He knew that the philosophy of liberty, when explained persuasively and with conviction had a universal appeal. Every group to whom he spoke heard a slightly different presentation of that message, as Ron showed how their particular concerns were addressed most effectively by a policy of freedom. Because he was a perceived threat to the progressive machine, the attack dogs of the media made him appear eerie, detached. Of course one of the best ever examples was "The Gipper," Ronald Reagan. He is gone now, but his legacy will continue to live on within those of us who believe in the liberty which was originally established in this nation, and also who have believed

Chapter Two — When Government Becomes Evil and Destructive

in the man Ronald Reagan, because he loved the liberty and freedom this nation afforded also. You can certainly learn much about liberty by reading his speeches. Many of his earlier speeches from his early days as a private citizen through the first two years of his presidency are available under one title, *A Time For Choosing*.[16] And it is a time for choosing, for if we do not change direction soon, we will forever lose our beloved democracy. Immediate steps of action must be taken simply because our government is exponentially causing the problem of poverty that it is claiming it can solve later.

Government is not the answer to the problem of destruction — Government is the problem.

Supporters of warfare, welfare, and Wonder Woman cheered as Congress passed a one trillion dollar "omnibus" appropriation bill [the week of January 15, 2014]. This legislation funds the operations of government for the remainder of the fiscal year. Wonder Woman fans can cheer that buried in the bill was a $10,000 grant for a theater program to explore the comic book heroine.

That is just one of the many outrageous projects buried in this 1,582-page bill. The legislation gives the Department of Education more money to continue nationalizing education via "common core." Also, despite new evidence of Obamacare's failure emerging on an almost daily basis, the Omnibus bill does nothing to roll back this disastrous law.[17]

Apparently, due to the feeble and frail knowledge of how money operates within an economy keeps the social justice enthusiasts from campaigning against the government, except for bias in their flavor of politics. There should be politicians, social commentators, religious leaders, welfare agency heads and anyone who cares about keeping people whole in their bi-weekly pay checks. The protestors are silent, absent or both in spite of the inflationary habits of government with the consequences of "highway robbery" where the masses are concerned. Either that or the call for social justice is just empty promises.

The current system of fractional reserve banking and central banking stands in stark opposition to a market economy monetary regime in which the market participants could decide themselves, without state pressure or coercion, what money they want to use, and in which it would not be possible for anyone to expand the money supply because they simply choose to do so.

The expansion of the money supply, made possible through central banks and fractional reserve banking, is in reality what allows inflation, and thus, declining income in real terms. In *The Theory of Money and Credit* Ludwig von Mises wrote: "The most important of the causes of a diminution in the value of money of which we have to take account is an increase in the stock of money while the demand for it remains the same, or falls off, or, if it increases, at least increases less than the stock. A lower subjective valuation of money is then passed on from person to person because those who come into possession of an additional quantity of money are inclined to consent to pay higher prices than before."[18]

When there are price increases caused by an expansion of the money supply, the prices of various goods and services do not rise to the same degree, and do not rise at the same time. Mises explains the effects:

"While the process is under way, some people enjoy the benefit of higher prices for the goods or services they sell, while the prices of the things they buy have not yet risen or have not risen to the same extent. On the other hand, there are people who are in the unhappy situation of selling commodities and services whose prices have not yet risen or not in the same degree as the prices of the goods they must buy for their daily consumption."[19]

The simple truth is that when wages of worker increase at a slower rate than the price of milk, bread, eggs, or peanut butter the relationship between income and assets are what I call a financial death spiral. Today, because of the inflationary cycle, heads of households will work two or three jobs and have less net take home dollars in real spending power than years ago when he had just one job. We should say no to these ways of managing our money. We are supposed to be the government. What we say goes; at least that is what we were told in school. That is surely a bait and switch, since now that one who sits in the presidency is betting that we will blink before he does. The result of us not standing up and making him blink, the madness continues. It is time to make him blink. But while the madness continues, there are several ways that will bring financial impoverishment to most people with an inflationary money supply that goes unchecked.

The Cantillon Effect

The uneven distribution of price inflation is known as the Cantillon effect: purchasing power moves away from those who hold old money to whoever gets new money. Those who receive the newly created money first (primarily the state and the banks, but also some large companies) are the beneficiaries of easy money. They can make purchases with the new money at goods prices that are still unchanged. Those who obtain the newly created money only later, or do not receive any of it, are harmed (wage-earners and salaried employees, retirees). They can only buy goods at prices which have, in the meantime, risen.[20]

History has produced accounts of "hyperinflation" like that of Nigeria in the 1990s. In 1995, inflation in Nigeria reached an unprecedented annual rate at 72.8%. This was caused mainly by rising prices associated with higher wages and excessive monetary injection the printing of money by the federal government into the economy.[21]

The Cantillon effect was in full force as the spending power of workers continually worsened so rapidly that some reports from the country showed that pay cycles of bi-weekly had to be shortened since their purchasing power with their currency would not buy but a reduced percentage what it could at the start of the pay cycle. Eventually, as the report went, some workers were being paid twice daily. Yes, that is right. They were paid at noon and at the end of the work day, because inflation was reducing spending power so rapidly. Said differently, what could be purchased at noon in 1995 with 100 *naira* had increased in inflationary price well beyond the 100 *naira* by the end of the day.

The Destruction of Asset Price Inflation

Investors with greater assets can better spread their investments and assets and are thus in a position to invest in tangible assets such as stocks, real estate, and precious metals. When the prices of those assets rise due to an expansion of the money supply, the holders of those assets may benefit as their assets gain in value. Those holding assets become more wealthy while people with fewer assets or no assets either profit little or cannot profit at all from the price increases.[22] Participles were dangling at terrible angles.

Currently precious metals especially gold and silver are being purchased and traded daily at record amounts. Those who hold greater amounts of currency are advantaged over those who have little. Thus the expanse between the two groups grows larger with the inflationary price on assets.

The Credit Market Amplifies the Problems for the Disadvantaged

The effects of asset price inflation can be amplified by the credit market. Those who have a higher income can carry higher credit in contrast to those with lower income, by acquiring real estate, for example, or other assets. If real estate prices rise due to an expansion of the money supply, they may profit from those price increases and the gap between rich and poor grows even faster.

Boom and Bust Cycles Create Unemployment

The direct cause of unemployment is the inflexibility of the labor market, caused by state interference and labor union pressures. An indirect cause of unemployment is the expansion of the paper money supply, which can lead to illusory economic booms that in turn lead to mal-investment. Especially in inflexible labor markets, when these malinvestments become evident in a down economy, it ultimately leads to higher and more lasting unemployment that is often most severely felt among the lowest-income households.[23]

The Destruction of the Expanding State

Once the gap in income distribution and asset distribution has been opened, the supporters and protectors of social justice will speak out, not knowing (or not saying) that it is the state itself with its monopolistic monetary system that is responsible for the conditions described. Said differently, they want the fox which caused the problems to guard the henhouse.

It is a deceitful "business model" in which the state creates social inequality through its monopolistic monetary system, splits society into poor and rich, and makes people dependent on welfare. It then intervenes in a regulatory and distributive manner, in order to justify its existence. The economist Roland Baader observed:

> "The political caste must prove its right to exist, by doing something. However, because everything it does, it does much worse, it has to constantly carry out reforms, i.e., it has to do something, because it did something already. It would not have to do something, had it not already done something. If only one knew what one could do to stop it from doing things."[24]

The state even exploits the uncertainty in the population about the true reasons for the growing gap in income and asset distribution. For example, The Fourth Poverty and Wealth Report of the German Federal Government stated that since 2002, there has been a clear majority among the German people in favor of carrying out measures to reduce differences in income.

The reigning paper money system is at the center of the growing income inequality and expanding poverty rates we find in many countries today. Nevertheless, states continue to grow in power in the name of taming the market system that has supposedly caused the impoverishment actually caused by the state and its allies.

If those who claim to speak for social justice do nothing to protest this, their silence can only have two possible reasons. They either do not understand how our monetary system functions, in which case, they should do their research and learn about it; or they do understand it and are cynically ignoring a major source of poverty because they may in fact be benefiting from the paper money system themselves.[25]

The Plot Deepens with War on Private Property

It appears our government has advanced to the stage of full collectivism in their war on private property owners. It was Clarence Carson in the 1970s, after watching Lyndon Johnson wage his so-called "war on poverty," that he published his *The War on the Poor*, an obvious takeoff on Johnson's war. Any actual war the government wages is not against circumstances but against a definable segment of people, as Carson noted. The policies that Johnson pursued, as predicted by conservatives and later analyzed by credible financial analysts, put a target on the backs of the poor, and they were indeed impacted the worst by government pursuits. In every

CHAPTER TWO — WHEN GOVERNMENT BECOMES EVIL AND DESTRUCTIVE

new initiative of the Great Society, the effect of those policies was to raise prices on various products, which caused the poor in America to suffer while a few selected special interests prospered.

The only change in America in this activity by our government is that things are worse now than there were then under Johnson. Personal property owners have become the target over the years. Most of the political initiatives center on personal property attacks, but it is all done in the name of alleviating all our troubles. No matter how severe the pain and misery we feel from these lingering policies, every election brings a new busload of politicians claiming their plan will fix the ailments if elected. Bill Clinton's famous statement, "I feel your pain," certainly comes to mind. Of course, incumbents not only argue their policies will work, given enough time, but they always blame the political opposition for it not working. How many times has Barack Obama blamed his opponents for derailing his promised feats, the Tea Party, NRA, Christians, or anyone else, for his ideas not working? Moreover, they tell us that they have been hindered in the performance of their promised feats because of the activities of their political opponents. Alternatively, challengers argue that only their proposed interventions will work to produce the desired economic prosperity. And so it goes, as each pursues the needed votes to ensure election.

Unfortunately for our aspiring magicians, the media does not take the process very seriously but devotes a great deal of time to favoring just certain candidates during the debate, namely the ones who favor socialism, collectivism, or Marxism, without asking any serious questions as to whether intervention of any sort is a prudent course of action. The media thus gives no credibility to the process that would not exist without their endorsement. The media makes claims that the government is like a genie, able to produce something from thin air and unthinking people in the towns and suburbs around the country begin to believe it. To date this seems to be the case, since the failures of past policies are generally not pointed to unless they belong to those from across the political aisle as a reason for doubting current political promises.

There is, of course, one issue that our political aspirants never wish to discuss at any length: the costs of their proposed legislation. If they are forced to discuss this topic at all, they simply argue that the many benefits of their scheme will vastly outweigh the upfront costs. Moreover, they invariably promote a plan saying they will impose the costs upon the so-called rich people because they can afford it. Since no one knows any of these very rich people, many feel secure that the politician's plan will ultimately prove beneficial to them.

The magician, or politician, lives by his deception. If the audience is ever able to see the reality of what the political class is actually doing, then these magicians would have to practice their magic craft privately. But this kind of fraud exposes them to the danger of spending time in prison. Bernie Madoff comes to mind. If they were not willing to risk jail time, the political class would instead have to work in the private sector, and produce results for a change. No longer would it be possible for them to live off of the fruits of other peoples' labor. They are ready to keep the average citizen in the dark so they can keep their own gravy train rolling.

Actually, the sleight of hand and deception of the modern day politician is nothing new. It is a very old practice, and history is full of cases where governmental authorities lived off the production of others. In *The Wealth of Nations*, Adam Smith observed that "[t]here is no art which one government sooner learns of another, than that of draining money from the pockets of the people." It is their very favorite practice by the way.[26]

The theory and process of looting citizens has clearly gained momentum with the newest administration. It has embarked on a full-scale assault on the American public, aimed not only at ravaging the poor for a few special interests, but vastly increasing the number of people consigned to poverty. Whether we look at Obama and the Democrats' cap-and-trade legislation or their health care reform or their pork barrel stimulus bill, in each case they intend to raise prices and increase taxes on us all. A few corporate interests will benefit majestically from such nonsense; the vast majority of us will be impoverished. The saddest part of all of this is that no one seems to care that the economic impact will be most heavily felt by those weakest among us. The gross immorality of this oppression and tyranny should be evident to anyone who would but casually look at the situation. However, thus far the mainstream media has given Obama a pass, and the general population has chosen to remain blindly ignorant.[26]

It is nothing new. In the political game, it seems that everyone is hoping to be numbered among the few beneficiaries. Moreover, it seems that people are basically unwilling to face a rather obvious economic truth: in this world there are only a few ways for each of us to obtain the things that we desire. We can produce the things ourselves starting from scratch, produce something valued by others and use that in trade for what we want, take the things from others by fraud or at gunpoint, or receive them as gifts of charity. Only the first two of these are economic. Theft and charity cannot be universalized, because each can be achieved only by the prior production of others. It is this fact that led H. L. Mencken to note in his day that elections in America were nothing more than advanced auctions on stolen property. Or, as he quipped, "A good politician is quite as unthinkable as an honest burglar."[27]

Indeed, redistribution of property and money by government is simple systematic theft, whereby the politically well-healed steal from the masses. Whether it was the orchestrated financial bailouts or the takeover of two auto makers by the Obama administration, government theft of private property is alive and well. It matters little to these people whether their actions impoverish others. Rather, they selfishly act upon their own greed and pursue political means to steal what they want from others. In truth, everyone whose hand is out begging for some government favor is participating in this immoral and unjust activity. Government is simply incapable of creating something out of nothing.[28]

Regardless of what some newsmen evidently believe, Barack Obama is not the Almighty, capable of calling things into existence *ex nihilo*. It does not matter whether it is Woodrow Wilson, Herbert Hoover, Franklin Roosevelt, Lyndon Johnson, Richard Nixon, Jimmy Carter, Bill AND Hillary Clinton, or Barrack Obama. A thief is a thief, and all thieves impoverish their victims.[29]

Destruction Caused by the Federal Reserve

The Democratic Party gained prominence in the first half of the nineteenth century as being the party that opposed the Second Bank of the United States. In the process, it tapped into an anti-state sentiment that proved so strong that we wouldn't see another like it until the next century.

Its adversaries were Whig politicians who defended the bank and its ability to grow the government and their own personal fortunes at the same time. They were, in fact, quite open about these arrangements. It was considered standard-operating procedure for Whig representatives to receive monetary compensation for their support of the Bank when leaving Congress. The Whig Daniel Webster even expected annual payments while in Congress. Once he complained to the Bank of the United States President Nicholas Biddle, "I believe my retainer has not been renewed or refreshed as usual. If it be wished that my relation to the Bank should be continued, it may be well to send me my usual retainer."[30]

No wonder these people were often pummeled with canes on the House floor.

It is little wonder that early Democrats garnered such popular support and would demand Andrew Jackson end America's experiment with central banking. Jackson called it "dangerous to the liberty of the American people because it represented a fantastic centralization of economic and political power under private control."

But the courtship between the political classes and their cronies would continue in the decades following Lincoln's assassination. Those politically well-connected groups that benefited from early central banking continued to benefit from government finance, especially off of "internal improvements," which is the nineteenth-century term for pork. National banking would appear during the War Between the States, setting in place a banking system in which individual banks would be chartered by the federal government. The government itself would use regulations backed by a new armed U.S. Treasury police force to encourage the banks' inflation and protect them from the market penalties that inflation would otherwise bring them, such as the loss of specie and the occurrence of bank runs.

The boom and bust cycle... became worse and worse in the period leading up to 1913. And with the rise of Progressive Era spending on war and welfare, and with the pressure on banks to inflate to finance this activity, the boom and bust cycles worsened even more. If there was one saving grace about this period it would be that banks were forced to internalize their losses. When banks faced runs on their currencies, private financiers would bail them out. But this arrangement didn't last, so when the losses grew, those financiers would secretly organize to reintroduce central banking to America, thus engineering an urgent need for a new "lender of last resort." The result [brought forth the creature from Jekyll Island — the Federal Reserve.[31]

This was the implicit socialization of the banking industry in the United States. People called the Federal Reserve Act the Currency Bill, because it was to create a bureaucracy that would assume the currency-creating duties of member banks.

It was like the Patriot Act, in that both were centralizing bills that were written years in advance by people who were waiting for the appropriate political environment in which to introduce them. It was like our current health care bills, in which cartelized firms in private industry wrote chunks of the legislation behind closed doors long before they were introduced in Congress.[32]

It was unnecessary. If banks were simply held to similar standards as other more efficient industries were held to the rule of law, at the very least, and then far fewer fraudulent banks would ever come about. There were market institutions that would penalize those banks that over-issued currencies, brought about bank runs, and financial crises. As Mises would later write: What is needed to prevent further credit expansion is to place the banking business under the general rules of commercial and civil laws compelling each individual and firm to fulfill all obligations in full compliance with the terms of contract.[33]

The bill was passed fairly easily, in part because the Democrats had a larger majority in both Houses of Congress than they do today. There were significant differences that were resolved in conference, with one compromise resulting in the requirement that only 40 percent of the gold reserve back the new currency. So instead of a 1-to-1 relationship between gold and currency issued, a ratio that defined sound market banking since the time of Renaissance Italy, the new Federal Reserve notes would be inflated, by law, at a ratio of 1-to-2.5. Notice the word inflation.

The bill that was first drawn up at Jekyll Island was signed by Woodrow Wilson in the Oval Office shortly after the Senate approved it. At one point during the signing ceremony, as he reached for a gold pen to finish signing the bill, he jokingly declared "I'm drawing on the gold reserve."[34] Truer words were never spoken.

Central banks always result in feeding those forces that centralize and expand the nation-state. The Fed's policies in the 1920s, so well documented by Rothbard, would provoke the Great Depression, which, in the end, wrenched political power from cities and state governments to the swampland in Washington. Today people take seriously the claim that there can be a viable federal solution to every problem thanks to the money printed up by the Fed, while each decade has seen a larger proportion of the population become dependent on its inflation.[35]

Chapter Two — When Government Becomes Evil and Destructive

Yet Andrew Jackson's beliefs about the malfeasance of the Second Bank of the United States are just as applicable to the Federal Reserve today.

Here is hoping we will see Jackson's hawkish nose and unkempt hair on a gold-backed, privately issued currency in the not — too-distant future.

Destruction by Keynesian Economics

Americans, by the millions, think the Nazi economic regime was successful, but closer examination tells something different: a tale of rationing, shortages, and starvation. Learning why their economy failed can teach us how to avoid the same fate.

Background To Understand

There's a myth which still endures that after Hitler inherited a country ravaged by the Great Depression in 1933, his aggressive policies turned the nation around and created an economic powerhouse and utopia. But the truth, as Professor Evans of the University of Cambridge argues in his seminal history *The Third Reich Trilogy*, is something far different.[36]

Evans, a Marxist sympathetic to Keynes and state intervention, nonetheless tells a story of rationing, shortages, and misery in the Third Reich. The Reich Food Estate, the state-controlled corporation responsible for agricultural production, regularly failed to feed its people. Agricultural output rarely surpassed 1913 levels, in spite of 20 years of technological advancement. Demand outstripped supply by 30 percent in basic foodstuffs like pork, fruit, and fats. That meant that for every ten German workers who stood in line to buy meat from the state-owned supply depots, three went home hungry.[37]

The same story was retold when it came to cars, clothing, and iron. New houses had to be built with wooden plumbing, because iron was so scarce. Nationalized iron depots could not produce enough for the army, let alone civilians. Clothing was rationed. Fuel and rubber shortages led to what one U.S. observer called, "drastic restrictions on the use of motor vehicles."[38] Of course, because the state dictated which car and truck models could be produced; there were not very many motor vehicles in the beginning, or variations in the models. The overall tale is one of misery for the average German citizen. The conclusion is this: the Nazis hurt their people. We should learn valuable lessons from that experience. Here are at least a few.

Lesson 1: Military Keynesianism Produces Austerity

Hitler's rearmament program was military Keynesianism on a vast scale. Hermann Goering, Hitler's economic administrator, poured every available resource into making planes, tanks, and guns. In 1933 German military spending was 750 million Reischmarks. By 1938 it had risen to 17 billion with 21 percent of GDP was taken up by military spending. Government spending all told was 35 percent of Germany's GDP.

Many liberals, especially Paul Krugman, routinely argue that our stimulus programs in America are not big enough, so when they fail it is not an indictment of Keynesianism. Not true, but let's continue. But no one could say that Hitler's rearmament program was too small. Economists expected it to create a multiplier effect and jump-start a flagging economy. Instead, it produced military wealth while private citizens starved. Employed on the largest scale ever seen, military Keynesianism created only ruin.

Lesson 2: Production, Not Jobs

Economist Joan Robinson wrote that, "Hitler had found a cure against unemployment before Keynes finished explaining it." And indeed, rearmament and nationalized industry put every available German to work. There were so many jobs that the Nazis complained of a labor shortage and brought women in to the workplace, even though they were ideologically opposed to it. Unemployment had been cured. And yet, the people routinely suffered shortages. Civilian wood and iron were rationed. Small businesses, from artisans to carpenters to cobblers, went under. Citizens could barely buy pork, and buying fat to make a luxury like a cake was impossible. Rationing and long lines at the central supply depots the Nazis installed became the norm.

Nazi Germany proves that curing unemployment should not be an end in itself. No doubt, jobs are important. But they are important for what they produce, not just by virtue of existing. Real growth means production of what people demand. It means making cars, growing food, building laptops, or commercial planes. Private production grows the economic pie and helps everyone to prosper. Without production, all that a job does is change a man from starving and unemployed to starving and employed.

Moving Forward

There are a thousand lessons to be learned from the Third Reich, from the evils of totalitarianism to the dangers of racial thinking. A key economic lesson is that, rather than curing the Great Depression, Hitler's military Keynesianism on a massive scale left the German people starving and short of goods. It's a lesson advocates of building tanks to make us rich, from John McCain to Paul Krugman, would do well to learn.[38]

Can anyone say Crony Capitalism?

A writer with the *New York Times*, David Brooks a neoconservative by their standards, urged Obama to ignore both his collectivist/egalitarian base and the "conservative tradition that believes in limiting government to enhance freedom." Obama already has nothing but hateful contempt for the latter tradition he learned from his mentors: Marx, Soros, Alinsky, Mao, Stalin, Lenin, Ayers. He does not need any thoughts from a right-wing thinker like Brooks, who said, "The president should also abandon his life-long infatuation with and devotion to socialism as well," advises David Brooks. "In its place he should pursue an agenda of crony capitalism disguised as a "social mobility agenda" with the help of professional propagandists and perverters of American history such as Brooks and his fellow neoconservatives. Of course, Brooks doesn't use these less-than-flattering words to describe his Machiavellian agenda. He talks of "a third ancient tradition" in American history, namely, "the Whig tradition, which begins with people like Henry Clay, Daniel Webster and Abraham Lincoln." (Source: Thomas DiLorenzo, "How David Brooks Panders to Power by Perverting History," LewRockwell.com, February 5, 2014)

Either Brooks knows nothing at all, whatsoever, about the Whig Party tradition in American history, or he is lying through his teeth about it. He describes it as having been devoted to "using the power of government to give marginalized Americans the tools to compete in a capitalist economy." The Whigs, says Brooks, "fought against the divisive populist Jacksonians" who supposedly sought to "pit classes against each other." Every bit of this is exactly the opposite of the truth. The Whigs were the party of crony capitalism, of government of plutocracy, by the plutocracy, for the plutocracy. That is why so many historians have marveled over how a man such as Abe Lincoln, who grew up so poor, would become the political water carrier for the Northeastern moneyed elite in American politics.

The most divisive economic issue in American politics during the heyday of the Whig Party (1832–1852) was the battle over free trade versus protectionism. If the Whigs stood for anything, they stood for corporate welfare in the form of high protectionist tariffs that would plunder the masses for the benefit of the few. This meant, for the most part, plundering Southern farmers more than anyone for the benefit of Northern manufacturers who would be protected from international competition by high tariffs. As John C. Calhoun once said, what "protectionism" protects the public from is low prices. Next to slavery, protectionism was the biggest assault on property rights in America during the first half of the nineteenth century. The Whigs did not believe in "sacred" property rights, as Brooks foolishly writes. Their entire political agenda was based on the government-enforced attenuation of property rights for the benefit of the wealthy and politically-connected.

Next to political plunder through protectionism, the Whigs stood for the worst sort of crony capitalism in the form of needless corporate welfare for road-, canal-, and railroad-building corporations. This was euphemistically called "internal improvement subsidies" at the time. Private capital markets financed thousands of miles of private roads during the first decades of the nineteenth century. As of 1800 there were 69 privately-financed road-building companies in America that would build more than 400 private roads over the next 40 years, as economist Daniel Klein has documented. The great railroad entrepreneur James J. Hill also proved that government subsidies were not needed to build a transcontinental railroad as he and his investors and business partners built and managed the Great Northern

Railroad without a dime of government subsidy, not even "land grants."

When the Whigs did get their way by deceived state government into funding "internal improvement subsidies" it was an unmitigated financial disaster. Very few, if any, projects were ever finished; taxpayers were stuck with enormous government debts to pay off; much of the money was simply stolen; and by 1860 every state except for Massachusetts had amended its constitution to prohibit the use of tax dollars for corporations with which to do anything, according to economic historian Carter Goodrich.

Edgar Lee Masters, the famous 1930s-era poet, playwright (author of *The Spoon River Anthology*), and law partner of Clarence Darrow, perfectly described the Whig Party on page 27 of his book, *Lincoln the Man*. Describing the leader of the Whigs, Henry Clay, Masters wrote:

"Clay was the champion of that political system which doles favors to the strong in order to win and to keep their adherence to the government. His system offered shelter to devious schemes and corrupt enterprises. He was the beloved son [figuratively speaking] of Alexander Hamilton with his corrupt funding schemes, his superstitions concerning the advantage of a public debt, and a people taxed to make profits for enterprises that cannot stand alone. His example and doctrines led to the creation of a party that had no platform to announce, because its principles were plunder and nothing else."[39]

This is exactly correct, and exactly the opposite of what David Brooks wants his *New York Times* audience to believe. Clay's agenda, which Alexander Hamilton originally labeled "The American System," was really an Americanized version of the corrupt mercantilist system the American Founders had fought a revolution against. The Hamilton/Clay/Lincoln "American System" included protectionism, corporate welfare, and a central bank to dispense even more corporate welfare subsidies to politically-connected businesses. It was a recipe for political power based on using taxpayer dollars to line the pockets of the (mostly Northern state) business plutocracy at the expense of the general public. Some things never change in a democracy.

It is equally outrageous for Brooks to claim that the Jacksonians were "divisive" and wanted to "pit classes against each other." This was the function of David Brooks' beloved Whigs, who were simply an early version of the neoconservatives; it was the libertarian Jacksonians who *opposed politicized divisiveness* and the pitting of classes against each other. This is exemplified in President Andrew Jackson's famous veto of the re-chartering of the Second Bank of the United States, a precursor of the Fed.

The Whigs championed a central bank. The Bank of the United States (BUS) even paid both of Brooks' heroes, Clay and Webster, many thousands of dollars as bribery money to promote the continuation of the bank despite the fact that it was well known that the BUS had corrupted politics and generated boom-and-bust cycles. In vetoing the re-chartering of the BUS (which was not overturned), Jackson wrote: It is to be regretted that the rich and powerful too often bend the acts of government to their selfish purposes. In the full enjoyment of the gifts of Heaven and the fruits of superior industry, economy and virtue, every man is equally entitled to protection by the law; but when the laws undertake to add to these natural and just advantages artificial distinctions, to grant titles, gratuities, and exclusive privileges, to make the rich richer and the potent more powerful, the humble members of society — the farmers, mechanics and laborers — who have neither the time nor the means of securing like favors to themselves, have a right to complain of the injustice of their Government. In the act before me [the bill to re-charter the BUS] there seems to be a wide and unnecessary departure from these just principles.

Neither Jackson nor the Jacksonians were "perfect" libertarians, but by their motto of "equal rights" they meant equality under the law and opposition to the use of the state to dispense "exclusive privileges" and special favors to special interests. They stood for exactly the opposite of what David Brooks claims they stood for, in other words.

Brooks' commentary turns to slapstick humor at one point when he claims that the Whigs, who were, after all, politicians, were somehow "family-oriented in their moral and social attitudes." (I assume that he threw this into his article to further dupe the "evangelical Christian" base of the Republican Party into accepting his thesis). The leader of the Whigs, the slave-owning Kentucky hemp plantation patriarch Henry Clay, was "family oriented" in that he had 11 children. But he was also a notorious gambler who rang up $40,000 in personal debt *in the 1820s* and was famous for staying out late carousing and dancing with women other than his wife while he was in Washington and the wife was back home in Kentucky, according to several biographies.

Armed with this absurdly false history of American politics, Brooks argues for an explosion of governmental central planning by Obama during the rest of his term. He wants Obama to employ "social entrepreneurs" to fundamentally transform American society by "improving family patterns," expanding early childhood education, "structuring neighborhoods," paying "young men wage subsidies so they are worth marrying," training "middle-aged workers" for jobs, and generally micromanaging everyone's life from cradle to grave. In his words, government should promote "[social] mobility issues from the beginning to the end of the lifespan." Something very much like this has been tried before. It was called totalitarian socialism and it failed miserably.

The Destruction by New Taxes Used in "Preserving" the Environment

For those who were of age at the time, they can remember exactly where they were and what they were doing that day on December 7, 1941 when the Japanese bombed Pearl Harbor; exactly where they were and what they were doing that hour when John F. Kennedy was assassinated; or exactly where they were and what they were doing in 1986 when the Challenger exploded killing 14 astronauts; or where they were and what they were doing when they heard the news more than a decade later of the Columbia shuttle burned up on re-entry killing seven astronauts. There was a revival of our nightmares over Challenger with the made for TV movie on that shuttle disaster which focused on Richard Feynman, the great physicist who was selected to work on the president's panel that tried to answer the question of "What happened?"

While all four are both personal and national tragedies, I was alive for the latter three of them, able to recall precise details of my where and when. They all rocked my world in their own unique way. The two shuttle tragedies were unique among them. There is something depressing about both. The government's environmental policy fingerprints are all over both disasters. Environmentalism not only killed 20 U.S. astronauts, but it killed them in a most horrible way on public television.

News reports pointed out that the wreck of the Columbia was almost certainly due to a chunk of insulating foam coming loose and hitting some heat-protecting tiles, scattering them and leaving the spacecraft vulnerable to the intense heat it would experience upon re-entry into the earth's atmosphere. That is all that the mainstream news and NASA have been willing to report. What they have not said is that the particular foam that was in use at the time was an environmental substitute replacing a material that had worked well. However, the previous foam used to insulate the Columbia's external fuel tanks contained Freon, which is a chlorofluorocarbon (CFC) that the EPA banned because of the ozone depletion scare.[40]

As Steven Milloy reports, NASA could have sought an exemption. Freon, after all, is inert and nontoxic, and its connection to ozone depletion is tenuous at best. However, having been burned by the EPA once before (as I will point out), NASA succumbed to what Milloy calls "PC foam." He writes, "PC foam was an immediate problem. The first mission with PC foam resulted in 11 times more damaged thermal tiles on Columbia than the previous mission with Freon-based foam."

Furthermore, the damage was obvious and quite severe. Milloy writes that following the 1997 Columbia mission, "more than 100 tiles were damaged beyond repair, well over the normal count of 40."[41]

The Challenger accident occurred in the winter of 1986. Everyone recalls the failure of the O-rings, which were designed to keep gases inside the rocket but in this case allowed the fuel and the fire out that turned into a fireball that enveloped the shuttle.

Cape Canaveral was cold that morning, freezing cold, and as it turned out, too cold for the O-rings to perform as designed. While that is old news that everyone knows now because of the attention; what most people had not known until the TV movie came out last year, is that O-rings were made out of a substitute material.

Chapter Two — When Government Becomes Evil and Destructive

The original product had to be replaced per the Environmental Protection Agency. It had banned because it contained asbestos.

As Richard Feynman has written: The original O-rings used between the rocket joints came from an over-the-counter putty that had been used safely and effectively for a long time. However, in its war against the use of asbestos anywhere, anytime, the EPA forbade NASA from using that product at all after the space agency had sought an exemption. The EPA, not surprisingly, refused that request, something that would ultimately lead to the next disaster 17 years later. The new product, not surprisingly, failed and we know the rest of the story.

In normal situations, this would be a scandal of epic proportions. A government agency requires the use of unsafe materials that lead to the very public deaths of 14 individuals. Had a private firm permitted these kinds of unsafe working conditions, the situation would be worthy of a *New York Times* investigative report. Instead, all we hear is silence, interspersed with "the show must go on" comments about the future of the space shuttle program. Even the news reports on the foam disaster have ignored the reason why NASA used such an unsafe product; in fact, mainstream reporters are not even asking the pertinent questions.[42]

Reagan's appointment of Richard Feynman to the council looking into the Challenger explosion was a godsend as it turns out. If it had not been for Feynman's apolitical approach to problem solving in that group, we might have not discovered what we did about the "Environmental Protection Agency" when he opened the door to its role. Innumerable writers in papers, periodicals, and books have pointed out the high costs, and low benefits, of environmental laws and regulations. But that is taboo, since environmentalism has become an official liberal religion in America, revered and protected from its sanctified position in government. The EPA goes wherever it wants no matter how much people object. Anyone who questions it is considered anti-government.

Yet, we see once again that applied environmentalism can be disastrous. Granted, we are talking about the lives of "only" 14 people, compared to the hundreds of thousands that have died of malaria following the banning of DDT, which once effectively killed the mosquitoes that carry the disease. Whether we speak of 14 astronauts, or 14,000 people in a remote African nation, we speak of the same thing: death by environmentalism. The verdict is in; environmentalism has become a sacrosanct religion is not only hazardous to our health, it threatens our very lives.[43]

The environmental movement, which is another radical religion, has received worshipful support from the leftist media for the movement's heroic process of rescuing this planet from us humans. And in this church of environmentalism, the EPA resounds as Lord, with the many missionary testimonies regarding the fights for the fruit flies and snail darter fish they claim to be saving. Like so many other stories of regeneration (Hugo Chavez freed the media in Venezuela, Castro liberated

Cuba, World War I made the world safe for democracy, and Lincoln freed the slaves), this one is a lie. However, it has become standard fare in the American academy, and, as one would expect, in the salons of the political classes.[44] These monumental lies have come from the enemy camp of the environmentalists. They have severely damaged our country, our economy, and millions of citizen's lives. If you live long enough, you have regrets in choices you made. The ones that bother you the most are the ones where you knew the data said environmentalists were wrong and you chose not to speak out against them, stopping them short of their goals.

With environmental regulations came the blame of countless capitalistic entrepreneurs for causing disasters, everything from cancer to the destruction of the planet. This list of phony environmental scares is so long, that any rational, thinking person should routinely assume that everything the organized, political environmental organizations say as a lie. Among the more infamous phony environmental "scares" have involved acid rain; asbestos; DDT; the hole in the ozone layer (which has always been there); global warming; global cooling; the fruit preservative Alar; electromagnetic fields; "cancer-causing" cellular phones; chlorine which, according to the Discovery Channel and environmental groups like the Sierra Club, has caused a "crisis" of shrinking Alligator penises (This is no joke; first the 'gators, then us, is the message); and hundreds of other beneficial chemical products.[45]

For a full half-century now, April has harbored the environmentalists' favorite holiday on which to do war dances against all these enemies of our planet. It is called Earth Day. On one weekend each year, Americans go forth to celebrate "Mother Earth" or the Big Lie where we are literally asked to worship the earth. Little children are coaxed each year to "worship" by doing their deeds of paper recycling and sending hand-written letters to politicians begging them to save the earth from the capitalists. We are told that all of us are in immediate peril due to pollution, global warming, climate change and a plethora of other slogans. We are reminded each year that only the EPA and its environmental activists, all government led, are the only ones knowledgeable and powerful enough to do the things necessary to fix mother earth. For example, California celebrations on this 2014 holy day included such services as interactive song and dance by the "Snail People" at Sausalito, an eco-fashion show at Palo Alto illustrating "inspirational ways to repurpose and reuse a variety of items into wearable clothing," and the penultimate stage presentation, the "Trashion Fashion Show" in San Jose! This religion in nothing more than the ancient Baalism repackaged and apparently now having edible worship garments made from banana peels, soggy lettuce leaves, old cheese, used paper towels, other garbage with hemp and steroids thrown in for taste. We are told that these Leftists are the only ones with the appropriate voices "in tune" enough to sing in the choir, and the biceps powerful enough to lift the sacrifices onto the altar and ultimately fix the problems with mother earth.

The celebration of Earth Day has led up to a new holiday announced by Socialist Evo Morales in his speech of April 2009 to the United Nations, International

Mother Earth Day, a resolution unanimously passed by Morales and his buddies to celebrate this event each year.[46] I suppose he is saying, "This is the mother of all religions now." In his accompanying speech, Morales explained to his colleagues that "Mother Earth was now having her rights recognized" and expressed his hope that the present century will be known as the "century of the rights of Mother Earth." He explained to the UN that its member states "now had the opportunity to begin laying out a Declaration on the Rights of Mother Earth."[47] Morales and the Bolivian government will table a draft UN treaty recognizing and enunciating the rights of the Earth (Sounds like a religion to me.).[48] Environmentalists from various activist groups are meeting at the UN for the debate entitled "Nature Has Rights," where a treaty is being pressed forward recognizing that and tell us that Mother Earth has rights. The treaty recognizes the Earth as a living entity (person) that humans have sought to "dominate and exploit." To prevent this exploitation, the draft treaty will "[grant] the Earth a series of specific rights that include rights to life, water and clear air; the right to repair livelihoods affected by human activities, and the right to be free from pollution."[49] The treaty establishes a "Ministry of Mother Earth" to hear the Earth's complaints against those who continue to dominate and exploit it. An "Earth Rights Doctrine" is being developed. It is primarily a doctrine aiming at the total control of man, and the extinguishment of human rights. Its power to accomplish this consists in two simple facts:

- that the Earth encompasses all resources that humans deal with, and these resources form a part of the "body" of the Earth; and;
- that the Earth is incapable of expressing any desires pertaining to its own alleged rights (since it does not actually have any desires), and it requires some human "representatives" to speak "on its behalf."[50]

In examining what they mean by the earth's rights, we must become aware of not only the context of the argument, what content they mean, but also the kinds of entities to which they accrue. To properly grasp a complete understanding of these entities, we should consult someone who knows the concept of rights, to whom rights apply, and from where rights are derived. 20th century philosopher Ayn Rand gives the best explanation. "The concept of rights is a part of moral philosophy, its purpose being to provide moral guidance on how to treat others."[51] According to Rand, the notion of "rights" is a moral concept: "the concept that provides a logical transition from the principles guiding an individual's actions to the principles guiding his relationship with others — the concept that preserves and protects individual morality in a social context — the link between ethics and politics."[52]

Before breaking out all the balloons and party favors, including the bibs to catch the BBQ burgers with sauce you were prepared to eat while dripping some onto the soil, be clear there are Mother Earth thought police in this nation state that will tell us there are more appropriate ways to celebrate this holy day. The implication of the new UN Treaty and the reverence which will be paid to earth is that humans must not interfere with the body of the Earth in any way without its permission, just as a person cannot interfere with the body of another person without their permission. It stands to reason that since all physical resources required for human survival come from the Earth, and are a part of this "living system," this implies that humans cannot do anything; they cannot even exist on Earth, without first asking, "Mother Earth, may I." Wanting to drill for oil? Nope! We must properly ask for approval. Want to build a road across a section of land? The answer is "No" to that thought too; not without your notarized permission slip!

We have come to a point in history where governments have secretly worked in promoting and establishing themselves as the official representatives of the Earth. In fact, they consider themselves as priests for the earth, in exercising its rights and making decisions for the planet, which is a spiritual service in this Baal-like religion. These priestly self-promotions certainly imply that people cannot do anything without the permission of their government. Therein, you find the purpose of the doctrine and the purpose of the entire environmental movement; it is to become an environmental hangman's noose if you do not comply. Fines, seizures of property, or even worse are in store for those who do not comply. To strip you of your rights, to eradicate them in front of your eyes is the goal, meaning government is now in control. For example, you wanted to plant a tomato garden: excuse me, but have you asked permission of the Earth yet? If not, forget it! You want to build a concrete slab for a driveway or a garage. I do not think so, not without Mother Earth's permission first! So while your children are being taught this earthy religion, celebrate Mother Earth Day as you are directed. Bow down to your government.

Speaking of your children's experience in government school, each year the project essays come from public school children in dutiful worship to the faith. For example, an 11-year-old fifth grade student at a Greenville, South Carolina, middle schools recently wrote in his Earth Day essay, "If there was no Earth Day, the Earth would rot and die and there wouldn't be enough trees or oxygen." A classmate writes, "You should save the world and not pollute."

Lest we think this is simply foolishness from only the mouths of babes, consider this from David Whitman, a reporter for *U.S. News*: "At the time of the first Earth Day, America was a place where oil-drenched rivers caught fire, loggers lopped down great swaths of national forests, recycling was rare, motorists routinely littered, and fabled icons like the bald eagle were headed toward extinction in the lower 48 states." He said further: "The Environmental Protection Agency did not exist, and industry and government casually dumped millions of tons of hazardous wastes." But like Mao's China in 1974, all-powerful central government has come to the rescue of the people and the land and has saved us from the greedy capitalists.[53]

From the mythical libraries of liberalism, many of us have heard the stories of those individuals and firms which were brought to the altar for repentance, confessions, and baptism into the Mother Earth way, all monitored by the government priests. Each story is always the same recipe, lots of propaganda, lies, fake witnesses, and loads of emotion blended together. Oh, and the flavor is variable. There are many testimonies of salvation made by the government officials, which come out of this naked city. Every story follows the same script as told by some liberal or Marxist. Each comes with shovels of propaganda the likes of which would have given Dr. Joseph Gobbels, from Hitler fame, great pride of authorship. When the associated lies are accepted as truth, they would bury America in a 1,000 year layer of dust. Just listen to some of these lies.

One liberal lie goes this way; unless the government executes socialist laws in America, we will drown in our own garbage and waste, suffocate from a lack of oxygen due to deforestation, or die from heat exhaustion due to global warming. Every century in every generation and practically in every decade has brought forward members who predicted an environmental catastrophe. You may have thought the environmental movement was just a "Johnny Come Lately" but late in the 19th Century, city planners warned of the impending danger of horse manure covering all the streets several feet deep. This was forecast because of the population boom of both men and horses. The rumors spread and soon every city was seen as endangered by the manure. The despicable automobile, with smog from its internal combustion engine, running on that magnet of liberal hate, oil, saved us from that horrible fate, only to move into another generation and create another nemesis that of global warming created from the capitalist fumes of the dreaded oil.

Then there is the unforgettable Club of Rome's screed, *Limits to Growth*, which appeared in 1974 and warned that unless the world immediately converted to socialism that humanity as we had known it would virtually disappear by the end of the 20th Century?[54] In their push for global socialism *Limits to Growth* reported, "Their inescapable conclusions are beyond anyone's grimmest fears. Possibly within as little as 70 years, our social and economic system will collapse unless drastic changes are made very soon."[55] Jimmy Carter's Global 2000, which environmentalists hailed, was another gloom and doom report that predicted chaos in 20 years unless the madness of free markets was replaced by "orderly" government planning.[56]

Ronald Reagan and his policies led to the fall of the Iron Curtain in 1991, and because of Reagan, the entire western world was not drawn into Socialism or Marxism over one evening. When the news reports finally leaked out about the environmental holocaust which had been going on behind that curtain in "Socialist" and "Marxist" nations, the environmental movement should have closed their doors. They had been preaching for a century that the only "solution" to the environmental madness in the world was to turn to socialism, and get away from capitalism, which they said had caused the entire environmental wall into which we were about to crash. Said differently, their solution, Socialism, was the culprit all along. A normal group of beings would have been embarrassed; but not them, they doubled down on their conclusions.

That leads us to our next big lie told by Leftists. It deals with the EPA, one of the denominational churches of this Leftist religion. They said without the EPA, America's rivers would be flaming sewers and life as we knew it most likely would have disappeared. The EPA is seen as the regulatory "thin, blue line" that separates the civilized world from chaos.[57]

However, as Bruce Yandle of Clemson University has so eloquently written, "environmental regulation in the United States did not begin with the formation of the EPA (in 1970)." Yandle points out, "America's pre-federal experience with environmental regulation is as diverse as the country's population and geographic regions. Almost a century longer than the federal period, it was a time of experimentation with and development of ways to control polluter actions."

The commonly held belief is that environmentalism is a new movement and that there were no attempts to control emissions into the air and water until President Richard Nixon and Congress created the EPA. In fact, dating back to the 19th century people had long acted both through the courts and through the legislatures to deal with pollution problems.

The most effective tool was the appeal to property rights as protected by common law. Citizens who found their property and personal health damaged by nearby factories could find redress from the courts and often were successful. However, as the state authorities began to see industrialization as something in the "public interest," the courts began to side with polluters without proper redress given to those whose health and property were harmed. (See Murray Rothbard's "Law, Property Rights, and Air Pollution" for an excellent discussion of common law and environmental issues, from *Economics and the Environment*, edited by Walter Block.)

In fact, the destruction of private property rights and the metamorphosis of private property into common property has been a central reason why industrial pollution had reached nearly intolerable levels in some municipalities by 1970. For example, the famous 1969 fire in Cleveland, Ohio's, Cuyahoga River would never have happened had the law recognized private property rights of waterways instead of having them declared "public" (or common) property. The same goes for the atmosphere above one's property.

Instead of continuing strict property rules, which would have allowed for bargaining and solutions that would have satisfied all sides, government resorted to a zero-sum game with the faulty economic analysis of the Kaldor-Hicks efficiency rule. This rule assumes one will know the paradigm of benefits and costs for obtaining the optimum efficiency of any economic outcome. Thus, "the winners" will supposedly have such a huge surplus from the outcome that they will theoretically be able to compensate the "losers" and there will still be huge piles of "public welfare" left over. When schemes such as this are used for welfare payments, as they are, and probably reparations, it is no wonder people become suspicious of government economic analysis.

Yandle notes that states and communities across the nation had experimented with various laws and regulations to deal with problems of emissions, with the results being a "rich diversity." As Yandle and others have also noted, environmental protection, which economists rightly portray as a normal good of which people demand more as their wealth increases, was on the rise even before the advent of the EPA.

In more recent years, the EPA has scrapped any sensible laws under the direction of the Socialist administrations over the years in the Oval Office. In particular the current administration is using the EPA as not only a threat to private industry but as a private sector "cop" to write large fines. This amounts to nothing but a tax. There have also been horrible substitutes for reasonable laws put in place resulting in horribly inefficient methods of command and control. What most people do not realize is that the law, in mandating "minimum levels" of discharge, actually requires private business, private property owners, and municipalities alike to employ uniform anti-pollution equipment whether or not that equipment actually does what it is supposed to do. This is another form of a tax.

Take your average automobile catalytic converter in the exhaust system, and other required pollution gear under the hood such as EGR valves and air pumps for most every car. The costs of the equipment and upkeep are very expensive and unless everything is working perfectly, most of the emissions equipment will not burn fumes properly and therefore takes out only marginal amounts of toxic discharges. The greatest improvements in emissions reduction have come from simple measures such as the positive crankcase ventilation system (PCV) that was enacted in the 1960s. However, even the most sophisticated anti-pollution devices are of little value if the car's owner fails to have regular tune-ups.

In truth, government has mightily contributed to the problems of air and water pollution by destroying common law property rights, which were the best defense against unwanted discharges into water and air. By insisting upon a rigid and inefficient command and control scheme, the EPA forces Americans to employ wasteful methods to clean up industrial and municipal discharges. Like Mao's communist state, the EPA is the emperor without any clothes. Of course, since the EPA and other government agencies are the main source of news to media outlets, the larger public will never be told the truth. Thus, the Big Lie continues.[58]

The Destruction of the Energy Crisis by a War on Oil

Federal government officials have been warning of an impending energy crisis ever since the dawn of the oil industry, roughly 1866. In that year the U.S. Revenue Commission warned that the nation may run out of oil at any moment. In 1885 the U.S. Geological survey forecast no chance of oil being discovered in California; some ten billion barrels have been pumped from that state since then. By 1914 the U.S. Bureau of Mines was predicting that only 5.7 billion barrels of oil were left;

more than 50 billion barrels have been pumped since then. In 1947 the U.S. Department of State warned that "sufficient oil cannot be found in the United States;" in 1948 more than 4 billion barrels were discovered. This was the largest discovery in history up to that point and twice the volume of U.S. consumption. In 1951 the U.S. Department of Interior forecast that oil reserves will last only until 1964. All of these gloomy (and false) forecasts were (and are) accompanied by proposals for more government control of the energy industry to "assure" a more adequate rate of development.[59]

The Destruction of Regulation and the Resulting Political Blackmail

Government regulation, or even the threat of regulation, is often a crude form of blackmail designed to bilk huge amounts of cash out of affected industry. When the threat is made, the campaign contributions start rolling in from those companies that would be hit hardest. Also the lobbyists go to work with pockets of favors and money to dissuade passage of such legislation. For example, federal regulators routinely show up at corporate headquarters with their ticket books, writing failure notices for being out of compliance with regulations for which no human could comply. Take for example the EPA's requirement for how corporations handle "hazardous materials;" keep a written record of where each and every container is located at every moment. There is no way a corporation can do that. Think about it; if a railroad cannot always keep track of the location of all its boxcars during a month, how much more difficult it would be to track waste products at all times, especially when they are being moved on a regular basis.

Here is why it is hard to track each container of hazardous materials. These "hazardous materials" include products such as the common window cleaner Windex, according to the EPA. That is an impossible task even for an army of company "trackers." This particular regulatory practice, according to former New York state environmental protection commissioner Thomas Jorling, is nothing more than what he calls "a kind of extortion." EPA regulators will enter a corporate office and impose huge fines on corporations that could not possibly maintain the EPA's huge paperwork burden, even if they wanted to. (What government can never understand is that a company has to make a profit to stay in business. To hire this army of individuals to track all containers at all times, would bankrupt the firm.) When the EPA threatens criminal indictments, they are assured payment of the fines. In 2014 speak, with this administration, it amounts to little more than an arbitrary tax that can be used to extort revenue at a given moment.

Blackmail and extortion are integral features of the modern regulatory process, at least that is the argument of Cornell University law professor Fred McChesney. In his book. he tells how political "entrepreneurs" threaten legislation and regulation that will either impose price controls or increase costs (both of which negatively impact profit margins when in place), that is unless the "targeted" companies and industries compensate the politicians with campaign contributions or other sorts of payoffs. The "other sorts" can be the speaking honoria, jobs for relatives, paid luxury vacations at world-class resorts, etc. While progressives argue these to be footprints of capitalism, urging a faster plunge toward socialism, McChesney's discoveries are not marks of capitalism at all. They are marks of human nature, trying to take advantage of others. History shows however that socialism, Marxism, Stalinism, Communism have much worse examples of extortion of their proletariat.[60]

There are special names politicians assign to legislation they or their peers design specifically to extort campaign contributions from a business or industry; they are called "milker bills" or "cash cows." One California legislator said: a politician "in need of campaign contributions, has a bill introduced which excites some constituency to urge [the legislator] to work for its defeat (easily voted down), pouring funds into his campaign coffers..."[61]

Some politicians go straight for the jugular to get as much quick cash as they can as quick as they can through legislation that is seen as a threat of intimidation. They nickname such legislation "juicer bills" or "pumper bills" because they do just that — they pump or squeeze the cash out of the pockets of corporate entities who pay to keep the hammer from being dropped on their business. Still other bills are referred to as "fetcher bills" because they are intended to go get tons of cash from private firms who might be harmed if the bills passed.

This is not a once in a lifetime occurrence. These bills are introduced periodically within the House or Senate, or even come from the White House. In his last term, Obama threatened legislation that would put severe limits on the oil industry. Almost immediately, there was billions in financial support given to him and his party in hopes of avoiding the penalty box into which he might put the oil companies. Once re-elected, Obama went ahead with his plans anyway. Back in 1999, Thomas DiLorenzo reported on another classic case: Rep. Jim Leach quietly introduced a bill . . . aimed at reducing speculation in financial futures. Barely 24 hours later, the Iowa Republican learned that Chicago commodity traders were gunning to kill his proposal. Rep. Leach said one Illinois lawmaker told him the bill was shaping up as a classic "fetcher bill" . . . Sure enough, one of the first to defend the traders was Rep. Cardiss Collins of Illinois, recipient of $24,500 from futures-industry political action committees.[62]

More Examples of Political Blackmail

One recent example in the U.S. of a proposed regulation that seems to have been purely designed to "fetch" perpetual campaign contributions is the battle over reducing the legal blood alcohol content (BAC) level from .10 to .08. The federal government's Office of Substance Abuse Prevention has declared that its goal is to eventually have .04 as the legal limit, which can be attained by an adult male who consumes one or two beers. Congress failed to pass such a law in 1998; the law that it did pass, however, creates a slush fund of highway grant money that can be used to bribe states into passing laws that reduce the legal BAC level. However, the law is to be renewed every year, which guarantees that the alcoholic beverage industry will be forced to make campaign contributions indefinitely in order to defeat this neo-prohibitionist legislation.[63]

In 1992 Congress authorized the Federal Communications Commission to impose price controls on cable television. Since, the cable industry has poured $ millions into campaign contributions into Washington annually in an apparently fruitless effort to eliminate the price controls.

One of the more notorious examples of political blackmail in recent years involved the Clinton administration's proposals to impose price controls on doctors, hospitals, and the pharmaceutical industry as part of its failed plan for socialized medicine, or what was called "Hillarycare." Once price controls were proposed, reported the *New York Times*, members of Congress and the president were receiving vast campaign contributions from the medical industry, an amount apparently unprecedented for a non-election year. While both plans were being hotly discussed, "big pharma" and the AMA were making winners out of members of Congress. Representative Jim Cooper, who proposed legislation that was slightly less onerous than Clinton's, received nearly $1 million in campaign contributions in the first four months of 1994; overall, campaign 1993 contributions were about one-third higher than in the previous non-election year of 1991.[64]

It was also widely reported at the time that the handlers of Hillary Clinton's not-so-blind trust were selling her pharmaceutical stocks short every time she would make a highly-publicized speech demonizing the pharmaceutical industry, which she did quite often. In his book, *In Defense of the Corporation*, Robert Hessen documented how Ralph Nader had long engaged in the same, shorting the stocks of companies that his numerous think tanks and organizations routinely demonized with highly-publicized "studies" claiming corporate wrongdoing.[65]

During the Clinton health plan fiasco of 1993-1994 the value of pharmaceutical stocks dropped by over $40 billion according to one account. After the pharmaceutical industry poured millions of dollars into the coffers of Washington politicians the price control plan was defeated.

Politicians also play a role that is essentially no different from the role played by organized crime in demanding protection money from businesses in return for "protection" from being robbed or beaten by the thugs. Sounds like Al Capone. Rather than threatening to break anyone's kneecaps, however, Congressmen frequently demand campaign contributions and personal payments in return for the granting of a business license.[66]

For example, after access to long-distance telephone markets was closed to the "Baby Bells," the companies made almost $10 million in campaign contributions during the 1984-1993 period and "hired scores of former federal officials" as lobbyists to help them gain governmental permission to compete in the long-distance telephone market.[67]

The "tobacco settlement" reached between the state attorneys general, the federal government, and the companies, might well be considered to be the Mother of All Political Shakedowns. In return for being allowed to stay in business, American tobacco companies are being forced to pay almost a quarter of a billion dollars to trial lawyers and federal, state, and local governments. The media have already begun reporting on how the initial installments of this money is being spent on anything and everything by state and local governments, not only "health care costs," as was promised.[68]

Obama is the King of Regulation and the Pharaoh of Blackmail

Since 2008, Obama has designed hundreds more government regulations that are working similar to a bulldozer in a china hutch, regulations of the past were making a mess of our daily lives. Now he has made it much worse. Whether it is banning the products that are effective or requiring second-rate functionality in our appliances and fixtures through regulation, the Obama government's role here is unarguably to degrade our quality of life.

Yet, to hear President Obama claim exactly the opposite in a February 2011 speech to the U.S. Chamber of Commerce is stunningly absurd. It proves moreover how he is working against America instead of for America. In his speech, he mocked those who predicted disaster from government regulations as far back as 1848. "It didn't happen," he said. "None of these things came to pass." Then he went further to say that government regulations "enhanced" industry and "made our lives better." Regulations "often spark competition and innovation."[69]

Obama's claim really goes further than saying that somehow industry overcame the costs of regulation. He suggested that we are actually better off than we would otherwise be because of regulations. And he gave the specific example of automatic defrosting freezers. Actually he did. Here is the statement: "The government set modest targets a couple decades ago to start increasing efficiency over time. They were well thought through — they weren't radical. Companies competed to hit these markers. And they hit them every time, and then exceeded them. And as a result, a typical fridge now costs half as much and uses a quarter of the energy that it once did — and you don't have to defrost, chipping at that stuff and then putting the warm water inside the freezer and all that stuff. It saves families and businesses billions of dollars."[70] This is a precise claim by the president that deserves the scrutiny of a "truth meter." Thanks to Jeffrey Tucker and other commentators for the Mises Institute we can verify the truth. Here it is:

Back in 1928, the U.S. Patent Office issued a patent for 'defrosting of the cooling element or unit of a refrigerating system." Because invention is one thing and production, marketing and sales is another, it was quite some time before these would be seen in real kitchens. All throughout the 1920s and 1930s, many more patents were issued by the government, though the innovative products could have appeared more quickly without the patents. Regardless, an article in *Chain Store Age* in 1947 writes as follows: "Auto Defrost," a recently developed electronic circuit for automatically controlling water defrosting of refrigeration coils has been announced by the Bush Mfg. Co., Hartford [founded 1907], Conn. Advantages claimed for this device are its low price, its ease of installation on existing water defrost systems, and it works independently from the refrigeration system.

Recall that Obama spoke of how the relevant regulations came about "a couple of decades ago." Well, his timing is off by some 63 years! Besides, these items were on the retail market by 1948.

By 1958, it seems like the great innovation was already old news. An advertisement in *Life Magazine* from 1958, this time from Westinghouse, refers to a "frost-free, Auto-Defrost Refrigerator" as if it was nearly a standard feature. The main pitch here is that the refrigerator has a "cold injector" that chills food faster. It is also styled in the "Shape of Tomorrow."[71]

Life Magazine 1958 — Westinghouse "frost free Auto Defrost Refrigerator"

As a child in the 1950s, I remember watching my mother defrost our small Sears Coldspot refrigerator. There were some problems with freezers then, not with ours it turned out. With that in mind, it is not crazy to remember some of the regulatory environment of the 1970s that brought on the universal move of making all freezers frost-free. And the government made a push for saving energy, so manufacturers were required by government to meet some particular targets, as the president said in his speech. But there is a serious problem as Jeffrey A. Tucker explains: An automatic defroster increases, not decreases, the overall energy use of refrigerators and freezers. As this government report said in 1998: "Refrigerators with automatic defrost have higher occupant consumption (on a label-normalized basis) per unit of occupant activity than refrigerators with manual defrost." In other words, the more straightforward way to meet regulations would have been to take defrosting

Chapter Two — When Government Becomes Evil and Destructive

devices out, not put them in! The devices therefore exist not because of standards but in spite of them.

All evidence suggests that the truth is precisely the opposite of what Obama claimed. Frost-free freezers came about in the normal market way. A company found a way to package it as a luxury good available in some markets. Another company saw the advance and emulated it, offering it to still other markets (though the process was likely slowed by the government regulation called the patent). Other companies saw the potential for solving a monstrous household problem and began making them more cheaply and more efficiently, as the target market gradually went from luxury to mainstream. Over time, the improved product was ubiquitous.[72] The case is that free capitalism working in an unshackled way was able to improve lives with innovations, not the regulations of the central government as liberals try to claim. That is the way the market works with just about every innovative product in the history of the world. From a stone wheel on a cart, to rubber tires on an automobile, to a sewing machine to the devices for phone and Internet use, private sector companies press innovation to the maximum each year to out-perform the competition in serving customers. Even without patents in the eons gone by, they learned from each other what makes the customer sing with joy.

Free enterprise and the market-driven economy have delivered the life and conveniences we enjoy in the U.S. every day. It was not the Socialist machine that did so with their onerous regulations. It was freedom fueled by human choices, entrepreneurs working hard and smart, and the relentless learning from mistakes, private property, and the freedom to trade. We also need to be aware of the opposite [like Obama, Marx, Soros, and Stalin], the gargantuan apparatus of compulsion and coercion called the state that operates on principles that are anachronistic to the core. Its principle is violence, and its contributions to the social order are prisons, economic upheaval, and war. It is lumbering, stupid, and angry as hell, and it is the main drag on the world today. The contrast with the market is overwhelming there is nothing that the state does that either needs to be done or that can be done within the matrix of voluntary action and exchange.[73]

There he stands, Mr. Obama, making his speeches about limiting regulation and with the other hand increasing regulation faster than any president in U.S. history; in effect saying to us "Go figure. See if you can see what's in my mind about what role my government is going to play in limiting and controlling every aspect of your lives." Well, I think I see inside his thoughts fairly well, since he is a Marxist following Karl's doctrine in lock step, it is fairly easy to see. He hates private industry, since that is a part of capitalism. Capitalism creates gizmos which just keep coming up with new advances in technology. He sees this private enterprise as "taking advantage of the masses of people which needs government to come to the rescue" giving them those things for which they wish not to work, like Obama cell phones. Private industry does not care about people, only profits he thinks. Only government cares about people enough. So in his mind if he can wipe out the profit motive, give it to people who do not wish to work, and the problems of the world will be dealt with and the day will be saved: by government.

Unfortunately, hundreds of millions of people have been murdered by leaders of governments like this in the not so distant past; Germany, USSR, China, Venezuela to name a few. We forget what fuels our economy forward. We lose knowledge from one generation to the next as if it were an old pair of shoes. It is all because we are a people are a species that has lost its memory. Knowledge in human history is so easily lost or destroyed. The cure for scurvy was known several millennia ago, then lost and had to be rediscovered again, only to be lost again. Such has happened several times in our brief history. The same is true with human freedom. Most of the truth of its creative powers were known millennia ago by the ancients but had to be rediscovered again and again. Through each millennia and each occasion where freedom stuck its head out of the slavery of some government, it was as if some ancient foe was fighting the will of human society who wanted to see God's creation either in chains or destroyed, never free to do what was right, but forced to do only that which the state of the time called legal.

So probably in Obama's mind, he sees himself saving the proletariat through rigid restrictions, government regulators riding into town with white hats. After they have scoured the consumer products to find opportunities for improvement and innovation, they focus on the problems and shortcuts in the manufacturers processes. After calculating their plan to extort monies in the names of bribes, they march into manufacturing plants packing heat. And he must imagine they read from the script which he personally has prepared, "Listen up underlings: our citizens have a problem with ice building up their freezers. According to my directive, you will find a solution, some solution to fix these problems. You have until next winter to figure it out. If you do not, you are dead meat."

Then in his mind because he has spoken, he sees the reaction of industry, complying under his will, scrambling to improve products only because government bureaucrats demand it. Under the Obama-nation edict, enterprise makes the improvement to their product, and all glitches vanish. This process is repeated for one gizmo after another until we are gradually made better off, all thanks to the central planners and wise public servants who know better than everyone else. Under this model, the entire developing world might be improved in just two terms of his reign!

Pipedreams are made of fantasy. So is Obama's claim that we should be grateful to him and his regulators for all the blessings that flow downhill to us. How many freezers did bureaucrats invent? Did the president invent the IPhone? Could be, at least Al Gore claimed he invented the Internet.

The truth is Obama is not happy just giving Americans the vast resources of a crippled mindset, from stimulus plans to bailouts to embargos, to Obamacare. He is after a more sinister plot than even that. He wants to redesign every appliance in your home having total control of your life from rising in the morning to hitting the sack in the evening.

Ben Lieberman shows how the Obama administration started meddling with every room in your house when first elected:

The Basement
New standards for water heaters and furnaces: for water heaters, the Energy Department estimates price hikes from $67 to $974, depending on size and type.

The Bathroom
The same 1992 law that gave us those awful low-flush toilets also restricted the amount of water showerheads could use to 2.5 gallons per minute. Some consumers who disliked the resulting weak trickle opted for models with two or more showerheads, each using the maximum 2.5 gallons. But Team Obama has now eliminated this "loophole" by requiring that the total flow must comply with the limit.

The Kitchen
Think remodeling a kitchen is expensive now? The cost of these regulations target refrigerators, dishwashers, microwaves, ovens and ranges. Costs will only be propelled upward by regulations.

For refrigerators (at least), this is a clear case of overkill. The American fridge has already been hit by several rounds of tighter standards, with each new rule saving less energy than the last; but boosting the price and compromising performance and reliability. Even the Energy Department admits that most consumers will lose money on its latest refrigerator regulation.

The Laundry Room
New standards are on the way for washers and dryers. When the last clothes-washer regulation hit in 2007, *Consumer Reports* lamented several ultra-efficient models "left our stain-soaked swatches nearly as dirty as they were before washing" and that "for best results, you'll have to spend $900 or more." The Obama rules mean even worse news.

Any Air-Conditioned Room
Both central air conditioners and window units received new regulations. When the Energy Department rolled out its last round of central AC rules back in January 2001 (one of those last minute Clinton administration "midnight" regulations), it admitted that many homeowners would never recoup the added up-front costs. New standards follow the same "logic" — and thus should make for another lousy deal.[74]

Obama regulations have continued non-stop. In the first three days of 2014, he and his staff wrote 141 new regulations alone as presented on Regulations.gov, all posted there from the various federal agencies. 119 of these are "rulemaking," meaning they establish new rules for each; 23 are "non-rulemaking" but reinforce and put teeth in earlier rules. Most are in the area of energy and environment; bringing new taxes as the EPA will enforce them.

The EPA, under Obama, is cracking down on new emissions for coal plants and other carbon-heavy fuels and materials. The agency is also working on 134 major and minor regulations that will take effect in the coming years, thus raising the bar probably beyond reach. In particular, the agency has established a rule, capping carbon dioxide emissions from power plants; for all intents and purposes banning coal-fired power plants from being built. "If these regulations go into effect, American jobs will be lost, electricity prices will soar, and economic uncertainty will grow. We need the federal government to work as a partner, not an adversary, and to invest in America's energy future," said West Virginia Democratic Sen. Joe Manchin.

Another new regulation from the Energy Department that has been listed since a new year established "test procedures for residential furnace fans." The Energy Department under new leadership from Secretary Ernest Moniz has been less of a lightning rod for controversy, but the department has still been active in pushing for more regulations. The Energy Department has 82 regulations listed in its latest Unified Regulatory Agenda for 2013. Many of its new rules have to do with energy efficiency and conservation efforts. This is a major shift in priorities from President Obama's first term where the DOE focused on renewable energy development.[75]

Evil politicians in America, as the system stands now, will always use their position to extort money from the private sector for their own pockets. Proof was seen twenty years ago, when the *Washington Post* wrote stabbing articles about Bill Gates and what they called his naiveté by focusing his energy on this job rather than becoming a player in Washington; aka, caving in to the establishment's extortion racketeering. Gates stayed above the fray for a time, but finally caved hiring dozens of lobbyists and attorneys. He ended up spending millions in contributions to campaigns for many politicians who were poised to spring on him.

Regulations increase the cost of doing business; drive up the price of end products, because business owners will pass along this cost to the consumer. So while Obama boasts that he is helping America, only the low-information crowd does not see through the shell game that it is all just a tax to make the rotten politicians richer.

The Extortion Hits the Beverage Industry

For most of the twentieth century, legislators have periodically extorted bribes (i.e., campaign "contributions") from the alcoholic beverage industry by threatening to increase excise taxes. The myriad industries now engaging in electronic commerce are undoubtedly concerned about all the proposals to tax e-commerce, and will be diverting more and more of their profits to Washington in the future, if they are not already doing so.

CHAPTER TWO — WHEN GOVERNMENT BECOMES EVIL AND DESTRUCTIVE

During 1986, the year of an historic "tax reform," members of the tax-writing House Ways and Means Committee tripled their "take" from the previous year, as industry groups sought to defend themselves from punitive tax treatment. At least a portion of the sadness of this activity is that people now accept it as business as usual in Washington. Blackmail is just a part of doing business now in what was once the greatest God-fearing nation in the world.[76]

What We Really Need Is for Government To Get Out of Our Way!

Defenders of liberty and other conservatives are often challenged by the Progressives to supply exhaustive descriptions of what would happen if some aspect of our increasingly government-dictated lives were returned to people's free choices. What would happen if government did not educate our children? What would happen if Social Security did not force people to "save" for retirement or Medicare and Medicaid did not provide health care? What would happen if the Fed did not control the money supply and the FDIC did not insure bank deposits? What would happen if the FDA didn't ensure that food was safe and the EPA did not protect us from pollution? What would happen if the SEC did not rein in Wall Street and the FTC and antitrust laws did not protect us from monopolies and collusion? These questions, and many more like them, make up an almost unending list. In the face of such questions, it is nonetheless important to recognize that such questions are rhetorical traps designed to put an unachievable burden of proof on voluntary arrangements, short-circuiting the need to deal with the many valid criticisms of coercive policies. The questions are always asked in an attempt to prove the current level of government enforcement that is so intrusive is not sufficient, but a "doubling down" of the same starting immediately is the only answer to provide the fix to our problem of an uneven playing field.

The trap set by Progressive Liberals usually works because some conservatives either feel the need to play the liberal game, or they have little basis of information and data from which to draw as they choose to attempt an answer. **The answers to all the typical liberal questions above are very easy and basically the same answer for each. "Everything improves," is the appropriate answer to each of their ridiculous questions.** Said differently, when we are asked what in the world will we do if government is not in charge of everything in our lives. We will thrive and survive. **Any answer is better than the one government provides.** Truthfully, the same questions should be asked of liberals asking why things would not improve if government were out of the way in each area. Take education for example. It is hard to imagine a situation that would not be better if government were out of the education business. Anyone who has had any dealings with public education, equal employment opportunity commission, or any other department, knows with certainty that almost everything is much worse, more burdensome, and much more expensive when government is driving.

"I don't know," is also an acceptable answer to a liberal. Therefore, an accurate answer to "What, precisely, would freedom produce?" is "I don't know; no one knows." But failure to satisfactorily answer the unanswerable in no way detracts from justified confidence that voluntary arrangements will do things better. In fact, the inability to answer helps explain why freedom works so well. It allows previously undiscovered beneficial arrangements that serve people more effectively to develop, though no one knows exactly what will happen in advance.

The sky is the limit on what can be produced, when you move government out of the way and let freedom reign. Just look at what it has done in the past. The manufacture of earth-shattering positive results has been done because of freedom, not because of socialism. Ask yourself why people want to come to America. It is because of the time tested results when government is limited; the sky is the limit on what individuals can do. That is the overwhelming testimony.

If you disagree, take a microcosm which most adults are familiar. Compare the U.S. Post Office with any of the other independent forms of message or material delivery and communication. If you can get the Post Office to deliver without losing your item, it is more times than not very late, a speed worse than a snail's pace. The comparison becomes a contrast. Freedom produces near miraculous results with innovation. It is amazing what happens when you get the government out of the mail delivery business. Just about everyone has more multiple horror stories to share in dealing with the Post Office, because it is operated like a union, with no penalties to pay for bad service. Think about it. If your package gets lost, and IF it is covered by insurance, and IF you are reimbursed, because it is run like a government operation, you end up funding the bad service by higher taxes and higher prices to deliver. The genesis of innovation has come from private industry, faster, better, and less expensive. Imagine that. We need only revisit the revolutions involved to see that no one ever knew exactly what would happen beforehand. If people had only pursued what could be clearly foreseen, none of those miracles would have happened and we would be immeasurably poorer.

But how do we know that freedom's results will be improvements when "anything could happen?" First, self-interest, the desire to improve the circumstances we currently face. This means that improvements are sought. Second, when people's rights are protected, the need to get others' voluntary agreement means no one can force worse results on others, but leaves plenty of room for results to be not only better, but unimaginably better. Neither is assured under government's heavy hand.

As Leonard Read's famous "I, Pencil," illustrated, market miracles are everyday occurrences. Pencils are cheap and plentiful, even though no one knows everything involved in making them. And so are staggering arrays of other things.

In addition, no politician who oversees, or bureaucrat who administers, one of the many government enterprises that have grown to surround us could have met the same burden of proof when the government overrides voluntary arrangements with their dictates. Moreover, questions posed to the government of "what would happen" in the face of some new proposed government program, such as Obamacare, are often tossed aside with impunity.

The initial promises made with such conviction for new government "solutions" have been unrealized pipedreams. And unlike self-ownership and the jointly beneficial market arrangements it allows, which has produced uncountable successes without theft, there are no such "success stories" that demonstrate miraculous improvement from the intrusion of government that can match the historical successes of the market. In fact, the only real examples of government-produced miracles, those produced by stringently restricting its reach, as with the "thou shalt nots" of our Constitution's Bill of Rights, only reinforce a legitimate belief in freedom and corollary distrust of government.

One of my professors once said that "I have been an economist long enough to realize 'I don't know' is an intellectually respectable answer." In fact, when predicting the future, that is virtually always an important part of the answer. But when people are free, the results of their voluntary arrangements will be as good as they can discover, even if they are unknown in advance. In contrast, public policies based on what Friedrich Hayek called the "pretense of knowledge," backed by coercion, are neither intellectually respectable nor a guarantee of improvement, however frequently or adamantly such promises are made. In fact, if the burden of proving its effectiveness was put on government, rather than liberty, vanishingly little of government would survive, and the shackles binding the miracles that are possible would be loosed.

Democracy within a Representative Republic Is What People Want

The question facing Americans is not whether Congress will ever cut spending. The question is will the spending be reduced in an orderly manner that avoids inflicting massive harm on those depending on government programs, or will spending be slashed in response to an economic crisis caused by ever-increasing levels of deficit spending. Because politicians are followers rather than leaders, it is ultimately up to the people what course we will take. This is why it is vital that those of us who understand the dangerous path we are currently on do all we can to expand the movement for liberty, peace, and prosperity.

History shows that democracy is introduced to a nation is the best form of government to be benevolent and provide the best moral choice which is understood at the time for all the people. While that notion is challenged by socialists, a democracy is going to function properly only when moral-minded persons are selected as representatives to represent the people. And as we have shown in earlier chapters, morality stems from an understanding of responsibility to and ultimately answering to God, just as our Founders accepted. Democracy is a flawed form of government. In fact, in spite of what the current day Collectivists, Socialists, or

Marxists will say, all forms of government are flawed. Winston Churchill probably expressed it best in his capacity of service while observing the various forms of government in the world, "Democracy is the worst form of government in the world, except for all the rest of them."

It is interesting to observe that our representative form of government, while having its many flaws, worked reasonably well for nearly two centuries. I believe that is because for that time period the thought of doing that which was moral was an overbridging thought in government process and legislation. And that thought process was prevalent since the underpinnings of government culture was the culture and morals as are taught in Scripture. And in that atmosphere, candidates for office were typically weeded out using good business practices and the morals as had been established. However, there were problems which erected their ugly heads through the years.

One obvious issue that has plagued this country is in the area of the selection of candidates for various state or federal offices. This problem has existed in both national parties, but the greatest majority of anti-democracy issues have surfaced with candidates in the liberal, or Democrat party. And then there is the issue of trying to disqualify candidates. Both parties do it. While in the past I have voted at times for persons on either side of the aisle, for the past 40 years, I have sought conservative candidates. I see them being attacked by today's liberal, socialist and progressive machines; not usually because of a moral problem, but rather because they are conservative and have sworn allegiance to the Constitution and the founding principles of the nation. For that reason, they are attacked by the liberal socialist machine, with its attack dog media will seek out any perceived or possible weakness of a conservative, even going so far as to dig through the family trash in the driveway. This has been supplemented by firms of lawyers who spend hours on end investigating backgrounds, even fingering childhood friends of a candidate, to report silly things like 5th grade skirmish on the playground, or a bad grade in high school. Basically they have harassed in every possible manner a responsible candidate who may be a credible threat to the socialist regime. As a result, many faithful Americans refuse to put themselves or their families through the scrutiny of a "political cat scan," which is then reported publically by this liberal fiasco machinery as a fear of having the American people find out the truth about some mysterious skeleton that may be in their closet. And all the time, this same media refuses to report even the lowest-hanging political fruit in a liberal candidate's life. The reason: they are not to be even questioned since they are liberals, and we know the urban myth: liberals never lie. Even if news of one of their candidate's illicit sex life leaks out by mistake, they either ignore it, or will say something like, "It's just all about a person's personal sex life." Sex scandals are a resume enhancer for a Liberal. All the background checks, reading past emails, and dumpster diving conducted by the Progressives is a horrible characteristic, not of democracy, but of the evil regime that is inflicting treason from within.

Chapter Two — When Government Becomes Evil and Destructive

This dumpster diving, et al, by the Left becomes a facilitator for another problem, elections. It goes back to human nature; individuals tend to focus on their own interests that benefit themselves, and not so much the public. For example, if an individual is in the process of buying a new car, he or she will do much data crunching in an attempt to determine which type of vehicle they need or want. Once that is determined, then the models are explored for the best service history, best MPH, best resale value, etc. all reported by Consumer Reports. It is time consuming, much data reviewed and by the time a purchase is made, and the buyer can be extremely well-informed on most of the traits of an automobile.

When it comes to voting, say for the President of the United States, the same person may throw up their hands saying something like, "It doesn't matter how you vote — they're all crooks anyway." After all, the reasoning may go; their vote is just one out of 68-70 million votes that will be cast. So they tend not to dig for data on which model they want based on criteria like foreign policy, economics, Constitutional views, and, **here is the key problem: the only real information they may have on a candidate is what the liberal media may be saying about the person.** Therefore, the smart car buyer turns out to be a negligent voter because they not what the candidates really do or are.

The end result, given many other problems that surface, the U.S. House of Representatives, the U.S. Senate, and the U.S. Presidency can be filled with not only lack luster individuals, but downright treasonous individuals, with regard to the most important requirement: on how they align with the Constitution. Think Nancy Pelosi. Think Harry Reid. Think John McCain. Think Jay Nixon. And we have only scratched the surface in mentioning these poor performers. Most of them appear to have been elected due to emotional issues, like a Viet Nam POW, as in the case of McCain, or being a normal "conservative" citizen of San Francisco as with Nancy Pelosi. I guess they viewed her like her comments on Obamacare: They had to "pass her" on to Washington that is, "to see what's in her." Need I say anything more?

Another problem existing in the current political arena is that politicians, once elected, tend to start building their empires. They are interested in their own political future. Most of them focus on their own fiefdoms. The only focus on the voters' concerns seems to be when they are running for re-election. Citizens are awakening and starting to demand term limits. Good results will come from term limits. First, it will free up the Senators, Representatives, et al to focus on their job, instead of constantly campaigning for the next term. Second, we will not have to listen to the career building machines in Congress who stay all their lives. Third, it gives us fresh blood every few years to do the people's work.

The political landscape was not supposed to appear like it appears today anyway. There were no career politicians in the wings as the Framers saw it. Representation in the federal government was to be none other than the farmers, business owners, retired workers at home, who would serve. This means they would put their lives on hold for the time they were in Washington serving citizens inside government for a time. When finished, they would return home to reopen the business or take over the management of it from a family member. Or they could go back to school, or whatever was their next step in life. The key is there would be no career politicians. Career politicians count on their constituency possessing a lack of concern about issues, or a lack of knowledge of the real issues, or just accepting what they the politician tell them. Passivity is a culprit. With regards to government that is an upside down travesty.

The Systematic Legal Destruction and Plunder of Our Rights

In *The Law*, an 1848 epic analysis of his government gone tyrannical, Frédéric Bastiat presented the unquestionable maxim that man's rights existed prior to the founding and formation of the state. Therefore, as his reasoning went, the collective action of the state cannot conflict with man's pre-existing rights. According to Bastiat, man can delegate to the state only those powers that he himself already possesses. His belief was that a person could not force another to give up his right on giving to the charity of their choice. Since I cannot coerce you to give to the charity of my choice, it only follows sound reasoning that neither should government be able to force you to give to the charity of its choice. Yet that is exactly what it does. Let us say that you object that government gives money to a charity that you personally abhor. You would not get very far arguing that you have a right to reduce your tax payment by a prorata amount. If you persisted in withholding payment, government will confiscate your assets. If you try to protect your assets, government will kill you. Yet, from the context of natural rights, government has no justification in forcing you to pay for a charity of which you disapprove and would not fund voluntarily.[77]

Bastiat's warnings of the dire effects of legal plunder are as relevant today as they were the day he first issued them. The system of legal plunder . . . will erase from everyone's conscience, he wrote, the distinction between justice and injustice. The plundered classes will eventually figure out how to enter the political game and plunder their fellow men. Legislation will never be guided by any principles of justice, but only by brute political force. The great French champion of liberty also forecast the corruption of education by the state. Those who held "government-endowed teaching positions," he wrote, would rarely criticize legal plunder lest their government endowments be ended.[78]

The end result is that the law of the land has become perverted and directed away from its original intent of serving people to now pursuing people. It is now the tool for the state's avarice. God has given us our life and liberty. The state must be stopped from taking it away.

Citizens Want the Government To Simply Do Their Job

We face many potential disasters in the days ahead. Many of them are daunt-

CHAPTER TWO — WHEN GOVERNMENT BECOMES EVIL AND DESTRUCTIVE

ingly dangerous to the population and are becoming worse threats every day. Why? All because while the government, led by Mr. Obama, is saying he and his administration are in charge; Americans are now discovering that actually no one is in charge. Why? A day of golf, followed by a day of fund raisers, followed by another day of golf, followed by another day of fund raisers, and so on. . . .

In my opinion, look at the example of what could be the worst disaster of the administration which stands at the door of our country. It is pandemic, probably one of Ebola. While the World Health Organization (WHO) and especially the Centers for Disease Control (CDC) state that this virus is in control, with no one in control that is most likely not true at all. At this writing, not only does it appear the CDC is not working hard on protocols for treating potential patients in this country, they are stating that all is safe. Don't worry, they say. Please believe me on at least this one subject. The Ebola virus and possible pandemic it can cause will make any Bird Flu virus seem like a walk in the park.

Citizens want our government to become involved with its own job description . . . to get seriously involved with its number one priority; that of protecting "we the people." Unfortunately, the priority seems to be everything but what is good for citizens.

Take the studies which the CDC has led the past few years at the behest of the administration. Instead of working on developing centers to deal with serious diseases, such as Ebola, they have focused on,

Video games and TV violence. Following the shooting in high school in 2013 Obama ordered the CDC to do studies of violent video games and media images including an assessment of "existing strategies for preventing gun violence and identifying the most pressing research questions, with the greatest potential public health impact." This is a $10 million study that if done, should have been done by another group. The CDC does not exist for this purpose.

Playground equipment at parks and schools. The 13 CDC Injury Centers, ordered to do so, have crafted a "national action plan" and funded countless studies to prevent scrapes and cuts as well as major accidents on American playgrounds. The cost was many millions and should have not involved the CDC while they were to be devising plans to fight deadly diseases.

"Social norming" in schools. Again being ordered to do so, the CDC has funded studies and campaigns "promoting positive community norms" and "safe, stable, nurturing relationships (SSNRs)" in homes and schools. More proof the government is moving into the business of parenting all citizens.

Mandatory motorcycle helmet laws. Dr. Thomas Frieden, the CDC Director, appointed a 15-member "Community Preventive Services Task Force" to promote pet Obama Administration projects. An obscure Obamacare rule - Section 4003(b)(1) - stealthily increased the task force's authority to study "any policies, programs, processes or activities designed to affect or otherwise affecting health at the population level." The CDC should not be involved in motorcycle issues — that is not a disease.

The 2014 annual budget of $7 billion the CDC has for its work, which grows exponentially every year, is being used to focus on these issues rather than working on projects dealing with diseases which has been its charter. Why the administration has people within this department working on "these projects" seems more than strange. Those "projects" listed above and many others, is an example of how far afield we are in a management scheme. To use the CDC for such work, when much more serious work is left on the table, such as preparing to defend the nation against a pandemic, is a serious failure of management.

It truly appears that in today's America, we have no qualified leadership to handle even the basic tasks before us.

The Destructive Problem with the Current Youth: Youth = Inexperience = Liberalism

Bill Russell famously said, "Youth is wasted on the young." A rough translation would wield a sentence that high energy and high levels of stamina are wasted on a time in life when you hardly need it. It would come in handy when you are much older, stiffer, stove up from arthritis, but also experienced enough to have learned very beneficial lessons which, given the energy and stamina of yesteryear, could be put the youthfulness into full effect.

Having been a youthful, wayward person at one time in my life and then watching the young people of this nation over the past couple of generations, against the backdrop of my own youth, I recognize a few very poignant tendencies between the two. The trend of the last couple of generations, I have noticed, is to confuse the knowledge of and use of technology with wisdom from life experience. It is not! And looking at someone who is a whiz at texting or using an IPhone to surf the Web, do mail, do videos of a group, etc., does not make them a marvelous leader. It only means they can use some technology.

I remember when a group of us who were so unhappy with the dismissal of one of the professors that we challenged the college administration in their move. We did more than challenge the decision. We made it personal and called for the firing of the president of the university and some other faculty members, all without knowing the details of what led to the dismissal of the faculty member. We were sure foolish thinking we could get the president dismissed, especially when we discovered the facts of the case.

That has been the trend of the last couple of generations, I have noticed, is to mistake the knowledge of and use of technology as being wisdom from life experience. It is not! What life experience is there in pushing a button or sliding a finger across a screen?! Technology will not make anyone wiser in a philosophical

Chapter Two — When Government Becomes Evil and Destructive

approach to life. It is a tool that appears to have the ability to divert attention away from reality. And looking at someone who is a whiz at texting or using an IPhone to surf the Web, do mail, do videos of a group, etc., that does not make an individual a marvelous leader in life. It only means they can use some technology.

That said, it is obvious that throughout history, evil people have used the naiveté of younger people to accomplish murderous acts and treason in the world. So many are easily duped partially due to their lack of experience: The result: a level of trust that is placed in younger proposed leaders, who speak their language, such as Obama himself. Six years ago, many younger people were talking about him being the Second Coming. Now the proof is available to make it abundantly clear that he is not, nor is he related to anyone that is, some seem to be lost as they look for a new leader. Mistakes of judgment are so easily done when in the tender bud of life. Look at just one more example:

The men and women who established and ran the terror systems of the Third Reich were startlingly young. When the forty-three-year-old Hitler was appointed chancellor of Germany in January 1933, more than two-thirds of his followers were under the age of forty. The future chief of the Reich Security Main Office, Reinhard Heydrich, was thirty-seven years old when he presided over the Wannsee Conference and unveiled Nazi plans for the mass murder of Jews in Europe. The legion of secretaries who kept the mass-murder machinery functioning, were only eighteen to twenty-five years old. The nurses who worked in the war zones, assisted in medical experiments, and administered lethal injections were also young professionals, most were in their late teens. The lovers and wives of the SS elite, whose task was to ensure the future purity of the Aryan race with healthy offspring, were, as required, of fertile, childbearing age. The average age of a female concentration camp guard was twenty-six; the youngest one was a mere fifteen years old when she posted at the Gross-Rosen camp in Nazi-annexed Poland.

Terror regimes feed on the idealism and energy of young people, molding them into the obedient cadres of mass movements, paramilitary forces, and even perpetrators of genocide. Male Germans who had the bad fortune of maturing at the time of World War I became a distinctive lot, deformed in ways that we are still trying to diagnose. One historian has identified this generations of young men as "uncompromising," hard-core ideologues and self-convinced professionals who realized their ambitions in the SS elite as developers of the Holocaust machinery in Berlin. A generation of young women also played their part in the genocide, not at the helm, but as the machine's operatives. What distinguished the female cadre of young spouses and professionals who made the Holocaust possible, the women who went east during World War II and became direct witnesses, accomplices, and perpetrators of murder there, was that they were the baby boomers of World War I, conceived at the end of one era and the start of another.[79]

Destruction can come from many avenues and certainly one more when government is gone astray.

"I fear for our nation. Nearly half of our people receive some form of government subsidy. We have grown weak from too much affluence and too little adversity. I fear that soon we will not be able to defend our country from our sure and certain enemies. We have debased our currency to the point that even the most loyal citizen no longer trusts it."

— Roman Senator, AD 63

Chapter Three

Destruction by Betrayal of the Free Press

WHEN MY MATERNAL GRANDFATHER WAS WORKING every day in the last decade of his career, I remember that he had the habit of watching the 6 PM news religiously every day he was not out of town. There had to be "quiet on the deck" during that time period in the house so as not to interrupt a message of the broadcast. That was back in the 1960s. I followed in his footsteps, in watching the evening news that is, though my sources were and are different. It is sickening to hear and witness visually the horrible news of the drift of our country every day, so much so that I starting turning off the TV to read, work on a project or play with the dogs. Of course, in Grandpa's days, the only news was found on the NBC or CBS, the only channels you could get. The national news which he always watched was the Huntley Brinkley Report on NBC each evening. It started as a 15-minute program at first, then eventually swallowed an entire 30-minute format time period in the later 1960s.[1] Grandma and some neighbors finally convinced grandpa to give up using his 40 foot antenna which stood along-side the house on its own tower. Grandma wanted Cable TV so she used the town's "professional lobbyists," better known as wives of businessmen among the town's citizens. They were also Grandpa's friends and they worked on him relentlessly for several weeks until he cried "uncle" and finally acquiesced.

The early days of Cable TV service, at least the one with which I was familiar, offered a whopping total of 13 channels from which to choose something for Grandpa and Grandma's viewing pleasure. The number seems so puny compared to the many hundreds, or thousands, which are available in today's market. Hearing Grandpa's initial comments were laughable as he switched around quickly to each channel the first week of service, "They told me I would have 13 channels, but they didn't tell me the same program was on every channel." Also, "I got two channels with the antenna. At least they had different shows." His statement coupled with his extremely dry sense of humor was the stuff for which stand-up comedy was built.

Young adults find it hard to realize there was no Internet in the days I describe. The only news was found on NBC, ABC, or CBS. Somewhere along the way, in the

1960s or 1970s, the network executives learned the power they had through television and how they could sway public opinion toward the liberal socialists by the way they presented news stories. As a result, the news broadcasts over time ceased being news, which was kicked to the curb and left to die. The networks continued their broadcasts but over time they became nothing but a commercial for socialists, secular humanists, and progressives promoting their tenants. They seemed to be learning how to effectively attack conservative leaders, since conservatives were the only thing between them and their goal line. About the same time, the network execs decided they would stop reporting all the news, and rather report only some stories that backed or promoted their positions that upheld their propaganda. Compared to now, they were in a fledgling state in reporting half-truths, leaving some stories off the docket totally or reporting totally misleading information to the public. One of Grandpa's statements which turned out to be almost prophetic was one at which we laughed during his news-watching decades. "I see the Big Boys in Moscow," he muttered, "are telling the little boys in Washington what to do today!" The prophetic part was that the guys in Washington were for the most part just immature progressives compared to their mentors in the Soviet Union. But they were learning and would someday graduate to the big time liberal stage sooner than we hoped. Grandpa was angry at what he described as the liberal trend of the news. The truth is, most of America was angered, which eventually led to the development of other news sources. Competition for the three networks eventually became competitors such as Fox News, The Blaze, providing a more truthful, thus conservative message. With the development of the Internet, the Progressive Left is in a dilemma. They want to use it for their subversive message, but as of yet, they cannot control the truth on conservative sites. Thus, you hear Obama or one of the liberals railing regularly against one of the many conservative news sources available. He has threatened to do what he can to shut down certain Internet News Sites. Those of course are the ones who will bother to tell the reality in news stories, refusing by their actions to carry water for the elite liberals.

Back to Grandpa. His rants about the liberal media back then sounded humorous and a little like slapstick to us kids in our separate world of fun, partly because we knew it torqued him, and partly because we were about to hear some verbal gems that would provide a great belly laugh. Over the last four or five decades, we grew to realize we were not as close to the political fire in those days as him, and what we see happening now is not laughable to any caring adult. Sadly, we have arrived at a day when it appears, the media's coverage of stories has become so atrocious and so treasonous that you cannot trust what they report. <u>Fabricating facts, eliminating data, burying some stories altogether, editing tapes to change recorded words. These are just a few of the crimes which put a question mark behind every sentence they make.</u>

Grandpa was not alone in his view. Presidents have reviled the press from their eras. Lincoln complained of them, as did Thomas Jefferson. Reagan at times even battled the national media. But it is obvious for all but the uninterested, that over

Chapter Three — Destruction by Betrayal of the Free Press

the last 60 years an extremist and anti-democracy shift crept into this media. A trickle at first, it became a torrential flood by the time of Bill Clinton. Currently the media is totally submerged in the Marxist doctrines with Mr. Obama. For the first time in our nation's history, the press is allied with anti-freedom lovers. They have careers now that are built upon the stoking of fires under prejudices and going so far as to frame some citizens (George Zimmerman is an example) changing the story or ignoring facts in order to advance a liberal demagoguery. In many cases it has aligned itself with the government against the American citizens. The government stance is defined by Obama and then communicated by media.

Many in the media and many liberals have a problem with the concept of evil. When Ronald Reagan called the old Soviet Union the Evil Empire, the media became livid and went berserk. They will bludgeon anyone not in lockstep with their viewpoint. Their goal is to bring every citizen into submission of their viewpoint so that actions are altered and accepted immediately.

As an example the press runs with the story in 2014 that black America is being hunted and killed by cops. In truth the real plague to black people is other black people. At least that is what the crime data shows. Members of the media and the leader of race-baiting, Al Sharpton, say that we don't put enough value on the lives of young black people. Well they do not put much value on the lives of black youths. If they did, they would be in Chicago, camping out, marching against the deaths in South Chicago every week. The civil rights establishment and white liberals look the other way when black people kill black people. The liberal media fails to tell us that while 13 percent of the country's population is black, 49 percent of the crime is committed by blacks. Neither will they tell us that 90 percent of the black murders in America are at the hands of other blacks. All this points to an important fact, if George Zimmerman had been black, we would never have known the name of Trayvon Martin. The media inflames stories such as Michael Brown and Trayvon Martin to keep the heartbeat of an agenda going.

What was believed and partially known by Grandpa in the 1960's, is known in full in 2014 by us now. That fact is the liberal elite media promote an agenda of treason, which Grandpa's "big boys in Moscow" would have held in high esteem. And these current liberals suffer from a false sense of superiority because they, as a group of liberal elites, try to follow in the footsteps of their elder and more polished Soviet counterparts in supporting progressive, socialistic, and communist platform reporting. But the network media personnel stumble in their reporting in that it is sloppy, obviously trimmed to leave out critical details, segmented and obviously falsified.

Don't Worry about Facts!

The media does more than contribute to and promote the heinous acts of racism. The media can also be unforgivably sloppy. Take Diane Sawyer's ABC World News Report, on Thursday, September 5, 2013. Jason Howerton, of the Blaze tells how her report contained a story about a huge 9-day traffic jam in China: "Diane Sawyer and her ABC News team gave critics of the mainstream media even more ammunition after Sawyer reported on a three-year-old story as if it were current during "World News" on Thursday evening. The story was about a massive Chinese traffic jam outside Beijing "now entering its third week." After noting that traffic had come to a standstill and people were eating noodles on the roadside, Sawyer reported that the jam would end on around Sept. 17 following the completion of scheduled construction. The huge problem? The original report is from August 2010."[2]

If it is not sloppy work, then it may be poorly researched work. Otherwise, one is faced with trying to determine into what sort of conspiracy the media is involved. Such as code language alerting team members of their plan of attack! Not being a conspiracy theorist, I lean on Occam's razor, seeing the simplest explanation as the one preferred, this time with a twist. The media is sloppy "and" they are poorly prepared to go on the air with the real facts of a story.

Gorilla Dust

Diversionary tactics are used sometimes in an attempt to pull the public's attention away from real stories, by finding small insignificant stories to report, which support their flawed theory of life. It is like sleight of hand; these diversions are what I call "gorilla dust." Take the "headline" story from one month during 2013, the story of the rodeo clown who donned an Obama mask at the Missouri State Fair. NBC News and their correspondents flew into high gear burying important stories of treasonous activity all by making this story not only their front page news, but their only news for weeks: "The rodeo clown at the Missouri State Fair who on Saturday wore a mask of President Barack Obama has been permanently banned from performing at the fair ever again, according to fair officials. . . . Officials on Monday apologized for the incident, which drew condemnation from elected officials on both sides of the aisle. They said they are reviewing whether to take any actions against the Missouri Rodeo Cowboy Association, the contractor who organized the Saturday rodeo event. . . . Video footage of the stunt aired by KSHB shows the rodeo announcer saying, "We're gonna smoke Obama, man.""[3]

Michelle Malkin has commented, "Oh, what a tangled web libs weave when first they practice to aggrieve! Let's review: Democrats and civil rights leaders are busy conducting a ridiculous witch hunt against a harmless Missouri rodeo clown who dared to wear an Obama mask. Oprah played the race card on a Swiss shop owner, whom she dubiously accused of denying her a look at a $35,000 handbag because she is black. P.C. mau-mau-ers steamrolled Paula Deen over three-decade-old comments. And feminists continue smearing Republicans as "War on Women" misogynists, while enabling Democratic perv predators Bob Filner and Anthony Weiner for years."[4]

Claire McCaskill, playing her part of Liberal Lap Dog well, played the race card when hearing about the Missouri State Fair incident, saying, "I hope they didn't do this out of racism. I so greatly denounce acts of racism like this."[5] Just think of it, thousands of people are dying around the world due to torture by the Muslim Brotherhood, but because McCaskill supports their position, she says nothing about that terrorism. Instead, it is: "Let's focus on the clown." And of course the lap dog media grab this sort of statement up. They chase after her or any other politician who voices an opinion in line with the Left, all with cameras and microphones to catch the latest dribble. Their statement is absolute worthless assertions to keep their hearers and readers in the dark; away from the truth. The reporting supports the agenda of keeping Americans divided into different groups. You can hear it when they talk of polls or votes. They always express how many African Americans supported a particular issue, or how many women were opposed to a directive, or how the Hispanics "feel" about another popular subject.

It is interesting that McCaskill was nowhere to be found to comment about the racism when a man wearing a George H. W. Bush mask was run over by a big black bull.[6] Or when George Bush, a doll of him that is, was burned in effigy during his presidency and that was considered nothing more than just "free speech" according to McCaskill. Got to keep the party line going, so of course the media breathlessly pants as they follow her bus in their own bus just to report whatever she and other liberals want them to report.

When George Bush was in office, liberals regularly compared him to Hitler, speculated that he was behind 9/11, fantasized about murdering him, talked about killing him on the talk shows, and generally talked about him like he was the Son of Satan. Media elites called this "speaking the truth to power." Then Barack Obama came into office and ironically, dissent toward the Oval Office is not patriotic anymore. Suddenly these same liberals became irate, humorless scolds who believe that the President of United States is beyond criticism. This came across during his initial campaign; he made it clear he was not to be questioned about his stances. Some said indeed he should not be questioned, they feared criticizing him openly because he is a Democrat; some because he is a Muslim; and some because he professes to be black. Of course, the truth is they are afraid, they do not stand for truth; they are just hypocrites.

When All Else Fails — Tell a Lie

The media will when they want, fabricate and falsify the content of stories (AKA, lie) to support the liberal agenda. In other words they lie. Liberal progressives define a lie as follows; an abomination for a conservative, but for a liberal, an ever present fluid to help promote the progressive agenda. The proof of this is seen in the George Zimmerman case of 2013.

George Zimmerman, as you will probably recall, is the Hispanic man who shot and killed a black man, Trayvon Martin. The story was set up by MSNBC, NBC, and the rest of the media to accomplish their evil liberal purpose from the start. Here is how they set it up:

First, they deliberately and falsely identified Zimmerman as a "white" Hispanic. White is the code word used in a shooting to get the racism apparatus in gear for national attention and subsequent disturbances.

Second, in his circumstance, the media (MSNBC and NBC) were caught playing an edited version of the 911 tape of Zimmerman calling for advice and help regarding Trayvon Martin. It turns out they deliberately distorted the facts of the case. Their version of the call had George Zimmerman singling out Martin as being suspicious for being "black," when he called 911. However, in the actual phone call, Zimmerman responded to the questions asked by 911 operators. MSNBC made it sound as if Zimmerman immediately stated the suspect was black, but the question was asked later in the call. The purpose of the question is to give a physical description of a suspect that also includes race. Regardless, MSNBC deliberately distorted the facts, and did much worse! They edited the tape by moving the words and statements within the whole conversation to make the story more inflammatory as to race. A person singling out and shooting someone because of their race makes a better story for a progressive media than someone calling in a suspicious person and answering a dispatcher's question as to what race they are. Regardless of whether or not Zimmerman found Martin suspicious due to his race and profiled him, he did not single him out for being black on the 911 call to police. The charge was a lie; the tape was spliced, doctored, and then reported by MSNBC and told to the world! **It certainly appears the purpose was and is to support the liberal progressive agenda.** My contention is that the agenda is part of the war that progressives have waged upon the underpinnings of America, and thus it is treason from within.

NBC's "Today" show ran the edited audio of Zimmerman's phone call to a police dispatcher, which showed Zimmerman saying, *"This guy looks like he's up to no good ... he looks black."*[7] Shown below is the difference between what was actually said by Zimmerman and what was reported. Then decide for yourself if NBC and MSNBC "make up stories" and have a treasonous bias. Here is what he

Zimmerman: *This guy looks like he's up to no good. Or he's on drugs or something. It's raining and he's just walking around, looking about.*

Dispatcher: *OK, and this guy — is he black, white or Hispanic?*

Zimmerman: *He looks black.*[8]

The **altered** NBC News version simply ran this way:

Zimmerman: *This guy looks like he's up to no good. He looks black.*

An official transcript of the complete 911 call shows that Zimmerman said,

CHAPTER THREE — DESTRUCTION BY BETRAYAL OF THE FREE PRESS

"This guy looks like he's up to no good. Or he's on drugs or something. It's raining and he's just walking around, looking about."

This segment of this tape within this news story is a nearly perfect "microcosm" of how the media will take recorded statements from anyone, alter the tape by moving or removing words, or take them out of context, all to support their purpose and agenda. And they do so in a bald-faced and unapologetic manner.

To accept the altered story from NBC and MSNBC without becoming annoyed or infuriated by their actions, translates into the viewer having one of the following demeanors: 1) he believes the media's story, 2) he is "unplugged," meaning he pays no attention to such news, or 3) he just does not care. In any case, the viewer becomes part of the problem, rather than part of the solution. Watching one reporter on the Florida street as he ran breathlessly from one black person to another interviewing them, was incredulous. He asked each interviewee about their "feelings" regarding the news of Zimmerman and Martin. Feelings? The only thing that feelings will do following a shooting is the "gin up" support for the shooting victim. When a reporter combines an edited tape with the neighbor's feelings, the produced response will be exactly what the reporter wanted, outrage. It is maddening to witness how pro-socialistic and pro-Communist reporters will offer up data to be pumped through TV channels for misinformed and under-informed people so they can be emotionally drawn further into the liberal machinery. Rush Limbaugh correctly calls these individuals "low-information voters." Remember P.T. Barnum and what he said about suckers.

Media Members are Mostly Progressive Liberal

Statistics are a wonderful tool, at least when they are used appropriately. I always loved statistics. Data when used honestly, will show a picture of what is real or valid. And statistics over time reveal trends. The following statistics provided by Bernie Goldberg in his book, *Bias*, show how different the media is from average Americans: "Eighty-nine percent of Washington journalists voted for Clinton in 1992, compared to just 43 percent of non-journalists; 23 percent of the public describe themselves as liberal, compared to 55 percent of journalists; 49 percent of the public is pro-choice, whereas 82 percent of journalists are; 75 percent of the public favors the death penalty, compared to 47 percent of journalists. The differences go on and on." He then added, "I said out loud what millions of TV news viewers all over America know and have been complaining about for years: that too often Dan, and Peter and Tom and a lot of their foot soldiers don't deliver the news straight, that they have a liberal bias, and that no matter how often the network stars deny it, it is true."[9]

The media elite (media ownership and management) do not resemble in any fashion "average Americans." They differ dramatically. They have a level of liberal progressive bias and dishonesty which is so far off the charts it is tragic. Goldberg addressed this concern in a meeting with Andrew Heyward, president of CBS News. Since CBS does so many investigative reports, Goldberg wanted to do one on media bias. "Look, Bernie," Heyward said, "of course there's a liberal bias in the news. All the networks tilt left." When the meeting ended, Heyward warned, "If you repeat any of this, I'll deny it."[10]

Race relations are manipulated in the mainstream media to present a slant to fit a Democrat Party and Liberal agenda. Goldberg shares again another example, *"Andy Triay, a producer at the Miami bureau of CBS News, was covering a story of two white men who abducted a black man and later doused him with gasoline and set him ablaze. Triay scripted the victim as a black man in an e-mail to his bosses at 'CBS Evening News' in New York. A senior producer told him to change the description from black to African-American. Triay told the producer that the man was from Jamaica. The producer said, 'Change it to African-American or the story doesn't get on the air.' Triay made the change."*[11]

How should Americans respond to the media bias? The solution is the vote with your finger on the remote control. In this way, "The free market is taking care of it. According to the Nielsen ratings, in the 1979–80 season 75 percent of all television sets turned on in the early evening were set to ABC, NBC or CBS news. Today, their audience share has fallen to 43 percent. When Walter Cronkite turned over the CBS Evening News to Dan Rather, it was in first place. Now CBS is in last place, having lost half of its ratings. Americans are responding to major media bias and dishonesty by voting with their remote controls, and a beneficiary has been FOX News, whose motto is 'fair and balanced.'"[12]

Americans should be thankful for the occasional reporter like Bernie Goldberg who wrote a *Wall Street Journal* editorial publicly uncovering the media bias, hypocrisy, and arrogance. Of course when Goldberg did that in 1996, CBS management exterminated his career with light speed. That tells a sad story of how much the media elite appreciates free speech, especially when the speech is truth and differs from their opinion.

The "news" story headlines illuminate this point. They are all from the past several months:

- NBC AND MSNBC DELIBERATELY DISTORTED AND FABRICATED THE CONTENT OF THE ZIMMERMAN 911 CALL TAPE IN THE TRAYVON MARTIN CASE[13]
- If It's Muslim Lies In The Holy Land, It's On PA-TV[14]
- HEY, SHARPTON: Five Charged With Attacking 77-Year Old Man, But It's Not a Hate Crime[15]
- CBS's Garrett Hints George W. Bush is A Serial Vacationer Compared to Obama[16]
- What?! Piers Morgan Falsely Claims Virginia Had Highest Murder Rate in U.S. for 2009[17]

Chapter Three — Destruction by Betrayal of the Free Press

- ObamaCare Suffers Another Setback, ABC and NBC Ignore[18]
- NBC, CBS Minimize Coverage of Jesse Jackson, Jr. Sentencing; Skip Party ID[19]
- On MSNBC, USA Today's Page Preemptively Blames Republicans For ObamaCare Failure[20]
- Censored! IRS Scandal Being Buried by Big Three Networks[21]
- AP's Nicole Evatt Covers For Oprah Winfrey's Dubious 'Apology'[22]
- NBC 'Nightly News' Portrays North Carolina Blacks in 'Fight to Vote' Against GOP[23]
- Ed Schultz Slams Religious Hypocrisy Before Lapsing Into It[24]
- After Obama Criticism of Reality Show Culture, Kardashian-Obsessed NBC Suddenly Agrees[25]
- NYT Columnist: Pro-Life Legislation Promotes Violence Against Women[26]
- Piers Morgan Still Manages to Praise 'Very Intelligent' Anthony Weiner[27]

The truth is this: "All reporting," by the Liberal Left media, not some, all, will favor a political agenda leaning left which leads away from the public square and all the way down the road to the city square of their preferred village named Marxistville. Their stories would possibly be allowable if done as commentary, but their commentaries are reported as "news." They learned long ago that a con-man gains a crowd because he has just a kernel of truth buried in lies in the story he tells. However the lies nullify their charter. Poorer folks in the 21st Century resemble my Grandpa of the 1960s; they only have the major networks from which to get their news. Most do not realize what they are hearing is full of lies and half-truths. What they hear is what they believe, and what they believe, they share as gospel with their neighbors. Over time, with enough repetition, it becomes fact and a prism through which other news is then viewed.

The end result is the liberal media produces propaganda, not truthful reporting, pure and simple. They pump it out every day, 24/7. They find small insignificant stories to report around which they can build their story of how life "ought to be." And that story is pumped full of their flawed socialistic theories. One day, it is a rodeo clown who they insinuated was racist. The next time it was a Hispanic man who overnight became a "White Hispanic." Poor guy, being white is such a crime; at least according to the elite media these days, who are also white. Next time, instead of a rodeo clown, it will be some other diversion to trumpet a message of falsehood. The subliminal message of their story will always be how great socialism is compared to free-enterprise.

In fairness we should note that NBC did apologize to Zimmerman and the world for the tape incident. Here is what they said, "During our investigation it became evident that there was an error made in the production process that we deeply regret. We will be taking the necessary steps to prevent this from happening in the future and apologize to our viewers." This apology sounds suspiciously similar to the apology I gave my uncle for swiping some of his pipe tobacco and one of his pipes when I was 10 years old. Both "apologies" appear to be made not for a lie, or theft in my case, but for getting caught.

Bury the Tough Stories

Often the media will simply grow tired of lying, especially after being caught, and simply bury reports of incidents or crimes with which they are uncomfortable or because the report would do damage to their agenda, or not support their liberal agenda.

Expose White on Black Crime; Hide the Black on White Crime

Most readers have become aware of the 2013 school bus incident involving black on white crime, having been referred to the video of the incident that went viral. Strangely, the report was not seen on the major networks in any timely fashion. A cell-phone video captures the 13-year-old boy's screams for help as he was pummeled with fists and kicked by three bigger, older youths who "ganged up" on him as he was getting off at his bus stop. The black teens beat the white sixth-grader for a minute before opening the emergency-exit door and fleeing the bus.[28]

Episodes of crime fitting the category have been buried for years by the media. Incidents of black-on-white violence similar to which the bus video covered have been epidemic in our society for years. You would not know it however if you get your information from the establishment media. Unfortunately for everyone, and contrary to what those holding most positions of power in our society would have you believe, black males, especially younger ones, are extremely more likely than peer members of other demographic groups to be violent criminals; to attack, rob, and even murder, for a few dollars or merely for sport. According to NYPD data, as long as blacks commit crime in numbers wildly disproportionate to their representation in the population, police data are going to show higher involvement with blacks than with whites. According to victims and witnesses, blacks committed 68.5 percent of all murders, rapes, robberies, and assaults in New York in 2012, though they are only 24 percent of the city's population. Whites, who make up 34.5 percent of New Yorkers, committed 5.3 percent of those crimes. Blacks are nearly 13 times more likely to commit violent crimes than whites.[29]

According to FBI statistics, including Uniform Crime Reports and National Crime Victimization Surveys from across the country, young black males commit upwards of 50% of all murders and other violent crime in the United States, while the young black males represent only about 3% of the country's entire population.[30]

In 2010 alone, homicides committed by young blacks were at a rate nearly 14 times higher than that of young whites. Blacks are 39 times more likely to commit a violent crime against whites than vice-versa, and *136 times* more likely to commit armed robbery. Even though many in our society are already aware of these facts, the media and other progressives "in authority" are engaged in a politically-correct conspiracy to hide the data. The data shows "the extent of the situation that there are still those millions and millions of brainwashed liberals who rush to join the hand-wringing over the number of black men in prison, alleging that such is the result of "institutional racism" in our criminal justice system, and endlessly bemoaning "the perpetuation of negative stereotypes" about black males.[31]

The phenomenon practiced by so many young black males known as the "the knockout game" or "knockout king" is nowhere to be discussed on CNN, NBC, CBS or ABC, or in the *New York Times* or *People* magazine. This is a widespread, sometimes deadly game wherein a group of young blacks sneak upon some random, unsuspecting white or sometimes Asian person in a public place; then one or more of the group suddenly starts punching their victim in the face/head to knock them unconscious. This achieves them credibility in the gang, or "street cred," and bragging rights among their peers.

The lack of reporting cannot be for isolated incidents, for the cities of Chicago, Minneapolis, Kansas City, St. Louis, Los Angeles and others have been infested with the problem. The lack of reporting comes from the media's agenda, to promote the evils of whites on blacks. However, hiding the flash mobs hides what amounts to all-out melees in which victims are struck with iron bars or other objects, stomped, and kicked in the face and head repeatedly by numerous, swarming "youths." Incidents sometimes feature random, innocent motorists being dragged out of their cars and beaten to a bloody pulp by large crowds of young blacks.

Whether it is a school bus incident with its disturbing videos showing an attack of blacks on a defenseless white kid, or the random street crimes against pedestrians revealing the statistics showing disproportionately high involvement by black men, or a You-Tube of a black flash mob beating an old person drinking coffee in a cafe — this all proves a point. While the color of the attacked individual is not critical, though they are beaten and disfigured mercilessly, the media will show "official indifference" toward the crime if the perpetrator is African American. If they ever do cover the story, these same media members will outright rally to the side of the attackers, standing beside members and leaders of the black "community. Official indifference means that the government does not want to overturn a good thing.

Saying "Amen" to Crime — aka, If You Don't Understand, Just Ask

By now, most folks know the media story of the Jena Six back in 2006. White students at Jena High in Louisiana hung nooses on a tree to warn black students not to sit under it. After a fistfight over this racist outrage, black kids in the fight were indicted for attempted murder, while the white racists who hung the nooses walked away with a verbal spanking. Pat Buchanan reports that in September 2007, 20,000 people traveled to Jena to march against this prosecutorial outrage. Fortunately, however, there are still a few real journalists around. Among them are Craig Franklin, assistant editor of the *Jena Times*, whose wife teaches at Jena High, and Charlotte Allen, who wrote an extended piece for the *Weekly Standard*. According to Allen and Franklin, here are the facts and chronology you have been denied by the Mainstream Media.

There never was a "whites-only" tree at Jena High. Both races sat under it, though whites congregated there. The nooses, or lariats, were the work of three young teens that got the idea from watching "Lonesome Dove" on TV, where rustlers are hanged. Franklin says they were a joke aimed at white friends on the rodeo team. As they were painted in Jena High's gold and black, Allen reports that the kids said the nooses were directed at a rival school's Western-themed football team. When school officials confronted them, all were remorseful. All had black friends, and none knew the nooses were offensive to blacks.[32] Instead of being seen as criminals representing a failed subculture of violence and social breakdown, the "Jena Six" were treated as heroes by broader black society and by the white Left. Two of them were brought onstage at the annual Black Entertainment Television Hip-Hop Awards show to a standing ovation, personally presenting Kanye West with the Video of the Year award.[33]

It has been easy for infiltrators to demoralize and corrupt this country: it is a simple matter encouraging people to selfishness. We are naturally inclined to selfish pursuits. Therefore, with the right combination of propaganda pressures applied consistently over time, progressives have changed the U.S. into a seething mass of selfish adolescents interested only in demonizing others to keep the revenue flowing into their pockets. They do not care that is false.

Chinese General Sun Tzu, one of the greatest philosophers and military strategists of all time, said: "If you know your enemies and know yourself, you will not be imperiled in a hundred battles ... if you do not know your enemies nor yourself, you will be imperiled in every single battle." (Sun Tzu was the author of *The Art of War*, written in the 6th century B.C.) The simple fact is we no longer know ourselves, and we certainly do not know our enemies. We can thank decades of demoralization, planted by our enemies and nourished by homegrown progressives. Two sources of information help to illustrate the point. First, look at the game plan promulgated by The Frankfurt School in the 1920s. These German Marxists, along with legions of like organizations, had one goal: destruction of Western civilization, followed by the installment of worldwide Communism. They would accomplish this through Cultural Revolution or cultural Marxism: infiltration and systematic overthrow from within. Today, the American media is ready to carry water for these Marxists, while refusing to report the real crime; all done to promote their cause.

The script is universal with these mainstreamers from the media. It is set in concrete. Play stories that help Democrats. Play them hard, thoroughly, repeatedly. Stories that help conservatives or Republicans, if they can be ignored, then ignore them. If they cannot be ignored, they should be delivered quietly. And in our day, if they hurt the president, Hillary Clinton, or one of the minions, then report it for no more than one midnight news cycle at most.

Thirty years ago we were accustomed to hearing Soviet propaganda from *Pravda*, but it was nothing to the level of crude we are seeing and hearing now from the American counterpart. In fact, it seems worse than *Pravda* ever was. Ironically, *Pravda* has more editorial truth now than the *Washington Post*, *New York Times* and the *LA Times* collectively. There is no journalism taught in this country any longer, not in the classic sense that journalism was once taught in places like Missouri University, one of the premier schools for journalism. Now, what is taught is playing propaganda for the Progressives, which by definition are patient Communists. Possibly we should start sending journalism students to Moscow or Leningrad to keep their minds free and able to do critical thinking. Of course I jest, but we must wake up to what has been happening. Do you see now why I say the enemy is here living among us? Not only are they here. They have microphones, pens and paper.

Hitler pumped out the same kind of dribble to sway Germans in the 1930s. His "lies" of course always showed his opposition in a horrible light. He called them liars and extremists. His claims would contain a small kernel of truth which was used to make him more believable, and therefore a good conman. That is the character you have in the entity, Barack Obama. The problem: the media supports him to a fault just so long as the Liberal Progressive Agenda and the Secular Humanist Manifesto is upheld.

Enemy Combatants

Through history, any media, replacing the facts, bending the truth, telling lies has been considered an act of war against the nation's people, I guess not any more. We really do not have anything close to "media" in America with the major networks any more. It is little more than campaign central for the Democrat or Progressive Party. Listening to them should put a question mark behind everything they say; because their credibility has sailed from port many years ago. As such I consider them no less than an enemy to our nation.

These numerous examples of bias and dishonesty have occurred in the past and are happening now. To understand the volume of the progressive lies, one can multiply the few events cited above by hundreds of times to approximate a real number and are just too numerous to count. They are obviously too plentiful to be errors, slips of the tongue, or slips of the pen. They picture a group of elitist charlatans with microphones and pens in hand, who have an aloof arrogance and defiance for the ordinary citizen. And their pomposity would fill the books in just about any public library.

In Covering for Muslims' Attacks on Christians

Take for example the news from the Middle East in August, 2013. Over 600 people were killed during the August 14-17 clashes between the Egyptian military and the Muslim Brotherhood. In the aftermath, the media and the political class have focused on the military's crackdown while giving the Muslim Brotherhood a total pass. The reason: Barack Hussein Obama has backed the Muslim Brotherhood to the hilt with American tax dollars. The American/Egyptian relationship has been damaged for years to come due to the actions of the president in the Oval Office.

Two U.S. Senators, Sens. John McCain (R-AZ) and Lindsey Graham (R-SC) released a joint statement to Obama the same week urging him to suspend aid to Egypt due to the actions of the Egyptian military but they made no mention of the Muslim Brotherhood's purposeful targeting of Coptic Christians.

Then on August 16, Investors.com reported that the Muslim Brotherhood was using the clashes with the military as "cover for ongoing persecution" of Christians: "Amid the raging violence in Egypt, a less-publicized war is being waged against Egypt's long-persecuted Coptic Christians, this time using the excuse that they were somehow involved in the military's ouster of the Muslim Brotherhood's Mohamed Morsi from power."

There have reportedly been "39 incidents of violence against churches, monasteries, Coptic schools and shops in different parts of [Egypt] within the past few days." This includes "the torching of the Prince Tadros Church in the province of Fayoum."[34]

And such attacks have been going on for months. In May 2011, Islamists stormed into Virgin Mary Church in Cairo, shouting, "With our blood and soul, we will defend you, Islam." They also attacked and burned the homes of nearby Coptic Christians, "killing a dozen and wounding more than 200."[35] What did Senators McCain and Graham said about this? Nothing. What did well-known media elites said? Nothing. The only news source I could find saying ANYTHING in a timely manner and it was not much: CNN. It is unclear what brought them out of their cocoon.

In Dumbing Down the Public

Life in America during the socialistic push is tragically similar to life under an 18th Century Latin American caudillo; while the leader is not a military leader; the people are viewed as little more than pawns or property of the state. So many fellow citizens seem to be in a stupor, do not care, have no ambition to do or be anything else, or are unaware of the surroundings just living in a bubble, and have become complicit with the progressives in doing to our country what they are doing. Complicit is also a great word to use with the so called media, as it places an indictment squarely on them for these treasonous acts. The treason enters the picture because

CHAPTER THREE — DESTRUCTION BY BETRAYAL OF THE FREE PRESS

their role is to "dumb down" their readers or listeners so much that these masses walk through life like clones, never objecting to the government's dictates, just looking for a government tit. Having become totally dependent upon the regime for a monthly check, food stamps, medical care, public assistance for utilities, and public transportation, they have long ago surrendered their human dignity to become a peon serving the caudillo. The public school system for sure has been one primary tool of liberals in accomplishing this goal, but the media has volunteered to serve, going above and beyond the call of duty, in carrying the liberal water in order to get the treasonous business completed. If Americans could awaken from their stupor, examine their surroundings with a libertarian eye, they would certainly and suddenly become enraged. Enraged at what the nightly news anchor, the media bosses, the progressive liberal party, and the current regime were collectively doing; keeping them uninformed and working hard to make ends meet.

Liberal media have promoted a form of psychological bankruptcy which is shameful. What they do every day, would bring a verdict of guilty and a sentence of hanging by the neck until dead in any American Colonial society. They especially would face a death sentence in a Muslim country, a system which by the way they claim they love so much. I am still waiting for the mob of loyal Americans to come as a swarm with pitchforks to deal with the aristocratic and plutocratic HQ news network executives.

It is a disastrous and devastating sight to see how this government has turned on that private sector like it has through poor education and a media who tries to mislead. NSA's domestic spying apparatus indicates that the people in government do not trust the law-abiding citizens for which they work. It appears having citizens poorly educated is not enough.

Indeed, the ruling elite have turned the military's attentions inward on the citizens. This has terrified the thinking American who values a less tyrannical government than, say, the East German Stasi under the Communists. But for those who are among the less knowledgeable in the nation, they will do anything to please an elder brother who wants to know everything you are up to. I mean they really do want to control what you think as much as what you say. Those of you who are "not doing anything wrong" will, of course, be able to change your eye color, skin color, parents' surnames, religious practices and political voting record to conform to the ruling elite's perception of reality, and thereby remain free of IRS persecution and multiple government prosecutions of newly invented hate crimes.

But of course the news media has done its job in misdirecting attention away from real stories. You need real proof of the media working its deliberate attacks to support the Obama train wrecks of the world? The world is in such a mess, the media does not know what to cover, does not know what it is covering when they attempt to cover it; especially they do not know how to cover it. Consider the following,

For example, there is "Fighting the Caliphate." The Caliphate controls portions of both Iraq and Syria. In Syria, the fight involves in part the effort to overthrow Bashar al-Assad. Our efforts may be a humanitarian response but it is unclear and unstated putting the United States in an impossible position. In Syria, after all, the U.S. is with the rebels pushing to oust Assad too. Result: the U.S. is allied with ISIS in Syria and fighting ISIS in Iraq. This puts the U.S. on both sides of the Syrian civil war while pretending to have nothing to do with it.

Consider the Veterans Administration Hospital disaster. That has been a train wreck for years, with our veterans dying due to a lack of care through a government version of Obamacare. Obama gave a speech at Fort Belvoir, Virginia on August 7, 2014. "Over the last few months, we've discovered some inexcusable misconduct. . . . It was outrageous." Obama said. "We're instituting a critical culture of accountability." It appears that portion of the speech was the total plan to fix of the problem. The media looks the other way.

Take Obamacare. To call its rollout a disaster would be an understatement. Mr. Obama has been terrifically inconsistent, unilaterally changing the rules after he said the act was law and could not be changed. The media looks the other way.

What about when union leaders rejected Obamacare saying they were "fed up" with the Affordable Care Act since it would be too expensive for their members? Three leaders of America's largest unions, including Jimmy Hoffa, wrote a jaw-dropping letter to Harry Reid and Nancy Pelosi, saying in part: "When you and the President sought our support for the Affordable Care Act (ACA), you pledged that if we liked the health plans we have now, we could keep them. Sadly, that promise is under threat. Right now, unless you and the Obama Administration enact an equitable fix, the ACA will shatter not only our hard-earned health benefits, but destroy the foundation of the 40 hour work week that is the backbone of the American middle class. . . . On behalf of the millions of working men and women we represent and the families they support, we can no longer stand silent in the face of elements of the Affordable Care Act that will destroy the very health and wellbeing of our members along with millions of other hardworking Americans."[36] In light of their veiled threat to discontinue their support to him, Obama granted them an exemption. The media was silent on this story too.

What about the CIA mess? Its infiltration of computer systems belonging to Congress was excusable according to some. Not! The story was covered up by major media sources.

What about the intelligence boss deliberately lying to Congress when asked a direct question on dragnet surveillance of Americans? Excusable? No. The media refuses to cover the story by looking the other way.

How about all those green jobs? Obama shoveled billions into the pockets of friends and their start-up companies in the "green market." Problem is, they have all filed bankruptcy. The media refused to cover the story.

CHAPTER THREE — DESTRUCTION BY BETRAYAL OF THE FREE PRESS

All these policies and more started as train wrecks, then only got worse. The media stays away from analysis of the policies of Obama because it smells like a disaster.

America's political Richter scale has been jolted by scathing criticisms of historical corruption within the executive branch, by executive order and otherwise; but one would never know it by media coverage. Instead, they are practically like a tree falling in an empty forest, because the corrupt broadcast networks are not reporting them. Can you imagine if America's biggest union leaders had delivered comparable blasts at the economic policies of Presidents Bush, Bush, or Reagan? The network amplifiers would have been turned up so loud, as they opened each news broadcast with a mocking ridicule of a president, they would have blown their fuses. We would still be watching re-runs of this 10, 20 and 30 years later. Come to think of it, many of their broadcasts are reruns. They all seem to say the same thing, "This is all George Bush's fault."

The media has declared a knowledge war on Americans; from Big Labor's complicit moans, to the IRS's corruption, to the NSA spy game crimes, to the Mideast crises. Many of these crises are facilitated by Mr. Obama and his backing of the Muslim Brotherhood, and other criminal elements within Islam. There seems no end to the media con game that shifts from silence to farce and back to silence again; whatever they believe helps to support their war. Congressional hearings have revealed the scheme to target conservative groups was directed out of the current administration and the Office of the IRS Chief Counsel. The Chief Counsel is one of only two agency employees who are appointed by Barack Obama! And White House Visitor Logs show that this chief counsel visited the White House more than 180 times in one year. While the smell of corruption is rancid in that scandal, the IRS scandal is not the story of stories from the networks' talking heads. Their story focuses on what they call the Republicans' hatred for American people and the tenor of their questioning during these hearings. Their other story is the heroic answers the ranking members of the IRS, CIA and others gave to the questioning.

Hang 'em High with Gun Control

The "bell of the ball" stories which the liberal media loves to cover are actually stale notes dealing with gun control, the evils of oil, abortion rights, and the special rights of the LGBYT movement. Of course the "Johnny come lately" story is the adoration the media has for anything Muslim. That adoration is obviously based on their illicit love affair they have with the head of Muslim activities in America, Mr. Obama.

A recent study by Obama's own Justice Department concluded that gun control laws are ineffective in reducing gun violence. But that fact will likely never cross the broadcast microphone of Chris Matthews. Hence we are forced to listen to more emotional drivel about "more gun laws are needed now to save lives."

An EPA study that failed to link "fracking" (hydraulic fracturing) with environmental contamination will not cross the sleek slips of Brian Williams. So the silence of the media will keep oil and coal on the Top 10 most wanted list of villains to the uneducated public.

Coverage of abortion rights must emphasize that the pro-life position is "extreme" while abortionists pro-choice is "reasonable" or "normal." You will never hear the network big-hairs try to pin down Democratic politicians on extreme positions or defying public opinion on things like late term abortion, partial birth abortion, parental consent, or many other vulnerabilities of the National Organization Advocating comprehensive information on Reproductive Rights in America (aka NARAL or "pro-choice) Democrats. It is not in the media playbook. No, they will stalk and bait and quiz pro-life Republicans, eagerly hunting the next gaffe that can go big time.

The LGBYT movement has had a special place in the heart of the media, if for no other reason than it irritates the traditional Judeo-Christian morality. And they hate those morals.

The media has totally done a two-step around murders of Americans on American soil by an Islamic follower, Ali Muhammad Brown. The media is afraid of displeasing Muslim leadership, being called Islamaphobics. They also want to from their demented view, make up for America's past sins of slavery; so they do not even mention the news story. Frankly, this story should shoved news from Ferguson, MO off the stage. But the media, in spite of not knowing who is crossing our southern border, responds with a collective yawn. They must believe some murders are deserved. Facts are inconvenient to the media.

The cynical thing about all this is that even though the public knows it is being played by cosmopolitan liberals, the game still works. Average Americans might not trust the media further than Barack Obama can throw a game-opening pitch, but the networks still set the agenda and control the subject. Face it — Barack Obama has failed in his policies both domestic and abroad. Excuses are offered by the media, instead of reporting the news of that failure.

Partisans of right and left seek their favored outlets; but the consciousness of the non-political middle is shaped by the legacy media, and the legacy media is a corrupt PR arm for the Democratic Party.

Could You Please Pass Me a Copy of the "Memo of the Day?"

I recall many years ago during the presidential campaign of 2000; George Bush had just selected Dick Cheney to be his running mate. Rush Limbaugh discovered that the various media personalities were all using the same exact phrases on particular days. As an example of media getting specific directions from their headquarters, he showed that changing channels on radio or television revealed that the identical key word was being used in describing, or reporting, in this case it was Bush's decision on Cheney. Shown below are the exact words used by the reporters in that case, all of which Limbaugh put together in a montage to show how obvious it was that a centralized memorandum was being followed. You can read below and then be the judge for yourself:

Al Hunt: He meets all of George W's weaknesses, lack of gravitas.

Juan Williams: We see the son, who is seeking some gravitas.

Claire Shipman: They were looking at candidates with gravitas.

Steve Roberts: But he has the gravitas and you can sum it up in one word, stature.

Vic Fazio: It may go to the gravitas.

Jeff Greenfield: We're to use the favorite phrase, gravitas.

Lester Holt: This is a vice president who brought gravitas.

Wolf Blitzer: This will give some gravitas, add some credibility.

Ed Rollins: I think the gravitas that Cheney brought to the ticket.

Jonathan Alter: What he gets is gravitas, a sense of weight.

Bob Kerrey: He does not need anybody to give him gravitas.

Margaret Carlson: It means that, you know, gravitas.

Mike McCurry: I think he also needs some gravitas.

Sam Donaldson: To give gravitas.

Eleanor Clift: Well, he brings gravitas.

Walter Isaacson: He does seem to bring some gravitas.

Al Hunt: It's called gravitas.

Mark Shields: A little gravitas!

Judy Woodruff: You certainly have gravitas tonight.

Sam Donaldson: He displayed tonight a certain gravitas.

Mario Cuomo: I think gravitas is the word. Unfortunately for the Governor, you can't graft gravitas. He has gravitas.[37]

Over the years, Rush Limbaugh has come across this type of reporting throughout what he calls the "drive-by media" time and time again, on different and independent political stories, but in each and every case this so-called "independent media" outlets have all used the same identical words or phrases in reporting the story. How is the world can this be just coincidental? It cannot be. Someone is sending out a memo, a liberal someplace within the Democratic HQ framework that rests either in Washington, D. C. or in one of the news outlets.

Another example of this type of reporting has shown up in supporting Hillary Clinton for president. The Democrats and the *New York Times* are trying to grease the skids in preparation for her presidential run in 2016. They recently released a story in follow-up to Benghazi, where they are trying to revive the story that an American-made video bashing Muslims was responsible for the whole incident. You should recall that under oath, Hillary had lied about her role in that disaster where four Americans were murdered. She yelled back to the interrogators regarding the deaths, "What difference does it make now?" So, *The Times* did a story on Benghazi in which they maintained two things: there was no Al-Qaeda involved in Benghazi, and it was all caused by a video.[38] Now everyone who has watched this incident develop knows that it was Al-Qaeda that was involved and that they said they did not know about any video. By the way, about the video; nobody ever really saw it.

So when the *New York Times* ran this story, the media outlets picked it up, on the memo someone sent out, telling them what phrases to use, and it appears, in what order they were to say the phrases. They are shown below:

> **John Berman:** Al-Qaeda was not behind the 2012 attack. The attack was likely carried out by independent Libyan militias and that those fighters were, in fact, infuriated by that anti-Muslim movie.
>
> **Mike Jerrick:** It really was an anti-Islam film that sparked the attack that killed four Americans.
>
> **David Gregory:** There was no involvement by Al-Qaeda. The attack was, in part, fueled by anger over an American-made video.
>
> **Jonathan Karl:** No proof Al-Qaeda played any role at all, and that many of the attackers were in fact motivated by that anti-Muslim web video.
>
> **Chris Wallace:** No evidence that Al-Qaeda or other international terrorist groups had any role in the assault. It was fueled in large part by anger at, yes, an American-made video.
>
> **Anderson Cooper:** No evidence that Al-Qaeda or other international terrorist groups had any role. His reporting assigns essential role in the tragedy to the American-made video denigrating Islam.
>
> **Don Lemon:** There is no evidence that Al-Qaeda or other international terrorist groups had any role in the assault and it was fueled in large part by a video denigrating Islam.
>
> **Jill Dougherty:** There is no evidence that Al-Qaeda had any role in the attack. An anti-Muslim video did play a role.

Chapter Three — Destruction by Betrayal of the Free Press

Dave Briggs: There's no evidence Al-Qaeda was involved in the Benghazi attack at all and it was all sparked by that YouTube video.

Victor Blackwell: Al-Qaeda was likely not involved in the attack.

Christi Paul: It was fueled in part by a US-made, anti-Muslim video.[39]

Conan O'Brien got in on the act of building his own montage of what media talking heads have been saying about a story during the holiday season, this one about Christmas shopping for oneself. And in reporting this, he thinks he has discovered something very unique about the media. What remains unspoken is that Conan himself hints that all the local reporters are reading the same memo, they have to be.

O'Brien: Judging by local news -- and I've been looking at a lot of local news -- there is an even bigger story that's sweeping the nation right now.

Local Anchor: Who are you really shopping for this holiday season? It's okay. You can admit it if you bought an item or two, or 10, for yourself.

Local Anchor: Well, it's okay. You can admit it if you've bought an item or two, or maybe 10, for yourself.

Local Anchor: It's okay. You can admit it. You bought an item or two, or 10, for yourself.

Local Anchor: It's okay. You can admit it, if you bought an item or two, or 10, for yourself.

Local Anchor: It's okay. You can admit it if you bought an item or two, or 10, for yourself.

Local Anchor: It's okay. You can admit it, if you bought an item or two, or 10, for yourself.

Local Anchor: It's okay. You can admit it. If you've bought an item or two, or 10, for yourself.

Local Anchor: It's okay. You can admit it. If you bought an item or two, or 10, for yourself.

Local Anchor: It's okay. You can admit it, if you bought an item or two, or maybe 10 for yourself.

Local Anchor: It's okay. You can admit it, if you bought an item or two for yourself.

Local Anchor: It's okay. You can admit it, if you bought one or two or maybe three or four, maybe even 10 items for yourself.

Local Anchor: It's okay. You can admit it.[40]

Whether you laugh or are disgusted, while some of this was offered as humor, it should show you a thread that runs through all three stories. The thread is: memos are created to keep all the reporters on the same page so that a story, any story, gets told the way the "big brother" wants it to be told.

Media — A Mere Propaganda Machine

Coverage of domestic terrorism such as a Fort Hood massacre or school shootings are a good gauge to the extent of the transformation of our mass media into a mere propaganda apparatus for the Progressive liberals. An Aurora, Colorado theatre shooting in 2012 got the mainstreamers in an immediate chaotic chatter. They blamed conservatives, conservative talk radio hosts, or the NRA, and even the guns themselves. On live television, one broadcaster went through the local phone book after obtaining a membership list of the Tea Party from the area and found a person with the same name as the accused perpetrator. He went so far as to say he was relatively assured it was the same person who did the shooting, "though we need to investigate further."[41] What should have been an embarrassing incident when it was proved that the shooter was not a Tea Party member, but actually a Democrat, a liberal. This was simply buried from the public by the media.

Take the Gabrielle 'Gabby' Giffords (US Rep. from AZ) shooting in Arizona. Immediately, blame was placed on the conservatives by reporters. Reporters also blamed Sarah Palin for a target scope "+" she drew on a map advertising the event. Truth revealed the shooter was a liberal who was confused and angry.

Take the August 2013 Oklahoma shooting of a 22-year old white man from Australia by three black teenagers. Immediately it was the gun market, which is associated with conservatism that was blamed by media members. When the dust settled, it was the Facebook pages of the three accused of the killing that revealed their allegiance to rappers with their "kill the whitey" culture. That is the wrong stuff for the media to cover. It does not support their agenda. And besides, the White House would not appreciate such a message coming from the steely lips of a liberal broadcaster.

The message which the liberal media gave to these events; there were two. The first message was just a black hole treatment. Stories that should be run around the clock for days are just swept into a dark closet. The shooting at the Family Research Council last year has been consigned to obscurity by the main stream media. The media could not be bothered by even reporting on the truth of each story. It must have been another memo from HQ from which they were reading.

The second message the media gave was their primary intent; that of gun violence. For them to blame guns for these shootings is like blaming a rope on a western movie for the public hanging. The point the liberal media wants each of us to understand is this; unless the crime fits into their world view, it will not be reported truthfully, in part, or at all. Unless of course it is altered to fit; blame someone other

CHAPTER THREE — DESTRUCTION BY BETRAYAL OF THE FREE PRESS

than the criminal, especially if that person is a person of color or a Muslim.

The propaganda filled narratives have to change. The American public must speed up their defiance for a media which is so biased to lie, cheat and steal to get an anti-American message broadcast. One favorite narrative of the propaganda-filled media is telling that right-winged Americans across the country are hording guns in order to use them on innocent victims. They operate from a fraudulent framework, managed by fraudulent media elites, who are controlled by a fraudulent political view that offers nothing but chaos. They present a message by jumping to conclusions before checking facts.

Though it is not possible, if I had the power, I would get into our time machine and ask it to take us back to a specific time, a specific place, to meet a specific person. The reason for our trip: the integrity and honesty of the media has unfortunately receded into the past. The purpose of our trip: interview a past member of the media who embodied the integrity, the honesty and the American spirit of the past for which we all year. I already know who, because he will be a breath of fresh air and a contrast to the chicanery we witness today with mainstreamers. His name: Rowe Findley. The place: his high school, Willow Springs High, sitting within his English literature classroom in Willow Springs, Missouri. The time: following his retirement from the National Geographic in 1990 after he received the Society's Distinguished Service Award.

Briefly, Rowe would tell us first of his love for America, especially the principles for which the country has stood for 200 plus years. He would tell of his commitment to "fresh air" in journalism, the integrity needed by journalists to speak truth and provide readers and listeners with no unkind interpretations; rather straight forward, bald facts. As former assistant editor for National Geographic, he would be for those who are choking on the smoggy air of the current media. He would recall a statement made by El Paso artist Russell R. Waterhouse about the American West as it to the media's coverage, "It's a country where you can see clear into forever."[42] Rowe thought journalism should be handled that way, crystal clear, so all the facts are known. Not made up, not misconstrued, and not propagandized, just clear as the western sky. In particular, Rowe had great respect for leaders who led. He thought highly of Ronald Reagan, our 40th President, who over thirty years ago led America during dark days, during a bad economy, a serious energy crisis, and foreign enemies who threatened our freedoms. At a time when Americans were told there was a crisis of confidence. He changed that because he believed in America, the American people, and in freedom. When he was first sworn in as president, he was told he might want to ask the press what they thought about what was going on in America. Ronald Reagan replied, "I tell them, they don't tell me." Those who heard Reagan that day knew he must be taken seriously because of his strength of character and his determination.

Reagan said he did not know everything, but like Isaiah Berlin's essay, *The Hedgehog and the Fox*, the fox knows everything, but only knows it from a 30,000 foot view, or rather superficially. The hedgehog knows only a couple of things, but knows the details of each and knows them very well. Ronald Reagan was similar to the hedgehog in this story in that he knew a couple of things very well. He knew and loved the American people. He also knew the truth about the Soviet Union and despised that for which it stood. He wanted the challenge and the chance to destroy that Soviet empire, and he wanted to return the country to the good sense of the American people. He was reviled by academic elites and in particular by members of the media. The media members tried in every way to sink the mission of that president, but Reagan could also shut out the buzz in Washington, he was underestimated, and he was able to accomplish much for America. Reagan saw America as the great land of opportunity. Rowe loved that about Reagan, felt the same in his soul, and wanted only to report truth.

We need media members with the integrity of a Rowe Findley again who will take their place in reporting truth about today's news stories; not becoming the news story themselves, or by taking on a mission to rewrite the news so they can tell the world what to think. Rather we need reporters who have the "courage" to tell truth, this is so lacking among those who count themselves as "media." As C. S. Lewis stated, "Courage is not simply one of the virtues, but the form of every virtue at the testing point."

"I don't think you can make a lawyer honest by an act of legislature. You've got to work on his conscience. And his lack of conscience is what makes him a lawyer."

— Will Rogers

Chapter Four

Destruction by Bad Barristers and Bad Court Verdicts

The other day my house caught fire. My lawyer said, "Shouldn't be a problem. What kind of coverage do you have?" I said, "Fire and theft." The lawyer frowned, "Uh oh. Should be fire OR theft." — Alan King

ON SEPTEMBER 5, 1993, AT APPROXIMATELY 5:30 PM, a deadbeat dad named Randy Long was spotted alongside a rural and remote section of a highway by the state's highway patrol officers. Turns out, Long, who was liquored up, had been trying to keep a "borrowed" pickup going down the highway in the right lane, but ran it off the road hitting a tree. Having attempted to avoid officers of the law for some months, Long stepped out of the truck and attempted to negotiate the uneven grassy berm beneath his feet. Discovering that too much of a challenge that day, he crawled on eventually finding it necessary to use the grass as a hideout, passing out, face down. The officers, seeing the wrecked truck stopped to investigate the scene. They found Long lying in the grass approximately 15 feet away from the pickup with crumpled front fender half embracing the oak tree and the other half "sticking to" the barbed wire fence it had removed from tree trunk. Further investigation within the truck, surfaced a stolen hand gun, some hemp, an open container of an adult beverage and a few rounds of illegal ammunition. While Randy slept off his whiskey sours from the Oasis Bar on his open-air grass bed, he was securely cuffed, loaded into the patrol car, and was carted off to spend some social time at the local slammer.

One other feature about Randy was disconcerting to the HP, running a background on his license, across the screen in their cruiser ran the words, "Wanted — warrant issued." Long was wanted for some earlier DUIs and for five years of continued non-payment of his child support. He also had an unpaid parking ticket as well as an assault complaint on his record.

Randy's father, upon getting the phone call from his son saying he was incarcerated within the jail three towns away, walked his fingers through the yellow pages, found the name of and called an attorney whose presence was requested forthwith at the jail. Presently attorney and Long were standing in front of the judge, with the list of charges read against him, as well as the newly added DUI charge. The judge called for meeting in chambers with prosecutor and defense counsel. When the hammer came down back in court, Randy was surprisingly fined only the sum of $200 for the DUI; and having spent all his dollars on his whiskey sours and tips for the cute bar maid, his dad was summoned to pay the fine and the attorney's fees. Then Randy was released under his own recognizance and rode home with daddy in the truck.

Some will ask, "What happened with all the other charges: the child support, parking ticket, DUI, the assault charge; what happened to them? Another will say, "I want the attorney's name and number; I may need it since he appears to be able to do miracles." What did happen to the other charges? Let's see. No one outside of the judge, prosecutor, defense attorney, the court recorder and of course daddy knows for sure. It appears the charges were brushed aside due to the work load at court, the luck of having a liberal judge, a good defense attorney, and possibly some fatigue on the part of the justice system, or possibly some records were just mishandled.

There are millions of stories in "the naked city." This has been one of them. Here is another.

At 2:30 A.M. on March 22, 1997, a convicted felon named Anthony Dye was racing his Corvette through the streets of Elkhart, Indiana. The police were in hot pursuit. Dye pulled into his mother's driveway, got out of the car, and made a run for it. When the police caught up with him, Dye took a semiautomatic pistol from his waistband and opened fire. At that critical moment, a valiant police dog named Frei leapt into action, fastened onto Dye's leg, and, as it were, took a bit out of crime. Dye was arrested.

Having been injured in the course of his arrest, Dye did what any red-blooded American would do. He brought a lawsuit, against Frei, the police dog. Dye argued that dogs are "persons" who can be sued, at least when they work for the police. Dye fought his way to the second highest court in the land, the United States Court of Appeals, which dismissed his claim.

Dye's theory that a dog is a person is not as far-fetched as you might think. In fact, he was not even the first person to sue a police dog. And some very respectable lawyers have argued that the legal distinction of "person" ought to be expanded, at least to include other primates. Laurence Tribe, Harvard's leading Constitutional scholar, has argued for years that chimpanzees should be considered persons under the Constitution.

That the country's best legal minds can be about whether the word "person" includes dogs or chimpanzees tells a lot about lawyers. But it also tells us a lot about the language of the law. Nothing in the realm of legalese is quite what it seems.[1]

The fact is that when involving lawyers, the written and spoken language can go from non-understandable to bizarre. And when confronted by "legal" documents from these, whom many call the most educated people on earth (laugh),

Chapter Four — Destruction by Bad Barristers and Bad Court Verdicts

"All this would be of purely academic interest if it weren't for the fact that the legal documents are a part of the basic infrastructure of life. Isn't it odd that the most important events in our lives require slogging through language that almost nobody understands?"[2]

Welcome to the world where some of these great legal minds reside: that is the United States Congress and White House, as well as the various federal and state court systems of America. For when select members of these lawyers moved from private or corporate practice into government work, the language and activities become nuttier. Consider the fact that Congress once passed legislation declaring that "September 16, 1940 means June 27, 1950 . . . At one time or another, the law has defined "dead person" to include nuns, "daughter" to include son, and "cow" to include horse. It has even defined white as black.[3] "Connecting the dots," following the line of logical progression, and piecing together these declarations of Harvard's leading Constitutional scholars and other legal brain trusts regarding who is a person. If chimpanzees can become persons, that is a real problem. They could also become lawyers and be elected to public government service. I know what you are thinking; however, I will not give any further explanations.

This is a tiny glimpse of one of the many problems which seems to be systemic with our American legal system today. Government bureaucrats have turned into legal barristers who distort the law. The law is simply an inconvenience to many attorneys, who use it for running up billable hours for clients. Some really do not want to follow the law at all. Couple that with the testimony of the arrests and court cases indicate that a court experience could turn into potluck, based on what legal advice is given, what attorneys are involved, how laws are interpreted, and how judges react to the evidence. Their activities not only point toward but are a mockery of justice. It shows the possibility of an uneasy ground beneath the feet of any person who may be standing accused of something within this justice system. It can be potluck or a perfect trifecta depending on whether a person gets the right judge, the right legal counsel, and the right timing of the court's workload. I get so concerned about it at times, it seems that it could conceivably be possible for exactly the opposite scenario to happen; an individual is arrested for a simple speeding ticket could get an outlandish sentence of say two years in prison, from the progressive court system. And in the case of Anthony, it is the same roulette possibilities are in play, looking for a sympathetic judge, jury, and interpretation of the law, no matter how guilty one may be. Since Randy's and Anthony's stories are both true, the possibility of justice going wrong in this system is quite possible. When right becomes wrong and wrong become right, anything can happen. Anecdotal evidence, but it is evidence.

There are good and great things which have obviously come from the law and some very good and great attorneys; many of them should be mentioned. While there are volumes dedicated to some of them, possibly it would be best to save many of those layers of stories for another separate volume. Suffice to mention one here, who comes from history. That story revolves around a specific account of a faceoff with eight British troops on March 5, 1770. The citizens of Boston were growing weary of all these British troops who had been occupying the city since 1768, all there to protect the elected British officials who were overseeing local affairs and Colonist's daily life. Tensions were rising and building a foundation hotbed for the revolution yet six years off. The British called the event the Incident on King Street; we call it the Boston Massacre. Hundreds of colonists began surrounding one British soldier, following a physical exchange between a young colonist and the soldier. A crowd gathered, church bells were rung, indicating an emergency, causing a few hundred colonists to gather around the soldier. The soldier was soon joined by eight others. Feeling threatened, some of the soldiers began firing, killing three colonists immediately and wounding two others, who died later that day. The soldiers were arrested, indicted by a Grand Jury and seven months later put on trial. During the time between the incident and the trials, local citizens held their own verbal trials and hangings in the local cafes. Paul Revere did an engraving of the incident, which heightened tensions even more, resulting in more inflammatory language such as claims that Capt. Preston had ordered the soldiers to fire their weapons on the unarmed citizens. Each soldier tried to secure legal representation, but to no avail as no one was willing to defend them. Finally, John Adams stepped forward and represented Captain William Preston in a first trial on October 24, 1770. Preston was found not guilty, the jury proclaiming Preston innocent on the basis of what the judge called "reasonable doubt." That was the first time that phrase was used on American soil. There was a second trial that started on November 27th, for the remaining soldiers. Adams also represented them. They were also acquitted of all guilt. Mob action had caused the deaths according to the jury. It was ruled self-defense.

It is worth noting what John Adams said about the trials, years later after he became president. Adams said, "The part I took in the defense of Captain Preston and the soldiers, procured me anxiety, and obliquely enough, it was, however, one of the most gallant, generous, manly, and disinterested actions of my whole life — and one of the best pieces of service I ever rendered my country. Judgment of death against those soldiers would have been as a foul stain on this country, as the executions of the Quakers or witches, anciently."

While this case from history speaks of doing the right thing, we have before us still the problem with legal framework when wrong becoming right. It is happening before us. Some individuals are being charged, tried and found guilty of hate crimes because of the color of their skin, while others with a different skin tone do the things but are not charged with anything because of protection. This is in no way equal protection under the law. It is a timing issue. An example such as in California; some convicted rapists are receiving sentences of community service only. No other time is served. The sentences handed out depend on overcrowding in prison or the politics of the day as with Obama and Eric Holder. They want fewer blacks and other ethnic persons in prison which would result in a higher percent-

Chapter Four — Destruction by Bad Barristers and Bad Court Verdicts

age of white people in behind bars. So it is a lottery, or roulette, based on "legal" factors: on color, race, on sexual orientation, and the luck of the draw it would appear. And what about the guys who have been in prison for 25 years because they were caught with marijuana on them too many times? It is obvious by the new hemp laws; they were just born too early.

And this seems more like the light from a signal fire indicating that our great nation is coming into a time of its own death throws. One of those signals is the nationwide discrimination, those who are aristocratic and politically connected to the regime in power, and those who are not.

Attorneys are not always willing to uphold the laws they have been sworn to uphold, once in office. Take a current situation, where in the House of Representatives, a bill labeled "Enforce the Law Bill" has been presented for discussion and a vote. It is a bill stating that the President of the United States must uphold the law of the land. Getting word of this, the president has spoken out, saying he will veto such a bill if it reaches his desk.[4]

In 2013, one news source writer documented some of this activity in what they called "Lawless in the White House," a blog showing the ways of Barack Obama. Included in that report was a list of thirteen separate grievances that only tell a portion of the tale of abuse on the Constitutional limits of presidential authority. This list is now out of date due to the many, many more recent grievances that have occurred. Plus we have the invention of new "executive order" laws which totally ignore existing law. The president is hired to administer laws and follow the Constitution. Article 2, Sec. 3 of the Constitution clearly makes its case by charging the president that he "shall take care that the Laws be faithfully executed." It does not say that he "should" execute the laws of the United States; it uses the imperative "shall."

The editors at *Investor's Business Daily* picked up on the issue, too. Following is short sampling of what they call "just a small sampling" of a *"Lengthy Legacy of Lawlessness."*

> **Aug. 14, 2013:** *The Obama administration delayed the provision in ObamaCare to cap out-of-pocket health care costs, picking and choosing parts of the law to enforce, which is to exceed its authority.*
>
> **July 17, 2013:** *The 4th Circuit Court of Appeals joined the federal appeals courts in D.C. and Philadelphia in ruling President Obama›s National Labor Relations Board recess appointments (who by law must be approved by Congress) were unconstitutional. Thus far, the president has ignored the ruling.*
>
> **July 1, 2013:** *The Obama administration unilaterally decided to delay the employer mandate provision of ObamaCare for a year, which is to provide information to the feds about the extent of an applicant›s insurance. Never mind that the law states the mandate must go into effect on Jan. 1, 2014; they are now relying on the "honor system" from applicants to determine if they are qualified for subsidies.*

June 25, 2013: *The Supreme Court ruled in Shelby County v. Eric Holder that Section 4 of the Voting Rights Act is «unconstitutional» and that "the formula can no longer be used as a basis for subjecting jurisdiction to preclearance." Instead of complying with the ruling, Holder filed suit to order Texas to submit to preclearance, in defiance of Congress' authority to legislate and the Supreme Court›s authority to rule on the constitutionality of the law.*

June 15, 2012: *The Obama administration announced it will stop deporting illegal immigrants under the age of 30 in a "deferred action" policy to circumvent immigration laws. This comes after Congress rejected a similar measure about a year ago. Since then, more than 500,000 illegals have received the deferment and only 20,000 have been rejected. As for the law-abiding applicants who have been waiting in line, well, that›s Obama›s idea of "lawfulness."*

May 20, 2013: *A Washington Post article revealed that Fox News reporter James Rosen was investigated by the DOJ, which subpoenaed his phone records and emails in direct contravention of the First Amendment under the pretense of a leak investigation.*

May 13, 2013: *AP reported the DOJ secretly collected phone records of AP reporters and editors, a move completely outside the realm of law. Even the AP, which up until then had been pretty submissive to the Obama agenda, was appalled by the breach.*

May 10, 2013: *The IRS revealed it targeted conservative groups applying for tax-exempt status beginning in March 2010, a direct targeting of political opponents through the tax laws. It›s one of the crimes that led Congress to impeach President Nixon.*

May 3, 2011: *When asked when he first heard of Operation Fast and Furious, Attorney General Eric Holder falsely testified, "I›m not sure of the exact date, but I probably heard about Fast and Furious for the first time over the last few weeks." Head of the National Drug Intelligence Center Michael Walther told Holder about Fast and Furious in a July 2010 memo. Subsequent revelations showed he knew all along.*

March 27, 2012: *EPA issued final rules regulating greenhouse gas emissions on electric utilities that require power plants to use non-existing carbon capture-and-control technology to meet new emission standards, in defiance of the Congress› rejection of cap-and-trade legislation.*

April 23, 2012: *The administration postponed Medicare Advantage cuts by calling them a "demonstration project" and used funds not approved by Congress to delay effects of those cuts before the election.*

March 1, 2011: *Attorney General Holder lied to Congress, saying "decisions made in the New Black Panther Party case were made by career attorneys in the depart-*

CHAPTER FOUR — DESTRUCTION BY BAD BARRISTERS AND BAD COURT VERDICTS

ment." Associate A.G. Thomas Perrelli, an Obama political appointee, overruled a unanimous recommendation for prosecution by DOJ attorneys.

Feb. 3, 2010: Judge Martin Feldman held the Obama administration in contempt for re-imposing an offshore drilling moratorium that was struck down by the courts.

These statements resemble the hallmark of a junta leading a banana republic. In America, the president is required by law to win the consent of Congress first. "At stake is not some constitutional curlicue. At stake is whether the laws are the law. And whether presidents get to write their own."[5]

Several columnists and writers have in the last several months opined on this issue. Their thoughts follow, however, given the attitude of Obama we have not seen the end of unilateral changes made by him. He is obviously feeling empowered and authorized to create a new law about anything at any time.

Charles Krauthammer, was one who said the lawless ways of [an attorney elected to public service] Barack Obama are "fitting of a caudillo, which are found in Central or South America, rather than an American President. That's banana republic stuff," he said and went on further:

> "Such gross executive usurpation disdains the Constitution. It mocks the separation of powers. And most consequentially, it introduces a fatal instability into law itself. If the law is not what is plainly written, but is whatever the president and his agents decide, what's left of the law."[6]

George Will is another reporter who jumped in on the story in a column in the *Washington Post*, where he blasted Obama and his administration: "Nowadays the federal government leavens its usual quotient of incompetence with large dollops of illegality." Will opined further that the Obama Administration is full of: "... small, devious people putting their lawlessness in the service of their parochialism and recklessly sacrificing public safety and constitutional propriety."[7]

The District of Columbia U.S. Court of Appeals, and in particular Judge Brett M. Kavanaugh, reprimanded Mr. Obama's Nuclear Regulatory Commission over what they called "flouting the law." This was in regards to a Yucca Mountain decision that was two years delinquent at the time. "It is no overstatement to say that our constitutional system of separation of powers would be significantly altered if we were to allow executive and independent agencies to disregard federal law in the manner asserted in this case."[8]

Elected because he was a self-proclaimed Constitutional attorney, Mr. Obama indicates he will enforce only certain laws. Deroy Murdock, a nationally syndicated columnist concluded that in the world according to Obama, " ... the Constitution is for chumps, and the law is for losers." Murdock, having loosened up in the bullpen, delivered some blazing fastballs next, "Slowly at first, then all of a sudden, the Obama Administration has devolved into the Obama Regime. Obama does whatever he wants. Those pesky impediments on his predecessors — namely, federal law, the separation of powers, and the Constitution — have proved as tough as tissue paper in containing Obama's ambition to impose statism on America. From Obamacare to unions to telephones, it's basically another day, another decree."[9]

One might ask, "Why are you writing about Obama here?" Answer: He is an attorney. That is what he says anyway, and while he has been elected President of the United States, he has absolutely no regard for the law. That Obama disregards, even disdains, the Constitution and the Law should come as no real surprise. While still a state senator in Illinois in 2001, he publicly criticized the Founding Fathers for creating a Constitution that he described as a "charter of negative liberties" that limited what "the federal government can't do to you." [In this interview,] Obama maintained that the Warren Court›s decisions on civil rights in the 1960s failed to go far enough; that they should also have sought "redistributive justice." His opinion was that the court needed to break from the "essential restraints" of the Constitution.[10]

Americans have long understood this much about liberal attorneys; that while they have lobbied their way to being in control of writing and interpreting law, they pose a serious threat to American freedom. That the Founders saw ahead to a time when government could be the biggest menace to individual freedom is obvious by their separation of powers. They labored hard for months and years in developing and writing a Constitution that checked the power of government. They cherished that Constitution; not so with Barack Obama. He has longed for the opportunity to "break free from the essential constraints" placed therein by the Founders that limit government's ability to accomplish what he sees as the most important objective: "the redistribution of wealth." Whether you agree or disagree with the Obama agenda, every citizen who loves America should be deeply concerned with the abuse of power by this president and his administration that have set the precedent of wanton disregard of the Constitution. I told you that lawyers do not always like the law.

We live in the day of what many high-ranking Americans call "high crimes and misdemeanors." The American people should be livid after these past years of seeing freedoms diminished, laws broken, and a U.S. diplomat murdered which brought a response of "What difference does it make now?" These actions and these statements were made by attorneys.

Attorneys from the Past Weren't Always Keen on Following the Law Either

Roger Nash Baldwin, a cofounder of the ACLU which he helped frame in 1920, was a social worker, pacifist, and a socialist. He traveled into the Soviet Union but became disillusioned by Soviet-style communism, calling it "A NEW SLAVERY."[11] Though Baldwin loved the idea of a level playing field for socialistic framework and platform that he thought would develop a level playing field, he did say of the

Soviets that it was "the inhuman communist police state tyranny."[12] The ACLU's website has concealed this side of his character, because it hurt the agenda of their organization. Baldwin's true agenda was social revolution in the US, by what he called "social [government] ownership of property."

But Baldwin, like many early socialists in the 1920s and 1930s, learned by the 1950s that it was preferable to be seen as liberal progressive, more in the spirit and tradition of Theodore Roosevelt, who was interested in social justice and social transformation over time, not outright revolution. He and his comrades learned that the legal system with attorneys, judges and courts was one of the best ways to achieve his ends.

Baldwin helped lead the way in pushing the progressive agenda. Over time, liberal lawyers and politicians learned to move slowly in changing society, similar in moving chess pieces in a long game of chess, so as to win the game. Progressives really want to "check-mate" democracy-lovers. They attempt to impact society in a steady, incremental and programmed way, steering the country to the left.

Social justice and transformation of society are the continual battle cries of the untamed liberal ideologue on an idealistic search. Social justice, that of taking from those who have and giving to those who have not, is always achievable in "leveling the field" in the theoretical world. Within the typical classroom where free speech is quashed, it is an unchallenged dream. But when social justice is assembled and tried in the real world, it brings layer upon layer of misery to people rather than equal joy. Liberals often broadcast that conservatives are opposed to the poor having success; that they care only for the rich. Nothing could be further from the truth. Conservatives want every individual to be able to walk out of poverty and to have all the physical blessings each person wants in his own life. But conservatives want that award to be reached by each person by them learning "how to fish" themselves, then providing for themselves and their families by "actually going fishing," rather than always asking someone to provide the fish to them.

The Trouble with the Courts

Questions on how to achieve social justice the liberal way are being asked by Leftists: the qualified answer is to stack the courts with Progressive and Liberal judges so guaranteed results will start coming, slowly but ultimately down the road.

Liberals did just that. They started stacking the courts with liberal judges, the most liberal ones they could find; the ones whose Fascist and Marxist positions had been proven by their lives; they were appointed in order to start their Fascism and Marxism seeping into society by their decisions, much like a hose trickling water into a garden. FDR put this initiative in high gear during his administration. He tried to increase the size of the Supreme Court from 9 to 18 justices, so as to stack the court with Progressive voices; in doing so he would fix the game to get all his legislation passed. The effect would be to turn the nation on its ear embracing the ideologies we had fought for two decades. Overturning local elections of God-fearing people by judicial decisions was one initiative. As a typical term in office for a politician is measured, FDR had four terms in the presidency and therefore moved methodically over time in order to bring about his wretched order of things, so no one would notice quick sudden changes over the years. The result was and is war: it has been and is being waged in our courtrooms against America.

There are two diametrically opposed worldviews operating within the communities of our national leadership, both supported by lawyers in courts. One follows the path set by the Founding Fathers. They want the Constitution to be our ultimate authority. The other is a brutal, stealth-style paradigm that seeks to rape our religious liberty and our sacred freedom. Some people prefer to stay politically correct so as not to have to admit that such diabolical activities are currently directed from the very top of our political echelons.

Leftists recognized long ago, as we said, that America could not be taken down by a frontal assault and revolution, so they decided on an incremental or progressive assault: Stealth and patience in appointing liberal judges on the courts have brought them this far.

A couple of those "Thus far" times include the following shocking accounts:

- The self-professed communist and obvious atheist, Madalyn Murray O'Hair, decided to bring down school prayer. She did it in court using liberal and progressive judges.

- When Imam Feisal Abdul Rauf organized in 2009 to build the Park 51 Islamic Cultural Center Project two blocks from the 9/11 terrorist attack site. The point is that Judeo-Christian believers in this country and especially the 9/11 victim families were left out of the process. They were in effect, kicked to the curb by the side of the road, and abandoned. It is as if political leaders gagged the American public while a tribute to Islam was built, then opened in 2011. That was taken by 9/11 survivors as if it was a tribute to radical terrorism on the site of the worst terrorist attack in American history. Our Founding Fathers aptly reminded us, only a Christian people can build upon Constitutional democracy and only a moral people can preserve the liberty required to build a bright future for America in which individual initiative and free enterprise can thrive once again. Good Samaritans are found in a Judeo-Christian nation. But beware of being a Good Samaritan in a Progressive political culture with the ACLU "robed lawyers" building the results, such as Project 51. They will most likely persecute you, then prosecute you. If not, they will simply rob and beat you, leaving you to rot in the ditch beside the road.

The American people are not knowledgeable about the back stage story of Muslim activity regarding Project 51. The true story is that Muslim conquerors and their modern day followers have a historic pattern of appropriating other religions' holy places in celebration and building mosques on these sites of "victory." These mosques supposedly have become monuments to their victories, though they will deny it. For example, they turned the Hagia Sophia church in Constantinople into a mosque, as well as the site of the Ayodhya temple in India. The point is twofold: it is happening here in America, and it is all brought to you by those smiling attorneys.

Treasonous activities like this point to an eventual time in the future where the last of our freedoms will be threatened: 5 minutes from now, or 15 years from now when the exponential swelling of our federal government, intrusive as it is in everyone's life today, will bring an end to our society. This is all sanctioned by Socialist, Fascist, Communist, and/or Progressive judges who hope they will overwhelm the system. People are slowly beginning to wake up and smell the coffee as the tyrannical moves of these Progressives are tipping the scales. This is not just some agenda of arguments for a Sunday TV news show like "Meet the Press" or "Face The Nation." Freedom is disappearing. Rights are being lost. People are hurting, as a direct result of Barack Obama, his party, his czars, his judges, his attorneys, and his policies. They are all getting a strangle hold on the people of this nation. There is a faint cry that is growing louder by the day for smaller, less expensive and less intrusive government.

For six years, we have observed a president, Barack Obama successfully promote the following 'redistributionist' and 'reparationist' agenda for building an economy. His agenda is to take from some of the most productive to stimulate the economy by redistributing money. This is often accomplished with much political back scratching. He has promoted the idea of bureaucratic alumni to pick winners and losers in the market, generally with the same political back scratching by awarding stimulus money to friends. New tax revenues are raised through unilateral decree, facilitated through federal agencies such as the EPA issuing new restrictions and fines against energy companies and other selected 'losers' he wished to punish. Obama's feel-good, top-down regulations have cost jobs and did little to improve conditions. He dictated the terms of health care with ObamaCare, a planned train wreck and monstrosity and placed one-seventh of our economy under the control of the federal government. All of this, brought to you by liberal robe bearing attorneys, declaring it 'legal': the good guys have been sold out in court again.

Attorneys are like hired guns; they go where the money is. While that alone is not evil, since anyone who works is looking to set up a revenue stream. However, there should be moral and ethical guidelines. Our government, consisting mostly of lawyers and law graduates, has been building a framework by which everyone will need an attorney, no matter what the particular need. And where you find attorneys, you need judges to make decisions. The tobacco settlements were a good case in point. An attorney from Oklahoma, who is an acquaintance of mine, summed up the usual methodology of attorneys. He said, "Everybody needs an attorney to review every document they have." Talk about a revenue stream! Another attorney, from the dark side of the force talked of his revenue stream in another venue. He said, "My clients are always innocent, until they run out of money."

Well, the results of all these policies are in. The attorneys and judges have sentenced us to the worst economic recovery since World War II. Unemployment remains high, with the real numbers hidden by the Oval Office. So many able-bodied people are dropping out of the labor force that the "labor force participation rate" remains near a 30-year low. This alone means there is no recovery. Then there are the taxes.

In 1900, government at all three levels took about 10 percent of our income. Today, government takes nearly 50 percent, or twice as much as people say government should. Yet when pollsters ask Americans how much money should government, at all three levels (state, local and federal) take from them, their answer has been consistent for decades: 25 percent. You may ask, "What do attorneys have to do with this?" Well, they are the politicians that have helped facilitate all this.

The problem in Washington and every state capitol is that the Framers of the Constitution never intended to have offices filled with professional politicians, especially attorneys. They designed the Constitution so that farmers, business men and women, would go and serve for a time, usually at great sacrifice, then return home after another election to take up where they had left their business or farm. That means and meant fewer attorneys. If Americans would enforce the Framer's wishes, politicians in Washington, D.C., would cower under their desks, as angry constituents pound on their doors.

Always in the abstract, people talk about freedom and liberty. But government has for the past century been run by professionals (mostly attorneys) who have led us down a road of dependency upon them. That has become so widespread that we accept the benefits, unaware that the costs are much higher than we think.

Nearly half of the federal budget goes to the three major entitlement programs: Social Security, Medicare and Medicaid. All of these programs address problems that the Constitution never intended the government to address. However, judges and courts have grown the federal government by their decisions in courts at every level. Earlier presidents, citing constitutional reasons, rejected congressional attempts at growing the government. However, over the past several years all this has come about through the attorneys in the courts. With the legal system as is built in this country, if you want to slow the giveaways in government, you would be advised to make it more profitable for attorneys to limit the giveaways rather than extend them.

There are obviously two different and distinct world views operating within the parties of our national "leadership." One of them, the conservatives (not necessarily Republicans) tries to follow the trail plowed and established by the Founding

Fathers. The other is a cunning emotionally based and serial-killer type doctrine that attempts to stomp on and destroy freedom, individualism and religious liberty. This is all being directed from the upper floors of the political left, the mahogany lined walls of media elites, the extremist liberal-end of the Democrat Party. Many of those live in the posh areas of the country, the various vacation spots of the White House. And so with these two world views in mind, we must return to the one that was cemented into place by our Framers. To show the problem with court decisions and to see behind the curtain look with me back in history at some of the worst decisions made in our Supreme Court:

One of the worst decisions, and some think the worst because of the slavery issue, the Supreme Court ever made was *Dred Scott v Sanford* **in 1857. Their decision upheld the repugnant Fugitive Slave Act.**, in this most scandalous case. Dred Scott, who was born a slave but brought to live in several states where slavery was illegal, was not only returned to slavery by the Court, but held to have no rights as he and all Americans of African descent were not citizens, contrary to the laws of several states and the federal Missouri Compromise. I think the Court's ineptitude and political bias, which it shows on many different occasions, speaks for itself in this case.

Chief Justice Roger B. Taney's opinion would have been atrocious coming from anyone, let alone a member of the Supreme Court. It was beyond racism, totally devoid of humanity. Blacks were "an inferior order and altogether unfit to associate with the white race," Taney wrote. "They had no rights that the white man was bound to respect." Moreover: "The Negro might justly and lawfully be reduced to slavery for his own benefit." They were not citizens and could not claim the "rights and privileges" of citizenship even if their masters took them to free states.

Absolutely the worst action taken by United State Supreme Court was in upholding most of the provisions of the Patient Protection and Affordable Care Act, commonly known as ObamaCare. The decision as the Act as it was presented in court was a narrow 4-1-4 decision. Chief Justice John Roberts held that "the individual mandate to purchase health insurance was not justified under Congress's power to regulation interstate commerce, or by the Necessary and Proper Clause." His four conservative colleagues joined him in this decision. But Roberts, for whatever reason, was not finished. Some believe he was bombarded by administration pressure or even threats. Whatever the reason, Roberts went to great lengths in finding authority for the mandate. He said he finally did under Congress's power to tax and spend. That was music to the ears of his four liberal judges. In doing this, Roberts carved out a weird, strange and even questionable legal island on which not one of his fellow judges or any of the parties in the lawsuit reside. Through his eleventh hour alteration of the very plain meaning of the statute, Roberts created a needle, threaded it with his action, and the result was a newly created tax delivered on a silver platter to Obama. Attorneys in robes did this, I remind you.

Another very egregious decision in my opinion was *Grutter v Bolinger* in 2003. It upheld racial preferences and basically affirmative action in the area of law school students being accepted at Michigan Law School. Writing for the Court, Sandra Day O'Connor found that the University of Michigan Law School had a compelling interest to promote class diversity that justified a series of racial preferences. While not expressly overturning the Court's rejection of racial quotas in the landmark 1978 case, *Regents of the University of California v. Bakke*, *Grutter* did give affirmative action supporters a pretty clear road map to evade *Bakke* and continue to discriminate among prospective students based on the color of their skin.[11]

Among the most egregious court decisions that has impacted this entire nation; setting it on fire with revolutions and killings was the famous *Roe v Wade* decision in 1973 by the Supreme Court. The liberal attorneys and judges managed this case along the path of women's rights. That gave the rights for legal abortion much greater chances for approval, because who in their right mind wants to say women cannot have rights about what they do? Most people do not realize that Roe v. Wade was made possible because of an earlier case, *Griswold v Connecticut* in 1965. In rejecting a Connecticut law prohibiting the use of contraceptives, the Court created a Right to Privacy previously unnoticed in the Bill of Rights. This novel interpretation of the Constitution stemmed from the Court's apparent desire to strike down the laws passed by the Connecticut Legislature without limiting government authority. So instead of basing its decision on principles limiting government power, it instead created a vague new right that would supersede state authority, at least when the Court decided it did. The privacy right led directly to the far more controversial ruling. Waiting in the wings was the critical *Roe v Wade* decision. The *Griswold* ruling's big fault is not that it struck down a rather onerous and unenforceable law, but that it did so by inventing a new right out of a whole new bolt of cloth, one of that would be impossible to define and subject to endless future litigation.

In the last ten years, one of the worst decisions by the Supremes (I refer to the court, not the singers) was made in the *Kelo v New London* case of 2005. Kelo saw the Court extend government's ability to seize private property under eminent domain, even when the only purpose was to provide more tax revenue and enrich the Treasury. The Fifth Amendment contains a "Takings Clause" which prohibits the seizure of private property for public use without "just compensation." In spite of the law, the City of New London argued that by condemning a number of privately owned lots, transferring ownership to New London Development Corp., the city would receive more revenue through property taxes.

Public outcry on this decision was great. The radio talk show hosts spent days doing little but fielding calls from people expressing outrage; some wanting revolution. And they were right. To think that in America that the high court could expand the eminent domain for whatever company or group that would come along promising more tax revenue for the state. The case remains a high water

Chapter Four — Destruction by Bad Barristers and Bad Court Verdicts

mark for the Court's support for unlimited government power, finding that "public use" need only serve a "public purpose" and that "public purpose" could mean anything the government wanted. I recall one developer calling a national talk show to state that if the law was going to be used to hurt little people like this, he was prepared to make a proposal to the Feds for taking the Kennedy Compound in Hyannis Port, Massachusetts under eminent domain to build a hotel and shopping center and produce more tax revenue for the state and the federal government. Because the Kennedy Compound is totally established in a special trust, the tax liability is minimal. While the caller indicated he had the necessary revenue to make the project happen, it seems probable the same government which would approve taking others' property would take large strides to protect the Kennedy's for the same law. Interesting how the Liberal causes are only appropriate with just certain people's rights; others do not count as much with them. The case remains a high water mark for the Court's support for unlimited government power, finding that "public use" need only serve a "public purpose" and that "public purpose" could mean anything the government wanted.

While attorneys have become a part of everyday life in modern America, there are a host of decisions made which have severely injured the freedoms of citizens of our nation over time. Another of the problems and reasons for asking, "Where did my country go?"

*"You and I have a rendezvous with destiny.
We will preserve for our children this,
the last best hope of man on Earth,
or we will sentence them to take the last step
into a thousand years of darkness."*

— Ronald Reagan

Excerpt - televised speech, Oct. 27, 1964

Chapter Five

The Trouble with the "Great Pretender"

IN *THE HITCHHIKER'S GUIDE TO THE Galaxy*, Arthur Dent learns that the plans for a new galactic highway, calling for the demolition of his own house, have been "on display" for quite a long time in the basement of a government building at the bottom of a locked filing cabinet which has been moved into an abandoned restroom with a sign on the door that reads "Beware of the Leopard."

The humor of this scene suddenly fades into dour gloom when realizing it is a fairly apt description of what Obama meant when he said his administration would be the most open and transparent in the history of man. During his campaign of 2008 when he touted the pre-advertised openness of his upcoming administration, he bragged that all proposed legislation would be up and posted in print for public review on C-Span days before actions were taken in Congress. This he promised would be his personal trademark of "the most transparent administration in the history of the nation." Gives a whole new meaning to the phrase, "the most open and transparent," let alone ethical. Who does he think he was kidding?! More accurately, just the "Beware of the Leopard" sign with no other trappings would be the best description of his austere destructive work and deceptive administration with regard to the Constitution.

And when that "Beware of the Leopard" sign is indeed envisioned, laughter must ensue since we have nothing like a leopard, or a tiger, or a puma, a bobcat, or even a neutered housecat. No, we have a weakling kitten who shudders when the doorbell rings. Refer to any of the red lines which Mr. Obama has drawn now in several countries. His so-called policies and everything else he has touched has melted away or turned to garbage. Above all, his foreign policy is kaput; one of inaction, unless the Muslim Brotherhood is in question. Then he jumps into gear. The Obama administration's lack of understanding of true foreign affairs is most disconcerting. It seems clear that foreign policy to Obama means rhetoric; rhetoric about anything that can be substituted for action. This was made clear from his press conference on October 21, 2011. At that time, he gave his "The tide of war is receding" speech, stating that the U.S. was moving forward from a position of strength. It is not clear what the forward motion meant in his reference, nor, in comparison, what made up his "so-called" strength. Any strength he claims to exert is a glaring weakness, in response to the power of foreign leaders, especially that of Putin in Russia.

Exploring that comparison further, the weakness of Obama and the power of Putin are clearly evident. Putin has been in office now for thirteen years. He is powerful externally as well as internally, in Russia. Putin has a background that is clearly visible, unlike Obama. Prior to being elected leader of Russia, Putin was a 16-year member of the KGB, including five years, 1985-1990, as a lieutenant colonel in East Germany. During that time, Putin became accustomed to the use of power. Obama to his credit had two years' prior experience hanging curtains in South Chicago apartments.

Within Russia, Putin has controlled public opinion and political life. With the law in September 2011 having changed the presidential term from 4 to 6 years, Putin, elected in 2012, can be expected to be in power another decade. After being president and then prime minister since 2000, he is expected to serve two six-year terms and be in office until 2024. Putin has built a strong group of advisers around him, many were subordinates employed at the KGB, who reported to him directly. On the world stage, Putin has emerged from "junior partner status" he had with the U.S. in 2000, to one now of near equality, in spite of the differences in economic resources, military strength, and population of the two countries. His presence and strength on that world stage is visible. Speaking fluent German and almost fluent English, Putin hosted the talks devoted to the Syrian Crisis at the G-20 summit at St. Petersburg in September 2013. In the US, Obama has exercised control over the executive golf course.

Putin also displayed arrogance while keeping western leaders waiting. He did this with John Kerry, keeping him waiting for three hours in the Kremlin, and when he took his Labrador dog to his first meeting with Chancellor Angela Merkel, who was bitten by a dog when she was a child. His policies, divergent from those of Obama, have been displayed in a variety of issues: Libya, Syria, Iran, Georgia, Abkhazia and South Ossetia, Afghanistan, and Central Asia, and on anti-missile defense. Obama, to his credit, showed his leadership by saying he was "out of the loop" on Benghazi. However, he was there to provide help to Morsi and the Muslim Brotherhood in taking over Egypt. Morsi and the Muslims lasted one year, before they were thrown out by Egyptian citizens who saw through their rule of terror. An interesting note is that the Egyptian people are stronger now exhibiting more willingness to revolt over criminal leadership within their country.

To carry this comparison a step further, Putin has made no secret that his objective, while not being clear about restoring the old Soviet Union, is to create a kind of Euro-Asian Union that can counter both the EU and NATO. The problem now is whether he can act unilaterally in areas such as the Crimea, which he, or

Chapter Five — The Trouble with the "Great Pretender"

some of his supporters, consider Russian. In view of Obama's inaction, it is likely that Putin now believes that NATO is a paper tiger, and that Obama is not to be taken seriously. "One of the alarming features of the crisis on Ukraine's Crimean peninsula is the staggering confidence with which Vladimir Putin is pursuing his agenda there and in eastern Ukraine," read the opening paragraph of the Observer's editorial on one Sunday.[1] [2] Of course, Obama showed how serious he viewed the situation by offering up a "reset" button to Russia.

Nothing is shocking anymore about the contrast between these two, unless you are straining and staggering from the weight of the six years of baggage from supporting Barack Obama. Putin branded Obama for the toady he was from the first day. The Russian leader will only provide us with more of the same activities, the same we have seen over Syria, Iran and a multitude of other countries. The exception: the Ukraine that looks like it can be taken like an over-ripened fruit setting against the fence of Putin's yard, with only another red line drawn by Obama.

Guardians of Obama, with their unabridged inanity, point to his command of drone strikes as confirmation that he's tough as he sounds in speaking before an NAACP Convention. But the use of drones in place of a genuine foreign and defense policy is like a reconstituted pinball machine. Even Obama can act all tough and macho when he is maneuvering the flippers to hit the bumpers on his game, when the worst thing that can happen to him is a demonstration in Peshawar after he's accidentally taken out a wedding party. Drop the virtual reality and he's like a person wandering across the lanes of freeway traffic.[3]

In reality, our difficulties with Russia and Putin were restarted the day Obama was elected. Putin is clever enough to see through the thin veneer of Obama that he is one of the weakest presidents the U.S. has ever had. This is something many Americans could not see since they were too busy in adoration of Obama calling him such names as "Savior" and "The Black Jesus."

The "innocent" days of Bill Clinton in comparison to the days now seem so far away. Those were the days as some described when our worst worries were the various definitions of what the word "is" is and which bimbo was about to erupt. Actually Clinton's foreign policy was just as bad. Most liberals have that in common. He bombed an aspirin factory while Obama nailed a wedding party. But with President Obama's second term inaugural address, our new worries have advanced to bigger words and their new definitions: like the word "liberty." His evil plans to demolish our homeland, to build a Marxist and Muslim Collectivist highway through it are becoming clearer every day. However the plans are not in a filing cabinet in a disused lavatory in the White House basement; they have been on his desk in his office. Someone needs to erect a sign over the office door that reads "Beware of the weakling kitten."

That this former "constitutional lawyer" would argue America has outgrown its need for our founding documents because we no longer define liberty in exactly the same way seems unfathomable. But actions are usually louder than words. Obama's actions speak how he has nested with political dissidents, radicals, and other Marxists, encircling himself with their advice. In doing so the Constitution is a primary target for destruction. With Obama it is laws be damned. Executive orders are the order of the day, printing more money becomes the refrain for each new morning, and he refuels the steam shovel for dumping more dollars into welfare and reparation. As a nation, we are still headed down a one-way street the wrong way: lots of spending; lots of debt piling up; lots of attacks on the Constitution; lots more welfare and lots of divide and conquer exhibited by Chicago style politics.

Today, the Leftists' work continues with a rapid mix and plethora of bad political decisions; legislation and executive orders to push Marxist, anti-Christian, pro-Muslim, and radically liberal ideologies down our throats. This comes from tribal tactics whose leaders emulate African dictators. In fact, what is happening in America would make African tribal leaders proud; it resembles how they control the lives of their people through the art of distraction. In Africa and in many other parts of the world, the tribal chief or dictator controls the administration of the tribe, and when challenges threaten his control, he has many distractions at his disposal. For instance, militants can set fires to crops outside the village. As that threatens the food supply, attention is immediately drawn by villagers to put out the fire. He can starve one portion of the population into submission and feed others who bend to his rule; as happens in North Korea. In America, the leader can "create" a plethora of problems; border crises, foreign floods of illegal children, catastrophes for Israel, American citizens murdered by Muslims, spy scandals on private citizens, attacks on conservatives by tax authorities. These have a two-fold purpose; like the African chieftain, he believes events will divert negative attention away from him, and at the same time each will further weaken the nation. Whether here or there, the leaders share a common trait; they despise America.

We have witnessed an unprecedented number of attacks upon American life and distractions to keep the activity going by the current administration. It may have started with the Fast and Furious scheme to run guns on the border, but has been followed by a plethora of other scandals, for which there has been continual stonewalling. The stonewalling has worked at least temporarily with what seems like weekly scandals now. Here are just a few which must receive legal attention at a minimum and probably are worthy of impeachment;

- NSA and Prizm scandal: Using social networking, email, phone and other communications to spy on Americans under the Patriot Act;
- IRS: the targeting those on Obama's "enemy list." The IRS targeted conservative and pro-Israel groups prior to the 2012 election. There should be more than just questions raised about why this occurred. There should be subpoenas to recover "lost" emails, discovery of "who" in the White House ordered these attacks;

CHAPTER FIVE — THE TROUBLE WITH THE "GREAT PRETENDER"

- Benghazi: There are several events to investigate including the failure of the administration to attempt to protect the Benghazi mission. The changes made to the talking points to falsely suggest the attack was motivated by an anti-Muslim video. The refusal and stonewalling of the White House to say what President Obama did the night of the attack. If the death of Michael Brown in Ferguson deserves an investigation and trial, Benghazi trumps it;

- Spying on the Media: The Justice Department performed a massive swipe of Associated Press reporters' phone records as part of a leak investigation. This also extended to MSNBC employees

- Rosengate and the first potential perjury of Eric Holder: The Justice Department claims the Fox News reporter James Rosen is a criminal for reporting about classified information via a Justice Department source. The DOJ subsequently monitored his phones and emails. Attorney General Eric Holder told Congress he had never been associated with "potential prosecution" of a journalist for perjury when in fact he signed the affidavit that termed Rosen a potential criminal.

- The ATF "Fast and Furious" scheme and the second potential perjury of Eric Holder: The Fast and Furious plan was to give weapons to known representatives of Mexican drug cartels and then follow them to their source in America. The source would be named as particular gun retailers, thus appearing the administration wanted to garner more support for gun control. It ended with the murder of a U.S. Border Patrol Agent and multiple scenes of massive violence in Mexico. The potential Holder perjury came in May 2011 when Holder told Congress that he had just recently heard about the Fast and Furious gun "walking" scheme when there is evidence he knew much earlier.

- Former HHS Secretary Kathleen Sebelius demanded and solicited donations from companies the HHS would later regulate. The money would be used to help her sign up uninsured Americans for Obamacare.

- Solyndra and other "Green Energy Rat Holes": Republicans charged the Obama administration funded and promoted its poster boy for green energy despite warning signs the company was headed for bankruptcy. The administration allegedly pressed Solyndra to delay layoff announcements until after the 2010 midterm elections when the company was imploding. Following its bankruptcy in 2012, the company's liquidation benefits went little beyond Argonaut Ventures, part of a foundation run by Obama fundraiser George Kaiser. Considering that suspicious connection, no wonder the White House defied an earlier deadline to provide 12 categories of Solyndra documents to the House Energy and Commerce Committee. Many other Solyndras have come to light, the latest being Sapphire Energy. Its pond-scum-based biofuel still costs over $26 a gallon, but that doesn't matter when your executives give almost solely to Democrats.

- Lisa Jackson: Former EPA Administrator used the name "Richard Windsor" when corresponding by email with other government officials drawing charges she was trying to evade scrutiny.

- The New Black Panthers: The Justice Department was accused of using a racial double standard in failing to pursue a voter intimidation case against Black Panthers who appeared to be menacing voters at a polling place in 2008 in Philadelphia.

- Waging war without Congress: Obama may have violated the Constitution and both the letter and the spirit of the War Powers Resolution by attacking Libya without Congressional approval.

- Biden bullies the press: Vice President Biden's office has repeatedly interfered with coverage, including forcing a reporter to wait in a closet, making a reporter delete photos, and editing pool reports.

- Sestak, we'll take care of you: Former White House Chief of Staff Rahm Emanuel used Bill Clinton as an intermediary to probe whether former Rep. Joe Sestak (D-Pa.) would accept a prominent, unpaid White House advisory position in exchange for dropping out of the 2010 primary against former Sen. Arlen Specter (D-Pa.).

- I'll pass my own laws: Obama has repeatedly been accused of making end runs around Congress by deciding which laws to enforce; including the decision not to deport illegal immigrants who might have been allowed to stay in the United States had Congress passed the "Dream Act."

- Open borders and immigration threats with children crossing the border. In addition to Nancy Pelosi making an appearance at the border to welcome illegal aliens into the U.S., there is the whiff or aroma of the administration's role in getting actively involved south of the border to get children bused to the U.S.

- The Veterans Administration (VA) patient scandal: Dozens of our service veterans have died waiting for medical treatment due to administrative incompetence, willful neglect, or deliberate acts within the halls of government.

Benghazi, the IRS targeting scandal, the NSA spy scandal, the VA patient scandal, Global climate change scandal used to launch Cap and Trade, illegal immigration scandal, open borders and influence-peddling supporting the illegal immigrant children flooding the southern border and others. All of these and more are

CHAPTER FIVE — THE TROUBLE WITH THE "GREAT PRETENDER"

followed by one scandal after the other. All seem to be for that dual purpose; to weaken the nation further, and pull attention away from Obama. Each new scandal pulls resources into attempting to fix each crisis and further away from investigating the "Who" behind each scandal. Just think, creating each new scandal could help hide the sinister and treasonous work which is ongoing behind the scenes in Washington.

Obama Provides New Definitions

Contrary to liberal speak, our Founders gave us words with appropriate definitions. One of their finest was a brilliant word, "Liberty." The ink they used dried eons ago on their definition: it is the right of individuals to pursue their own interests with minimal interference from a "limited" government. Now the suggestion has been offered by Obama, that after all these years of having him in the White House, this word has always meant something completely different. It is shocking for at least three reasons: First, he is one claiming the title "constitutional attorney." Second, he has a tremendous lack of understanding about America's founding principles. Third, he has total disdain for the Constitution. Obama seems intent on taking the wild and crazy "Clintonesque" dictionary in providing new definitions for almost everything in sight. Herein lies the rub: the convolution and lack of understanding of a community organizer turned president. He is an ideologue whose language, life, and executive orders all contradict the Constitution he promised to uphold.

If the ultimate goal is to shake up, tear down, and fundamentally transform America into a genuine collectivist society, Obama's allegiance to Muslim doctrines and Sharia Law, will certainly be one of the main ingredients in what he cooks up for this country. It is clear there is no Constitutional authority for him to lead in this remaking of America. Remaking requires unmaking, but it matters not to him since his heart has never been that of an American, not even for a moment. "Obama speak" is always dripping with Muslim or Marxist faith principles, and he is driven by mentors to remove this country from its long standing position as the nation of choice for capitalists. As such he views the Constitution, our bulwark from the past, as a living document that must be challenged and then changed drastically, shoehorning it into "Socialistic speak."

Given Obama's focus and legislative actions trying to transform a great nation downward into a Marxist state, he is one of the driving forces behind the current treason from within. Obama's inaugural speech words echoed similar thoughts from his book, "The Audacity of Hope," signifying the Constitution "should not be static but rather a living document, and must be read in the context of the current ever-changing world." That doctrine calls for continual change to it. If that perspective is true, we should rewrite Marx's Communist Manifesto diluting it with components of capitalism. The only problem with that is the breathless worship Progressives give it today.

Conservatives tried to tell Americans about him several years ago, when many Americans were falling all over themselves in adoration as they called him "The One," giving him the rock star status the media claimed were his. Years ago, in the Illinois Senate, when he was being supported by radical socialist contributions, he was interviewed on a Chicago radio station. It was there at WBEZ-FM, Chicago; he made his case for wealth redistribution and social justice, stating he could make a case for it in what the Constitution did not say. At least he is consistent in that claim. Citing a previous court case, Obama said, "the Constitution is a charter of negative liberties" mandating "what the states can't do to you" and "what the federal government can't do to you, but it doesn't say what the federal government or the state government must do on your behalf." With the focus on radical change, he is certain to change the definitions of the words, liberty and freedom. Individuals such as Obama are a concern since they tend to be little more than a political Jim Jones, having some Kool-Aid close for us to drink. In this arena, Obama become more like a leopard than a kitten.

Listening to Obama requires the use of something akin to a secret spy "decoder ring" to interpret his words. The ring will require at least two different translations since in domestic policy speeches he seems only to know "Marxist speak." For foreign policy speeches he seems only to know "Muslim speak." For example, his first inaugural speech was chockfull with duplicitous and eerily conservative words like "equality." That hid his intended wealth redistribution. In a Newtown speech he used the word "safety" to mask his planned unilateral gun control. Students are trained through "Liberal speak" that any conservative thinking is extremely dangerous for their future. They are taught and therefore just cannot imagine a world where some Progressive and Liberal entity, like an Obama or others from the same Marxist mold, are right there to spoon feed and protect them.

Hearing a pluralistic, secular humanistic, and a demoralizing message from the Progressive media and Progressive Liberal leaders like Obama; the messages they leave has resulted in bureaucratic rubble. Any hidden and secret UFO information the government may be protecting from us, as some people focus upon, is not our real problem now. The real problem is that Liberals have hidden our liberty, our freedom, and our rights. Attempting to find those amidst the rubble of the bureaucracy is a challenge, except for those who grasp our genuine U.S. History. The Founders of our nation gave us wonderful definitions, especially for freedom; the ability of citizens to live without government interference. Making your own decisions is risky; but there is a joy in living your life the way you want to live it. Conversely, government today is frightening and intimidating people into thinking it can provide a perfect world without risks. No government has the ability to build such a world. Deluded Marxists striving for a totalitarian society alone make that claim. Liberty means simply that we are free in all kinds of weather, and during events that are good or bad. The beckoning to trade your liberty for a hot meal and a government security blanket is made only by a dictator and his government.

CHAPTER FIVE — THE TROUBLE WITH THE "GREAT PRETENDER"

Transformation — Remaking the Country - She Is a Comin'

The 2008 election returns come in that November evening for the Presidential election; many thoughts ran through my mind. It was an evening of reflections as I began to express genuine concern for America's future. The Republicans nominated John McCain, albeit from manipulation from the liberal media during the primary campaign. McCain is a war hero from Viet Nam POW days; tortured and beaten during war, leaving him with an obvious physical disability. Appreciating his conservative stands, the "I can reach across the aisle" demeanor which was the theme throughout his campaign was not what the country needed. I reminded myself why I had left the Republican Party in 1988. Sadly, the American political scenery has lately devolved into having to vote for poor presidential candidates, at times the lesser of two evils. This election had reached a crescendo of preposterous and outrageous proportions. By the way, predictably the media abandoned McCain during the election campaign.

The electoral results announced that evening, I was struck by a couple of scenes. The first was a Chicago couple on TV, cheek to cheek with a glimmer in their eyes which translated for those watching a "breathless anticipation that "The One who had finally arrived." The second scene was recalling Tom Brokaw's comments while watching this "unknown" new president elect which the media had collectively hailed as the most prominent leader to appear on earth in over 3,000 years. While he and the rest of the media had refused to vet any segment of his life during the campaign, here was Brokaw speaking brashly that night, "What do we know about Obama — his foreign policy? Nothing at all." On October 31st, Tom had appeared on the Charlie Rose Show on PBS, "We don't know a lot about Barack Obama and the universe of his thinking about foreign policy . . . what books he's read . . . [his world view] . . . there's a lot about him we don't know."[4]

Brokaw was not completely correct. They did know Obama was the most liberal politician ever to step on the national stage in America. But they loved him because he wore the important badge; a capital "D" for Democrat. That made everything in the world right for Brokaw and team. This of course was preceded by Obama looking stoically stern through his black eyes, staring at the crowd with a look that many identified as stating, "I'll show you peons now."

Despite Chris Matthews' comments when he mentions the name Obama, or when a picture of Obama was visible to him, while the lasting impression of Obama is favorable to him, it is not impressive to the majority of Americans. The missing vetting would have shown so many tragedies which could be avoided. To see what he supported in the Senate in Illinois and then in the U.S. Senate is appalling. From partial-birth and post-birth abortions, to his stands on welfare giveaways called reform, his anti-military stand, to pro-Muslim stands, it is enough to make a reasonably liberal person run in fear, but not the progressives. There we were on election night with the media screaming "Hallelujah" out of one side of their mouths, and out of the other telling us "We don't know anything about Obama, except that of course he claimed to be black."

Actually, they had that one wrong too, since Obama has very minimal African American blood in him, about 10%. For example, we know that his father while having lived in Kenya, his heritage is mostly of Arab descent. His mother was white. But the point should not be what color his skin is, it does not matter at all. What matters are the color of his heart and the color of his politics. And that color is not good for America. It is good for the Muslim Brotherhood with every move; it is good for the enemies of America, for Marxists nations, but not America. As mentioned, I would not have been impressed if McCain had been on that stage that night. It was never white vs. black. It was the poor, poor quality and yet poorer quality in the candidates. The last thought that ran through my mind that night was the thought that ran through my mind in July, "God help this nation now."

The Cast of a Media Which Hates America

At least a portion of the pretense of this one now known as "The One," being called that by Oprah Winfrey, is to be laid at the feet of the media, the Northeast academic elite, and the Hollywood Left; they 'encouraged' this dangerous delusion. Micah Tillman, a lecturer of philosophy at The Catholic University of America, said: "Barack Obama is the Platonic philosopher king we've been looking for, for the past 2,400 years." The *New York Times* called his election "a national catharsis." His hometown newspaper, the *Chicago Sun-Times*, wrote, "The first African-American president of the Harvard Law Review has a movie star smile and more than a little mystique. Also, we just like to say his name. We are considering taking it as a mantra."[5]

Several of Obama's disciples continued to come up with new and lightning-charged statements about his proposed deity, attempting to get more and more Americans to see this fraud as some sort of god-like creature.

> **Chris Matthews of MSNBC:** "I've been following politics since I was about five. I've never seen anything like this. This is bigger than Kennedy. [Obama] comes along and he seems to have the answers. This is New Testament."
>
> **Newsweek editor Evan Thomas:** "In a way, Obama is standing above the country, above the world. He's sort of God. He's going to bring all the different sides together."
>
> **Film director Spike Lee:** "You'll have to measure time by 'Before Obama' and 'After Obama' . . . . Everything's going to be affected by this seismic change in the universe."
>
> **Jonathan Alter in his book,** *The Promise: President Obama, Year One:* Rabbi David Saperstein, reading from Psalms in English and Hebrew, noticed

from the altar that the good men and women of the congregation that day, including the Bidens and other dignitaries, had not yet stood. Finally Bishop Vashti McKenzie of the African Methodist Church asked that everyone rise. At that moment Saperstein saw something from his angle of vision: "If I had seen it in a movie I would have groaned and said, 'Give me a break. That's so trite.'" A beam of morning light shown [sic] through the stained glass windows and illuminated the president-elect's face. Several of the clergy and choir on the altar who also saw it marveled afterward about the presence of the Divine.[6]

Not to be overly judgmental, but there is something Biblical here. If light was coming through stained glass windows and illuminating Obama's face, while choirs were singing in the background and one reporter said that "the scene was apocalyptic"; all that is a sign of something. The sign is that of either Leftists who cannot interpret signs correctly who are prophesying or the light is truly showing the face of one found in Scripture, one who parades falsely as an angel of light.

The absurd, and even blasphemous, comparison of Obama to the Almighty became so outrageous and embarrassing that several people around the White House would not comment. Except for Vice President Joe Biden who could not resist the opportunity to tease the president about his messiah complex; speaking at the 2009 white-tie Gridiron Club Dinner, Biden said, "[President Obama] can't be here tonight because he's busy getting ready for Easter. He thinks it's about him."[7]

Serious News Coverage Tells of Crimes of Treason Which Are Examples of Malfeasance in Office

In spite of the admiration tossed at Obama by his admirers and by himself early in his administration, he is guilty of unilateral crimes against the Constitution and the law, some of them which are impeachable. It may take some time for the public to catch up with the truth, but eventually they will if they look at the evidence.

Whatever his fans claim to artificially jack up the polls, Mr. Obama is flush with many unlawful acts and empty promises which have in effect left the American people standing at the altar. We can start with his broken campaign promises, primary of which was his repeated promise that families making less than $250,000 a year would see no form of tax increase. Another pledge he broke his first week in office was his promise to post upcoming legislation on C-SPAN for several days before any legislative action would be taken. He promised green jobs everywhere; yet the companies he push forward as if they were chips in a poker game, all went bankrupt. He claimed there were "shovel ready jobs" waiting if taxpayers would simply provide $1 Trillion in stimulus — it was nothing but a rouse. His claim that citizens would see a reduction in medical insurance premiums with "his" medical legislation would be laughable, except for the pain and disaster he has brought to many individuals and families with his fraud. He promised to uphold and protect the Constitution, but from the start he has led a continual attack on most every amendment. He promised to uphold America in the world; within a week of taking office he was off on a Muslim country tour, apologizing for American excellence. He claims to be a leader: but a true leader does not blame others and/or make excuses saying they are out of the loop. They do not bemoan misfortune. They find ways to overcome it. A true leader does not have to tell you he is "the man" or "the buck stops here" with him; only to dodge questions at press conferences and not provide answers when asked the tough questions. He made a commitment to work hard, but it appears obvious now that he is on an eight year vacation, all at taxpayer expense.

While promising hope and change, the administration has brought about an amazing amount of destructive change, all with no hope. He not only failed to deliver on his promise to cut the deficit in half during his first term, he doubled down four times and built more debt than all other presidents combined. He has not put more people back to work as committed; that has been nothing more than a shell game to hide the pea that tells the true unemployment rate. He did not keep companies or cities from bankruptcies, especially Detroit which he said he would he not allow to go insolvent. He did not fix Middle East problems as promised. He only fixed a firm foundation from which the Muslim Brotherhood could operate in each country. They are the only ones benefiting from his foreign policy. He has not created a better heaven and earth as was predicted by his adoring media. His claims, they out strip his production. However, like a bull in a china shop, if not stopped our country will lie in shambles, broken on the ground if he is not stopped. Evidence says Obama is an epic pretender.

When Obama does keep a commitment, it is the Muslim Brotherhood that stands in the front of the recipient line well ahead of the American people. Therefore, there are many more problems we face today because of the lack of attention to the real problems before us, such as employment.

As of 2014, the current forecast of the deficit by the CBO, with the added burden of Obamacare, will rise from $1.65 Trillion (under Bush), to over $17.55 Trillion in 6 years. Though George Bush spent money like it was water, he was a rank neophyte compared to Obama. Either way, budget estimates in the future will require a Richter scale to measure the shaking to collect new taxes, and a depth meter to measure the depth of the crash resulting from the giveaways, Presidential vacations, and bonuses for agency staffs.

Under Obama's leadership, race relations and racism in America have hit the bottom and are growing worse as the weeks go by. The reason? He is not a leader who has the resolve to bring a solution to the table. Despite what the administration and the media dictate, racism is not just a problem which white people possess, it is a two-way street; blacks and other ethnic groups are infected too. Daily headlines post the reality of race relation issues. The temperature of this problem has never been more feverish in my lifetime. If divide and conquer is Obama's objective, then he is being extremely successful.

Unemployment and work force participation rates hit 60-year highs under the guidance of our current leader. Some people call him the "Lord of the Flies." That could be an appropriate title since the true numbers are massaged to reach a fabricated number that is artificially low. Whatever a person wants to believe is subjective. What we need is objectivity in reporting. Nearly 100 million Americans are out of the workforce over the past several years. <u>Remember the formula that has been used by the President: Fewer people looking for work + Fewer jobs available = Lower Unemployment.</u>

The many cities in America which have declared bankruptcy over the last six years is staggering, including the city which was promised protection by Obama, Detroit. My, what is happening to these mission targets as promised by Obama? The only response by the Democratic leadership to Detroit's financial petition was to blame the Republican leadership running Detroit. That has to be counted as a ridiculous statement by any liberal anywhere. Only scratching the surface in Detroit politics reveals that Republicans or any conservatives do not register on any scale of leadership in the city and frankly have not for over 40 years. It seems convenient to blame anyone and everyone when you blow your budget. And the ever-friendly media will make certain no Democrat is ever injured in the press from this debacle.

Increased Welfare and extended Unemployment would be a draconian medal to have on the chest of any presidency. While I am always in favor of helping, assisting anyone to get back on their feet so they feel self-pride and can produce and participate in the American dream, we have made a serious mistake in treating welfare so that it can become a way of life. We have 3rd and 4th generation welfare families now living in America. They have been robbed of their initiative by a "big daddy" form of government which is a death sentence in itself. To rob someone of their humanity and sentence them to years of servitude in a "take it — it's free from the government" program, is certainly as destructive as dropping bombs. All ambition and industry stirred into days, months and years of time, is eventually sucked out of life, as you are in effect told "you don't need to work; just await the check from the government." Much of our society over the years has grown to fit into an ancient and sacred writer's thoughts. The book is The Message, "Some people dig a fork into the pie, but are too lazy to raise it to their mouth." (Prov. 19:24)

"To criticize Obama or his results is to be a racist," that at least according to Al Sharpton, Jesse Jackson, Eric Holder, or any liberal.

Nevertheless, here is where I refer to Jessie Mumford's statement from 48 years ago: "Words mean things!" Saying one thing and doing the opposite, as this leader has done, puts you on a dung pile too: this one is hypocrite pile, also known as "imposter" or "liar." Here is also where I refer to my words again about Mr. Obama

6 years ago, "You can't fool me, Mr. Obama, with your campaign rhetoric. Looking at your record in the U.S. Senate speaks of your values. Looking at your life-long friendships with radical communists and Muslims, which you have continued to cultivate while you deny you do so, also speaks of your values. From those alone, I know that you are a Marxist and a Socialist, and probably a Muslim as well. Your actions betray your words, in spite of what your apostles say!"

Sadly in retrospect, Obama clearly meant some of his words. The words uttered to Muslim leaders and African leaders in apology for America were heart-felt. Obama has made at least two apology tours to tell the world in effect, "I am sorry for what America did." On July 25, 2008 during his campaign, Obama stopped by Germany to say this, "People of Berlin, people of the world, this is our moment. This is our time. I know my country has not perfected itself. At times we struggle to keep the promise of liberty and equality for all of our people, we've made our share of mistakes, and there are times when our actions around the world have not lived up to our best intentions."

Seems strange that America should apologize to Germany, but Obama was apologizing for the U.S. attempting to bring peace and democracy to other nations long under Old World style dictators. Possibly Mr. Obama has forgotten about two World Wars, in which Germany was responsible for the deaths of tens and more likely hundreds of millions of people. No, America owes no apologies to Germany or Europe. It is Europe who should thank God every day for an America who has always stood by them, twice against German militarism, more recently against communist barbarism, and most recently against Islamic Terrorism asking nothing in return except friendship.

Nevertheless, to Obama, the U.S. must be made to pay for some sins of creating wealth and using it. Some other nations have not been so fortunate. The lifestyle in America must result in an apology from him on behalf of us. He believes that having a nice home, a newer car, air conditioning, etc. is a sin against the world.

Most have noticed that the words he has spoken to Muslim kings were words of apology, not for him, but for us. And that was for burning more fuel and using other resources than some other nations. While saying those things, he has been a champion of champions spending and using resources faster and more often than any one who can come to mind. What a carbon footprint! So what if it is an $180,000,000 vacation! This combined with his work in raising taxes and shooting the economy in the foot shows the many predictions back before he took office seems on target. That prognostication said he has meant all along to bring harm (aka, no good) to the freedom and direction of this country.

His word "transformation" is becoming clearer as the Federal government takes more personal property, as it takes over the health care industry, and as it increases federal taxes, or in Obama's word about all of this, "Transformation" we have learned means government control, government takeovers. Obama has been giving citizens a government "facial," of all things government in your face. Karl Marx would have been proud of his protégé. "Well done my son! You are on track and doing a great job! By the way I am not a Marxist either."

In examination of his record, the correct title for, Barack Hussein Obama is, "the Great Pretender." To hear his speeches read from teleprompters from either side of the stage serves as a lobotomy to the logic portion of the brain. However, to listen to his speeches and see his actions and the direction he is steering this country is what can be called "treason from within."

Reasons for Impeachment

I am just not falling for Obama's banana in the tailpipe routine. Therefore, I submit the following as evidence for what I call the treason within; the high crimes and misdemeanors and a few other offenses which he has committed against the U.S. Constitution, the citizens, and the limits of his office. From "fusion centers" to data mining to drones to alarming Department of Homeland Security power grabs, it is obvious U.S. citizens are fast arriving at the train terminal called "the virtual surveillance stop." Add rank corruption, cronyism and fake green jobs funding, all these add up to horrible misuse of public funds. That Obama has done serious and sustained damage to American society by abusing the powers of his presidency is a titanic understatement. Obama has also made America weaker both domestically and abroad by supporting the Muslim Brotherhood at the drop of a hat, emboldening our enemies, spurning our allies, and bringing a deeper threat than ever to Israel.

Last of all, whatever your bent, conservative, liberal, Democrat, Republican, Independent or Libertarian, you should have a serious concern about the president's limitless seizure of power, all the lies and cover-ups, and the abuses of authority. Here is an abridged version of the list.

Impeachment Reason #1 – Collusion with a Foreign Interest over Oil

Yes, I said oil in connection with Obama. Through the Department of the Interior (DOI), he placed a moratorium on offshore oil drilling or exploration off both the Atlantic and Pacific coasts of the United States and in parts of the Gulf of Mexico. He has also prohibited new drilling exploration on federal land in any states in the United States. These actions by the DOI have continued in direct defiance of several court orders issued by Federal Judge Martin Feldman in New Orleans, Louisiana declaring that the department had no authority to issue such a moratorium on drilling in the Gulf. The administration has claimed to be complying, but has tied up the drilling permits in so much red tape that the effect is the same. Now this is old news, at least 4 years old, but some have forgotten and need to be reminded.

Strange coincidence, instead of allowing American companies to drill domestically, Obama betrayed all of us by authorizing loans of billions to countries like Brazil and Mexico so they can drill for oil where we were drilling. The plan is they will sell the oil to the U. S. But the story takes a more suspicious turn, since Obama's mentor, George Soros, has invested heavily in BraxBrazil, a huge Brazilian oil company which is doing the drilling. And then even stranger, they are given a contract to drill in the gulf.

Obama fights the approval of the keystone pipeline from Canada to the United States that would not only lessen our dependence on oil from countries like Venezuela and Saudi Arabia, but create thousands of new jobs in the United States. He first emphatically said, "NO!" The decision on the pipeline is one that belongs in the hands of the members of Congress, not the President. Bad business — yes! The smell of collusion — yes! Impeachment? — yes!

Impeachment Reason #2 – Promoting Illegal Immigration

Obama sidestepped Congress and already granted largely unreported de facto amnesty to millions of illegal aliens using illicit interagency directives and executive orders. He has abdicated his responsibility to enforce the laws of the United States in protecting our borders against illegal immigration. He has ordered the border patrol not to arrest most illegal immigrants entering the U.S. He also stopped deportation proceedings against thousands of individuals who are here illegally. He has single-handedly in effect instituted the so-called "dream act" bypassing the United States Congress which by law has sole authority over immigration matters.

Then as a slap in the face of each American citizen, Obama and his Attorney General have clearly violated their oaths of office by joining with foreign countries of Mexico, Bolivia, and Columbia in lawsuits against the sovereign states of Arizona, Georgia, and Alabama to stop them from enforcing the federal immigration laws. To call this treasonous is a waste of words.

Under Obama, being an American citizen is not a positive thing any longer; it carries a negative connotation. Also, citizens believe they have fewer rights as a citizen than you do if you are an illegal. In New York for example, research shows one can get on all the available welfare programs and possibly get an income of over $50,000 per year. And that is without any production or work. So tell me where is the incentive in this scenario to work or to produce?

Impeachment Reason #3 – Fast and Furious Gun Running

Obama has used illicit edicts on gun control actions in addition to the deadly "Fast and Furious" gun-running operation intended to collect fraudulent data on gun activity and therefore change popular opinion against guns. Compounding his problems, he improperly used executive privilege to block a congressional investigation of Eric Holder's participation in the illegal Fast and Furious gun-running scandal.

Independent and reliable sources have widely reported that acting through the Bureau of Alcohol, Tobacco, and Firearms, the Obama White House was for months doing "straw purchases" of guns from legitimate gun store owners along the southern U.S. border to supply weapons to the drug cartels in Mexico. The reason? They wanted to have a sting operation against the cartels producing this fraudulent data showing that large numbers of weapons were "illegally" going from the United States to Mexican drug dealers. The data was going to be used then, and is being used today, in an attempt to justify more 'new' gun control regulations. The administration has refused to cooperate with committees in the House of Representatives that are investigating the scandal. Obama has blocked any access to documentation verifying this program, thus defying Congressional subpoenas to investigate emails, memorandums, and other papers from the White House dealing with this "fast and furious," their name for the operation. Defiance took the form of "executive privilege" by Obama.

The U.S. House of Representatives voted to hold Attorney General Eric Holder in contempt of Congress, for his stonewalling to questions. Holder not only stonewalled, he lied. U.S. Attorney Ronald Machen chose to ignore the criminal resolution and not bring charges against Holder.

Impeachment Reason #4 – Benghazi Scandal and Cover-up

The king of all the scandals for Mr. Obama is the tragedy of U.S. Ambassador Christopher Stevens being brutally murdered on his watch. While the president's activities while this happened have not been accounted for, there have been multiple stories spun as an explanation. There were lies told and it now appears there is a cover-up for some other activities. Besides being unforgiveable, this is the worst of the Obama scandals.

"When a president lies to the American people and is part of a cover-up, he cannot continue to govern," said Rush Limbaugh. At least that was the case with Richard Nixon. It seems that could be the case with Obama too. "And as the facts come out, I think we're going to see something startling . . . In fact this dwarfs Iran-Contra, about which the media spent three solid years trying to take out Ronald Reagan. The latest shoe to drop in the Benghazi disaster is the news that the State Department was e-mailing about the attack on the consulate and the terrorists who they thought were behind it within two hours, and the e-mails went to the Situation Room of the White House. Obama knew . . . And before it's over, I don't think this president will finish his term unless somehow they can delay it in Congress past the next three and a half years," says Rush Limbaugh. (Source: Rush Limbaugh radio program, May 7, 2013)

And Then the Media Cover Up

From the beginning, U.S. media reports on the events in Benghazi were misleading. The vast majority of media coverage worldwide referred to the U.S. facility that was attacked as a "consulate," even though the government itself has been careful to call it a "mission."

A consulate typically refers to the building that houses a consul, who is the official representative of the government of one state in the territory of another. The U.S. consul in Libya, Jenny Cordell, works out of the embassy in Tripoli. Consulates at times function as junior embassies, providing services related to visas, passports and citizen information. On Aug. 26, about two weeks before his was killed, Ambassador Stevens attended a ceremony marking the opening of consular services at the Tripoli embassy. The main role of a consulate is to foster trade with the host and care for its own citizens who are traveling or living in the host nation.

Diplomatic missions, on the other hand, maintain a more generalized role. A diplomatic mission is simply a group of people from one state or an international inter-governmental organization present in another state to represent matters of the sending state or organization in the receiving state. However, according to the State Department investigation, the building was a "U.S. Special Mission" set up without the knowledge of the Libyan government.

Withholding, Misleading

Two days before the November presidential election, CBS posted additional portions of a Sept. 12 "60 Minutes" interview in which Obama made statements that contradicted his earlier claims about the attack. Remember what I said; the media is our enemy. In the released portions of the interview, Obama would not say whether he thought the attack was terrorism. Yet he would later emphasize at a presidential debate that in the Rose Garden on the day of the attack, he had declared it an act of terror. Reuters was also implicated by WND for possibly false reporting.

The Benghazi Timeline

As time went on following the Benghazi attack on September 11, 2012, within a couple of months a timeline of the events leading up to the massacre became clear. From this timeline, we can now dig for the tough answers, find responsible parties, and hold them accountable for the deaths of four Americans. Here is the timeline,

> June 6, 2012 – A bomb was planted at the U.S. compound in Benghazi, ripping a huge hole in the outer wall.
>
> June 11 – The British ambassador's motorcade was hit by a rocket-propelled grenade, wounding two people.
>
> June 12 – The British Ambassador left the country and the British Embassy was closed.
>
> June 12 – The Red Cross had a second attack; they shut down and fled the city. This left the U.S. as the only foreign flag flying in Benghazi.
>
> August 15 – An emergency meeting was convened at the U.S. compound in Benghazi. The agenda was discussion of 10 Islamist militia groups that were in training camps in the immediate area.

CHAPTER FIVE — THE TROUBLE WITH THE "GREAT PRETENDER"

August 16 – Ambassador Christopher Stevens signed and sent a cable to Hillary Clinton in the State Dept. telling of the imminent danger to the embassy. He stated they were unable to defend themselves and would help in case of attack.

September 11 – A cable was sent again to the State Department that the embassy was under attack. Ambassador Stevens died that day by the hands of members and elements of Ansar al-Sharia and al-Qaida.

September 12 – President Obama spoke to the nation from the Rose Garden saying in part, "The United States condemns in the strongest terms this outrageous and shocking attack. We're working with the government of Libya to secure our diplomats. I've also directed my administration to increase our security at diplomatic posts around the world. And make no mistake, we will work with the Libyan government to bring to justice the killers who attacked our people. Since our founding, the United States has been a nation that respects all faiths. We reject all efforts to denigrate the religious beliefs of others. But there is absolutely no justification to this type of senseless violence. None. The world must stand together to unequivocally reject these brutal acts."

Later Catherine Herridge of Fox News uncovered the Aug. 16 cable, calling it the "smoking gun" of the Benghazi attack.

September 16 – U.N. Ambassador Susan Rice announced, "Our current best assessment, based on the information that we have at present, is that, in fact, what this began as, it was a spontaneous — not a premeditated — response to what had transpired in Cairo," that the Benghazi attack was not premeditated but was due to Muslims watching an anti-Muslim video.

September 25 – Obama spoke to the U.N. and spoke about the attack in part saying, "... conflicts arise along the fault lines of race or tribe. And often they arise from the difficulties of reconciling tradition and faith with the diversity and interdependence of the modern world. In every country, there are those who find different religious beliefs threatening; in every culture, those who love freedom for themselves must ask themselves how much they're willing to tolerate freedom for others.... That is what we saw play out in the last two weeks, as a crude and disgusting video sparked outrage throughout the Muslim world..."

October 11 – During the vice presidential debate, Joe Biden asserted, "We weren't told they wanted more security there."

After the President and his staff blamed a video for the Benghazi attack, we have learned other facts since then. For example, in real time the State Department was following the Benghazi attack. Three separate email messages came from the compound that night; the first described the attack, the second came as firing stopped, and the third reported that Ansar al-Sharia was claiming credit.

We also learned from an October 26 Fox News report by Jennifer Griffin there were two drones over Benghazi the night of the September 11 attack capable of sending pictures to U.S. commanders in the immediate area, to the CIA, the Pentagon, and the White House. We also learned that ex-SEAL Ty Woods in the CIA safe house just a mile away, was denied permission to go to the rescue of those in the compound. He disobeyed orders anyway, went and brought back the body of diplomat Sean Smith, one of those killed in the attack.

On November 2, 2012 we also learned further details as the truth has started coming out slowly, some of which was reported by Pat Buchanan. His analysis appeared in an article on TownHall.com. He stated in part,

> After the attack on the compound, the battle shifted to the safe house, for four more hours. Another ex-SEAL, Glen Doherty, made it to Benghazi from Tripoli. Seven hours after the initial assault that killed Ambassador Stevens and Smith, Doherty and Woods were still returning fire, when, having been abandoned on the orders of someone higher up, they were killed by a direct mortar hit. Due to stonewalling and the complicity of the Big Media in ignoring or downplaying the Benghazi story during the last weeks of the campaign, the Obamaites may get past the post on Nov. 6 without being called to account.
>
> Hillary Clinton said she takes full responsibility for any security failure by her department at the Benghazi compound. But what does that mean? Did she see the Aug. 16 secret cable sent to her by Stevens describing his perilous situation? Was she oblivious to the battle in her department over security in Benghazi? This failure that occurred in her shop and on her watch that Stevens warned about in his Aug. 16 cable, resulted in his death and the most successful terrorist attack on this country since 9/11. Why didn't Hillary explain her inaction and why she lied? She did step down but only it appears to prepare her campaign for 2016.
>
> The CIA has issued a terse statement saying it gave no order to anyone not to try to rescue the ambassador or not to move forces to aid Doherty and Woods, who died because no help came. Who, then, did refuse to send help? Who did give the orders to "stand down"?
>
> The president says he is keeping Americans informed as we learn the truth. But is that still credible? When did Obama learn that State was following the Benghazi attack in real time, that camera-carrying drones were over the city that night, that a seven-hour battle was fought, that desperate cries for help were being turned down. The CIA had to know all this. Did Tom Donilon of the NSC not know it? Did he not tell the president?

CHAPTER FIVE — THE TROUBLE WITH THE "GREAT PRETENDER"

Cause of Attack — A Film She Said

In the immediate aftermath of the attack, Reuters quoted a purported civilian protester by his first name who described a supposedly popular demonstration against an anti-Muhammad film outside the U.S. building. Immediately following the attack, President Obama and other White House officials claimed anti-American sentiment was fueled by the obscure anti-Muhammad video on YouTube and sparked civilian protests outside the U.S. mission that devolved into a jihadist onslaught. However, vivid accounts provided by the State Department and intelligence officials later made clear no such popular demonstration took place. Instead, video footage from Benghazi reportedly shows an organized group of armed men attacking the compound, officials said.

For weeks after the Sept. 11 attack in Benghazi, Obama and his surrogates proffered that the violence was merely an impromptu response to an anti-Muslim video. But reports which followed from several agencies including Reuters and CBS News reveal the administration knew precisely what was going on almost immediately, courtesy of emails.

Sharyl Attkisson at CBS says: "At 4:05 p.m. Eastern time, on September 11, an alert from the State Department Operations Center was issued to a number government and intelligence agencies. Included were the White House Situation Room, the office of the Director of National Intelligence, and the FBI.

"US Diplomatic Mission in Benghazi Under Attack" — "approximately 20 armed people fired shots; explosions have been heard as well. Ambassador Stevens, who is currently in Benghazi, and four COM (Chief of Mission/embassy) personnel are in the compound safe haven.'" (Source: Sharyl Attkisson of CBS Evening News, October 24, 2012)

Reuters reported that there were emails which specifically mention the Libyan group called Ansar al-Sharia had asserted responsibility for the attacks. In the meantime, there were members of the Obama Administration who were saying the attack was all based on reaction to a video about Islam. It was not only misleading, it was much worse than that. Rush Limbaugh in fact, "They lied, folks. I don't know how else to say it . . . They knew exactly what happened and who was responsible for it and they knew what was happening. They knew it was not a video, they knew it was not a protest that had gotten out of hand . . . It was a preplanned terror attack. There was real-time video of it." (Source: The Rush Limbaugh Show, October 24, 2012)

The controllable part of this disaster certainly appears that in the seven-hour attack on the embassy, there was no action taken, no troops sent in to rescue the ambassador and his people. History now shows there were enough military members and equipment in the region that boots could have been on the ground in a short time to assist the ambassador and his staff. But the government did not make one move to protect the Americans in the area, though they knew what was happening because they were watching in real time via monitors at the site. Still there was no to response to this attack by the president and the hundreds of his staff who sat and watched.

Limbaugh says most of the national media is now ignoring the revelations from the emails. "What we're watching here today is the equivalent of Woodward and Bernstein helping Nixon cover up Watergate," he said. "The mainstream media is Woodward and Bernstein. Watergate is Benghazi. Except this time, Woodward and Bernstein are helping Nixon cover it up." "It's just maddening," he continued, "and to have the story basically ignored and covered up today is evidence to me of just how devastating it is. I think the regime is barely holding its campaign together. I think this campaign is leaking. Imagine a dike with all the holes in it, and the holes are the states, and the regime has got people plugging the holes with fingers and doing everything they can to stop the flow. I think they're very close here to being swept away by a tidal wave. I think everybody involved knows it."

He suggested several theories as to why the events have transpired as they have, including "gross, unbelievable, incalculable incompetence;" "bald-faced lying;" and a political calculation since Obama has been claiming al-Qaida terrorists have been decimated under his watch. "There's another possibility here," added Limbaugh. "It could be very simple. Obama simply wasn't engaged when this was going on. He wasn't around. He didn't want to be engaged. He didn't want to be told. He didn't want to have to do anything. And therefore, they were paralyzed. Nobody knew what to do because he didn't care." (Source: The Rush Limbaugh Show, October 24, 2012)

Reconfirmed

World Net Daily has reconfirmed with multiple knowledgeable Middle Eastern security sources that the U.S. special mission in Benghazi was used to coordinate Arab arms shipments and other aid to the so-called rebels fighting in Libya and later in Syria. And now, knowledgeable security sources have reconfirmed *World Net Daily's* original reporting on the use of the Benghazi mission in aiding the rebels who are known to be saturated by al-Qaida and other Islamic terrorist groups.

In late September 2012, World Net Daily carried a story linking the slain ambassador in Libya for coordinating jihadist fighters. Aaron Kline writes, "Christopher Stevens, the U.S. ambassador murdered in Libya, played a central role in recruiting jihadists to fight Bashar al-Assad's regime in Syria, according to Egyptian security officials speaking to WND. Stevens served as a key contact with the Saudis to coordinate the recruitment by Saudi Arabia of Islamic fighters from North Africa and Libya. The jihadists were sent to Syria via Turkey to attack Assad's forces, said the security officials. The officials said Stevens also worked with the Saudis to send names of potential jihadi recruits to U.S. security organizations for review. Names found to be directly involved in previous attacks against the U.S., including in Iraq and Afghanistan, were ultimately not recruited by the Saudis to fight in Syria, said the officials."

Klein also reported, "One witness to the mob scene in Libya said some of the gunmen attacking the U.S. installation had identified themselves as members of Ansar al-Shariah, which represents al-Qaida in Yemen and Libya."[8]

While the White House has been largely mum on the alleged use of the Benghazi mission to aid the rebels, Obama administration officials did claim the White House rejected a plan to supply arms to the Syrian rebels.

If, indeed, President Obama rejected the arms plan, as reported by the *New York Times*, it would mean the White House went against the recommendations of outgoing Defense Secretary Leon Panetta; Gen. Martin Dempsey, chairman of the Joint Chiefs of Staff; Secretary of State Hillary Clinton; and then-CIA Director David Petraeus. The plan was said to have been generated by Petraeus and Clinton.

In Senate hearings on Benghazi, Sen. John McCain, R-Ariz., asked Panetta and Dempsey whether they had supported a plan "that we provide weapons to the resistance in Syria." "We do," Panetta replied. "You did support that?" McCain asked again. "We did," added Dempsey, who was sitting next to Panetta. Neither Dempsey nor Panetta elaborated on their positions.

The *New York Times* reported the White House rebuffed the Clinton-Petraeus plan developed last summer to arm and train Syrian rebels. The *Times*, citing unnamed Obama administration officials, reported the White House rejected the Clinton-Petraeus proposal over concerns it could draw the U.S. into the Syrian conflict and the arms could fall into the wrong hands. The plan reportedly called for vetting rebels and arming a group of fighters with the assistance of Arab countries.

World Net Daily reported Stevens himself was leading the vetting efforts, working with the Saudis to send names of potential jihadi recruits to U.S. security organizations for review. Names found to be directly involved in previous attacks against the U.S., including in Iraq and Afghanistan, were ultimately not recruited by the Saudis to fight in Syria. The scheme appears to mirror the Petraeus-Clinton plan as described by the *New York Times*.

Secret Activities

During the Libyan revolution against Moammar Gadhafi's regime, the U.S. admitted to directly arming the rebel groups. Stevens himself first arrived in Libya on a cargo ship to serve as the official U.S. liaison to Libyan opposition, reportedly working directly with Abdelhakim Belhadj of the al-Qaida-tied Libyan Islamic Fighting Group. At the time of the U.S. aid to the Libyan fighters, rebel leader Abdel-Hakim al-Hasidi acknowledged in an interview that a significant number of the Libyan rebels were al-Qaida fighters, many of whom had fought U.S. troops in Iraq and Afghanistan. He insisted his fighters "are patriots and good Muslims, not terrorists," but he added that the "members of al-Qaida are also good Muslims and are fighting against the invader."

House Republicans released portions of an interview with State Department whistle-blower Gregory Hicks, who took over as the top U.S. diplomat in Libya after Stevens was killed. Hicks told investigators that U.S. forces were prepared to fly in to provide support to the besieged embassy, but were told to stand down. The claim contradicts previous testimony from Obama administration officials who said all available resources in the region were utilized during the attack. "We've got a lot of Americans at risk and an administration that has pursued for four years now, a very weak policy. And even in the face of the murder of four Americans has not materially changed that policy." That's the conclusion of former U.S. Ambassador to the United Nations John Bolton, who is stunned that Obama didn't have a much stronger reaction to the murders of four Americans. Bolton said the governments of Egypt and Libya "failed miserably in their obligation" to protect U.S. diplomatic personnel and that Obama needed to make it clear American deaths are "unacceptable."

"We're not going to apologize for the American system. We're not going to tolerate these attacks on our interests. And we're not going to operate under the delusion that the rising wave of Islamic fundamentalism is anything like a democratic movement or an Arab Spring."

Bolton says the apologies of the administration for an Internet film critical of Muhammad that may not even exist sends exactly the wrong message.

"This is a reflection of the hatred they have for America and the desire of Islamic radicals to do us harm." Bolton is also incredulous that the U.S. media is far more interested in the mundane details of Mitt Romney's reaction to this crisis than in the crisis itself.

Impeachment Reason #5 – Criminal Prisoner Releases and Non-Pursuits

Obama's decision on releasing prisoners has within it a "three strikes and you are out" plan. The effects of his actions seem similar to accepting from a doctor a prescription for arsenic tablets. **Strike One:** Obama and his administration have recklessly endangered the American public by releasing criminal illegal aliens from federal prisons. **Strike Two** is this: the releases have been so many times more numerous than first reported. Like all Obama numbers, there are phases by which they are reported. The first numbers are reported to calm the public in the areas of unemployment, crime, GDP, etc., and make things appear better than they are. The second set of numbers always follow some time later, usually on a weekend so as not to attract attention, and tell something closer to the truth which is always worse than that which was first reported.

In their book, *Impeachable Offenses: The Case to Remove Barack Obama from Office*, Aaron Klein and Brenda J. Elliott cite ICE documents which state that more than

CHAPTER FIVE — THE TROUBLE WITH THE "GREAT PRETENDER"

8,000 criminal illegal aliens were released from prisons between fiscal years 2009 and May 2011 alone. The statistics cited indicate the agency released 3,847 convicted criminal aliens in 2009, 3,882 in 2010, and 1,012 through May, 2011. An audit by the DHS Inspector General found 809 recidivist Level 1 illegal immigrant criminals eligible for deportation were actually released from California and Texas jails in 2009. It's a note of interest that ICE defines these Level 1 criminals as the "most egregious criminal aliens, who pose a significant public safety risk."[9]

Offenses among these graduates (aka, criminals) include homicide, kidnapping, sexual assault, robbery, aggravated assault, extortion, sex offenses, cruelty toward family, resisting an officer, illegal weapons possession, hit and run, and various drug offenses accompanied by sentences of more than a year.

Why were the criminal illegal aliens released? The audit blamed the actions on "agent 'staffing challenges,'" which were vacancies and "increasing workload levels."

Strike Three: Obama is sworn to uphold the Constitution and protect the American public. He is not doing it. Obama has used this release it appears to rub the budget crisis into the collective faces of the public, i.e., he did not get his way so all will have to suffer the consequences. This is totally unacceptable, beyond what most of the public knows, and certainly a criminal act.

Added to this "Strike Three" portion Eric Holder who at Obama's behest has changed policy in pursuing and arresting drug offenders. The stated reason is that the offenses are not dangerous criminal activity. However, behind the action is the discussion the week before by the same players that too many minorities (Blacks, in this case) are being imprisoned for drug convictions. I mean if the bad guys are your "brothers" just change the rules so they do not get arrested any longer and they will not be counted as bad guys anymore! History shows that any past administration officials, including the president, would have been questioned ad infinitum ad nauseum before a special Senate Sub Committee in order to find the answers to such a catastrophe. Watergate comes to mind. Within the context of other ongoing scandals at this White House, every rock should be overturned to discover the whole truth.

Impeachment Reason #6 – NSA Spy Intrusion Scandal

According to the *Washington Post*, "The National Security Agency has broken privacy rules or overstepped its legal authority thousands of times each year since Congress granted the agency broad new powers in 2008, according to an internal audit and other top secret documents."

On August 22, 2013, even the pro-Obama, leftist, progressive, communist-loving *New York Times* was lobbied to report the confirmation that the president's National Security Agency, or NSA, has violated the U.S. Constitution. And the Democrats say, "So What?!" In its front page story headlined, "Top Secret Court Castigated N.S.A.

on Surveillance — Email from Americans — Judge Found Violations of the Constitution in a 2011 Ruling," reporters Charlie Savage and Scott Shane acknowledged:

> "The Justice Department told Judge Bates that N.S.A. officials had discovered that the program had also been gathering domestic messages for three years. Judge Bates found that the agency had violated the Constitution and declared the problems part of a pattern of misrepresentation by agency officials in submissions to the secret court."

It is rather obvious to a thinking person that the government establishment or official Washington (aka, the balance of senators and representatives in both parties) are all just sitting on this knowledge that the NSA has been spying on Americans without any reason, and they are basically covering it up to suit their own means. As bad as it sounds, we Americans are ready to start some hearings, to uncover how private information of citizens has been misused for coercive government purposes. It is time to channel Senator Sam Ervin from the past with all of his now famous Watergate vernacular. I can almost hear him now saying, "What did the government know about ordinary citizens and when did they know it?" And obviously the essential question, "In what manner or manners did you use this information?"

If Obama and his administration and the NSA are not going to be held legally accountable and soon, then every legal matter the U.S. Government is into should be summarily dismissed or overturned. In other words, if this is not a crime, this neither is about anything else. Throughout history, our society has always struggled to keep an appropriate balance between liberty and security. The internment camps of World War II speak to this. But one thing is for sure, there is a large percentage of "we Americans" who will fight to preserve, and in this case, restore our freedom. As Benjamin Franklin famously declared, "they who can give up essential liberty to obtain a little temporary safety deserve neither liberty nor safety."

Impeachment Reason #7 – NSA Actions: Illegal And Unconstitutional

It is somewhat encouraging to see the New York Times op-ed editors get in on some of this action. On June 27, 2013, in their article "The Criminal N.S.A.", contributors Jennifer Stisa Granick and Christopher Jon Sprigman made the case that the NSA actions are both illegal and unconstitutional.

"The twin revelations that telecom carriers have been secretly giving the National Security Agency information about Americans' phone calls, and that the N.S.A. has been capturing e-mail and other private communications from Internet companies as part of a secret program called Prism, have not enraged most Americans. Lulled, perhaps, by the Obama administration's claims that these "modest encroachments on privacy" were approved by Congress and by federal judges, public opinion quickly migrated from shock to "moi."

Chapter Five — The Trouble with the "Great Pretender"

Edward J. Snowden, the former N.S.A. contract employee and whistle-blower, has provided evidence that the government has phone record metadata on all Verizon customers, and probably on every American, going back seven years. This metadata is extremely revealing; investigators mining it might be able to infer whether we have an illness or an addiction, what our religious affiliations and political activities are, and so on. While all the "Inside-The-Beltway-Mob" of so-called representatives call Snowden a criminal, I don't think so. It appears to me that he should be elevated to the level of hero for informing the sheep of this country on what their government is really up to. We have nothing less than a King George III activity going on here.

The law under which the government collected this data, Section 215 of the Patriot Act, allows the F.B.I. to obtain court orders demanding that a person or company produce "tangible things," upon showing reasonable grounds that the things sought are "relevant" to an authorized foreign intelligence investigation. The F.B.I. does not need to demonstrate probable cause that a crime has been committed, or any connection to terrorism. Even in the fearful time when the Patriot Act was enacted, in October 2001, lawmakers never contemplated that Section 215 would be used for phone metadata, or for mass surveillance of any sort. What is almost humorous is that foreign leaders are voicing their anger over what Obama is doing in this secret surveillance program that has reached even into European government offices. Anyone want to bet that Mr. "O" does not have the Muslim Brotherhood offices bugged?

Let's turn to Prism: the streamlined, electronic seizure of communications from Internet companies. The government justifies Prism under the FISA Amendments Act of 2008. Section 1881a of the act gave the president broad authority to conduct warrantless electronic surveillance. If the attorney general and the director of national intelligence certify that the purpose of the monitoring is to collect foreign intelligence information about any non-American individual or entity not known to be in the United States, the Foreign Intelligence Surveillance Court can require companies to provide access to Americans' international communications. The court does not approve the target or the facilities to be monitored, nor does it assess whether the government is doing enough to minimize the intrusion, correct for collection mistakes and protect privacy. Once the court issues a surveillance order, the government can issue top-secret directives to Internet companies like Google and Facebook to turn over calls, e-mails, video and voice chats, photos, voice over IP calls (like Skype) and social networking information.

Lay aside the Patriot Act and FISA Amendments Act for a moment, and turn to the Constitution.

The Fourth Amendment obliges the government to demonstrate probable cause before conducting invasive surveillance. There is simply no precedent under the Constitution for the government's seizing such vast amounts of revealing data on innocent Americans' communications.

One of the most conservative justices on the Court, Samuel A. Alito Jr., wrote that where even public information about individuals is monitored over the long term, at some point, government crosses a line and must comply with the protections of the Fourth Amendment. That principle is, if anything, even truer for Americans' sensitive nonpublic information like phone metadata and social networking activity.

We may never know all the details of the mass surveillance programs, but we know this: the administration has justified them through abuse of language, intentional evasion of statutory protections, secret, unreviewable investigative procedures and constitutional arguments that make a mockery of the government's professed concern with protecting Americans' privacy. It is time to call the N.S.A.'s mass surveillance programs what they are: criminal. [10]

Being nothing less than an "electronic Watergate," the pencils writing for impeachment need to be sharpened.

Impeachment Reason #8 – IRS Attacks upon Conservative Citizens

If the Obama Administration were just running a radio station, we could simply say, "The hits-they just keep a comin'!" And what a hit this one is! Publicly released records show that embattled and former IRS Commissioner Douglas Shulman had visited the White House at least 157 times during the first three and one-half years of the Obama administration, more recorded visits than even the most trusted members of the president's Cabinet.

Contrast with this, Shulman's predecessor Mark Everson, who only visited the White House once (that's "1" time!) during four years of service in the George W. Bush administration, which is logistically comparing the IRS's remoteness from the president as Washington is to "Siberia." But the scope of Shulman's White House visits, which strongly suggests coordination by White House officials in the campaign against the president's political opponents, is even more striking in comparison to the publicly recorded access of cabinet members. What would really be interesting to see, is the number of times George Soros and/or members of The Muslim Brotherhood visited the White House during the same time period.

Analysis completed by the Daily Caller of the White House's public "visitor access records" shows that every current and former member of Obama's Cabinet would have had to rack up at least 60 public visits each to the president's home to catch up with Douglas Shulman! The visitor logs do not give a complete picture of White House access. Some high-level officials get cleared for access and do not have to sign in during visits. A *Washington Post* database of visitor log records cautions, "The log may include some scheduled visits that did not take place and exclude visits by members of Congress, top officials and others who are not required to sign in at security gates." Again I reference George Soros and the Brotherhood.

CHAPTER FIVE — THE TROUBLE WITH THE "GREAT PRETENDER"

Attorney General Eric Holder, President Obama's friend and loyal lieutenant, logged 62 publicly known White House visits, not even half as many as Shulman's 157 visits.

Former Treasury Secretary Tim Geithner, to whom Shulman reported, clocked in at just 48 publicly known visits. Former Secretary of State Hillary Clinton earned 43 public visits, and current Secretary of State John Kerry logged 49 known White House visits in the same timeframe, when he was still a U.S. senator.

Shulman has more recorded visits to the White House than former HHS Secretary Kathleen Sebelius (48), former DHS Secretary Janet Napolitano (34), Education Secretary Arne Duncan (31), former Energy Secretary Steven Chu (22) and former Defense Secretary Robert Gates (17) combined. What a statistic! It speaks of planning.

Impeachment Reason #9 – DHS Gate and Ammunition Grab

Shortages in ammunition within America started occurring in late 2012 which was immediately followed by the tragic shooting at Sandy Hook Elementary School, in Newtown, CT. Predictably Obama, Feinstein and the balance of the gun-grabbing choir immediately launched into a pre-prepared anti-gun refrain which had been reserved for just the opportune moment after Obama had been re-elected. Gun owners ensued in a panic by buying up available stocks of bullets so fast that shelves were bare. Rumors were flying. Then the news began to filter down to the public that the DHS was purchasing 7,000 AR fully automatic rifles (these are the 5.56 x 45mm NATO personal defense weapons [PDW], also known as "assault rifles" when owned by the general public) and specially ordered with those dreaded 30-round magazines (which the public is not supposed to even think about owning), coupled with purchases of somewhere between 1.6 and 3.2 billion rounds of ammo. (Source: Jason Howerton, The Blaze Network, June 26, 2013) Our economy is on life-support and is being presided over by a man whose only accomplishments seem to be in the realm of destroying whatever remains of American society under the title, "Change has come to America!," one is likely to ask "what the hell is this for?"

Then the other news began to filter down that 2,700 armored vehicles for use in the U.S., were being "ordered" by the DHS! The headlines were late in coming because the Department of Homeland Security (through the U.S. Army Forces Command) recently retrofitted 2,717 of these MRAP vehicles for service on the streets of the U.S. The vehicles were formerly used for counterinsurgency in Iraq and are specifically designed to resist mines and ambush attacks. They use bulletproof windows and are designed to withstand small-arms fire, including smaller-caliber rifles such as a .223 bullet. Does DHS expect a counterinsurgency here?

In 2013, a DHS officer, Robert Whitaker, stationed in El Paso, Texas, proudly described the agency's new armored toy as "Mine-resistant... we use to deliver our team to high-risk warrant services . . . (with) gun ports so we can actually shoot from within the vehicle; you may think it's pretty loud but actually it's not too bad . . . we have gun ports there in the back and two on the sides as well. They are designed for .50-caliber weapons." This is needed to serve warrants? Well, maybe along the Mexican border (or South Chicago), but what about serving warrants in Columbus, Ohio? Or Tulsa, Oklahoma? Or Aberdeen, Mississippi? Or Bend, Oregon? If so, then I want one when going to the grocery store in LA.

Some History on The Use of Tanks and Bullets

The question is what does the DHS need with 1.6 billion bullets, 7,000 Ar-15s and 2,700 armored vehicles? What are they, or more correctly what is Obama anticipating or planning for, and why are few in the media and Congress asking about it, particularly in the light of daily apocalyptic bleats from the administration about sequestration cuts? Read on and you will see the trend that I see.

It was Neville Chamberlain in 1939 who now famously said, "War wins nothing, cures nothing, ends nothing . . . [I]n war, there are no winners, but all are losers." [11] At approximately the same time, it was Adolph Hitler who stated, "My only fear is that some bastard will propose a peace conference." [12]

Impeachment Reason #10 – Civilian National Security Force (Army)

Now, we face a devastating loss of freedom at home in health care. It will be joined by controls on our lives to "protect us" from global warming, itself largely a fraud, if believed to be caused by man. Hillary Clinton signed on to a Small Firearms Treaty at the U.N. This is a back door gun control move. If this is approved by the Senate and a 2nd Amendment majority does not exist in the Senate now, it will supersede all U.S. Law and the 2nd Amendment. All citizen possession will be eliminated through confiscation. Just like Great Britain and Australia.

Mr. Obama knows Americans are getting wise and will stop him if he delays at all in taking away our freedoms. There is his urgency and our opportunity. Once freedom is lost, America is lost.

Mr. Obama said on November 11, 2008, "**We cannot continue to rely only on our military in order to achieve the national security objectives that we've set. We've got to have a civilian national security force that's just as powerful, just as strong, just as well-funded . . .** " There is a possible answer to what is going on, but not an acceptable answer. A bit of irony here, in proposing this national security force. This is exactly what Hitler did in Nazi Germany, exactly what the Soviet Union did, exactly what Augustus did in Rome.

At first the report was the rounds were being purchased for FEMA. Really? And at whom are they going to shoot? Then the word was passed down from on high that it was actually the DHS which were getting the rounds. Okay, and what do

CHAPTER FIVE — THE TROUBLE WITH THE "GREAT PRETENDER"

they need these shipments for now? I used to ask, "What in the world is going on here?" Now I know, and so will you if you keep reading.

Obama's speech of July 2008, look and see if you find a thread that runs through this and other stories which leaves you with a cold, chilling feeling from some evil in the past. Here is the content of the speech as given in Colorado during the presidential campaign:

> **Obama, July 2, Colorado Springs, CO:** *[As] president I will expand AmeriCorps to 250,000 slots [from 75,000] and make that increased service a vehicle to meet national goals, like providing health care and education, saving our planet and restoring our standing in the world, so that citizens see their effort connected to a common purpose.*
>
> *People of all ages, stations and skills will be asked to serve. Because when it comes to the challenges we face, the American people are not the problem — they are the answer. So we are going to send more college graduates to teach and mentor our young people. We'll call on Americans to join an energy corps, to conduct renewable energy and environmental clean-up projects in their neighborhoods all across the country.*
>
> *We will enlist our veterans to find jobs and support for other vets, and to be there for our military families. And we're going to grow our Foreign Service, open consulates that have been shuttered and double the size of the Peace Corps by 2011 to renew our diplomacy.* <u>We cannot continue to rely only on our military in order to achieve the national security objectives that we've set.</u>
>
> <u>We've got to have a civilian national security force that's just as powerful, just as strong, just as well-funded.</u> *We need to use technology to connect people to service. We'll expand USA Freedom Corps to create online networks where American can browse opportunities to volunteer. You'll be able to search by category, time commitment and skill sets. You'll be able to rate service opportunities, build service networks, and create your own service pages to track your hours and activities. This will empower more Americans to craft their own service agenda and make their own change from the bottom up."*[13]

One question here if you don't mind. Is this the kind of a force that could kick your door down after midnight and haul you off to a gulag or local prison for re-education? I guess, if nothing is done, we'll all have to wait and see.

A Little History To Show a Kindred Spirit

Given a comparison with world history alone, where this administration is going does not look good. Let's look at the history showing someone else who did this before that will possibly frame this picture. Bring back for a moment the ghastly shades of Germany following World War I. The war was over, Germany was in economic shambles. The German Revolution of 1918, known as the "Novem-

189

ber Revolution," was a civil war which came at the end of WWI, driven by politics and anger about the outcome of the war. It resulted in Germany's imperial government being replaced with a republic, the Weimar Republic in August 1919.

A movement called the "Freikorps" was formed into nationalistic groups made up from disenchanted and angry German combat veterans from WWI, who were opposed to the Weimar Republic. They were put in place by the government in January, 1919, following the start of the November Revolution to thwart any possible threat of the Communist revolution, since the perception was that Germany lacked the adequate troops to fight off the loyalists to the communists in Russia associated with the Bolshevik Revolution. From this birthright, the "SA," or "Sturmabteilung," arose. The SA was ready to be used by Hitler who promised economic recovery in his political platform that promised "hope and change." The SA or storm troopers were assault divisions which Hitler created out of the group. They were with him early in his rise to power from the 1920s and well into the 1930s.[14]

Hitler gave the SA several functions, most which the German public knew little to nothing about. Initially they served as his paramilitary force for the Nazi Party, much in the same way the Praetorian Guard served Augustus Caesar centuries earlier. The SA was also commissioned to provide guard service protection for all Nazi rallies, parties, banquets, assemblies and meetings.[15] Their job description had additional responsibilities including the work as "storm troopers" where they specialized in disrupting political meetings of any opposition parties. They would search and find the opposition meetings, when they went to work, breaking down doors, "shouting down" meetings, using brass knuckles on the opposition in the meetings to inflict black eyes or broken noses, especially on the leaders when possible; even shooting members of the opposition party with a trusty and concealed Schuler Reform Pistol or a Broom handle Mouser which was carried as a side arm. They would tear up and trash any assembly hall where these opponents to the Nazis might be meeting. (Sounds like liberal Democrat style politics now!) Hitler especially liked to use the group to frighten, intimidate, and beat up Jewish citizens, whom he ironically blamed for tearing up the joints his shadow troops had just trashed.

The SS and Hitler

These "assault groups," or "SA," were the first Nazi paramilitary group to use military rankings. Among the various SA groups Hitler used, was the renowned "Schutzstaffel," or "SS," an elite military guard that came from the ranks of the SA which he created in 1925. SA men were commonly called the now famous "Brown Shirts" because of their brown uniforms. The SA functioned as a private militia used by Hitler to intimidate any political rivals and disrupt any meetings of competing political parties, especially those of the Social Democrats and the Communists. The battles in the streets of Germany were so fierce it might appear at times to be scenes from the Old West movie such as the shootout at the OK Corral, only set in a more modern time. The violence became so bad between the parties;

CHAPTER FIVE — THE TROUBLE WITH THE "GREAT PRETENDER"

it helped to bring the destabilization of Germany's experiment with democracy to a quick end. In June, 1932, the violence got so bad there were more than 400 street battles and shootouts, resulting in dozens of deaths. The destabilization of the civil society was crucial in Hitler's rise to power, because as many Germans believed, once Hitler became chancellor, the violence would end.[16]

How did Germany descend so quickly into becoming a dictatorship you might ask? Well, when Hitler was appointed in January 1933, Germany was a democracy. Germany had fair elections; nobody had their rights to vote deterred; there were numerous political parties for which a person could choose to vote, etc. To pass a law, the Reichstag (Parliament) had to agree to it by a majority vote, after a bill went through the normal processes of discussion, arguments etc. Within the Reichstag of January 1933, over 50% of those who held seats were against the Nazi Party. It was fairly unlikely that Hitler would have gotten just about anything passed into law with kind of minority. Many saw Hitler as a fall-guy politician who would have to shoulder the blame if the economy got worse under his leadership.

Hitler had promised a general election for March 1933. In his mind, this was the perfect chance for him to show all opposition politicians where the true loyalties lay in the German people. In fact, 1932 had shown Hitler that there was a possibility that support for the Nazis had peaked as their showing in the November 1932 election had shown. Anything other than a huge endorsement of Hitler and the Nazi Party would have been a disaster and a gamble which it seems Hitler did not want to take.

One week before the election was to be held, the Reichstag building burned to the ground. Hitler immediately declared that it was the signal for a communist takeover of the nation. Hitler knew that if he was to convince President Hindenburg to give him emergency powers, as stated in the Weimar Constitution, he had to play on the old president's fear of communism. What better than to convince him that the communists were about to take over the nation by force?

To aid his plan, a known communist, Marinus van der Lubbe, was caught near the Reichstag building shortly after the fire had started. The Nazi officials who arrested him claimed that van der Lubbe confessed to them that the fire was really a signal fire to other communists to start a revolution to overthrow democracy in the country. The confession came after a beating with brass knuckles of course. Matches were allegedly found on van der Lubbe and those who arrested him claimed that he smelt of petrol.[17] With this "evidence," Hitler asked Hindenburg to grant him emergency powers in view of what he called the 'communist takeover." Using the constitution, Hindenburg agreed to pass the Law for the Protection of the People and the State.[18]

This law gave Hitler what he wanted a ban on the Communists and Socialists taking part in an election campaign. The leaders from both parties were arrested and their newspapers were shut down. To 'keep the peace' and maintain law and order, the SA (the Brown Shirts) roamed the streets beating up those who openly opposed Hitler.

The election took place in March. Hitler was planning for it to be the last election Germany would have. But he did not get the number of votes he wanted; 30% went to banned parties which spoke of defiance, but he did get enough to get over a 50% majority within the Reichstag. After the burning down of the Reichstag Hall, politicians had nowhere to meet. The Kroll Opera House in Berlin was selected to be a temporary place for the Reichstag to meet. The opera house was a relatively small round building, perfect for meetings. On March 23rd, elected officials were due to meet to discuss and vote on Hitler's Enabling Law.[19]

On March 23rd, when all elected politicians gathered to vote on the Enabling Act, the SS and SA jack-booted thugs made sure only Nazi politicians got in to vote. The vote was taken, and with a stacked deck, Hitler obviously won. The Enabling Law, now the law of the land, stated that any bill only needed Hitler's signature in order to become law, and it became law in only 24 hours after he signed it. He became a dictator with no one standing in his way. "Change and transformation had come to Germany." Whatever Hitler wanted was just one day away from being the law of the land. So, with Hitler's signature, on April 7, 1933, Nazi officials were put in charge of local government in every province. On May 2, trade unions were abolished, all their funds taken; their leaders put in prison. On July 14, legislation was passed making it illegal to form a new political party. This made the Nazi Party the one legal party in Germany.

So Hitler was off to the races, as making new laws go. From the SA, Hitler created the famous "Gestapo," who were his investigators. They were usually in plain clothes. These characters were given ultimate authority to do anything at any time to anyone, for Hitler of course, and nobody dared mess with them. From the SA also arose another famous division, called "SD." They were the advanced planners for the Third Reich, who wickedly forced people to cooperate with them, to coordinate future Nazi plans. They also served as spies, to closely watch the activities of neighbors, much as some of the current czars in Obama's administration do. There was also a group referred to as the "Einsatzgruppen." They were the volunteers from the "SS" who were assigned geographical areas for invasion and to kill assigned segments of the population which Heinrich Himmler and Adolph Hitler had assigned for them. Many Jews never made it to the death furnaces because they were executed in their own neighborhoods, earlier being targeted as non-useful for the Reich. Built upon the Nazi racial ideology, the SS, under Heinrich Himmler's command, was said to be primarily responsible for many of the war crimes perpetrated by the Nazis during the holocaust of World War II.[20]

The SD was named and these Nazi loyalists became those who furnished the forced labor for the Third Reich's construction projects, such as the Peenemunde site where the B-2 missiles were built and completed for use in the Second World

Chapter Five — The Trouble with the "Great Pretender"

War. If you were tagged to work at Peenemunde you had two options; die quickly or die slowly. You either went to work to support the Third Reich or you were executed in your home or in a back alley. Of course if you worked as told, you were on a prolonged death sentence, eating mostly a ration of bread and water, never to return to your family or normal life after being drafted by these, the SD. Enough Third Reich history for now, but I want you to see the realm of the entire elongated process Hitler took to accomplish his goals and most of the important steps he took.

While in full power Hitler would enact a paper agreement for peace with leaders like Neville Chamberlain at Munich in 1938, while at the same time he was making plans for continuing to take his Third Reich tyranny into other nations and eventually the entire world. He did so by making agreements, then breaking them. He made promises he never intended to keep. Usually this is called a lie, but in politics, it is called diplomacy. Chamberlain thought he had won a peace, when he returned to London waving the signed paper with Hitler's signature which turned out to mean nothing. "But the bloom was off the rose. A poll in October revealed that 93% of the British did not believe that Hitler had made his last territorial demand in Europe." [21]

Hitler had a ravenous appetite for more power even after he came into power in 1933. Most people saw this, except for the politicians in America and England. Horace Rumbold, the British Ambassador in Berlin wrote: *"Hitler believes it is the duty of government to implant in the people feelings of manly courage and passionate hatred.... The new Reich must gather within its fold all the scattered German elements in Europe.... What Germany needs is an increase in territory."* [22]

Being an ideologue, Hitler was ever pointed toward carving out new empire, 'transforming' old Germany into a perfect race of people cleansed of its impurities. As Pat Buchanan explains, *"Finally, Hitler intended to cleanse Germany of Jews, smash Bolshevism, and make himself a man of history like Frederick the Great and Bismarck. The anti-Semitism in which 'Mein Kampf' is steeped is his most consistent conviction."* [23]

Why do I tell you all this about Hitler? Because Obama has proved to be on a similar, steady push, assuming more and more dictatorial powers over apathetic American "sheeple." Obama has made promise after promise to the American people, from promising to be the most ethical administration in the history of America, to we'll post all legislation on C-Span so you can see it ahead of time, to "I'll create more jobs than have been created by past administrations," to "you can keep your own healthcare plan if you want, to you can keep your doctor if you want, to you can keep your guns — I won't take them, I promise."

The picture of Hitler and Chamberlain come to mind, as I contend he, Obama, has made most if not all of his promises never intending to keep any of them. Through all of this, the people's voice in their governance has all but been silenced. He has by-passed the U.S. Congress again, and again, and again ruling by executive orders, just as other two-bit dictators have done in the past. Opposition and even members of his own political party have been largely "afraid" of him, and I find the apparent reason really funny and sad at the same time; it appears they are afraid because he is black and because of his connection to the Muslim Brotherhood.

Now it could be they are afraid of the media too, since they have become more or less electronic storm troopers for the dictator. (By the way, when will the mainstream media start carrying guns?) It seems that even the U.S. Supreme Court has lost their collective backbone to stand up to the pressure of this African American dictator, Obama. If you weren't trained better, you would think that America is being replaced, or maybe "transformed" is the word; our republic swapped out for a total Marxist regime. And if he gets his way, he'll sit like a political sour cherry on top.

Now with the signing the U.N. Treaty, banning private ownership of weapons in America, what possible options does all the militarization of the DHS point toward, except for some calculated conflict with citizens down the road. If the government is armed and the citizens are not, what type of representation does that give us in this modern day parliament where our voices are not heard now? How many red flags do we need before we see the trend line and start to realize we have a very serious problem developing in front of us? Why else would he want citizens to be unarmed? Is it so that UN vehicles can roll down the streets, collecting whomever they want to go into a re-education camp, with practically no resistance? And all the while, the most that the citizens could do is throw rocks and sticks at them, just as they do in Haiti to voice their discontent over the lack of public service. Now do you understand why we discussed Hitler?

Don't think me silly for drawing some parallels with Obama now. Just tell me for what purpose would such a "brown shirt DHS" force be used for in America today? Just tell me what purpose all the armored vehicles have within the DHS? It is not a good omen for things to come in this country if unchecked. There is a pattern which is emerging with Obama trying to regulate private gun ownership within the US, having guns himself in a national militia, plus the nationalizing leading industries and even stricter regulation of key financial sectors of the U.S. economy. See a pattern?

When reading Obama's speech again from 2008, especially the section about the use of a national militia being fully armed and helping returning veterans to find jobs, one has to chuckle. If veterans are such an important part of the "future economy," why has he labeled them as "terrorists" who cannot be trusted with a gun?

Dictators have had a well-kept secret among themselves throughout history; that a private army is necessary to control the great unconverted masses over which they force their rule. "The things done in every Marxist insurgency are being done in America today." Those are the words of Lt. General (Ret.) William G. Boykin on a video he released in 2012. Boykin is a decorated former Delta Force Commander, U.S. Deputy Under Secretary of Defense, and a recipient of the Purple Heart. The

Chapter Five — The Trouble with the "Great Pretender"

General, or Jerry as he likes to be called, goes on to say in the video, "The reality is, I'm a special forces officer; I'm a Green Beret; I've studied Marxist insurgencies, it was a part of my training. The first thing that's been done is like when Castro took over in Cuba, when they have moved their nation towards Marxism, the first thing they did was nationalize major sectors of the economy."[24]

General Boykin said he is troubled by Obama's promise of a "Civilian National Security Force." Boykin indicates the formation of such a force is included in the thousands of pages of the Obamacare Law, also known as, "The Patient Protection and Affordable Care Act." Boykin says such a police force would be at Obama's beckoned call and disposal, and is very similar to national police forces socialist tyrants, like Hitler used to complete their revolutions. The list of those in denial that Obama would hide legislation for the Civilian National Security Force is a big one. No way, they say. Nothing like that could ever happen. This is America. There is no way that Congress would ever fund such a thing as that anyway, so there is no reason to worry about this.

If you believe this, then you might want to review the following: According to Section 5210 of HR 3590, titled "Establishing a Ready Reserve Corps," the force must be ready for "involuntary calls to active duty during national emergencies and public health crises."

The health-care legislation adds millions of dollars for recruitment and amends Section 203 of the Public Health Service Act (42 U.S.C. 204), passed July 1, 1944, during Franklin D. Roosevelt's presidency. The U.S. Public Health Service Commissioned Corps is one of the seven uniformed services in the U.S. However, Obama's changes more than double the wording of the Section 203 and dub individuals who are currently classified as officers in the Reserve Corps commissioned officers of the Regular Corps.[25]

The following is the previous wording of the act as of 2004, before Democrats passed the health-care legislation:[26]

SEC 203	PUBLIC HEALTH SERVICE ACT	10

Commissioned Corps

SEC 203 [204] There shall be in the Service a commissioned Regular Corps and, for the purpose of securing a reserve for duty in the Service in time of national emergency, a Reserve Corps. All commissioned officers shall be citizens and shall be appointed without regard to the civil-service laws and compensated without regard to the Classification Act of 1923,[1] as amended. Commissioned officers of the Reserve Corps shall be appointed by the President and commissioned officers of the Regular Corps shall be appointed by him by and with the advice and consent of the Senate. Commissioned officers of the Reserve Corps shall at all times be subject to call to active duty by the Surgeon General, including active duty for the purpose of training and active duty for the purpose of determining their fitness for appointment in the Regular Corps. Warrant officers may be appointed to the Service for the purpose of providing support to the health and delivery systems maintained by the Service and any warrant officer appointed to the Service shall be considered for purposes of this Act and title 37, United States Code, to be a commissioned officer within the commissioned corps of the Service.

This demonstrates, as it appears, that the passing of the Affordable Care Act provides Obama with the law to have the civilian force he wants. Section 5210 of the Patient's Protection and Affordable Care Act (aka Obamacare) may be the beginning of Obama's civilian security force. This section amends Section 203 of the U.S. Public Health Service Act. Why it was included in the massive health-care bill is a question in search of significant answers. Some deny that this language could ever apply to the National Civilian Police Force which Obama mentioned in his campaign rhetoric in 2008. Given his pension to deceive, to lie, and to build an ever larger and more complex national government, I'm not ready to put any weight in anything he says. He has followed Hitler step by step in what he has done so far, why should he quit now?[27]

The U.S. Public Health Service website describes its commissioned corps as "an elite team of more than 6,000 full-time, well-trained, highly qualified public health professionals dedicated to delivering the nation's public health promotion and disease prevention programs and advancing public health science."

According to its mission page, officers of the commissioned corps may:

- Provide essential public health and health care services to underserved and disadvantaged populations;

- Prevent and control injury and the spread of disease;

- Ensure that the nation's food supply, drinking water, drugs, medical devices and environment are safe;

- Conduct and support cutting-edge research for the prevention, treatment and elimination of disease, health disparities and injury;

- Work with other nations and international agencies to address global health challenges;

- Provide urgently needed public health and clinical expertise in response to large-scale local, regional and national public health emergencies and disasters.

Members are trained to respond to public health situations and national emergency events, such as natural disasters, disease outbreaks and terrorist attacks.

As stated in the health-care legislation, "The purpose of the Ready Reserve Corps is (a) to fulfill the need to have additional Commissioned Corps personnel available on short notice (similar to the uniformed service's reserve program) to assist regular Commissioned Corps personnel to meet both routine public health and emergency response missions."[28] (b) Assimilating Reserve Corp Officers Into the Regular Corps; Effective on the date of enactment of the Patient Protection and Affordable Care Act, all individuals classified as officers in the Reserve Corps under this section (as such section existed on the day before the date of enactment of such Act) and serving on active duty shall be deemed to be commissioned

Chapter Five — The Trouble with the "Great Pretender"

officers of the Regular Corps. (c) Purpose and Use of Ready Research. USES: the Ready Reserve Corps shall, (A) participate in routine training to meet the general and specific needs of the Commissioned Corps; (B) be available and ready for involuntary calls to active duty during national emergencies and public health crises, similar to the uniformed service reserve personnel; (C) be available for backfilling critical positions left vacant during deployment of active duty Commissioned Corps members, as well as for deployment to respond to public health emergencies, both foreign and domestic; and (D) be available for service assignment in isolated, hardship, and medically underserved communities (as defined in section 799B) to improve access to health services. (d) Funding; For the purpose of carrying out the duties and responsibilities of the Commissioned Corps under this section, there are authorized to be appropriated $5,000,000 for each of fiscal years 2010 through 2014 for recruitment and training and $12,500,000 for each of fiscal years 2010 through 2014 for the Ready Reserve Corps.[29]

Commissioned officers of the ready reserve corps are appointed by the president, and commissioned officers of the regular corps are appointed by the president with the advice and consent of the Senate.

Robert Book, a senior research fellow in health economics at the Heritage Foundation, said the service has been around some time but is not well known. In the past, its responsibilities have included work related to the National Institutes of Health, the Indian health service and providing physicians for Coast Guard operations, he said.

Remember what he said on July 2, 2008: "We cannot continue to rely on our military in order to achieve the national security objectives that we've set," he said. "We've got to have a civilian national security force that's just as powerful, just as strong, just as well-funded."

Just another note of history about Hitler and what he did with his Sturmabteilung. He ordered the "Blood purge" of 1934. Those three nights of June 30-July 2, 1934 will be known forever in history as the "Night of the Long Knives," or three nights of political murders. Adolf Hitler moved against the SA and its leader, Ernst Röhm, though they were part of the apparatus that supported Hitler. He did so because of his obvious feeling of insecurity and inferiority, and seeing the independence of the SA, the penchant of its members for street violence. The SA numbered well over 2 million men, as a direct threat to his newly gained political power.[30]

So in a shortened work week of evenings, Hitler reined in the SA. The final death toll is not known for certain, but it is estimated to be in the hundreds, with several thousand being arrested in addition to those killed. I guess he did bring hope and change to Deutschland. It was just not the same hope the German citizens had desired wanted nor the change for which they sought.

Birds of a Feather

Travel back much further in time, to the time of Roman Emperors and see another similar and select army. In the time when Jesus walked a portion of that Galilean hillsides, Augustus established the Praetorian Guard because he saw a need to have a large body of soldiers who would be loyal to just himself. These guards following the death of Sejanus, began to plan an exponentially ambitious and murderous game in Rome. For the right amount of loot, or just because they felt like it, they assassinated emperors, they bullied their own Prefects. Sometimes they even turned on the people of the Empire. In 41 AD, Caligula was killed by conspirators from the senatorial class and from the Guard. These Praetorians placed Claudius on the throne, daring the Senate to oppose their decision.[31]

From the time of Caesar Augustus until now, several other leaders in several other countries have, or had, their own forms of SS or Praetorian, under different names. These were countries like the Soviet Union, Cuba, China, North Korea, and Venezuela and are sure to include the Iranian Revolutionary Guard, or the "Elite Republican Guard" who were loyal to Saddam Hussein, which all seems to be like Hitler's SS. Notice the thread of similarity running through them. Notice them? "Civilian National Security Force," a vast militia sounds very similar or not unlike Iran's Revolutionary Guard, a personal army. Obama knows he will need to rule like the Ayatollah in Iran. He will need such a force to protect him and to enforce his will on the American people. And an army of domestic disciples of "the anointed one" would fill that need, assuming all other military and law enforcement agencies fail to resist such a horrible plan.

But the U. S. Military might just be the entity he wants, not as it has been, but as it is becoming, as Obama continues to replace all the Generals and other high officers who are not loyal to him. It appears as he has replaced some 30 different generals in the last several months, possibly putting loyalists in those positions. It is speculation by some that he wants to establish military leadership that is blindly loyal to him, regardless of replacing those who have stated openly their loyalty to the Constitution and their stated refusal to fire on American citizens if asked to do so.

Pretend you are one who just wandered into the voting booth and dropped a ballot for the person with a "D" in front of his name, which would be Obama. Ask yourselves this: Has Obama described a "New National Brownshirts" organization to make sure you conform to the "Change" he promised to bring, and IS bringing? Of course he is. If he were talking about only a police force to help with crime, he would have pushed for the initiation of such a state-wide force just in South Chicago years ago when he was a senator from Illinois. He is really only interested in fighting just certain crime. The crime of opposing his will.

Yes, it is called the "Civilian National Security Force." No one outside of his inner circle and George Soros knows for certain what their duties will be yet. But it does not take a rocket scientist to see that "The One" is mimicking Augustus, or

Hitler or Chavez, or Stalin, or Castro. He knows the resolve of the American people is slow to change course. He also knows that the American people are asleep and slow to awaken. You can bet that my bet is right on target. And if you reluctantly agree, but think such a thing would not get approval in a millennium, think again, because it already did. The approval was buried deep in the Obamacare legislation about which Nancy Pelosi was giddy when saying, "You'll have to vote for it to see what's in it." Well, we did not vote for it, but now we are seeing what is in it. And what's in it appears not to be a celebratory ice cream treat called a "bomb-pop" but rather a homeland military surprise full of brass knuckles and night sticks for Americans: this one is just for domestic use, just as strong, just as equipped, and just as ready to crack heads as the SD, I mean the U.S. Military.

Obama needs it to do his enforcing because the concept of Posse Comitatus, which forbids the use of the U.S. military to enforce some new kinds of laws within the nation. Getting ready for that is exactly within his desired realm. Because Obama has despised this country for years, with our exceptional work ethic, our free enterprise system, a people who were blessed with our spiritual heritage. As Edward Klein states, "... based on my reporting, I concluded that Obama is actually in revolt against the values of the society he was elected to lead. Which is why he has refused to embrace American exceptionalism — the idea that Americans are a special people with a special destiny — and why he has railed at the capitalist system, demonized the wealthy, and embraced the Occupy Wall Street movement." [32]

Obama, like Hitler or Stalin or Mao, has been on a march toward building power over power, growing the federal government to the point that it squashes individual liberty. He has assaulted the Constitution at every possible fork in the road, pushing forth executive orders and congressional legislation which will strengthen his stranglehold on the people. As Judge Andrew Napolitano puts it: "... Thomas Jefferson, warned that absent a revolution, it is the inevitable nature of things for government power to increase and for the liberty of the individual to decrease. Unfortunately, he was right."[33]

Ridding Utopia of the 2nd Amendment Idiots

Not only does it appear to be Obama's quest to wrest away from all the states their power and money, but he desires a regime that resembles his idol's prescription; a Marxist style welfare state.

To support his position, Few American gun owners are aware that both Obama and Secretary of State Hillary Clinton are leaning on the U.S. Senate to ratify the UN's Small Arms Treaty which would regulate private gun ownership in America, superseding the U.S. Constitution's 2nd Amendment. Even if the U.S. Senate does not ratify that treaty, how sure are we that the Obama administration will not find a way to do the same thing through a Presidential executive order?

Remember he has a pen and a phone. Some say the U.S. Supreme Court will never allow that to happen. Even after what the SCOTUS just did, by finding Obamacare constitutional. What is to stop our dictator President from regulating private ownership of guns in America by executive order?

Here is the bone chilling truth: SOME American citizens will be, as usual, completely happy to allow the government to do whatever it wants as long as nothing is required of them. Most Americans will not sit idly by and allow a President (or a Congress) to go "rogue" without resisting with whatever means necessary.

The country is ruptured now; and seething with anger. Citizens throughout the expecting another major attack of domestic violence. Obama's tossing of salt into the wound with his own "Praetorian Guard" will have no curative effect. In fact, it could easily ignite the smoldering powder keg that is America today. Obviously, something is going on in America which is not good. Hear his speech again, "It is important for us to develop a national police force just as armed and just as prepared as the U.S. military around the world.

When you see the individual who was in charge of buying the bullets at DHS, this individual also runs a website that openly states African Americans need to prepare for the war with white people who are horrible. How did this person, Ayo Kimathi, get into a position within the DHS without their knowledge his general background? Why would the government have someone like this aboard? The question marks grow bigger the longer one looks.

This case within the DHS points specifically to a very real problem that has been growing for years; many of our governments' practices are diseased and getting sicker every day. That is certainly true in hiring practices. That is an appropriate place to start. Interviewing and selection practices within the various agencies must be more solid than this; there must be very stringent background checks as the order of the day, especially for an agency such as the DHS. A visit to this person's website at waronthehorizon.org reveals a great deal about what he says. Some of it would be humorous, good lines for a Saturday Night Live routine, if the attacks were not in the context of the security of our nation. For example, he writes, "Oprah Winfrey is a wealthy lesbian mammy." About Mr. Obama, he claims he is "a treasonous mulatto scum dweller." He lists Al Sharpton as "a sadistic political white sex offender who advocates homosexual behavior among black people." Exploring further, he indicates the nation is about to explode with war on the horizon. The country is ruptured and seems ready to explode. Possibly it is not best to have officials within the bounds of government pushing it on. Whoever interviewed this individual and signed off on hiring him should be at a minimum mandated to attend classes on top talent selection processes. Like most people, I fear that many processes within our government, such as this hiring decision, are also at a minimum systemically warped.

Excuses may be offered for how this person was placed in his job, and many folks will suspect that his placement in the DHS was not an accident. God help those conservatives who are preparing now to clean up this cesspool someday and pick up the pieces which were made by progressives among Democrats and Republicans.

Over the past two years, while the Department of Homeland Security was buying up more than 3.1 billion rounds of ammunition, and 2,700 armored vehicles, at least one person in Congress has been trying to uncover the real rationale behind this; he is not willing to accept the stated reason of "they are needed to deliver subpoenas." Rep. Timothy Huelscamp, R-Kan., has been trying to discover what DHS plans to do with all that firepower, but he can't get an answer. A reporter for *We Are Change*" asked Huelscamp at the Conservative Political Action Conference why DHS needs weapons of war. "They have no answer for that question. They refuse to answer to answer that," said Huelscamp.

And multiple members of Congress are asking those questions. ATK, a manufacturer of ammo from Anoka, Minnesota as an example, was awarded a 5-year contract in 2012 to deliver 460 million rounds of .40 caliber hollow points to DHS and ICE.

Impeachment Reason #11 – Obamacare Legislation

Obamacare is unconstitutional, illegal because it bypasses Congress, infringes on states' rights, and marks an unprecedented and unauthorized expansion of IRS power. The push by Obama and Pelosi to pass healthcare in Congress in less than 24 hours was so elementary and what my children used to call "ridiculoso." It took weeks to find the White House dog. Liberal Progressive as it was, he was fully aware it was unconstitutional. To make things worse, he continued to use his executive privilege to implement the legislation despite the fact that a federal judge declared the entire law unconstitutional, and ordered that it not be implemented.

The fact that Obama buried his national police force as a big chunk of pork within the pages of the document may mean he does not care at all about the medical portion of the bill anyway. He may have been just trying to get his national police force in place so he can try to maneuver as he wants in forcing his will on the American people.

Worst Legislation in 75 Years

David John Marotta, a Wall Street expert and financial advisor and Forbes contributor, said in a note to investors, "Obamacare was the worst legislation in the past 75 years. Socialism is on the rise and the NSA really is abrogating vast portions of the Constitution. I don't disagree with their concerns."

In a 2013 note, he said that "Americans should have a survival kit to take in case of a financial or natural disaster. It should be filled with items that will help them stay alive for the first 72-hours of a crisis, including firearms."[34]

Impeachment Reason #12 – Seize the Internet

President Obama has ordered the FCC (Federal Communications Commission) to adopt regulations handing the federal government control of the Internet and all its contents, including providing Obama with a kill switch that gives him authority to shut down the Internet "if he sees fit." This is in direct violation of a decision by the United States Supreme Court that the FCC has no Constitutional authority to control the Internet. There were two bills pending in Congress to effectively give Obama the kill switch he wants over the Internet. When these two proposals, the Stop Internet Piracy Act (SOPA) and the Protect Intellectual Property Act (PIPA) were withdrawn amid public outcry, Obama announced he will sign an international treaty that purports to give him the same authority anyway. He has signaled his intention to do this as an "Executive Act" and not bring the treaty to the Senate for ratification as required by Article 2, Section 2 of the Constitution. He is taking the same action with the Internet as he is with the United Nations Small arms treaty and the UN Law of the Sea treaty that are both unlikely to get Senate approval.

Impeachment Reason #13 – War Powers Act

Amidst all the scandals circling the White House, Obama's insistence on acting unilaterally in helping rebels against national leaders all to place the Muslim Brotherhood in charge of those nations throughout the Middle East is most troubling. He has proceeded because he knows Congress would not give him the authority to go to war just to help solve internal problems within one or more countries. The president of the United States is not authorized by the Constitution to take our nation to war without the approval or consent of the Congress of the United States. Though his words have varied for each country, it does not take a rocket scientist to see what he has been doing in Egypt, and Libya, and now in Syria.

Impeachment Reason #14 – In Breaking Myriads of Laws

One of the paramount responsibilities of the President of the United States is to enforce and also defend laws adopted by Congress, except where declared unconstitutional by the United States Supreme Court. Obama has decided that he should ignore this Constitutional mandate, and that as President he is more powerful than either the Congress of the United States or the Supreme Court. For example, he has unilaterally declared that the Defense of Marriage Act passed by the Congress as unconstitutional, and further declared that he will not have the Justice Department defend it against lawsuits. His administration has also refused to enforce laws against voter intimidation and federal law that requires states to purge their voter registration lists of deceased individuals and those that are registered illegally.

Add to this, Obama and his Justice Department are refusing to allow states to enforce laws requiring proof of identity by voters at the polls. Some states like Texas have stated they will have their own laws regarding fair elections requiring ID. Obama through the DOJ is suing Texas on this decision. Obama has essentially said that he is the supreme ruler of the United States. In doing so, he has in effect announced that the Congress and the Federal Judiciary are irrelevant, unless of course he wants to use them for some reason.

Will Rogers used to say, "Nobody is as stupid as an educated man when you get him out of the department he's educated in." History is full of stories about men and women, who once removed from their area of expertise, disasters occurred.

The Great Depression of the 1930s made an indelible mark on my parents' and grandparents' generations. Their view of the world certainly changed forever and as one old timer down the block from my uncle's house said, "We just don't look at the world through rose tinted glasses like you younger people do." True as that probably was for most of their generations, there was a familiar story of one man who lost everything he had. As he walked down the street of his city one day, at every intersection he would thrust out his left arm. Someone stopped him and asked why he was doing it. "That," he said, "is all I have left of my automobile." Nothing was left but the gesture for turning left.

Let's go straight to "Double Jeopardy" and now we have Barack Obama who claims he knows all about how to get out of financial messes. Borrow money and spend it, is the theme, as fast as you can, on "shovel ready jobs." Wasn't that one a horrible trick on Americans? It appears the real motto is to follow the progressive code, spend money as fast as possible, cut jobs as much as possible, drive prices higher as much as possible, then break the system and start anew with government ownership of everything. Oh, and regarding foreign affairs, we can know that his experience trumps all others because he lived in Indonesia at one time (as a child); thus he believes he has more knowledge than all other respective minds that have ever assembled thoughts.

There is no pay dirt with Obama.

Impeachment Reason #15 – Cap and Trade

Few Americans are familiar with the term "Cap and Trade." They also have no idea what this law will mean to either our nation or to them personally, as citizens or consumers; so let's define this first. Large corporate interests and especially Government, have such a habit of creating acronyms and other terminology for internal use, which can seem baffling at first. A couple of reasons for the acronym thing: for quick reference within a group, saving language, and time; and a more sadistic one, for having and using a perceived power over those who are not aware of the terminology. However, with a little help they can be deciphered for everyday use and application. Simply put, cap and trade is a tax.

In cap and trade, the "cap" refers to the enforceable maximum limit of greenhouse gases a particular corporation or company will be allowed to emit into the atmosphere. Given the assumption that it will be easier for some companies to reduce their greenhouse emissions than other firms, a "cap-and-trade" system would theoretically allow companies that are able to reduce their greenhouse emissions below their budgeted allowance to then sell their extra "permits" to those companies having a more difficult time reducing their emissions. The federal government may opt to auction the emissions permits to those companies struggling to reduce their emissions; thus another revenue stream will be created for the U.S. Treasury. There might be goals set to reduce carbon emission by U.S. companies to a percentage of some specified target level, just as an example, cutting the carbon emissions in used in 2000 by 80 percent, by the year 2050.

Jerome R. Corsi, in his great book, *America For Sale*, lays out the case that Obama and his cronies are dismantling portions of our economy and basically selling them to the world. He says, "Economist Peter Orszag, currently the director of the Office of Management and Budget in the Obama administration, testified before Congress on cap-and-trade last year, when he was the director of the Congressional Budget Office. From his testimony, it was clear Orszag believed global climate change resulting from human causes was a serious, perhaps even catastrophic, problem.

"Human activities are producing increasingly large quantities of greenhouse gases, particularly CO^2," he testified. "The accumulation of these gases in the atmosphere is expected to have potentially serious and costly effects on regional climates throughout the world."

Corsi also adds, "The last thing we need is a massive tax increase in a recession, but reportedly that's what the White House is offering: up to $1.9 trillion in tax hikes on every single American who drives a car, turns on a light switch or buys a product made in the United States," Michael Steel, a spokesman for House Minority Leader John A. Boehner, R-Ohio, told the Washington Times. "And since this energy tax won't affect manufacturers in Mexico, India and China, it will do nothing but drive American jobs overseas."[35]

The truth about what Obama wants to accomplish with cap and trade is simply this; under the disguise of "improving the environment, reducing supposed "manmade" global warming, returning the ocean levels back to a pre-twentieth century level, saving the polar bears, the snail darter fish, the spotted owls, and of course the world from conservatism. The goal is really to make it so difficult, costly, and burdensome for American citizens and American companies to operate; it will reduce our market share in the world and our wealth. The proof of this is easy to see; every growing and expanding economy in the world runs on oil, coal, and natural gas. Those are the very things Obama is trying to "outlaw" in this country and make them more expensive.

That withstanding, what bothers most conservative Americans, is trusting that we have the straight story on climate change, aka global warming. Especially bothering is the question of not only how but if it is caused by human activity at all. Following Al Gore's presentations of his now famous PowerPoint® presentations, speeches, and movie, *An Inconvenient Truth*, the leftists raced forward introducing new plans to get money, tax money. Frankly, it appears to me the name of that party's website should be changed from Democrats.org, to "Its-all-about-the-money.com."

CHAPTER FIVE — THE TROUBLE WITH THE "GREAT PRETENDER"

Real data from over half the scientists, non-political data, non-liberal data, shows not the "hockey stick," Gore presented and preached. It shows we have peaked in warming and are now cooling. Besides, it was revealed a year or so after the sermons by Al and the Left, that the Scottish scientist who came up with the hockey stick, admitted he used not only, flawed data, but he manipulated the data to make warming appear to be happening when it was not. What he did was plug in data from an earlier month to make the temperature trend show an upward move, when actually it was not really moving upward at all. In street language, he lied! It is fairly obvious even to the scientists who study such data that the earth goes through warming and cooling trends or "cycles," regardless of the amount of human activity. Data derived from sources including tree-rings, lake sediments, ice cores and historic documents bear that position out. Indeed, it is abundantly evident that since the last glacial period ended, over 14,000 years ago, the Earth's climate has undergone multi-century swings from warming to cooling that occur often and with remarkable rapidity. And **not one but three** such radical shifts occurred within the past millennium.

During testimony before the Senate Committee on Environment & Public Works Hearing on Climate Change and the Media in 2006, University of Oklahoma geophysicist Dr. David Deming recalled "an astonishing email from a major researcher in the area of climate change" who told him that "we have to get rid of the Medieval Warm Period." Deming identified the year of that email as 1995 and the source only as a lead author of that month's *Global Climate Change Impacts in the United States* report. The truth is the truth. By the time most Americans received their first lesson in climate hysteria in the Albert Gore lecture hall that was the 2006 film *An Inconvenient Truth*, the MBH chart the professor stood before and offered as proof of impending doom was already held in disrepute by most serious persons of science.[36]

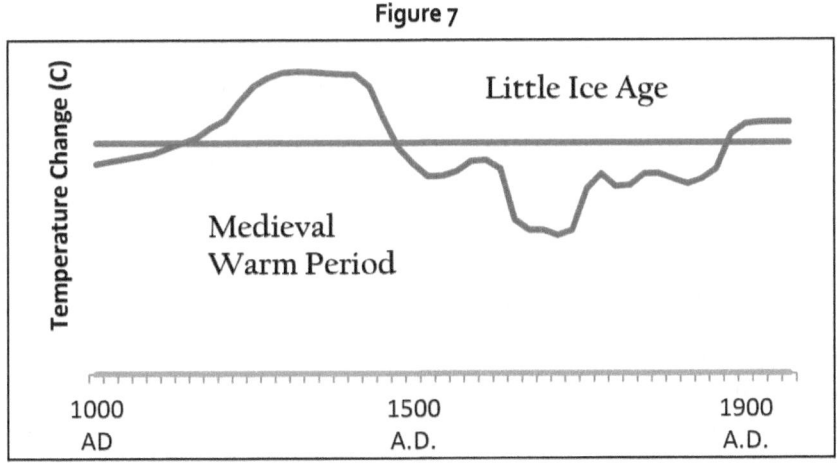

Figure 7

There are a whole host of events which can and do impact global weather and the subsequent temperature. Volcanoes have the most tremendous impact on raising the global temperature. Historically, the cooling which results from their blasts have outweighed the warming they produce. The 1991 Mount Pinatubo eruption in the Philippines lowered global temperatures by about 0.4-0.5 Celsius according to scientists. Compare that to the 2010 explosion of Mount Eyjafjallajökull in Iceland, which disturbed air traffic in some 20 countries while it ejected approximately 250 million cubic meters of tephra into the atmosphere. The video images were very dramatic, but the Iceland volcano was not in the league with Pinatubo.

The data gained from the 2010 explosion of Mount Eyjafjallajökull in Iceland proves it was relatively small for volcanic eruptions, though it caused enormous disruption to air travel across western and northern Europe six days in April 2010. Twenty countries closed their airspace to commercial jet traffic which impacted over 100,000 travelers. There was a second phase to the eruption, which lasted most of the summer and put in the atmosphere an estimated 250 million cubic meters of (330,000,000 cu yds.) (¼ km^3) of ejected tephra. The ash plume rose to a height of approximately 9 kilometres (30,000 ft), which rates the explosive power of the eruption as a 4 on the Volcanic Explosivity Index. They also produce carbon dioxide, a greenhouse gas.[37]

Almost laughable, are some weather reports, or predictions of global warming by Leftists. Listen to your next weather forecast, especially when the forecast is predicted "to break a record high." Then the next sentence or two usually is, "today's temperature will tie a record set in 1933," or "1896," or some such year. The next question then is what was going on in 1933 and 1896? Were the freeways jammed with SUVs those years? Was Al Gore sitting at some convention center with his SUV engine running while he made a speech? The truth is, temperatures have been rising and falling for centuries, and scientists, credible ones say that it is tied to sunspots. But do not present facts to a liberal. This global warming stuff is a religion to them, the worship of Mother Earth, and to question it. To challenge it, is to insult one of public proponents who are to them, god-like creatures. But just watch as we get into a period now of global cooling. Surely there is a tax in there someplace.

The New Weather Tax

There are two obvious and visible reasons why the "cap and trade" doctrine or law is being pursued by Obama the liberal elites. First, American businesses have to be punished for being successful, for using resources in a larger measure than other countries. This is something to which Obama referred in his original campaigning in 2007-08. He said America would not be allowed to continue using up the resources which it has done in the past. Obama clearly wants to limit this country, making it like all other nations. This results in nothing less than harm to our country. Obama's track record shows the evidence: going around the world apologizing for the U.S.; then he supports other countries in doing what he disallows for American interests. His attitude is that of an angry liberal, and his words smack with that aroma. I have always told people that elections have consequences. The last few point that out in an apocalyptic way. The second reason and foundational purpose of cap-and-trade is to establish a new revenue stream for government. What is so inconsistent are those who are speak of their concern over the supposed overuse of oil, gas and coal, while they travel the world in jets and SUV's, burning oil-based fuel products in record amounts. Once revenue streams are established, the progressive model is to collect more money each year by legislative measures increasing the percentage of tax a company, individual or family will have to pay. And this is all for those who want to 'control' America. Money is power and Obama is about the quickest I have seen at collecting and spending it.

Any start of a cap-and-trade program is therefore doing nothing more than starting an additional tax, a carbon tax. Leftists like Orszag are arguing that a cap-and-trade is a market-oriented approach to reducing carbon emissions that would be more efficient in producing results than what he calls a command-and-control approach. That is a disguise.

Despite the fact that the United States Senate refused to pass the Cap and Trade bill, the President has proceeded to order the Environmental Protection Agency (EPA) to use regulations, thus implementing key portions of the bill anyway, including those regulating so-called greenhouse gases. So unilaterally, **Obama himself has proudly acknowledged that this will force energy prices in this country to skyrocket.** Can you guess the result? The price of electricity generated by coal or oil will at least double, rising by a factor of at least two. Of course, he is taking these actions in direct defiance of the will of the people of the United States, the will of Congress, and against the Constitution.

Cap-and-trade will also increase all energy prices including the cost of gasoline and diesel. Conservative estimates say somewhere between 100 – 300 percent. That translates to the pump price between $6 and $10 per gallon in 2014 dollars. The actions of the EPA include regulations that are currently forcing many coal burning power plants to close. The cost of coal will be similar to gas, so the cost of electricity will skyrocket in the 25 states that get more than 50 percent of their electricity from coal. Businesses that emit carbon dioxide, including manufacturing companies, will face yet one additional cost of operations in paying cap-and-trade costs. Businesses are trying to compete in a global economy where multinational corporations are free to outsource operations to cheap labor countries (such as China); this at a time when it appears China and other nations have little intention of implementing cap-and-trade emission schemes on companies operating within their boundaries.

The imposition of a cap-and-trade tax will further depress the economy. Today's typical American family is at a point where they are struggling just to keep jobs; just to put food on the table; not lose homes and pay monthly living expenses, including those involved in raising children. Prices will go up if further tax increases are implemented on companies. Companies must pass on these costs to those using or purchasing their products however they are manufactured or produced. Initial statements of "I don't care" will soon change — the cost of your Big Mac would go to $10, and a gallon of milk would probably be $7-8. But proponents of cap-and-trade schemes do not care; they believe the economic costs are cheaper than the perceived "climate-change catastrophe" they say will definitely happen. One need only remember that behind the curtain is Obama, the disciple of Karl Marx, who taught it was necessary in a collectivist society to have an 80 percent tax rate. We are just getting started.

Czars, Czars, and More Czars

President Obama has appointed numerous people to cabinet level positions without the advice and consent of the U.S. Senate, as is required by the Constitution. These individuals are given extraordinary power and independent funding, and are not under the scrutiny of Congress. Most Americans do not even know about them. The fact that Obama calls them Czars does not make them legal. He has also made illegal recess appointments of other members of his cabinet that required Senate approval. He simply declared that the U.S. Senate was in recess despite the fact that there was no such recess or even a declaration of a recess. The President has no Constitutional authority here.

The end result is that there are dozens of individuals serving Obama wearing the title "Czar" who were not appointed lawfully, and many of whom appear to be running some sort of shadow government, heading up little fiefdoms. Most of these fiefdoms are being operated by the czar from behind a dark curtain, leaving their actions out of sight, with little to no knowledge of what is being done. Yet we know that each czar wields vast power in affecting change in domestic and international issues. All the following czars are/were Obama appointees:

Czar Name	Position / Department	Person in Position	Tenure
AfPak Czar	Special Representative for Afghanistan and Pakistan	Holbrooke, Richard [38]	2009 – 2010
AIDS Czar	Director, Office of National AIDS Policy	Crowley, Jeffrey [39]	2009 – 2012
AIDS Czar	Director, Office of National AIDS Policy	Colfax, Grant [40]	2012 – Present
Asian Carp Czar	Director of Office of Economic Opportunity	Goss, John [41]	2010 – Present
Auto Czar/Car Czar	Treasury Advisor, Head of Auto Taskforce	Rattner, Steve [42]	2009 Feb – July
Auto Czar/Car Czar	Sr. Advisor, President's Auto Task Force / Director of Recovery for Auto Communities and Workers	Bloom, Ron [43]	2009 – Present

Chapter Five — The Trouble with the "Great Pretender"

Czar Name cont.	Position / Department cont.	Person in Position	Tenure cont.
Bank Bailout Czar/ TARP Czar	US Asst Secretary of the Treasury for Financial Stability	Allison, Herbert [44]	2009 – Present
Border Czar	Assistant Secretary for International Affairs, Special Representative for Border Affairs in DHS	Bersin, Alan [45]	2009 – Present
Climate Czar	Special Envoy for Climate Change	Stern, Todd D. [46]	2009
Climate czar, Energy czar, Global Warming czar	Assistant to the President for Energy and Climate Change	Browner, Carol [47]	2009 – Present
Copyright Czar	Intellectual Property Enforcement Coordinator	Espinel, Victoria [48]	2009 – Present
Compensation czar, Gulf claims czar, Pay czar	Special Master for TARP Executive Compensation	Feinberg, Kenneth [49]	2009 – Present
Consumer Czar	Special Advisor, Consumer Financial Protection Bureau	Warren, Elizabeth [50]	2010 – 2011
Cyber Security czar, Cyber czar	Director of the White House Office of Cybersecurity, Cybersecurity Coordinator	Hathaway, Melissa [51]	Acting czar May–July, 2009; resigned
Cyber Security czar, Cyber czar	Director of the White House Office of Cybersecurity, Cybersecurity Coordinator	Schmidt, Howard [52]	Office created 5/31/09
Calif. water czar	Deputy Interior Secretary reports to Int Sec Ken Salazar	Hayes, David J. [53]	2009 – Present
Domestic Violence czar	Advisor to the President and the Vice President on Domestic Violence and Sexual Assault Issues	Rosenthal, Lynn [54]	2009 – Present
Drug Czar	Director / National Drug Control Policy	Kerlikowske, R. Gil [55]	2009 – Present
Economic Czar	Chairman of the President's Economic Recovery Advisory Board	Volcker, Paul [56]	2009 – Present
Ethics czar, Transparency czar	Special counsel to the president for ethics and government reform	Eisen, Norm [57]	2009 – 2010
Ethics czar, Transparency czar	White House Counsel	Bauer, Robert [58]	2010 – Present
Faith-Based Czar	Director, White House Office of Faith-Based and Neighborhood Partnerships	DuBois, Joshua [59]	2009 – 2013
Faith-Based Czar	Director, White House Office of Faith-Based and Neighborhood Partnerships	Rogers, Melissa [60]	2013 – Present

Czar Name cont.	Position / Department cont.	Person in Position	Tenure cont.
Great Lakes Czar	Special Advisor to the EPA Administrator	Davis, Cameron [61]	2009 – Present
Government Performance czar	Chief Performance Officer reporting to Office of Management and Budget Director Peter Orzag	Zients, Jeffrey [62]	2009 – Present
Green Jobs Czar	Special Advisor for Green Jobs, Enterprise, and Innovation at the White House, Member of the White House Council on Environmental Quality	Jones, Van [63]	2009 April – Sept.
Guantanamo Closure czar	Special Envoy, U.S. Department of State	Fried, Daniel [64]	2009 – Present
Health Czar	Director of the White House Office of Health Reform and Counselor to the President	DeParle, Nancy Ann [65]	2009 – Present
Health IT Czar	National Coordinator for Health Information Technology, Department of Health and Human Services	Blumenthal, Dr. David [66]	2009 – Present
Information Czar / Infotech Czar	Chief Information Officer at the White House	Kundra, Vivek [67]	2009 – Present
Intelligence Czar	Director of National Intelligence	Blair, Dennis [68]	2009 – 2010
Iran Czar	Special Advisor for the Persian Gulf and Southwest Asia (which includes Iran)	Ross, Dennis [69]	2009 – Present
Manufacturing Czar	Senior Consultant for Manufacturing Policy/ White House	Bloom, Ron [70]	2009 – Present
Middle East Czar	Special Envoy for Middle East Peace	Mitchell, George [71]	2009 – Present
Regulatory Czar	Director of the Office of Information and Regulatory Affairs / Office of Management and Budget	Sunstein, Cass [72]	2009 – Present
Science Czar	Director of the Office of Science and Technology Policy	Holdren, John [73]	2009 – Present
Stimulus Accountability czar	Chair of the Recovery Act Transparency and Accountability Board	Devaney, Earl [74]	2009 – Present
Sudan Czar	Special Envoy to Sudan	Gration, J. Scott [75]	2009 – Present
Chief Technology Czar	Associate Director of the White House Office of Science and Technology Policy, Chief Technology Officer (CTO), Assistant to the President	Chopra, Aneesh [76]	2009 – Present

CHAPTER FIVE — THE TROUBLE WITH THE "GREAT PRETENDER"

Czar Name cont.	Position / Department cont.	Person in Position	Tenure cont.
Terrorism Czar	Assistant to the President for Homeland Security and Counterterrorism	Brennan, John [77]	2009 – Present
Urban Affairs Czar	Director of the White House Office/ Urban Affairs Policy	Carrion, Adolfo [78]	2009 – Present
Weapons Czar	Under Secretary of Defense for Acquisition, Technology, and Logistics	Carter, Ashton [79]	2009 – Present
WMD Policy Czar	White House Coordinator for Weapons of Mass Destruction, Security and Arms Control	Samore, Gary [80]	2009 – Present

This is the latest listing of the forty-two (42) czars who were appointed by Obama, mostly by executive order. Very few have been presented for Senate approval. By and large, they represent the most liberal, the most Marxist, and the most Left-leaning individuals, other than those in the Senate and White House, this country has ever experienced. All were either appointed personally by Obama himself, or approved personally by Obama after they were short-listed for appointment. They have no accountability to the American people, only answering to individuals within this administration.

But even more questionable, if that seems possible, are the individuals in the chart on the following page. These individuals have all been appointed personally by Obama, in very key areas, and are Muslims. Some may think the previous sentence is a critical comment, but please see the chapter on "The Trouble With Islamists" for a true hearing.

Muslim Appointments	Position / Department	Person in Position	Tenure
DHS Advisor	Assistant Secretary for Policy Development for the U.S.; Department of Homeland Security (DHS)	Alikhan, Arif [81] (See Arif on p. 212)	2010 – Present
DHS Advisor	Homeland Security Advisor, U.S. DHS	Mohammed, Elibiary [82] (See Elibiary on p. 214)	2010 – Present
White House Advisor	Advisor and founder of the Muslim Public Affairs Council; currently its Executive Director	Salam al-Marayati [83] (See Salam on p. 214)	
Sharia Czar	Sharia Law Advisor	Imam Mohamed Magdid [84] (See Imam on p. 214)	
	Advisory Council on Faith-Based Neighborhood Partnerships	Patel, Eboo [85] (See Eboo on p. 215)	
	Special Envoy to the Organization of the Islamic Conference (OIC)	Hussain, Rushad [86] (See Hussain on p. 215)	

211

Troubling news it is that each of these appointments made by Obama has strong ties to the Muslim Brotherhood. If you are not concerned about the Muslim Brotherhood's ties to radical Islam, you should be. The appointments by Obama establishes a scenario which makes a long-term resident in this nation more than a little uncomfortable with this leadership model, based on what is known about the hardline Muslim Brotherhood and its allies.

Imagine having your home broken into by neighborhood thugs. You know where they live. The police are not able to accomplish much as far as you are concerned in solving the crime. Not only is your home break-in going unsolved, other homes are being broken into, and they too go unsolved. In a move to satisfy some politicians, there is pressure to place some members of the neighborhood thugs on neighborhood watch teams, and some of them are actually in charge of going home to home and inspecting security measures within family dwellings. It is advertised that the inspections will be done to help prevent future robberies, but you recognize some of the "inspectors" now wearing suits as those who have robbed homes in your neighborhood. Soon they will be visiting your home.

You would be shocked at such a turn of affairs. You would most likely sound alarms in the neighborhood as to who is on the committee for home security, knowing they are ones who have been busy causing problems for many families. You would be questioning the police and HOA association officers as to how they would allow such an event to take place. You would be calling your congressman, attorney, insurance agents, attempting to raise the issue as high as possible trying to get someone to stop the process, stall as long as you can, or get a monkey wrench to throw into the works to get the machinery stopped.

This is what is happening within the national neighborhood watch at this time. It is called "Homeland Security!" The enemy wearing the same name, who has bombed us with our own planes, attacked private citizens in many different settings with homemade bombs, has threatened the public if they do not convert to their odd religion, and declare themselves immune from many of the laws of the land, are helping to govern Homeland Security as you read these words. It is happening at the behest of the occupant of the Oval Office, the highest office in this land.

While liberals think nothing of seeing radical Muslims being placed in important post positions at the White House, especially since a liberal is doing the placing of such individuals, it appears to be more than just a heinous crime to conservatives. Consider the backgrounds of these individuals:

- Arif [81]: Consider the background resume of Arif Alikhan — named Assistant Secretary, Policy Development in the U.S. Department of Homeland Security (DHS).

    Arif Alikhan, whose last position was that of deputy mayor for the city

CHAPTER FIVE — THE TROUBLE WITH THE "GREAT PRETENDER"

of Los Angeles, was appointed as assistant secretary for the Office of Policy Development at DHS. Muslim Democrats were excited to hear of Alikhan's appointment.

His resume shows the following activities. At a banquet/fundraiser for the Islamic Shura Council of Southern California one weekend, the first speaker was Arif Alikhan. As Deputy Mayor of Los Angeles, he had been in charge of public safety for the city. He was bidding farewell, as he was going to take the post as **Assistant Secretary at the Department of Homeland Security**. Arif Alikhan is a devout Sunni and the son of Pakistani immigrants.

Professor Agha Saeed of the American Muslim Task Force (AMT) spoke of the aftermath of 9/11 and the struggle of the Muslim Community against the pervasive atmosphere of Islamophobia and hatred. It was a struggle against the tide, a very strong, tide, to prevent Muslims in America from being marginalized and silenced.

Professor Saeed issued five demands from Muslims to the Department of Justice. These demands included a cessation to the infiltration by spies of mosques and an end to the introduction of agents provocateur. In addition there was to be a cessation of attempts to undermine Muslim groups such as the Council on American Islamic Relations (CAIR).

This is where Alikhan spoke? He was comfortable with this terror talk? Why Alikhan? DHS Secretary Janet Napolitano at the time noted Alikhan's "broad and impressive array of experience in national security, emergency preparedness and counterterrorism." I am not sure what she is talking about (neither is she, I am sure.)

Arif Alikhan was appointed Deputy Mayor of Los Angles; picked from relative obscurity.

He began his career nine years ago, when he took a job with the Department of Justice hunting down computer hackers, crooks who were selling merchandise on Ebay at rock-bottom prices. In his former position as an assistant U.S. attorney, Alikhan consistently did his work accurately and silently, never producing any headlines. But then he suddenly became one of the most important men in Los Angeles, America's second-largest city after New York.

He took the position of Deputy Mayor in November 2006. The year that the Congress went Democrat and history and America took a disastrous turn. How does an obscure bureaucrat and a devout Muslim come to the position of Deputy Mayor of Los Angeles in charge of public safety for the city in a time of Muslim attacks? And now he is Assistant Secretary to DHS? In 2007, Alikhan was instrumental in removing the Muslim terror tracking plan in LA. The controversial Muslim 'Mapping' Plan of the Los Angeles Police Department is now "dead on arrival" according to Chief William Bratton.

This is clearly a case of the fox guarding the hen house. Can Americans not see what is happening to our country? We are giving our country away, piece by piece. When Law makers start pushing the one world government, we are getting to the end and it will not be long after that, the one world dictator will appear on the scene. You naysayers go ahead and balk but God's word says this is true. To all you unbelievers, I feel sorry for you. America is at the point where there will be no turning back. You may not be a Christian but even heathens will not like the type of government that the current Democrats want to come to power. Keep being apathetic to people that are in power now and making our laws. Our freedoms are slowly eroding. May God help us all.

- **Elibiary**[82]**: Mohammed Elibiary — Homeland Security Adviser** First we have Arif Alikhan, Devout Muslim, Assistant Secretary for Policy Development for the U.S. Department of Homeland Security. Now we have Mohammed Elibiary, Homeland Security Adviser.

  Elibiary has strong connections with Muslim terrorists and fundamental Muslim organizations. He appeared at a conference honoring the Ayatollah Khomeini. He has made attacks on prosecution efforts of terrorist fundraisers. He has actively promoted jihadist ideology godfather Sayyid Qutb. Also he threatened a *Dallas Morning News* journalist who repeatedly exposed his extremist views.

- **Salam**[83]**: Salam al-Marayati** – Obama Adviser; founder Muslim Public Affairs Council and its current executive director, and a Muslim leader who said that Israel should have been added to the "suspect list" for the Sept. 11, 2001, terrorist attacks.

- **Imam**[84]**: Imam Mohamed Magid** – Obama's Sharia Czar; President of the Islamic Society of North America (ISNA). Magid was born and raised in Sudan and immigrated to the United States in 1987. Imam Magid studied with his father, Al-Haj Majd Haj Mosa, described by one watchdog website as "a Cairo-trained Muslim Brotherhood scholar" who has served as the top cleric in the Republic of the Sudan, one of the most Sharia-adherent nations in the world. In 2012, ISNA hosted Dawud Walid who said, "One of the greatest social ills facing American today is Islamophobia, and anti-Muslim bigotry. And if you trace the organizations and the main advocates and activists in Islamophobia in America, you will see that all those organizations are pro-Israeli occupation organizations and activists."

CHAPTER FIVE — THE TROUBLE WITH THE "GREAT PRETENDER"

- **Eboo**[85]**: Eboo Patel** – Advisory Council on Faith-Based Neighborhood Partnerships; Patel is the founder and executive director of the Interfaith Youth Core, a Chicago-based international nonprofit that promotes interfaith cooperation. A source for more on the Muslims and Muslim Brotherhood infiltration into the White House can be found in Frank Gaffney's *The Muslim Brotherhood in the Obama Administration*. Read more at http://theblacksphere.net/2013/04/devout-muslims-in-key-positions-in-the-white-house/#SDUPdlTsV6mtjxb3.99

- **Hussain**[86]**: Rashad Hussain:** President Obama appointed Rashad Hussain to serve as his Special Envoy to the Organization of the Islamic Conference (OIC). Comprised of over 50 member states, the OIC is the second largest inter-governmental organization in the world. As Special Envoy to the OIC, Rashad Hussain will deepen and expand the partnerships that the United States has pursued with Muslims around the world since President Obama's speech in Cairo last June. Hussain is "a hafiz of the Qur'an". An individual earns this designation by committing to memory the Qur'an in its entirety and enjoys high status among Sharia-adherent Muslims who regard this feat as proof of a deep devotion to Allah. The OIC is headquartered in Jeddah, Saudi Arabia. It is dedicated in its documents to spreading Islamic law, or Sharia.

    President Obama said, "I'm proud to announce today that I am appointing my Special Envoy to the OIC—Rashad Hussain. As an accomplished lawyer and a close and trusted member of my White House staff, Rashad has played a key role in developing the partnerships I called for in Cairo. And as a hafiz of the Qur'an, he is a respected member of the American Muslim community, and I thank him for carrying forward this important work."

To most Americans, the "important work" our president mentioned is a mystery. It certainly cannot be peace or forward-thinking doctrines, since there is an obvious point made about clinging to Muslim traditions.

If anyone needed evidence that this administration, Barack Obama including Hillary Clinton, when she was Secretary of State, is in the pocket of the Muslim Brotherhood, the events of the last few years should be more than sufficient to point that out. On the anniversary of 9/11 in 2012, on what should be a day of shame for the Muslim world, the U.S. Embassy in Cairo issued a statement condemning critics of Islamofascism in language appropriate to the office of propaganda for the Muslim Brotherhood. Islamofascists launched violent attacks on Americans, repeating the outrages in miniature of the World Trade Center attacks of 2001. In the face of these outrages the posture of the U.S. government is one that would make Neville Chamberlain blush. In five years Barack Obama has turned the Middle East over to America's enemies.

Impeachment Reason #16 – Executive Order Laws

The last on the list of impeachable offenses, are the executive orders which President Obama has put into place since taking office in 2009. There are 923 of them and counting. Some he has appointed while Congress has been in recess; some pushed through Congress in the dark of night. In connection to the "ones in the dark of night" he has also used administrative actions taken by his departments to nationalize and control automobile manufacturers, banks, insurance companies, and now the healthcare system. These orders are designed to move our country away from a free enterprise economy to a socialist, state-owned economy. These orders/laws fly in the face of the Constitution of the United States. There is no authority, absolutely none, anyplace in the Constitution that allows this president to take these steps. It does not matter who did this before Obama arrived. If it is wrong it is wrong.

Article II, Section 4 of the Constitution provides as follows: "The President, Vice President and all civil Officers of the United States shall be removed from Office on Impeachment for, and Conviction of, Treason, Bribery, or other high Crimes and Misdemeanors." In fact, federal law at 5 U.S.C. 7311 in particular provides that violation of the oath of office includes advocating the overthrowing of our constitutional form of government. Moving our government from a free-enterprise to a socialistic form is treason. Specifically this is declared a criminal offense in 18 U.S.C. 1918 and is punishable by both a fine and imprisonment.

Among those high crimes and misdemeanors, it is my contention each is a willful and intentional violation of the oath of office sworn to by the President as well as by some other federal officials. In 14 areas I submit and believe therefore that Obama, Eric Holder, and some other members of his administration have engaged in the overthrow of our constitutional form of government. We have in fact gone well past that point. The goal seems to be replacing our representative republic with a dictatorship. For those reasons, I faithfully submit there is treason in our highest offices within the land.

Then There Are the Foreign Policy Lies

Ever since first hearing the term "Arab Spring," the press has fallen in love with the term; so much so that a person needs a meter to count. It has gone on ad infinitum ad nauseam. Visions of the old Ottoman Empire came to mind with long robed thugs swinging swords and killing Crusaders and other Christians throughout the Middle East and throughout Europe. With George Soros providing funding for the Brotherhood in Middle Eastern Countries, all to support this so-called Arab Spring, it spells trouble. Soros backs projects designed to bring money to his pockets in concert with destruction of economies he touches. With the backing of Soros, Obama's foreign policy has brought viewing our greatest ally, Israel, now as our worst enemy; and our old worst enemy, The PLO, as our best ally.

Chapter Five — The Trouble with the "Great Pretender"

All the activities in the Middle East seems to have been driven toward giving the Muslim Brotherhood control over nations, Sharia Law put in play, and the ultimate destruction of Israel. And current American Policy Hacks in this administration have supported moving toward a pro-Muslim posture at every turn, and an anti-Israel stance at the same moment.

Supporting Islamists in Egypt

Take for example, all the rosy predictions for Egypt's Islamic revolution, being like the 2nd coming, did not turn out very well, or at least as planned. Finding foreign rulers who totally agree with good American policy is difficult at best, just like trying to find a foreign word which translates 1 to 1 for an English word. It just does not happen, and when you have a disaster of a foreign policy like we do with Obama, you just knew that the howling mobs in Hahrir Square in 2011 would fail to produce any kind of peaceful democracy.

Egyptian President Hosni Mubarak was at least supporting U.S. policy, he had been using his military to fight the Muslim hoard and extremists, and he did something that the Muslim Brotherhood will not do; that is recognize Israel's right to exist. So naturally, Obama could not have that, and told him in January, 2011 he had to get out of town before sundown.

Liberal progressives were busy at the time spreading propaganda about the events in Egypt, calling it at that time this "glorious people's revolution." It was tainted with lies as you can see when reviewing just a microcosm of the liberal media, the *New York Times*:

- "(Egyptian) Officials blamed the Muslim Brotherhood (for the protests).... Even if the Brotherhood had a role — the group denies it; the truth seems more complex — it is easy to understand why Egyptians are fed up." (Editorial: "Mr. Mubarak Is Put on Notice," Jan. 26, 2011)

- "The mistake, which still emanates from think tanks stocked with neoconservatives, is assuming that democracy can come at the end of sword.... Now that some of the dominoes appear to be falling, this has more to do with Facebook and the frustrations of young, educated adults who can't earn enough money to marry than it does with tanks rolling into Baghdad, or naive neocons guiding the State Department." (Timothy Egan, "Bonfire of American Vanities," Feb. 3, 2011)

- "It's time to be clear: Mubarak's time is up." (Roger Cohen, "Hosni Mubarak Agonizes," Feb. 4, 2011)

- "What is unfolding in Arab streets is not an assertion of religious reaction but a yearning for democracy with all its burdens and rewards." (Ray Takeyh, "What Democracy Could Bring," Feb. 4, 2011)

Obama continued to support Morsi all during the time period which the people were moving to remove Morsi from office. It took less than a year and now we know the truth, that it was not "complex." The Muslim Brotherhood was behind the original revolution, the deaths, the rigged election and was planning to implement Sharia law. And, of course Obama and George Soros, with his billions, were behind this whole carnival. And it almost worked, until the Egyptian military stepped in on behalf of the Egyptian citizens and forcibly removed President Mohammed Morsi, the Brotherhood's henchman. In Arab countries, at least, it seems that democracy can come only "at the end of a sword."

Then Support the Islamists in Libya

Close to the same time in 2011, Obama ordered air strikes in Libya against Moammar Gadhafi, just when he had no power. As one outlaw said in the movie *The Outlaw Josie Wales* ". . . he is as harmless as a heel hound." Before you argue, look at the history. After Bush invaded Iraq, Gadhafi promptly gave up his nuclear program and even invited U.N. weapons inspectors in to prove it. He was not interested in becoming the next Saddam Hussein.

When Obama bombed Gadhafi, the NY Times excitedly jumped on board to support the action. After all, Gadhafi, was guilty of killing hundreds of his own people. (You should remember what the same media said about Reagan when he dropped some bombs on Gadhafi in the 1980s. Reagan was classified as a terrorist for that action.) Coincidentally, President Bashar Hafez al-Assad in Syria was left alone to preside over the slaughter of more than 100,000 of his people without so much as a bad word from the Liberal Media here. I guess it all depends upon which faction of Islam you follow.

After the Libyans had chased and killed Gadhafi out in the desert, a year later some happy Islamists murdered our ambassador and three other Embassy; but as Hillary Clinton explained so clearly, "What difference, at this point, does it make?" Apparently it makes no difference. The nonsense is seen in that we are railing against the democracies that existed in Egypt and somewhat in Libya. Then in Iraq, where we have earlier helped to start a democracy, we are told by the White House we must leave that nation immediately. The democracy in Iraq was starting to work, now with the U.S. Troops pulled out the radical al Qaeda is moving back in. Where is the sense in that move? Looked at Germany lately? We still have troops there, 30 years after the Wall fell and 70 years after WWII, but not in Iraq because Bush led us there. We cannot have that. For ones who may cry, "It's so dangerous in Baghdad!" Well, have you looked at south Chicago lately? It is much safer in Baghdad!

The one place Obama should have intervened was Iran. The moderate, pro-Western, educated Iranian people are wonderful people but were being shot in the street in 2010 for protesting an election stolen by Mahmoud Ahmadinejad, a self-proclaimed messianic individual in a Members Only jacket. There was a clear alternative in that case that did not involve the Muslim Brotherhood, to wit: the actual winner of the election. However, Obama just turned his back on the Iranians. Democrats are so opposed to promoting the United States' interests around the globe (unless it is a socialist interest or one of the Muslim Brotherhood), it does not occur to them that, sometimes, our national interests might coincide with the interests of other citizens of the country who live there.

Then There Is the "Ever-Hidden" Obama Doctrine

Liberals made fun of Sarah Palin for not being able to define "the Bush doctrine." Yet no liberal can accurately define "the Obama doctrine." They have no clue what it is. After watching the last six years of foreign policy, I can give the correct definition; **It is simply this: "What does the Muslim Brotherhood want? Then, damn it, give it to them!"** To practice that doctrine is to truly leap in only to make the rest of the world a more dangerous place. Well, at least Egyptians are safer now than they are away from Morsi; thanks to their military and no thanks to Obama.

Despite the killings around the world in the name of Islam, and there have been hundreds of thousands of them in just the last few years, Obama has been unable to pull himself away from vacations, the pool, golf course or the ice cream cone in his hand to focus on the problems. Finally, he did release a statement; but he just reiterated his support for the Muslim Brotherhood in Egypt. When Morsi was overthrown, Obama reacted in grandiose manner by announcing that he was cancelling the biannual joint military exercise in Egypt between that nation and the U.S.

This was Obama's foreign policy: retaliation for the Egyptian military's crackdown on the Brotherhood, despite the fact that the Brotherhood has been burning churches, terrorizing and killing Christians all over Egypt. Instead of backing the Muslim Brotherhood, he should have been punishing it with whatever power he felt he had, along with all the Egyptian protesters. I just wonder what doctrine he really learned in the Reverend Wright's presence. Oh, that's right. His claim to be a Christian was just a pretense. Actions speak louder than words. What a disaster in Egypt, a microcosm of his dealings throughout the Middle East. That has been the disastrous consequences in country to country where Obama has been backing the Muslim Brotherhood, in Jordan, then in Libya, in and around Israel, and now in Egypt.

In the midst of street fighting in Cairo, Obama had the un-mitigating gall to utter the bald-faced lie, "We don't take sides" in the Egypt conflict. That is way up the tree next to "I didn't inhale" and "I did not have sex with that woman, Miss Lewinsky," spoken by another famous progressive liberal. Memo to Obama: "We do take sides: The side of political freedom and individual rights. Or at least we've taken that side until you arrived." But Obama has chosen to take the opposite side, the side of the Muslim Brotherhood.

Obama has been a patsy for the Muslim Brotherhood; not all has gone well for him there. Now Egypt is calling him out on it. Current President Adli Mansour declared his intention to sign the U.N.'s resolution acknowledging the Armenian genocide; a clear slap in the face to the pro-Sharia, pro-Muslim Brotherhood, Erdogan regime in Turkey. To re-Islamize Turkey rapidly has come down now as a strong priority for the Brotherhood in response. Obama loves Erdogan, calling him his closest friend among world leaders. He does what Erdogan recommends, because he thinks it wins him more influence in the Muslim world. What is really happening is that the Obama is now helping Erdogan attain dreams of restoring the Ottoman Empire; just as he had backed the Islamic supremacists in Egypt.

Obama has done nothing to end the slaughter of non-Muslims under the Sharia or protect the Christians in Egypt. He did not say a word about Christians being murdered or the burned churches in his short address he has been too busy vacationing and making calls supporting the Brotherhood. Not one word!! Instead, his agenda shows that he supports the savages. His agenda is seen not in words but in his sins of commission and omission.

Obama has established a hallmark for himself as one who will abandon any religious group and help them to suffer tribulation under Sharia law. Christians and Jews in Egypt, Indonesia, Thailand, the Philippines, Lebanon, Malaysia, Libya, the U.S.A., or pick your country where these crimes of killing, oppression and ethnic cleansing are being done. According to Joseph Farah and World Net Daily, more than 40 churches were destroyed in one week in Egypt alone, all at the hands of the Muslim Brotherhood. It has become open season on Christians.

All these crimes go on without further mention from Obama. The Brotherhood's hideouts are being stockpiled with weapons and ammunition. They beat, torture, and kill any activists seeking to leave, plus they exploit women and children for their own purposes. The Brotherhood supporters took to the streets firing on soldiers and police. The Brotherhood supporters destroyed dozens of churches in one week, killing any Christians they could find, all the while chanting, "With our blood, our souls, we will defend Islam." Note they were not defending Egypt but Islam. It appears that in this apocalyptic theatre, that must be Obama's chant too.

When the Egyptian military (the new government) rolled into town, they had to clean out the Brotherhood's "terror camps," where these sub-human creatures were preparing for civil war in the midst of people being tortured and murdered. Obama shows his colors in criticizing the Egyptian military and not standing in solidarity with the soldiers and police officers who were being brutally murdered by the Muslim Brotherhood.

He, Obama, has supported this evil Brotherhood from day one of his presidency. In 2008, he said he had campaigned in all "57 states," literally that is ironically the exact total of all the countries of the Muslim empire. He was speaking of the 50 U.S. States, but his mind was back home with the Muslim Brotherhood. He has placed Muslim Brotherhood advisers in his administration, even within Homeland Security. He has invited this Muslim Brotherhood to places where before they have

Chapter Five — The Trouble with the "Great Pretender"

been forbidden to be, such as his notorious appeasement speech in Cairo on June 4, 2009. (They were banned from the site at the time and should not have been able to attend.) All this was done to be a pointed attack on Mubarak at that time. Obama's public and outspoken support of the Brotherhood in Cairo including his outreach to them in Egypt, set the stage for their coup in January, 2011. However, Obama has kept his administration's comments very low key. For example, his director of national intelligence, James Clapper, called Egypt's branch of the Muslim Brotherhood movement "largely secular." Obama then went further and threatened any opposition to the Brotherhood with withdrawal of billions in U.S. aid after he helped oust Hosni Mubarak.

At least the Simon Wiesenthal Center has called on the world to recognize the Muslim Brotherhood for what it actually is: a hate group second to none. Wiesenthal is one of the few legitimate Jewish organizations in the U.S., fighting for freedom and equality for all and speaking out against Islamic anti-Semitism, which is the gravest threat which Jewish people face today. If the threats had been made to illegal aliens, blacks, Muslims or Hispanics, the media would have been screaming "Racism!" Another sign the media is doing the bidding of Obama.

If Obama had done nothing, that would have been appalling by itself, but he has done much worse. He went so far as to remove the sections about religious freedom and religious persecution from the 'Country Reports on Human Rights' which the State Department has released. Frankly, Obama's metrics are terrible and gruesome. To call his actions amateurish is dead wrong. They are deliberate actions to support the evils of the Muslim Brotherhood which wars with righteousness, with Christians, Jews, etc. and with America. His bloody fingerprints are there. <u>Under any reasonable definition, it's treason from within.</u>

America cannot, must not, and hopefully will not continue to sanction a president who is favorably drawn to Sharia Law. The proof is seen in the Sharia czars he has appointed. Obama was elected not only to protect and defend America and our Constitution, but to lead the free world. He has abandoned both tasks: he despises the Constitution and has detached himself from dealing in the free world issues. He has filled the balance of his time by promoting the Brotherhood. But he has not. If you doubt it, then you must not remember the following narrative taken from a 2008 Sunday morning televised *Meet The Press*. It was on Sunday's Sept. 7, 2008 show.

> THE THEN Senator Obama was asked about his stance on the American Flag. General Bill Gann' USAF (ret.) asked Obama to explain WHY he does not follow protocol when the National Anthem is played. The General stated to Obama that according to the United States Code, Title 36, Chapter 10, Sec. 171: During rendition of the national anthem, when the flag is displayed, all present (except those in uniform) are expected to stand at attention facing the flag with the right hand over the heart. Or, at the very least, "Stand and Face It."

Senator Obama replied: "As I've said about the flag pin, I don't want to be perceived as taking sides. There are a lot of people in the world to whom the American flag is a symbol of oppression. . ." He added, "The anthem itself conveys a war-like message. You know, the bombs bursting in air and all that sort of thing."

Obama continued: "The National Anthem should be 'swapped' for something less parochial and less bellicose. I like the song 'I'd Like To Teach the World To Sing'. If that were our anthem, then, I might salute it. In my opinion, we should consider reinventing our National Anthem as well as 'redesign' our Flag to better offer our enemies hope and love. It's my intention, if elected, to disarm America to the level of acceptance to our Middle East Brethren. If we, as a Nation of warring people, conduct ourselves like the nations of Islam, where peace prevails — perhaps a state or period of mutual accord could exist between our governments . . ."

"When I Become President, I will seek a pact of agreement to end hostilities between those who have been at war or in a state of enmity, and a freedom from disquieting oppressive thoughts. We as a Nation, have placed upon the nations of Islam, an unfair injustice which is WHY my wife disrespects the Flag and she and I have attended several flag burning ceremonies in the past."

"Of course now, I have found myself about to become The President of the United States and I have put my hatred aside. I will use my power to bring CHANGE to this Nation, and offer the people a new path. My wife and I look forward to becoming our Country's First black Family. Indeed, CHANGE is about to overwhelm the United States of America."

All the while, the media such as MSNBC, NBC, ABC, CBS, and CNN have been an activist arm and literally campaign central for Obama and his administration. These so called media centers are nothing more than campaign offices to do the bidding of the White House. Even little Yahoo News has become the same, since it refuses to publish any event which can be perceived as negative for their "anointed one."

Too many Americans are woefully unaware of the catastrophic consequences of this rogue president, since these sources are where they get news, if they get any at all. If anyone dares to challenge his despicable activities, people will say, "It can't be — the news didn't report that!" If someone offers a big enough challenge, they are simply attacked by tentacles of the regime, the media, and are usually called "racists." It is a sign that America is in free-fall. When I look at this mess, it appears Winston Churchill's statement was right. While not intended to be comical he said, "The best argument against democracy is a five-minute conversation with the average voter."

Take the unemployment U-3 numbers in Figure 8, presented by this president in the summer of 2014:

CHAPTER FIVE — THE TROUBLE WITH THE "GREAT PRETENDER"

Figure 8

Measure	Not seasonally adjusted			Seasonally adjusted					
	June 2013	May 2014	June 2014	June 2013	Feb. 2014	Mar. 2014	Apr. 2014	May 2014	June 2014
U-1 Persons unemployed 15 weeks or longer, as a percent of the civilian labor force	3.9	3.1	2.8	4.0	3.5	3.5	3.2	3.1	2.9
U-2 Job losers and persons who completed temporary jobs, as a percent of the civilian labor force	3.8	3.0	3.0	3.9	3.5	3.5	3.4	3.2	3.1
U-3 Total unemployed, as a percent of the civilian labor force (official unemployment rate)	7.8	6.1	6.3	7.5	6.7	6.7	6.3	6.3	6.1
U-4 Total unemployed plus discouraged workers, as a percent of the civilian labor force plus discouraged workers	8.4	6.5	6.7	8.1	7.2	7.1	6.7	6.7	6.5
U-5 Total unemployed, plus discouraged workers, plus all other persons marginally attached to the labor force, as a percent of the civilian labor force plus all persons marginally attached to the labor force	9.3	7.3	7.5	9.0	8.1	8.0	7.6	7.6	7.3
U-6 Total unemployed, plus all persons marginally attached to the labor force, plus total employed part time for economic reasons, as a percent of the civilian labor force plus all persons marginally attached to the labor force	14.6	11.7	12.4	14.2	12.6	12.7	12.3	12.2	12.1

A closer look at the remaining statistics on the chart above is where one can find a closer approximation of what the real unemployment really is. The reported numbers against the backdrop of the real numbers are a good example of the lying done by this president.

Note the official unemployment number presented by Obama for June 2014 was a reduced 6.1 percent. It is in every rational way, a fake number: a lie. When you start counting all the people who want a job but gave up looking for one, all the people forced into part-time jobs who want a full-time job, all the people who dropped off the unemployment rolls because their unemployment benefits ran out, you get a little closer picture of what the true unemployment picture really is. That number is in the last row labeled above U-6, a much higher number at 12.1 percent. Both numbers are inaccurate and would be listed as much higher, were it not for the millions of former workers who have totally dropped out of the workforce, having given up on finding a new job; none of which Obama wants to even discuss. The result: unemployment numbers presented by this president are an absolute farce.

The ignorance of many voters has set the stage for the wool to be pulled over their eyes by such reports. The same ignorance has allowed Liberals to use the class warfare in this country on ALL the Democrats and many of the Republicans, which is unforgivable. Everybody in politics claims they want to get everybody out of poverty. What is the difference between the poor and any other class? Wealth. And what is often criticized by the left? Wealth. Wealth is one of the most misunderstood, mischaracterized states of being for a human being, because it is bastardized by politics. We want everybody to get out of poverty. But when someone does escape from poverty, they are ripped to shreds by leftists and Democrats. Wealth is a dirty word. Wealthy is an even dirtier word. Poverty is what is common. The wealth, the standard of living produced by the economy of this country, again is the exception.[87]

The summary of history shows that America became an exceptional nation due to its unique beginning on Biblical principles and a Puritan rigor and ruggedness that came here with the Pilgrims. Individualism was the engine of development within this society that built a system to ensure individual freedom through a system of law. Over the years, in spite of our blatant shortcomings and self-betrayals, our society became great; America evolved into a prosperous and exceptional nation. Since then, we have been about the business of deconstructing this great country through more than a few facilitators. Since the 1920s, individual responsibility began to be replaced by moral and cultural relativism. Since the early 1960s we have debilitated our public education system, removing the platform of morality and spiritual guidance. Since the late 1960s, we have begun listening to Liberals who among other things have been falsely claiming that white people are racist by nature and must confess to that national blemish.

For decades that Liberal Progressive harangue has been like an evil repetitious drumbeat getting into the minds of many who would listen. The result has been an artificial guilt that reached its penultimate when collectively the nation decided to elect a "black" man as president — all in a move attempting to compensate an ethnic group for their claim of mistreatment and loss. Make no mistake there was mistreatment, but they were not the only ethnic group mistreated. Whites, Indians, Asian, Pacific Islanders and Hispanic were all mistreated at various times. Enter stage right, Mr. Obama.

Alinsky's faith and rules for radicals had are a fact. Also a fact is that Alinsky was a hero to Mr. Obama, because of Alinsky's dreams for America. Wanting America to drop democracy and adopt a Marxist type regime, he wrote his "Rules." The most famous of the 13 rules are: (3) Attack your enemy to increase insecurity, anxiety and uncertainty; (4) Force the enemy live up to their own book of rules; (8) Keep the pressure on Conservatives; (13) Pick the target, freeze it, personalize it, and polarize it. Disciples following

Karl Marx was another liberal mentor ready for the following. The ten essential principles Marx held for a nation to become communistic were very appealing. To Obama, America must have seemed as a fruit ready to fall into the basket for what he called hope and change. The principles Marx taught were: central banking system, government controlled education, government controlled labor, government ownership of transportation and communication vehicles, government ownership of agricultural means and factories, total abolition of private property, property rights confiscation, heavy income tax on everyone, at a rate of 80 per cent, elimination of rights

CHAPTER FIVE — THE TROUBLE WITH THE "GREAT PRETENDER"

to inheritance through taxation, etc., and regional planning done by government.

Most of the problems, and there were many, making Obama an undesirable candidate were not known by the bulk of Americans. One problem, was the facilitator to the other problems; a lack of vetting. Obama received less vetting than an average town would do in selecting its village idiot. Second, there was his upbringing in a communist home with the communist mindset — the dreams of his father. Another is his close association with known terrorists and thugs such as Chicago based Bill Ayers and Tony Rezko. The transformation of the nation of which he spoke while leaning on those borrowed words "hope and change" marked his presidency as being something more than inexperience or a lack of character. Character was there — just not the type most Americans had hoped for. Mr. Obama was conditioned to be an adversary of American exceptionalism as he came of age in a bubble of post-1960s. In his mind America's premiere status of being named exceptionalism in the world came at a cost. It was a deal Americans signed with the devil. It was a trade to receive Satan's gifts of militarism, racism, greed, environmental neglect, and industry of sexism in order to gain the broad economic, military and even cultural supremacy in the world. Obama sees America's greatness as a fruit of evil much more than a devotion to freedom.

When Mr. Obama campaigned, he did not explicitly run on an anti-exceptionalism platform. Once elected however, it became clear that his ideas of when and where to apply the power of the office was going to be based on old East European Socialism. This is where he had literal worship and devotion for a philosophy; in big government, in his passion for redistribution of wealth, and ludicrous desire for reparations. He has gone about the sabotaging of American capitalism itself. He has a bent to punish the success of this nation while going out of his way to reward the brutality of the Muslim Brotherhood whenever and wherever he can, another of his devotions.

America's fate is to pay for its exceptionalism by being both defamed and burdened by a liberal false guilt. Others hate us, are envious, resentful, or admiring around us. We had a huge target on our backs since Muslims and especially al Qaeda despised anything more than tents and camels — they attacked on 9/11. They chose America because we are viewed as the leader of the western world. Thus we became a trophy for them that they could steal lives from America while they stole our exceptionalism.

Following that attack, liberals went to work again with their sick music that it is our fault they attacked. Their lyrics made many among us begin to feel anxious about our singular position among nations — guilty about racism, about homosexuality, about environmentalism, about Christianity, and even about making a good life. The old enemy of Marxism was being called the villain; that is capitalism. So we have moved from feeling certain about who we were, whose we were to that of uncertainty. And it all started by the Leftists taking a stand against the exceptional American spirit. They have continued to this day having a relentless attack on free-enterprise, naming it as the villain of imperialism, racism, global warming, and any other problem that arises.

However, with their ludicrous stance, the political Left is left with the position of trading what they call the weight of greatness for the relief of being mediocre. But that brings an unforeseen to now problem; mediocrity breeds a lack of action. Nobody comes around anymore; average does not attract attention or a crowd. The proof is seen in the empires of the history, something liberals do not learn well.

The big questions facing individuals, families, neighborhoods, communities, cities and even states today are these; how will we respond to the liberal choices Obama has given us? This is a pivotal time of decision: do we rise up in in rededication to and reaffirmation for what made us great from the beginning? Or do we slide quietly into that night letting go of those values and trademarks that lifted America above the remaining nations? The choice must be yours to make.

This administration is the latest in a parade of fools. In full blossom it has produced massive destruction: from the horrible murders of innocent Christian and Jewish people around the world by Islamists that not only continues but is growing; the unilateral abuse of power in the Oval Office displayed in the criminal activity against the American people shown above; and the culmination of a century-long attack upon Christian ethics and fixed moral standards leading to a breakdown and bankruptcy of the American culture. All this is a result of making poor choices in ethical standards which bled into selections in elections of these so-called leaders. If our nation survives, hopefully some historian in the future will have the courage to at least tell the truth about Obama and all the impeachable offenses he committed.

"A government is only to be supported by pure religion or austere morals. Private and public virtue is the only foundation of republics."

— John Adams

2ⁿᵈ *President of the United States*

"If ever time should come, when vain and aspiring men shall possess the highest seats in Government, our country will stand in need of its experienced patriots to prevent its ruin."

— Samuel Adams, 1776

Chapter Six

The Truth About: Discrimination, Prejudice, the Old and the New Racism, Slavery, and Reparation

> *"... I have a dream that my four children will one day live in a nation where they will be not be judged by the color of their skin but by the content of their character..."* — Martin Luther King, Jr.[1]

WHATEVER ONE MIGHT THINK ABOUT DR. Martin Luther King, Jr., and there are many views: good or bad, saint or villain, patriot or Communist, altruistic or fraud. As a young teenager, I had admiration for his messages because his words rang true both about civil and moral uprightness, especially as applied to establishing equality among the races; and for his words about personal responsibility for men to work and provide for themselves and his family. His "I have a dream" speech given in August 1963 in Washington especially resounded with me. While King primarily spoke that day of seeing " . . . one hundred years later [following Lincoln's Emancipation Proclamation] the Negro still is not free . . . "[2] most people heard that as a speech attempting only to propel the African American population upward. Maybe that is what he meant, but I saw and heard it differently then, as that thirteen year-old boy. I still see it differently today. In my hearing, King painted a portrait with his rhetoric of an integrated and unified America, true civil rights for all. It did not matter his or her race, income level, or status in society. As one business colleague said, "Today, unless mistaken, I believe those words apply to every race and every color of American."[3]

Questions may arise such as, "What do all these words and topics in the title of this chapter have in common?" Answer: they are all things that the media and Liberal Left has accused the Conservative Right of either inciting, using, being, causing doing, and in the case of the last word — needing to do. These answers and their conclusions are both wrong. The data shows that anyway, but the media and Leftists can only muster the one conclusion.

For those living outside the United States, looking at and listening to the television and radio broadcasts and commentary about activities regarding "race" and "race relations" in this country has to run the gambit from being confusing, hilarious, sad, and even maddening. It must have many people confused. It comes under the general category of insanity, sub-filed in the sub-section named, "I'm drinking the Kool-Aid." With regard to rhetoric about race, never has a society become so incensed with certain words and terminology. Many of the words are being used as a political whip by minorities all aimed at doing a money grab. Hearing all such talk on radio and TV makes one wonder about how long our society can really survive with the current mindset. Surely if there were aliens from another part of the cosmos monitoring broadcasts of America's radio and television programming, such as Carl Sagan suggested could happen in his novel *Contact*; the aliens most likely would refuse to provide any engineering schematics for a machine through which to we could reach them, thinking we are unable to negotiate complex or intelligent drawings. They would probably check our civilization off their list as not being able to hold any reasonable conversations. Possibly they would beam us a copy of Webster's 1887 unabridged dictionary along with a one-page note stating simply, "Read this."

Diving into our words in our title, we should examine each starting with their appropriate contexts.

1. Discrimination

Possibly a little definition and history of this word would be in order. "Discrimination" has been for generations a word used to describe the wise use of intellect and logic in discerning and making choices between not only good and bad, but also good, better and best. Case in point: a person in the 18th or 19th centuries could have well been described as having "discriminating taste" in reading material when focusing on the classics, the Bible, Shakespeare or Flavius Josephus, Thomas Aquinas, and Aristotle in studying ancient history. As late as the 1960s, the Muriel Cigar Company ran commercials on TV with Edie Adams as their spokesperson. Her provocative coaxing of male viewers in a singing sales pitch, noting she could see you were a man of distinction, good looking, and so refined; followed by "Hey big spender, spend a little dime with me," and "Pick one up and smoke it some time." While the word "discriminating" was not directly used, it certainly was implied in virile terms substituting the words "distinction" and "refined," (a requirement necessary for rhyming with the surrounding lyrics) and implied by Edie Adam's actions.[4]

Today, we can use that adjective, "discriminating" as descriptive of or modifying the positive actions of a person choosing a diet that is gluten-free or sugar-free as opposed to one that is filled with starches, refined sugar and fat. Or because I love classic black and white moves as opposed to watching the so-called "reality" TV shows of today, or even the popular game show Wheel of Fortune. It could be said that I too have discriminating taste, obviously meaning in this case something very constructive, cultural and therefore positive by my choice of viewing. In other words, discrimination, the verb discriminating, or the adverb form, discriminatively, all have a very positive connotation historically, and has for hundreds of years. It solidifies and classifies similar actions of a person, promoting them upward in society and culture, connoting a more judicious path.

Discrimination in its original form then is an everyday act about choosing, making a choice. But even in the act of making good choices, there can be both positive and negative results. When choosing one of Edie Adam's Muriel cigars for example, other marketed brands would be left in the wake due to our choice. When we choose to eat Italian food at an Italian restaurant, we perform what is called discrimination against any other food; Tex Mex, Greek, Chinese, Thai, or American food just for that evening. Granted, most people would say this type of discrimination harms no one, and most would say that this is not discrimination at all. But thinking about it longer, there is some harm that comes to other restaurants. There are decreased sales first of all. The stock and economic value of the various other restaurants is negatively impacted since Italian food was selected even if only for one evening. That impact can be much deeper if I have a party of 200 persons, for which I hire a catering company to serve Italian. I have then discriminated against the same American, Greek, Tex Mex, and Chinese catering businesses in a much larger way. Or if friends and I decide to stick with Italian food for weeks on end, we really do bring harm to other restaurants and segments of the food people in certain restaurants could lose their jobs, or some places close. Discrimination has both positive and negative impacts in cigar sales, in food sales, in other businesses, and in life.

We choose associates, friends, and relationships based on decisions those individuals typically make in life; how similar they are to ours. For example, where they go: such as the same church, same restaurants, same clubs, same university, same neighborhood, same golf course, same work; what they do: visit same places, same museums, play golf, softball, football, basketball, hike, bike, etc.; or what they are: same age, same race, male or female. Our lives are spent discriminating for something and against something, in just about everything we decide. In other words, choice necessitates discrimination.

When we modify the term to reflect race, sex, height, weight or age, we merely specify a stricter level of discrimination in the choice criteria. Even in employment, all hiring managers and interviewers make "discriminating" choices about candidates. Usually they do so in response to a series of questions; "Does the candidate have the skill sets? The necessary experience? Possess the motivation to do the job?" We have discrimination laws in the country for the employment arena, but note those are against the use of color, creed, ethnicity, etc. in making a hiring decision. Said differently, discriminating based on valid work history, skill sets, or capabilities is appropriate according to the law.

It would be ludicrous, not to mention even intolerable, if our government outlawed discrimination in our daily lives. Even if they did, you can bet the Senate, House, and White House would indemnify or exempt themselves from that law. It would not apply to them, and it would be applied with only political correctness in the public. But before condemning this statement, one should consider this possibility. Imagine starting to play a round of golf on the first tee, and being told by an official that you could not play with a person of the same skin color as you. Or just as you select a mountain resort for the perfect summer vacation spot, it is nixed by government regulators because you discriminated against the beach cities. Then, your choice of a thin dinner partner or of a friend is outlawed. Why? Because you did not choose someone who was heavy; the choice of a skinny person you selected is viewed as an act of personal discrimination against others not so fortunate. Imagine having the same charge leveled because you did not choose someone taller, or black, white, brown or other color of skin. Just about any action we could take would be turned into a ridiculous circus attraction, all because a government regulator said someone would be left out of the loop. No matter what the choice of person we make could bring a charge of active discrimination based on the government memo of the day regarding race, sex, height, weight, age, mannerisms, college selection, looks or some other trait.

Several years ago I was a national executive board member of a minority-based engineering association. The topic of about any day among many of the student members of the association was equal employment opportunity. That seemed natural since the employment arena has been saturated with affirmative action and most of them were either currently looking for employment, or soon would be. Over lunch one day when in the headquarters of the association, a group of five college students joined me at my table. I asked them if they believed wholeheartedly in equal employment opportunity. To a person, they all enthusiastically said "Absolutely, yes." Then I asked them when they graduated, whether they planned to give every employer an equal opportunity to employ them. Their answer was "No, probably not." Most of them said they planned on talking with just a select group of employers based on location, industry-type, advertised flex work schedules, benefits, etc. In a very real way, that is nothing less than discrimination. I asked them, if they were not going to give every employer an equal opportunity to hire them. When they said "No," I then asked "What is fair about requiring an employer to give them an equal opportunity to be hired if they will not reciprocate?" While the thought of this scene may seem ridiculous, and the actions of trying to fulfill it would be preposterous, it still speaks of discrimination. Obviously we live and work within the law. Those of us who have been in the business of identifying top talent for both external hire positions and internal succession planning in a firm will to a fault follow the law. We look for the best possible matches for the company to drive excellent results for customers, stakeholders, and profit motive.

Many people sustain the thought that certain forms of discrimination are OK. I am one of those. "But it is racial discrimination that is truly offensive," many will

Chapter Six — The Truth about Discrimination, Prejudice...

say. That is when I confess my own history of in this arena. Most of the time, those friends of mine, with whom I have spent most my time have been white, like me, though I am mixed race; white and Cherokee Nation. In my teenage years, while growing up in a predominately white area, my Cherokee heritage did not come in play at that time. I was always classified as white. Other friends and acquaintances are great people, some Mexican, Indian, Native American, Chinese, African, a Japanese man, and one great friend from the Middle East. He is from Arabic descent, and I spend some quality time with him when schedules match. But more times than not, I spend time with those who have the same schedule as me. I discriminate based on their proximity to me, their matching schedules, where they live and work, what they like to do. Those are the ones with whom I spend the bulk of my time. And so in the strictest definition of our term we are considering, I ended up discriminating against one or more of them at times. And the people I spent most of my time with were more like me in many respects, including color. It appears that most Americans act similarly by racially discriminating in setting up their friendships with people who tend to be like themselves. I wonder if the young blacks I see at shopping centers think of their actions as being discrimination, as they run together. Or the Hispanics, or Asians, or "Native Americans," as the Equal Employment Opportunity Commission classifies them, as they will usually socialize with people like themselves. Isn't that discrimination too? Or is it discrimination only when white people get together with other white people? The truth is it is all discrimination in one form or another since every one of these groups and individuals made a choice with whom they wanted to associate. It came down to a choice. College choices are the same. People discriminate in making the choice of their school based on a number of criteria. Marriages are the same with mates usually selected from the same race, not always but usually. According to the 1992 Census Bureau, only 2.2 percent of Americans were married to people other than their own race or ethnicity. To say that 97.8 percent of married folks are racists is the wrong interpretation of data.

Discrimination in choice is made when we select a college to attend, or a person to date, or fraternity houses to join, etc. Or the groups of students with whom we "hang out." Higher IQ individuals tend to hang out with friends and have gotten married to mates with high IQs. High-income people tend to mate with other high-income people. It is the same with education. To the extent there is a racial correlation between these characteristics, racial discrimination in mate selection exaggerates the differences in the society's intelligence and income distribution. There would be greater equality if there were not this kind of discrimination in mate selection.

With so much emphasis by our government to keep society from discriminating in schools, employment, friendships, etc., it is interesting to note, that the Feds and many state officials discriminate, too. Please allow me to illustrate in just a couple of simple ways. One, over the past decades I recall Washington politicians making loud speeches insisting that school age children throughout society be integrated, and bused around cities to make that happen when possible. However, when it came to their children, they chose to exempt them from such treatment.

A second example, I have a friend who performs weddings at a state prison in California. For obvious reasons the weddings are performed behind bars in the prison. The interesting thing to note is that prisoners held behind the walls are always segregated according to race. The prisoners choose to stay in groups of the same race, since this affords them more protection from individuals of a different race. You can classify this in several ways, but at the end of the road, you have state-sponsored discrimination. The same thing exists in federal prisons in California. I agree that the state and the Feds are doing the right thing, but it is still discrimination based on race. There are all kinds of the paradoxes here. One of which is that the federal government discriminately both actively and passively.

In today's society, many people choose to use the word discrimination in dealing with the subject of illegal immigrants; meaning that if someone is opposed to illegals coming into a country, they are discriminating against that group, and are therefore branded as racists. When individuals choose to be with someone of a similar color, creed, or religion, income bracket, etc., it is in the strictest sense discrimination.

Common sense rationale suggests that not all discrimination should be eliminated. So the question is, what kind of discrimination should be permitted? I am guessing the answer depends on one's values for freedom of association, keeping in mind freedom of association implies freedom not to associate.

Discrimination Grew Up To Become a 4-Lettered Word

In today's America, due to some of the poorest education that can be found on earth and in some instances, no education at all, many people have focused on only the baser elements of how the word can be used, resulting in it taking on only a nasty, degenerate state dealing with only those negative choices making it refer to race, color, creed, ethnicity, language, nation of origin, or birth place. Normally, religion is on that list, but I have selected to leave it off in this application. The reason: today's leftists apply their use of the term religion inconsistently, nearly always being negative toward any faith of conservatives, especially the "Christian" faith. Concurrently, liberals are usually positive in dealing with individuals of other religions, especially Muslims. Liberals are notoriously weak in identifying important traits in several areas of life. Religion is no different. And therein lies the problem since their particular discrimination is based on faulty thinking and ignorance. Professing themselves to be wise, they became fools because they could not distinguish a bad belief system for a good one. They have become guilty of "prejudice" based on their total lack of knowledge and understanding.

2. Prejudice

Prejudice is another extremely useful term that has often been morphed into a racial term, much like the word discrimination. Seeing the word defined in a 100+ year old dictionary and comparing it to the current definitions in modern dictionaries illustrates what time has done to this word. First the older definition:

Prej"u*dice (?) n. [F. préjudice, L. praejudicium; prae before + judicium judgment. See *Prejudicate, Judicial*.]

1. Foresight. [Obs.]

    "Measures will too often be decided according to their probable effect, not on the national prosperity and happiness, but on the **prejudices**, interests, and pursuits of the governments and people of the individual States." This quote from Federalist 46 demonstrates the use word with this definition in the late 18th Century.

2. An opinion or judgment formed without due examination; prejudgment; a leaning toward one side of a question from other considerations than those belonging to it; an unreasonable predilection for, or objection against, anything; especially, an opinion or leaning adverse to anything, without just grounds, or before sufficient knowledge.

3. Preconceived opinion that is not based on reason or actual experience.

Now the modern definition of the word according to Merriam Webster is as follows:

Prej·u·dice *noun* \'pre-jə-dəs\

1. An unfair feeling of dislike for a person or group because of race, sex, religion, etc.

2. A feeling of like or dislike for someone or something especially when it is not reasonable or logical.

Just a glance shows how the word has changed in its use over the last two centuries, and actually most of the change has occurred in the last 70-80 years. That is mostly due to the hijacking of the word by the Progressive Liberal Left. The word originates from the Latin; the root word is praejudicium, which means "an opinion or judgment formed with either not enough data or without due examination." Therefore, we might define prejudicial acts as decision-making on the basis of inadequate information. On that basis, we might say that a person who speaks first, without engaging the brain, in some instances could be "prejudiced." Using that definition, it is so easily seen that many so-called journalists, such as Chris Matthews are prejudiced.

Many Kinds of Prejudice

In today's world, there are several areas of prejudice that can be seen outside of the typical use of word in a race relations environment. For example, in the market place there is instant information and data available, providing an atmosphere for prejudice in educational opportunities. The Internet and so many other sources of information are available for those who want to attend classes remotely. People can in some opinions cheat their education opportunities where the experience of face to face gathering in a classroom, working in small groups with other students, could be beneficial but have been cut out. There is nothing wrong with going to school "on line" but one could be accused of — you got it — being prejudiced because they did not do college on a brick and mortar campus.

There are other types of prejudice, too. Visualize the following: You are on a camping trip with friends in the north woods of Wyoming near Yellowstone. After a hearty breakfast of bacon and eggs, you get ready to do some fishing. You open the front door, only to be greeted by a huge grizzly bear, his face two feet from yours. The bad news is he smells the bacon and eggs on your breath, along with the same aroma coming from your kitchen. The boring part of this story is your response in slamming the door. To make your action the least bit interesting or even humorous, we have to add actors like Dan Aykroyd and the late John Candy from a similar scene from the movie *The Great Outdoors* to get the average person to pay attention long enough to get a chuckle and eventually get the point of the scene.

Discussing why you or they would slam the door is a bit more stimulating, especially if sitting in a real classroom on a real campus in a real small group. It is unlikely that Candy's decision to slam that door was based on any detailed statistical models gained from studying a PowerPoint® presentation or data from an Excel® spreadsheet about grizzly bears and their habits, or some particulars of the grizzly bear species when he is standing at your door. More likely his decision to slam the door is based on bear folklore, bear activity in Looney Tunes cartoons, or how he has seen other bears behave. In short, he pre-judges, stereotypes, and is therefore prejudiced toward that particular grizzly.

If a person did not pre-judge grizzly bears, he would seek more evidence about this breed of bear prior to making his decision about closing the door. That is where you would see him enroll in a class with many different movie clips regarding various species of bears and their habits. Given an impression there is no urgency in closing the door, he could have an alternative approach. He might endeavor to pet the bear, feed him some treats, talk to him and then seek safety only if the bear responded in a menacing fashion. No, the normal person would not choose that path, surmising that the anticipated cost of getting more information about the bear through personal contact is of greater danger than the expected benefits package of slamming the door, thus concluding, "All I need to know is he's a grizzly bear, and he's probably like the rest of them." By observing this person's behavior, there is no way one can say unequivocally whether he likes or dislikes bears: grizzly bears, black bears, bears, panda bears, koala bears, Smokey the Bear, or any kind of bear.

Herein Lies the Rub

Being prejudiced in today's society is almost always viewed through a lens of negativity or guilt by association. For example, in the late 1990s, due to the high crime rate in that city, the taxi commissioner of Washington, D.C., warned local cab drivers against going into low income black neighborhoods of the District and picking up "dangerous looking" passengers whom she described as young black males dressed a certain way. During the previous decade in St. Louis, MO, pizza delivery drivers were complaining to their management about delivering pizzas to black neighborhoods on the north side of town because of robberies and pizzas taken with no payment. Can one say anything unambiguous about cabbies' or pizza deliverers' likes or dislikes for blacks?

Just before an accusation of racism is made, or discrimination charges are leveled, as would be the modus operandi of the elite media in yelling, "You're a racist" for saying that, one might want to know more about those making the statement, giving the warning, and doing the complaining in these news stories. This is where the Excel® spreadsheet, PowerPoint® presentation, or just the newspaper comes in handy in presenting the data in a "visual" format. In the case of the taxi commissioner's warnings, the commissioner was black and so were most of the cabbies to which the warnings were given. In St. Louis, approximately 85 percent of the complaining pizza delivery drivers were black. So with that data in hand, we need to ask, "Are they racists?" Before we jump to answer that question, we should recall brave journalists have been reporting on the magnitude of black crime for decades. As one wrote, "It's especially revealing when a black leader such as Jesse Jackson can admit being embarrassed when, walking at night and hearing footsteps behind him, he nervously looks back and then feels a sudden sense of relief upon seeing that the person behind him is white." (Source: Fielding Greaves, *The Coastal Post*, March, 1997) And, don't you think they all respond this way, not on the basis of some pie charts which they studied about crime statistics, all presented on a PowerPoint® slide, rather just folklore, of crime statistics, and how they have seen other blacks behave. This is very simple to understand; if white people were committing the vast majority of crimes, one would feel a deep sense of fear if white youth were seen behind them on the sidewalk at night. It is called guilt by association.

People pre-judge all the time. I did with the story of the bear at the cabin door. The cabbies, the pizza delivery guys and gals, and Jackson, they all pre-judged, too. They are using the least expensive data available. It is called observation of physical characteristics in lieu of sitting through classes studying the afore mentioned spreadsheets. Simple observation over time can tell more than pie charts and graphs. In the minds of cabbies, pizza deliverers and Rev. Jackson, race was associated with a higher probability of crime and being assaulted. In spite of what some government bureaucrat might say in speaking out and condemn, real life experience tells the average person something different. Neighborhoods with houses having bars on the windows speak of a higher risk than neighborhoods where there are no bars on windows.

I know the rule in today's society. If you criticize the culture, you are certainly going to be criticized, subjected to name-calling, and in some cases, racial slurs. Do not think for a minute that as I penned these words, I was not aware that the media would pursue with a passion in name-calling, branding, etc., any author who would dare tell the truth would be subjected to such treatment. This action is however "their shtick" with anyone they choose not to like. Before they or any other reader jump the gun in a tirade, thinking I am a green-toothed hillbilly who was raised in the hills of Tennessee, or wherever it is that racists are raised these days, consider the following bio.

I was born and raised in South Los Angeles, California, in what today is called Compton. If you know anything about the history of that area, it is the black area of Los Angeles. When I was a young school child, I was definitely a minority in that part of the world. Looking at my class picture from that day, it still seems strange and also humorous that of my class of 33, there were 3 of us that were considered white. Additionally, I recall that all my friends were black except one, a little girl. That trend continued in at least the educational portion of my life as I went to university on a basketball scholarship in those dark days of discrimination of the 60s. And as I lived in the athletic dorm for football, basketball and baseball players, I was the only white athlete who had a black roommate. By the way, that was not forced on me. When the coaches were talking to each other about the uneven numbers of colored athletes (that's black AND white) there was not the right number to pair off equally by race. They were concerned about the volatility of what could happen with mixed roommates. So I volunteered privately to coach that I would be glad to have a black roommate, if someone cared to room with me. I also recall after several weeks into the semester of having a black roommate, which were going fine for my roomie and me, three other athletes dropped out of school because of grades. That freed up some space, and my roommate chose at that time to go live with a friend of his, of the same color. It seems he was being intimidated by some black athletes who did not want him rooming with a white guy, or "cracker," and being a sort of Uncle Tom. Later when I worked in industry, I labored hard to go beyond what is called affirmative action. But when it came to hiring, I chose not to look at the color of skin in making a hiring decision. I tried to be color blind, which is not what government officials want a hiring manager to do. I sought and hired what were perceived to be the best candidates based on qualifications: that is technical skills, communication skills, best fit for the culture of the company, best fit for the job. Sometimes they were protected class citizens, sometimes not.

Someone might be prone to say that I have been one to have "white privilege."

Chapter Six — The Truth about Discrimination, Prejudice . . .

Allow me to be very clear at this point and say, Yes, I was and am privileged. I was privileged to hear my father tell me when I was a young boy to, as he said it, "Get your butt out of bed and clean the snow off your mom's car so she can go to work." This should give you a hint as to my privilege. Yes, I was privileged to work hard as a boy of 10 to 17 years of age to get up at 5:15 AM every morning and feed cattle, chickens, sometimes hogs when we had them, do all the supporting chores associated with feeding the animals. Then I would come inside, bathe, eat breakfast, get ready for school, and walk the one-quarter mile to catch the bus at 7:00 AM every day. That was my white privilege. I was also privileged to work hard in school, ride the bus for 1½ hours to get home at 5:05 PM and start the chores all over again. Because my father later told me he could not afford to send me to college, I had the privilege of earning and taking a scholarship, then working harder than ever in college. My typical day was classes 7:00 -11:00 AM; work off-campus in a job from 11:15 to 5:00 PM M-F (longer on weekends), then off to B-Ball practice from 5 to 7:45 PM daily. Following college, I had the privilege to get into the world of real work. In corporate life, my white privilege (at least a few years) consisted of rising at 4:30 AM and being at work by 6:00 AM for conference calls. Usually working through lunch and normal dinner time, I would leave the office around 8:00 PM with periodic conference calls taking place with off-shore personnel at 9:00 PM to 10:00 or later in the evening. That was my white privilege!

Possibly you understand now, when I say I tune out the journalists and media elites who are saying I have white privilege. I would love to have passed my privilege along to any one of them, or anyone else claiming I have been pampered in life because of my color. I speak out now, because you should know how ridiculous such a statement of "white privilege" is. The so-called journalists have the right to say what they want. However, when they say white privilege about me, it is a lie. Maybe it depends upon your perspective, but I choose to take the privilege to tell the truth about discrimination and prejudice.

When it comes to crime, no one says that all young black males, not even a majority, pose a threat, but people are assigning probabilities, even Jesse Jackson. Such an assignment differs little from that of a physician, knowing that incidences of cardiovascular diseases are 30 percent higher among blacks than whites and prostate cancer is twice as high, giving his black patients more careful screening for these two diseases. Why? I don't know, ask the doctors. Like the cabbies, the pizza deliverers and Rev. Jackson, the doctor is engaging in what some have tried calling racial profiling; using race as an indicator of something else in the area of health.

Analytical analysis is necessary to understand purposes for decisions made. It is important to correctly identify behavior, not just jump to assumptions. Asserting that a particular behavior reflects racial likes and dislikes, which it could, when in fact it does not, is to mislead and confound whatever problem or issue one is addressing. In my personal experience I have known some white people who can be the worst trash when trying to negotiate life. However, statistics, when complete, paint an overall picture which needs our attention.

Sentencingproject.Org reports 1 in 10 black males in their 30s are in prison on any given day. Alternet.org says 1 in 3 black men will go to prison during their lifetime. Right now 30 percent of African American males, ages 20 to 29 are in or under the direction of correctional facilities. Half of all black males and 40 percent of white males have been arrested by the time they are 23. The same statistic for whites is 4 percent. 39.4 percent of the total prison and jail population in the United States in 2009 was non-Hispanic blacks, while blacks and non-Hispanic blacks made up 13.6 of the total population. (Sources: Bonczar, T. 2003 Prevalence of Imprisonment in the U.S. population, 1974-2001 Washington, D.C. — Bureau of Justice Statistics. Also see the Huffington Post, Crime and Delinquency, August 18, 2014; See also the U.S. Bureau of Justice Statistics)

Sophia Kerby further reported in her article entitled *"One in three black men go to prison?: The ten most disturbing facts about racial inequality in the U.S. Criminal Justice System,"* appeared in *American Prospect* on March 17, 2012 that between 1970 and 2005, there was a 700 percent increase in the prison population in the U.S. That data is interesting because simultaneously in this country, we were fighting a war on poverty. We obviously lost that war.

3. Old and New Racists

For generations, the white communities of America, those made up of individuals and families who form cross sections of the socioeconomic layers of business, retail, restaurant, school, and retirement, have been accused of racism and indeed there have been times when some have been guilty of the charge. It's a fact. Please notice the word "some," indicating not all, as seems to be the mantra of the media. Also true, and something you will never hear either in the media, or in the political arena, is the fact that some black individuals and families have also been guilty of racism. Liberal politicians say it is impossible for any black person to be guilty of racist thoughts or activities, simply due to their race. Racism has been and is a problem among all races of the world's population. Shouts of superiority have been launched from various individuals of separate races. Al Sharpton did unapologetically in a public forum. Ted Kennedy did behind closed doors. Individuals from every race, color and creed have said some of these things since time immemorial. Unfortunately, it is a part of our brokenness in human nature displayed in these thoughts.

Southerners are typically pointed out as those who are the real villains in the racism charges. Granted, there was a time when that charge was probably true; genteel Southerners years ago would bow their heads in shame at such accusations. Today, many of them, are rejecting the stereotyping of their region and its citizens because things have changed in Ol' Dixie. It is not because the South is free totally from racism, but because it is more so than other areas of the nation. Integration is

Chapter Six — The Truth about Discrimination, Prejudice...

far more prevalent in parts of the South over other parts of the country.

In addition, black scholars, like Harvard professor Henry Louis Gates, Jr. (who a few years ago complained about racism in Boston, which you may recall led to the ridiculous "Beer Summit" in the White House garden), have questioned what they call the myth of Lincoln as the Great Emancipator and of the North as the savior of the black race — as did Frederick Douglass more than 100 years ago. Suddenly, the history of the question has become more complicated — and, consequently, a little less important. I would remind you however, that this subject of racism is not limited to black and white issues, since Native Americans, or "Indians," Hispanics, and Asians are involved in this discussion just as much. The only reason all of them are not front and center in the news is because they are not the darlings of the media light as African Americans, or blacks, are.

But let's get back to the South again. Tens of thousands of blacks who have little contact with formal history are expressing their own dissent in opinion and in behavior. Several years ago a Gallup Poll found that in only one region did a majority of blacks believe they were treated equally: that is in Dixie — also known as the South. A Harvard study reported that in only one region did a majority of white children attend integrated schools — that was in Dixie. And the 2000 Census revealed that, in recent decades, more blacks have moved into the South than out of the South, while the reverse is true in all other regions. If you had only data and facts to guide you, you might well conclude that the Northeast is the citadel of racism in America of today — and you most likely would be right.

Today, many Americans presume that the debate over slavery in the 18th and 19th centuries turned on the question of race. Though race was an ingredient in the Great Debate, it was no more than a pinch of salt. Both proponents and opponents of slavery tended to hold the same view of blacks. The superiority of the white race was a given from colonial times to long after the passage of the 13th and 14th Amendments. For example, Abraham Lincoln took great care in his ongoing quarrel with Stephen Douglas to suggest the ways in which he believed people were different from each other. In 1857, in a speech criticizing the *Dred Scott* decision, he said,

> "I think the authors of [the Declaration of Independence] intended to include all men, but they did not intend to declare all men equal in all respects. They did not mean to say all were equal in color, size, intellect, moral developments, or social capacity. They defined with tolerable distinctness, in what respects they did consider all men created equal— equal in "certain inalienable rights, among which are life, liberty, and the pursuit of happiness."

In 1858, he said the following during the first Lincoln-Douglas debate:

> "I have no purpose to introduce political and social equality between the white and the black races. There is a physical difference between

the two which, in my judgment, will probably forever forbid their living together upon the footing of perfect equality; and inasmuch as it becomes a necessity that there must be a difference, I, as well as Judge Douglas, am in favor of the race to which I belong having the superior position."

Serious students of history are not surprised by his statement. Lincoln was a man of his time and place. Just five years earlier, Illinois had passed legislation prohibiting any black immigration into the state. It was the third such Illinois statute directed against blacks *per se*. These laws, motivated by intense racial animosity, were common in the territories and newer states.

By the turn of the next century, much of the comment on race came from the South. In 1900, Benjamin "Pitchfork Ben" Tillman — whose statue, a gift in part of the South Carolina Democrat Party, broods over the State House in Columbia — said in a speech to the U.S. Senate: "We of the South have never recognized the right of the Negro to govern white men, and we never will. We have never believed him to be equal to the white man, and we will not submit to his gratifying his lust on our wives and daughters without lynching him. I would to God the last one of them was in Africa and that none of them had ever been brought to our shores."

All three men believed blacks were less intelligent than whites. All three advocated shipping blacks back to Africa rather than allowing them to remain among whites to "amalgamate" or "mongrelize" the races. And all three accepted without question the same stereotypical view of blacks—one that, until the second half of the 20th century, supported *de jure* segregation in the South and parts of the North, *de facto* segregation elsewhere.

Tillman thought he was speaking for all white Southerners speaking in a smarmy yet haughty tone. He especially thought northern state senators were just as prejudicial saying, "We are open and honest about our racial attitudes. You aren't."

Turns out he was at least partially correct. Northern states led the nation in recruitment when the **second** Ku Klux Klan was organized in 1915. The top five states were in number of members, per a report in Kenneth T. Jackson's *The Ku Klux Klan in the City, 1915-1930*, the period in which the Klan was at the height of its political power: Indiana, 240,000; Ohio, 195,000; Texas, 190,000; Pennsylvania, 150,000; and Illinois, 95,000. In 2009, the Klan was estimated to have a total membership of around 5,000. Don't dare forget the **first** Ku Klux Klan was organized before the War Between the States (aka, Civil War) by none other than the current Democrat Party — all designed to prohibit blacks from participating in our civilization as independent citizens. Democrats did not want blacks to have the right to vote, or any other rights. Later when Democrats saw the inevitable, they elbowed their way around Republicans to claim they were saving blacks. Now Democrats stand smugly claiming it was the Republicans were the ones who burning crosses in the front yards of blacks. Incredible claims with no conscience.

Chapter Six — The Truth about Discrimination, Prejudice . . .

Today, no senator, Northern or Southern, would admit to membership in an overtly racist organization or publicly endorse white supremacy. If he did, he might well be expelled from the Senate. Indeed racism, as it is called, is now the greatest of all political sins, and the N-word has replaced the F-word as the most obscene utterance in the English language. In fact, using the "N-word," may be worse than committing murder, unless of course it is a black person using the afore mentioned "N-word." Skin color in this day does provide a license.

Not to be outdone, the Nation of Islam, a militant branch of Black Muslims in America, calling themselves "Ideology-Black Separatists" are led by Louis Farrakhan and claim a 2014 membership of approximately 400,000 nationwide. The Pew Research Center claims that one percent of blacks in American claim to be "Black Muslims."

The substructure for this change in culture was laid in 1948, when a group of liberal Democrats captured their party's national convention and, with a series of high-decibel speeches, and made what they called "civil rights" the focal issue of the campaign. Franklin D. Roosevelt, Jr., of New York; Blair Moody of Michigan; and Hubert Humphrey of Minnesota led the charge, excoriating the South for its racism and Jim Crow laws, capturing the high ground for the liberal wing of the party. In reality, civil rights is a much bigger issue than only a black issue — our society is turned upside down now where people of all colors and creeds have their civil rights threatened.

Simultaneously, back in 1948, Strom Thurmond, then the Democratic governor of South Carolina, led 35 Southern delegates out of the convention and formed a third party, known by its nickname, the Dixiecrats. Seeing a fragmented Democratic Party, the far left formed yet a fourth party, the Progressives, and nominated former Vice President Henry Wallace, called Old Bubblehead because of his dreamy vision of a socialistic America. Harry Truman, who fell into the None of the Above category, ran on the civil-rights platform the convention had handed him — and won, to the surprise of just about everybody. Thus, the 1948 convention may well have signaled a new era, one in which the charge of "racism" played an increasingly important role in the political debate. The Democrats wrestled for the higher ground, though they had led the charge in earlier years as the true racists.

As Americans entered the second half of the 20th century, some Southern politicians were still defending *de jure* segregation, arguing that whites should not be forced to attend school with blacks, sit next to them in buses, drink out of the same water fountain, and eat at the same lunch counters. The implication of these Jim Crow laws was clear to both races: The law was affirming the superiority, and therefore the supremacy, of the white race. In that sense, legalized segregation may have been more mean-spirited than slavery, since it mandated an artificial separation of the races to protect the sensibilities of white folks.

It is interesting to note that, in Harriet Beecher Stowe's *Uncle Tom's Cabin*, Tom's second benevolent Southern master, Augustine St. Clare, defends the institution of slavery but reproves Ophelia, his New England abolitionist cousin, for her aversion to blacks, which is so strong that she feels uncomfortable in their presence and avoids their touch. In Mrs. Stowe's novel, then, it is the Yankee whose sensibilities are offended. Stowe was not the last writer to take the measure of Northern racism. (You should note, Simon Legree was a transplanted Northerner.)

The second and more important change in racial politics occurred when Congress passed the 1964 Voting Rights Act, which effectively ended the Democrats' disenfranchisement of blacks in the South. Suddenly, they were allowed to vote in the primary where "nomination was tantamount to election" — and with the Department of Justice standing behind them, pistols cocked.

A lot of Southern politicians were caught off base. Those who had ritualistically demonized "nigras" and "niggers" saw the Democratic precincts flooded with black voters. Like Old Pharaoh, many politicians got "drownded." Others, like Strom Thurmond and George Wallace, turned on a dime and began to reach out to the black community — hiring black staff members and delivering sides of pork and spare ribs to black constituents. Within a nanosecond of the passage of the Voting Rights Act of 1964, the Democratic Party in the South began denouncing Republicans as the party of racism and reaction. At last, Northern and Southern Democrats were on the same page again, singing as one harmonious choir for the first time since 1895. Of course they were singing a lie.

And it worked. Sort of. Blacks flocked to the Democratic Party, despite the fact that between 1876 and 1964 the GOP had been the welcome wagon of Southern blacks, who were the beneficiaries of what little patronage Republicans had ever offered.

However, the change ultimately proved an electoral setback for the Democrats. The essentially conservative nature of the Republican Party, coupled with the fierce anti-Southern rhetoric of Northern Democrats — which impugned the moral integrity of every man, woman, and newborn baby in the region — drove millions of white voters into the ranks of the GOP, once hated by Southerners as the architect of Reconstruction.

Liberal Democrats saw this shift as proof that Nixon's so-called Southern Strategy was an appeal to the South's immitigable racism — the true motive, they argued, for every conservative dissent to the inevitable march of America toward statism. And so we have arrived at today. Thus, criticism of Obama has become for left-leaning ideologues an expression of racial bigotry, whatever the stated motive.

In February 2012, Actress Janeane Garofalo, appearing on Keith Olbermann's show, called those who demonstrated against Obama's agenda "a bunch of teabagging rednecks," and then added that "this is about hating a black man in the White House. This is racism straight up." Colbert King, a *Washington Post* columnist, wrote,

CHAPTER SIX — THE TRUTH ABOUT DISCRIMINATION, PREJUDICE . . .

"There's something loose in the land, ugliness and hatred directed toward Barack Obama, the nation's first African American President, which takes the breath away." And Maureen Dowd, writing in the *New York Times*, said of Rep. Joe Wilson's now-famous outburst, "Surrounded by middle-aged white guys—a sepia snapshot of the days when such pols ran Washington like their own men's club—Joe Wilson yelled "You lie!" at a president who didn't. [But he did lie.] But, fair or not, what I heard was an unspoken word in the air: You lie, boy! . . .This president is the ultimate civil rights figure—a black man whose legitimacy is constantly challenged by a loco fringe."

It should be increasingly difficult for leftist Democrats to sustain the myth of rampant Southern racism and to explain electoral losses in the region on this factor. In the recent past, it has been relatively easy to play the race card. Here are some fresh comments gleaned from the airways as seen through the eyes of Rush Limbaugh:

> **Campbell Brown:** . . . vicious, racist imagery attacking our first African-American president.
>
> **Lawrence O'Donnell:** (newsroom noise) Gentleman Joe Wilson has done much to make the racist history of South Carolina jump back into our present consciousness.
>
> **Candy Crowley:** Critics think this is about resistance to a black man as president.
>
> **James Carville:** People are upset with President Obama because of the color of his skin. Who cannot believe that?
>
> **Chris Matthews:** Could there be a refusal to accept the legitimacy of Barack Obama as president because of his race?
>
> **Wolf Blitzer:** A small but disturbing minority within the Tea Party movement is also blatantly anti-black.
>
> **John Ridley:** When you talk about racial image, this is not just standard debate.
>
> **Elaine Quijano:** A small but passionate minority is also voicing what some see as racist rhetoric.
>
> **John Avlon:** Hitler. Communism. Racism. All this ugliness is bubbling up.
>
> **Anderson Cooper:** There is an undercurrent of racism in some of the criticism of the president.

Now remember this when you think of the above comments being called racism. Keep another thought in mind: Trent Lott lost his position as Senate majority leader because, at Strom Thurmond's 100th birthday party, he paid the old man a meaningless compliment: "I want to say this about my state. When Strom Thurmond ran for president, we voted for him. We're proud of it. And if the rest of the country had followed our lead, we wouldn't have had all these problems over all these years either." Trent Lott said that January 31, 2007.

Lott was no segregationist. He wasn't even a strong defender of his state's cultural conservatism. In the House and Senate he was a trimmer — a dealmaker who could reach across the aisle when principle was on the block. He was the last person to suggest that segregation was anything but wicked. As a Mississippian, he knew better. If, in his little speech, he meant anything at all, he was referring to Thurmond's fiscal conservatism and his support of a strong military. Lott's fellow senators and President Bush knew what kind of cautious animal he was. Yet they forced him to surrender his leadership post anyway — because a charge of racism, however farfetched, was still the hydrogen bomb of political warfare.[5]

Because they had the media's ear, the liberals charged forward claiming racism despite attempts to calm the waters. What is strange to some is to see real racism getting worse since the nation elected a person who is called a black president. It is much, much worse. And if, like a pair of French fops in the court of Louis XIV, the Reverend Jesse and the Reverend Al continue to make a profession of getting their feelings hurt, then it will be easier and easier to brush them off like a couple of houseflies. We may even be approaching a time when charges of racism will seem as bland and dull as unsalted oatmeal, when even the *New York Times* will read Maureen Dowd's name-calling, clear the phlegm from its magisterial throat, and yawn.

But the media keeps pointing the finger at anyone conservative as the problem — so we are not there yet.

4. The Truth about Slavery

Indentured servitude was a form of slavery, and frankly were the way the pilgrims and many early colonists came to this country. Individuals would sell themselves into service for a period of time; in early America that time period was usually seven years. Once the time of service was satisfactorily fulfilled, each was released with a bonus and usually a generous plot of land to work to begin to build their own fortunes. Make no mistake this was a form of slavery critical to the building of the nation's economy.

Chattel (rhymes with cattle) is also a word used for slavery, ignoble though it was; individuals were held against their will to work farms, residences, mills or factories sometimes for many years or the reminder of their lives. Reprehensible, yet it was viewed by governments, businesses, or family land-owners as a means of obtaining the necessary labor to support the local economy at the time. With a review of Biblical and other ancient literature, we are able to peer back in time to view both types of slavery. Usually in ancient days, the most common form of slavery was chattel. It was often enforced as a sentence or punishment for a crime. It also came as the result of war, with one nation dragging off citizens to serve in the courts of the victorious king. Often it was an attempt at destruction of a people, or simply a way of expanding personal territory and influence. The look back into history helps us to see the participants and the various impacts upon peoples and cultures.

Admittedly, chattel was a disgraceful and horrible thing as it existed in this country during the 16th and 17th Centuries, as it existed in other countries during the same time period, and as it exists today throughout the world. Slavery has been an age old contraption of mankind, revealing the evil side of homo sapiens, in making slaves of differing peoples, races or nations following conquests of territory, dating almost back to creation. It surprises many Christians to read that chattel slavery was common place during the Old and New Testament time periods; not good, but an everyday part of life in the Roman Empire. Many young students are shocked to discover that slavery is still being practiced in parts of the world, especially Africa, the Middle East, Asia, and in parts of the southern half of the Western Hemisphere.

The use of the "S" word as commonly heard in America today refers to chattel. The word is bandied about as a weapon, much the same way on a western movie set a villain will use a club, a bullwhip or a devious plot against the hero; all to maneuver him at will. Or it is used like a samurai's sword, to cut fast and deep. The use of the word now largely is for naming blame, attempting to cast guilt on a particular group of people, such as the "old white guys" of the population for their supposed involvement in that ancient ritual. Moreover the word is used attempting to leverage position in society, financially, politically, morally, or any way possible so long as it has a payday at the end of the road.

Regarding the slavery of the 16th and 17th Centuries in this country, the media and the remaining portions of the Left love to cast a shadow upon the people of this country; a shadow of proposed and horrible guilt that all white people should feel for the slavery which existed in pre-America and America during those two centuries. From my studies of history, I confess my discomfort in seeing this apparatus called slavery; I despise what it is in the present world today, and always have hated what role it played in the history of this country. It is offensive to me to think about any human being placed forcibly into the servitude of another individual or group. It is a fact, there were white Europeans who either owned or participated in owning these "chattel" slaves.

A Hidden Surprise

While many have been taught that all blacks in America were unanimously leveraged into this chattel slavery, what many high school and undergraduate history students are often amazed or shocked to discover is there were large numbers of free blacks (free African Americans) who lived in the ante-bellum period, not only in the North but also in the South. More serious students are often equally shocked to discover the large number of these free blacks that actually owned black chattel slaves themselves during that period. R. Halliburton, Jr. writes in his essay *Free Black Owners of Slaves*, that "Carter G. Woodson founded the Association for the Study of Negro Life and History in 1915. John Hope Franklin has described that accomplishment as "launching the era of 'the New Negro History.'" Franklin went on to write, 'Dr. Woodson and his associates went about the task of exploiting the myths of Negro history and of putting the Negro in his rightful place in the history of this country.'"[6]

Our current political climate today combined with the poor history that has been taught in the past century, many history professors are skeptical when they hear of the numbers of free black slaveholders and the sheer numbers of slaves they owned. Some blacks living in post-civil war days either were not familiar with this fact, or just refused to believe it. As Booker T. Washington wrote in 1905, "My own personal recollections bring no case in mind of free black men owning slaves, nor am I able to refer you to any books making reference to this phase of slavery, in case it did exist."[7]

It would be my suggestion to NBC, MSNBC and the rest of this media that say they love to report truth, that they do just that; report the truth. For if white people should be branded as guilty of slavery in this country, then so should black people, or African Americans as they are popularly called in culture today. The media needs to be held to answer for their broadcasting of half-truths until they are believed by people in the land, solely because they have heard it so many times. Perception then becomes reality. The liberal media has said so many times that white people are solely responsible for slavery that the average American now believes it — though it is a lie. Black people participated in the building of the slave market just as much as whites did, if not more. It was the black African people and Arab Muslims who sold other tribes into slavery, to white and black, and Arab slave traders. It becomes obvious to me that several unknown facts about slavery need to be laid out so people can see the truth, especially since there is so much guilt being laid out by the media. And in spite of what you have heard on the news, or from Rev. Jesse Jackson, or Al Sharpton, or anyone else, there is a lot of historical evidence which tells the real story and account regarding indentured servitude (slavery) as well as chattel.

As to the emotional appeal for white people to apologize for slavery, there are many possible responses. First of all, I am not personally apologizing for slavery in the past because of one fact. I never participated in slavery in the past in any way. I never owned slaves. Said differently, I am not responsible for what some ancient white person did 400 years ago. Second, none of my relatives I can find in my genealogy owned slaves either. At least there is no written or oral record of it, after much exploration by genealogists in the family. However, there is a record of a portion of my relatives fighting for the abolition of slavery. Since there is a solid record of evidence that some blacks owned chattel slaves, possibly they should write letters of apology for what their relatives did, if they truly insist that letters be written. Possibly they could write such letters to my family and me, since it was some of my family members who fought and sacrificed so that blacks could be freed. How about them apples?

Do I wish that this slavery never happened and that people were not sold into slavery? Of course I do. Do I wish that slavery was not going on now in the world? Of course I do. And if you think it is not going on now, then you must have your head buried in the sand.

However, I honestly do not believe that I am responsible for slavery any more than I believe that a couple of German families alive today in Stuttgart should today be held accountable for the death of my great uncle Hearl Smith, when a German sniper shot and killed him nearly 100 years ago. Sure the sniper that did the shooting was a relative, an uncle, cousin, father, or grandfather, of one or more individuals alive today, but these people today were not personally involved nor are they responsible for what the sniper did. But how in the world do you start in a good conscience to hold people responsible for what their relatives did that long ago? A reasonable, rational, sensible, ethical, sane person would not do such a thing.

Regarding indentured servitude, as it is defined today, it remains unknown at least up to now, to many Americans. Many people sold themselves into this slavery for a time under contract in order to pay for their trip to America, obtain land, money, status, paid education, or position so they too could do business in the new land called America. By the way, there is still a form of indentured servitude in our country today. It is practiced openly in our society, even encouraged by our government in times of war and peace. It is called military service.

We should review some of the facts about slavery, some of them rarely known or discussed, as it has existed in the world and as it existed in this country long ago.

History of Early Slavery in America

Once the colonies in the New World were established, "the Great Migration," as it was called started to this country between the years 1618-1623. While by today's standards it does not seem large, the population grew during those years from 450 to over 4,000 people. But because of malnutrition, exposure to diseases, lack of good medical treatment, and wars with Indians, the mortality rate was extremely high. Due to the high death rate, more workers were needed for the support and progress of the population. In 1619, the *White Lion*, a Dutch ship which had battled a Spanish galleon and captured 20 slaves from it, limped into port at Jamestown, Virginia for repairs from the battle. In exchange for food, supplies and repairs, the Dutch traded the Africans to the Colonists as indentured servants.[8] With that start, slavery in America had begun.

In America, indentured servitude consisted not only of Africans (black people), but there was a large majority of these servants who were Irish, Scottish, English, Germans, Swedish and other nationalities who were brought over from Europe.

History records that a man named Anthony Johnson, one of the early African indentured servants to have finished his contract of services, became a land owner on the East Coast and quickly became a slave owner himself. As he produced tobacco, over the years he became a wealthy farmer in early America.

However, as human nature tends to do in business dealings, it took over. Some masters were awarding land which was totally undesirable and nonproductive to their indentured servants who had completed their contracts. This practice of discrimination led to "Bacon's Rebellion," in Virginia, which was launched against William Berkeley, the governor who was an owner of indentured slaves. (Source: Juliet Walker-See Introduction; footnote 17)

Given the bad taste left over from the rebellion, the desire to keep more of their own land, and the option to avoid further conflicts, slave owners looked for a newer and different kind of agreement. Over time, the status of slavery changed in America, especially with Africans, from the indentured slave status, being gradually replaced by chattel slave status. Land disbursement in completed contracts was becoming unpopular with many land-owning masters since they themselves ended up awarding so much of their personal land to their servants, leaving them not as much land as they wanted. It appears that is where we get the oft used term, "giving away the farm."

In 1624, John Casor became the first legal black "chattel" class slave, held against his will in the American Colonies. Anthony Johnson, referenced above, who had been an African indentured slave himself, claimed John Casor as his slave. Northampton County ruled that Casor was now the legal property of Johnson. This made Anthony Johnson not only one of the first slave owners in America, but THE first slave owner owning a black slave in America. Since Africans slaves were not English, they were not considered citizens nor covered by English Common Law.[9]

Discovering that whites were enslaved more often than the Negros, is not only shocking to many but also politically incorrect to mention in today's marketplace where the subject matter is connected with African Americans and reparations. The truth is that African slaves were expensive while other ethnic groups like the Irish were considered cheap by market standards, or more of a bargain. The Irish also became targets for the English. This is easily seen through the centuries as the English and Irish have warred more often than not. James II started the Irish slave trade with the Americas in 1625 by selling over 30,000 Irish slaves to English settlers in the West Indies. Boatloads were sold to settlers in the English Colony of Virginia and in New England during through the late 17th Century, totaling close to 700,000 slaves in all. Tragically, during the middle of that century, over 100,000 Irish children, ages 10-14 were sold as slaves for the rest of their lives, most landing in New England, Virginia, and the Virgin Islands.[10]

White "chattel" was not limited to the Irish ethnic groups. Great Britain, wanting to rid herself of criminals, used their own version of "3 Strikes and You're Out" law, to send criminals to the Colonies. The English deported political prisoners into bondage through an English law in force in the mid-1660s, and banished to the colonies anyone convicted three times of attempting an unlawful meeting, a law aimed mostly at the Quakers. Hundreds of Scottish nationalist rebels, particularly after the Scottish uprising of 1679, were likewise shipped to the colonies as political criminals. A 1670 act banished anyone from coming to the colonies that had knowledge of illegal religious or political activity, which had refused to turn informer for the government. White criminal slaves were also sent to America from other countries. Some whites were made into bond servants; others were chattel, to be owned for life. Some slaves had horrendous living conditions and tried revolting or fleeing to improve their lives. Demands of the rebelling servants ranged from improved conditions and better food to outright freedom. The leading example was the servant uprising of 1661 in York County, Virginia, led by Isaac Friend and William Clutton. Friend had exhorted the other servants that "he would be the first and lead them and cry as they went along who would be for liberty and freed from bondage and that there would be enough come to them, and they would go through the country and kill those who made any opposition and that they would either be free or die for it."[11] White slaves grew by such numbers that one historian remarked, "It was almost as if the British merchants had redirected their vessels from the African coast to the Irish coast, with the white servants coming over in much the same fashion as the African slaves."[12] Another writer remarked how white slaves experienced "... sufferings on their voyage across the Atlantic that paralleled the cruel hardships undergone by negro slaves on the notorious Middle Passage — having as high as a 50 percent mortality rate in transit to America, with young children seldom surviving the horrors of the voyage that might last anywhere from seven to twelve weeks in horribly overcrowded and unsanitary conditions."[13]

Over the following years, the definition of slaves and their status changed in varied ways. It began in Virginia in 1650. The law stated that "Negroes are not allowed arms and ammunition." In 1662, a child's status, free or slave, depended on the mother's status. In 1667, it was ruled that baptism would not alter a person's status as to slave or free. In 1682, it was ruled that servants did not become Christian merely because they were purchased by a Christian master.

Emancipation in the Northern States

Following the Revolution with Great Britain, in 1777, Vermont, a territory at the time, completely abolished slavery. Note that Vermont was not a state yet. In 1780, Pennsylvania became the first state to totally abolish slavery. This makes sense when you remember the strong Quaker background, or reformation influence in the state. In 1781, New York's legislature voted to free those slaves who fought with the patriots during the Revolutionary War. In 1787, what is known as the 1787 Northwest Ordinance was passed by the Congress of the Confederation of that territory. This ordinance outlawed slavery in the region, however the northeastern states of New York and New Jersey still allowed slavery. Though in the region, slavery was illegal, people still lived illegally, owning slaves and indentured slaves.

In 1808, it should be noted that the US Congress banned the importing of slaves from Africa. And in 1827, New York took their earlier action to completeness, by totally abolishing slavery there.

Anti-Abolitionist Blacks in the South

Meanwhile down in "The South," it might come as no surprise that there were black, or African American, slave owners. Nicholas Augustin Metoyer for one, an African American land owner in Louisiana, personally owned thirteen slaves in 1830. He and his family members collectively owned 215 slaves.[14]

Historians will argue some of these facts, sometimes for logical reasons, more often for political ones. For example there is reputable and credible evidence showing that some free blacks, or African Americans, bought family members to protect them, being motivated by benevolence. On the other hand, as historian Carter G. Woodson puts it, some of these African Americans purchased black people "as an act of exploitation" to get the free labor for profit, just as the competition, the white slave-owners, were doing. Unfortunately, evidence shows that both cases are true. The African-American historian, John Hope Franklin proclaims this unmistakably, "The majority of Negro owners of slaves had some personal interest in their property." He also admits, "There were instances, however, in which free Negroes had a real economic interest in the institution of slavery and held slaves in order to improve their economic status."

This is all controversial in today's "the pendulum has swung the wrong way" culture, full of political correctness. R. Halliburton shows in his essay that free black people owned slaves "in each of the original thirteen states and later in every state that countenanced slavery." That was certainly true ever since Anthony Johnson, an African-American mentioned earlier, and his wife Mary went to court in Virginia in 1654 to legally procure the services of their indentured servant, a black man, John Castor, for life.[15]

In fact for a time in Virginia, black people could "own" white indentured servants. Many free blacks in the northern states owned their own slaves. By 1724 in Boston and 1783 in Connecticut free blacks owned slaves. In Maryland by 1790, 48 black people owned 143 slaves. Halliburton reported there was one particularly notorious black Maryland farmer, Nat Butler, who "regularly purchased and sold Negroes for the Southern trade."[16]

Those who it seemed fought hardest and spoke loudest in desperation to defend the right of black people to own black slaves on what turned out to be the eve of the War Between The States were free black people in New Orleans. They freely offered their services to the Confederacy to fight the North, it seems in part to play both ends against the middle for fear of becoming slaves themselves. As one historian states, "The free colored population [native] of Louisiana . . . own slaves, and they are dearly attached to their native land . . . and they are ready to shed their blood for her defense. They have no sympathy for abolitionism; no love for the North, but they have plenty for Louisiana . . . They will fight for her in 1861 as they fought [to defend New Orleans from the British] in 1814-1815."[17]

These people were opportunists to the ultimate. As Noah Andre Trudeau and James G. Hollandsworth Jr. explain, once the war broke out, some of these black men formed 14 companies of a militia composed of 440 men and were organized by the governor in May 1861 into "the Native Guards, Louisiana," swearing to fight to defend the Confederacy. They never had combat roles, but the Guards, reaching a peak of 1,000 volunteers, became the first Civil War Unit to appoint black officers. Bottom line: black soldiers and black officers were a part of the Confederate army.

You will never hear any of this on CNN or read about it in the *New York Times* or *Washington Post*. It is probably too much to hope that our school children would be taught these truths rather than the tripe they are being taught as history. Possibly we have gone too far to ever go back to hear truth. But know this — there is at least one of us who has researched and now knows the truth and wants to tell it like it is.

Does this data excuse slavery? Of course not. But it does scratch the surface for a few who will learn. And in learning, it will cause them to research more, learn more truth, and come to the realization that we are living in a time when nobody in the major media is speaking the truth about slavery, prejudice, and discrimination. I call it the true about this the true leveling of the playground, which the media always claims it wants.

About Abolitionism

There are persons noteworthy of mention who supported abolition, some rather well-known, some not so well. They worked tirelessly in the fight against slavery throughout their lives.

Harriet Beecher Stowe is one of the best known. In 1852 she published the anti-slavery novel, *Uncle Tom's Cabin*, which was the best-selling novel of the 19th Century. Because of its success, it helped fuel the abolitionist movement and cause in the 1850s.

William Lloyd Garrison prepared a weekly anti-slavery newspaper called the "Liberator" which he published for thirty-five years. Garrison's presses ran from January 1, 1831 to January 1, 1866, when the Thirteenth Amendment was finally ratified. The Thirteenth abolished slavery within the boundaries of the United States.

Fredrick Douglass was another abolitionist who inspired thousands to join the cause through his lectures. Douglass was a strong and passionate believer in equality among the various races and genders. Over the years, tens of thousands of people heard him speak, many on more than one occasion.

Harriet Tubman was also and an inspiring leader and worker in "the Underground Railroad."

You may recall that this railroad was an intricate network of secret tunnels and routes with stations (churches and homes of sympathizers) where slaves could hide while escaping to the Canadian border. It has been reliably reported that approximately 6,000 people escaped slavery via this railroad.

Slave Uprisings and Revolts

Through the years there were brave men and women who led uprisings and revolts against the slavery in which they were trapped. Over the last one and one-half centuries many of these rebellions became known through a name.

There was the New York Revolt of 1712, an uprising in New York City led by twenty-three blacks, or African-American slaves. The city was a perfect place for slaves to plan a rebellion. Unlike on plantations in the South where slaves far apart, in NYC they lived next to each other, which made communication between them very easy. During the rebellion it was reported that nine white people were shot, stabbed or beaten to death. Six more were injured. As authorities gained the upper hand in the revolt, seventy blacks were jailed, six committed suicide, and twenty-seven more were put on trial. Of those, twenty-one were burned to death.

Then came the Stono Rebellion of 1739. That year a flu epidemic rocked the country, affecting mostly those who traveled off of plantations, such as slave owners. With the epidemic at its height many slaves saw this as a time to strike for freedom. According to the local reports, an Angolan slave named Jemmy led the revolt by recruiting twenty other African American slaves, who met at the Stono River and marched down the river road. Seizing weapons and ammunition while burning seven plantations and killing twenty white plantation owners, they eventually recruited an additional sixty slaves and met at the Stono River Bridge.

Some Noteworthy Pastors Who Fought for Abolition

There were many other individuals, including a number of pastors who stood tall and preached loudly in society their messages for abolition. Two became very close friends with Abraham Lincoln, and undoubtedly influenced to some degree Lincoln's impressions upon slavery. Two of these pastors were Rev. Owen Lovejoy (1811-1864) and Rev. Joshua Giddings (1795-1864), the latter being known as the "Messiah of the Abolitionist Movement."[18]

Giddings lived and preached in Ohio and also served his state in the US House of Representatives from 1838-1859. There, Giddings is known for his firm and loud stance against slavery so much and so, that in 1842 he was censured for violating the standing "gag rule" against discussing slavery in the House of Representatives after he had proposed a number of Resolutions arguing against federal support for the coastwise slave trade. His proposals were presented in relation to the *Creole case*, whose elements demonstrates that slavery was vastly larger than just involving blacks, but involved most of the American Indian tribes in the eastern part of America. Giddings angrily resigned when censured, but was overwhelmingly re-elected by his Ohio constituents in a special election to fill his own vacant seat. He then returned to the House and served well for several more years, fighting for abolition.[19]

Lovejoy was clearly one who stood against slavery but took a less aggressive stance. Although Lovejoy advocated eventual emancipation of all slaves, he did not actually support immediate interference in Southern slavery. Lovejoy, though an ardent abolitionist and an anathema to more moderate Republicans, understood the need for Republican political unity and consistently supported Lincoln's entry into the Party, presidential nomination (despite the preference in his congressional district for Seward), and presidential policies. Like Mr. Lincoln, he opposed the compromise efforts of late 1860 and early 1861. He used his influence in the House to fight the Crittenden Compromise and the proposed constitutional amendment which would have prohibited interference with slavery in the South. Speaking of the secession movement in the Republican caucus, Lovejoy said: "There never was a more causeless revolt since Lucifer led his cohorts of apostate angels against the throne of God; but I never heard that the Almighty proposed to compromise the matter by allowing the rebels to kind the fires of hell south of the celestial meridian of 36°30'!"[20]

Lovejoy had served churches in southern Illinois for many years and had the occasion where he spoke in services, for a young country lawyer in attendance to hear the message. This lawyer named Abraham Lincoln who later became president often attended church services wherever Lovejoy was preaching. Reverend Lovejoy played a pastoral as well as a political role with Mr. Lincoln, reportedly visiting Lincoln when he was the president on several occasions to read the Bible with him. Former Illinoisan Brooks described Lovejoy as "stout, good-natured, bluff, and full of fun and Scripture quotations..."[21]

Before he died from cancer in March 1864, from his sick bed in late February, Lovejoy wrote abolitionist William Lloyd Garrison to "express to you my gratification at the position you have taken in reference to Mr. Lincoln. I am satisfied, as the old theologians used to say in reference to the world, that if he is not the best conceivable President, he is the best possible. I have known something of the facts inside during his Administration, and I know that he has been just as radical as any of his cabinet."[22]

Learning of Lovejoy's death later than month, Mr. Lincoln said: "Lovejoy was the *best* friend I had in Congress."²³ "Our friend, whom we all *so* loved & esteemed, has so suddenly & unexpectedly passed away — Mr. Lovejoy!" wrote Mrs. Lincoln to Senator Charles Sumner.²⁴

Mr. Lincoln's attitude toward Lovejoy had undergone an incredible transformation. He wrote John H. Bryant on May 30, 1864: "Many of you have known [Owen] Lovejoy longer than I have, and are better able than I to do his memory complete justice. My personal acquaintance with him commenced only about ten years ago, since then it has been quite intimate; and every step in it has been one of increasing respect and esteem, ending, with his life, in no less than affection on my part. It can be truly said of him that while he was personally ambitious, he bravely endured the obscurity which the unpopularity of his principles imposed, and never accepted official honors, until those honors were ready to admit his principles with him. Throughout my heavy, and perplexing responsibilities here, to the day of his death, it would scarcely wrong any other to say, he was my most generous friend. Let him have the marble monument, along with the well-assured and more enduring one in the hearts of those who love liberty, unselfishly, for all men."²⁵

A fellow Illinoisan, Republican Shelby M. Cullom recalled Lovejoy: "I was at the White House when the news of his death was brought to Lincoln, and I recall the kindly manner in which he spoke of him. Lovejoy had been something of a radical in the House, and, although his radicalism had in a way aided Lincoln, there were times when it grew to[o] strong for the good of the cause in hand. Speaking of Lovejoy on this occasion, Lincoln said, 'He was one of the best men in Congress. If he became too radical I always knew that I could send for him and talk it over and he would go back to the floor and do about as I wanted.'"²⁶

Another Lovejoy, Elijah Parish Lovejoy, a school teacher living in his native state of Maine, migrated to Illinois in 1827 and then across the Mississippi to St. Louis, Mo. There he taught in a high school for a few years when he "experienced a religious conversion, and entered Princeton Theological Seminary, and obtained a license to preach." In 1833, he returned to St. Louis and became editor of the *St. Louis Observer*, a Presbyterian newsletter, where he penned editorials opposing slavery. Residents of the area rejected his thoughts because Missouri was split on the idea of abolition, with many people in the area openly owning slaves. Over time, the threats grew louder against Rev. Lovejoy and his family, leading them to eventually move back to Alton, Illinois to seek safety in that "free state" while he preached his message of abolition.

Lovejoy raised the anti-slavery tenor in his tabloids after witnessing an incarcerated slave, Francis J. McIntosh, being burned at the stake by a mob without even so much as a trial. McIntosh had earlier killed two guards in a failed jailbreak. Though the leaders of the mob were prosecuted and tried for their actions, in a stunning reversal the judge blamed Lovejoy on stirring up the violence with his anti-slavery editorials published in the Observer. The tabloids now took on an

Chapter Six — The Truth about Discrimination, Prejudice...

even higher octave against slavery because Lovejoy was incensed that the mob was cleared and he was blamed in the judge's ruling. Simultaneously Lovejoy became the object of bodily threats by both Southerners and slave-holders everywhere who read his words, which had taken on the dedication and sound of an activist, screaming the unfairness and dishonesty of the judge. The mob dropped the hammer on Lovejoy in July, 1836, breaking in and ransacking his St. Louis office, destroying his press. This was the precipitating event for the Lovejoy family to move across the river to Illinois.

Over time with Lovejoy's active and open participation and support of the organization of the Anti-slavery of Illinois, the local residents in Alton were becoming enraged. But he continued writing and publishing the Alton Observer during the time of violence when three separate presses had been broken and thrown into the Mississippi River by mobs of thugs. But Lovejoy would not give up on his message. In Alton he became the Stated Clerk of the Presbytery in 1837 and the first pastor of the present College Avenue Presbyterian Church, continuing his abolitionist work from that position.

Lovejoy and the area pro-slavery mob continued on a collision course which reached a fever pitch one November night in 1837. Secret arrangements were made to receive and hide the new press by Lovejoy and 20 of his friends when it was delivered. As a steamboat delivered the press at approximately 3 AM on November 7, 1837, they quickly unloaded it. While moving it to the third floor of the Godfrey & Gilman warehouse, a few members of the mob saw them. They quickly raced around town spreading the word through the morning and into the late afternoon. When daylight was gone, the mob leaders and drinkers from the local bars gathered. The crowd swelled. Tensions also grew dramatically within both groups, inside and out. William Gilman, a co-owner of the building quickly and unexpectedly appeared in a third floor window.

The Alton Observer carried the entire fateful story. A portion of the remaining part of the account as was reported follows below:

> "Suddenly, William S. Gilman, one of the owners of the building, appeared in an upper window. "What do you want here?" he asked the crowd. "The press!" came the shouted reply. Gilman called back: "We have no ill feelings toward, any of you and should much regret to do any injury; but we are authorized by the Mayor to defend our property and shall do so with our lives." The mob began to throw stones, breaking out all the windows in the warehouse. The defenders retaliated by bombarding the crowd with a supply of earthenware pots found in the warehouse.
>
> Then came an exchange of gun fire. Shots were fired by members of the mob, and rifle balls whizzed through the windows of the warehouse narrowly missing the defenders inside. Lovejoy and his men, returned

the fire. Several people in the crowd were hit, and one was killed.

"Burn them out!" someone shouted. Leaders of the mob called for a ladder, which was put up on the side of the building. A boy with a torch was sent up the ladder to set fire to the wooden roof. Lovejoy and one of his supporters, Royal Weller, volunteered to stop the boy. The two men crept outside, hiding in the shadows of the building. Surprising the mob, they rushed to the ladder, pushed it over and quickly retreated inside.

Once again a ladder was put in place. As Lovejoy and Weller made another brave attempt to overturn the ladder, they were spotted. Lovejoy was shot five times, and Weller was also wounded. Lovejoy staggered inside the warehouse, making his way to the second floor before he finally fell. "My God. I am shot," he cried. He died almost immediately. By this time the warehouse roof had begun to burn. The men remaining inside knew they had no choice but to surrender the press.

The mob rushed into the vacant building. The press Lovejoy died defending was carried to a window and thrown out onto the river bank. It was broken into pieces that were scattered in the Mississippi River. Fearing more violence, Lovejoy's friends, did not remove his body from the building until the next morning.

Members of the crowd from the night before, feeling no shame at what they had done, laughed and jeered as the funeral wagon moved slowly down the street toward Lovejoy's home. He was buried on his 35th birthday, November 9, 1837, in an unmarked grave in the Alton City Cemetery, the location known by a black man, William "Scotch" Johnston, who assisted in the burial."[27]

The story of Elijah Parish Lovejoy and the Abolitionists, who joined in his work in both St. Louis and later in Alton east of the river, is a brief glimpse into a courageous and active faith. To herald this man and his love for eternal truth is only right. His stand and his lasting vigil were in a fight for an eternal cause: for freedom of thought, freedom of speech, freedom of action, as well as freedom of the press. On one dark night long ago in 1837, history does indeed show that little Alton, Illinois was the scene of a courageous battle for mankind's freedom, the tremors of which were soon going to be felt throughout the nation. The angry mob attack at the Godfrey & Gilman warehouse was realistically the first, though unrecorded shot fired in the battle of what is now called the Civil War.

An interesting side note in the story: Not one member of the mob was found guilty of the murder of Elijah Lovejoy and the ambush of his supporters in the warehouse. However, abolitionists everywhere used Lovejoy's death as a greater reason to end slavery. His name and murder became a flag and a rallying symbol for reformers of future years throughout the land. It still should be today.

Many more freedom lovers go unnamed in this book, not only black and white, but many other ethnicities, and in many other times. Thankfully they fought against slavery and in some cases made the ultimate sacrifice for their stated cause. With an army of blacks and whites who fought to destroy and rid the nation of the chattel empire, it was operated by both black and white plantation owners. We must stop the criminal activity of trying to coerce one race of people to apologize for activities of which they were never a part and never even witnessed. Given the current circumstances, it will be up to a modern-day Elijah Parish Lovejoy to step forward to lead that battle for truth against this evil coercion industry.

5. Reparations

Defined in its current politically correct context, reparation is the proposed payment of money to current residents in this country, all of them African American and descendants of slaves of the same race, in order to "make up for" or make reparations for the 17th and 18th Century national sins of slavery.

In response to pressure lobbying by individuals such as Jesse Jackson, Al Sharpton, and others, some time ago Representative John Conyers, Democrat-Michigan, introduced HR 40, legislation entitled "Commission to Study Reparation Proposals for African-Americans Act." HR 40 has 48 co-sponsors and a number of them, such as Jim Traficant, D-Mich., and Jerry Nadler, D-N.Y., are white. Do not worry about their eventual exposure, however, since if any misaimed legislation like this ever passed, members of Congress would be exempted from being held liable to make any payments.

With such a gross violation of human rights such as slavery, it would make sense to most that justice demands that all slave owners step forward to make compensatory reparation payments to slaves. What kind of sense does that make? Both the slaves and the slave owners are dead. They are dust and memories now. Justice states that compensation payments are beyond our reach in this life. But let's play the game of "What If!" What if reparation payments could be still paid? But who pays? Advocates for reparations do not want us asking many questions about this. They just want the U. S. Government, some wealthy families, or white families to pay the price. The problem is, the government does not have any money that it does not first take from some American individual or company. The second problem, there were more white slaves who were wronged than black slaves who were wronged. Keep reading and you will see the facts about that. Truth has to be honored here, not political correctness. So my first question still stands; who pays?

Another truth is illegal immigrants may turn out to be worth something here in terms of dollars and cents. How about making them pay reparation? They were not here you say? Well neither were the millions of Europeans, Asian, and other Latin American legal immigrants of the last half of the 19th century and the entirety of the 20th century. Yet it appears that Conyers, 40 other Democrats, et al, would want to make them responsible. But do not stop there. I have other questions. What about fifth generation descendants of Northern whites who fought and died in the war to win freedom of these slaves, both black and white? What about reparations being made by the 5th and 6th generation of non-slave-owning Southern whites, who by the way were the large majority of Southern whites. Let us have them all pay reparations. That would be fair would it not? The answer is, "No, it would not!" Somebody someplace is saying that we are guilty by association.

Let's not stop yet. We are not done. How about looking at the account ledger on the blacks who are seeking reparations? They want money. They want lots of it. There is some real thorny ground in this area. While some blacks purchased other blacks as a means to free family members; other blacks owned slaves for the same reason some whites owned slaves: to work farms or plantations. Are these descendants of these blacks eligible and deserving of reparations? How about having the descendants of black slave masters pay reparations to the other blacks who are descendants of the black slaves who were owned on these plantations? What about descendants of whites who were slaves to black plantation owners. Who pays reparation to those descendants? You have a real mixed bag when you play this game. One could end up having money go back and forth between whites and blacks, blacks and whites on this reparations game. And we have not even discussed the blacks in Oklahoma who owned American Indian/Native American slaves.

But wait. After we work that strategy out, there is another problem to solve. There is no way that white Europeans could have captured millions of African slaves, even if we were to pretend that blacks were the only slaves in America, and that would be a big pretense. History shows they did not. They had African, Arab, and Muslim help. Shouldn't Conyers haul representatives of Ghana, Ivory Coast, Nigeria and other Muslim states before Congress and demand they pay reparations if we are going to play this game correctly? By the way, there is another question: Is anyone prepared to make the argument that blacks in America today would be better off if they were in Africa? If blacks would not be better off, then why the reparations?

Reparations advocates, including their attorneys seeking another pay day, make the thoughtless yet publically unchallenged pronouncement that the United States became rich on the backs of free black slave labor. While it is tempting to agree, just stop and think about the nonsense of that statement, at least based on the historical evidence. I know that evidence has nothing to do with the argument, but play the game anyway. Slavery does not have a good record of producing wealth. Slavery was all over the South and scarce in the North because it became outlawed in most places within New England. Buying into the reparations nonsense brings the following conclusion: the antebellum South was rich and the slave-starved North was poor. The truth is just the opposite. In fact, the poorest states and regions of our country were places where slavery flourished: Mississippi, Alabama and Georgia. The richest states and regions were those where slavery was absent: Pennsylvania, New York and Massachusetts.

Adjoa Aiyetoro, a legal consultant to the National Coalition of Blacks for Reparations in America, says, "We're not raising claims that you should pay us because you did something to us 150 years ago. We are saying that we are injured today by the vestiges of slavery, which took away income and property that was rightfully ours." This vestige-of-slavery argument, as an explanation for the pathology seen in some black neighborhoods, is simply nonsense when you think about it. aka, "We want money, dude!"

Holding slavery as the culprit for why blacks do not do well today is an interesting argument. There is a culprit, but it is not slavery. It is the welfare state. Take for example: Illegitimacy among blacks today is 70 percent. Only 41 percent of black males 15 years and older are married, and only 36 percent of black children live in two-parent families. These and other indicators of family instability and its accompanying socioeconomic factors such as high crime, welfare dependency and poor educational achievement is claimed to be the legacy and vestiges of slavery, for which black Americans are due reparations. The truth: the welfare state produced the problems. Allow me to show you the trail of evidence.

In 1940, illegitimacy among blacks was 19 percent. From 1890 to 1940, blacks had a marriage rate that was actually slightly higher than whites. As of 1950, 64 percent of black males 15 years and older were married, compared to today's 41 percent.[28]

In Philadelphia, in 1880, two-parent family structure was: black (75.2 percent), Irish (82.2 percent), German (84.5 percent) and white Americans (73.1 percent). In the other largest cities of the time, such as Detroit, New York and Cleveland, the percentages were roughly the same.[29]

In *The Black Family in Slavery and Freedom, 1750-1925*, author Herbert G. Gutman reports on one study of black families. The reports show that "Five out of six children under the age of 6 lived with both parents." The study also found that, in Harlem for example, between 1905 and 1925, only 3 percent of all families were headed by a woman under the age of 30, and 85 percent of black children lived in two-parent homes and families.[30]

Historical facts on Gutman's study invites an ironic and quite disturbing question in the face of the claims of reparation advocates. If the residue and legacy of slavery is what we are viewing today in many black neighborhoods, why was this social pathology not worse when blacks were one, two or three generations removed from slavery? Said differently, are slavery's heritage and vestiges like Parkinson's or diabetes. That is can they skip a few generations before they appear again? A sensible, logical person, when looking at the data will realize the devastating 70 percent rate of black illegitimacy cannot be a delayed result of slavery skipping six generations — social pathologies just don't work that way![31]

Conclusion

We live in an age where racism is certainly worse than I ever remember it being in my lifetime. The new racism has now been elevated to be the greatest of all political sins; where murder is not the lead story of the news, because it been replaced with the new lead story. The N-word has replaced the F-word or the G-word (gun) as the most obscene utterance in the language. I do not uphold any of these words as being the promotional material a person might want to use in advertising a personal IQ, the emotional intelligence, or EQ, or a statement of where he or she wants to be in society. As I have heard some God-fearing people say, "What in the world has happened to our society?" The answer is a little good, but certainly mostly it is horrible. It is obvious that the seams of our world are coming unraveled.

But the beat goes on. NAACP President and CEO Benjamin Todd Jealous, in a prepared statement, said, "The apology for slavery and the era of Jim Crow is long overdue and is the first step toward healing the wounds of African-American men and women throughout this country." Words and phrases mean things: Note the language, "first step toward healing." Anyone care to bet on what the second step is?

The wounds of Jim Crow and slavery have been healed for black families; but these entrepreneurs of racial discord and "immersion into subversion" do not want any healing to have occurred yet. Reason? There is no payday in it for them, no financial quid pro quo if healing has occurred.

No, when the evidence is reviewed with any serious scrutiny, any of the arguments offered in the attempt to get money. Whether it is the wounds of Jim Crow or the theory of the effects of slavery skipping so many generations, only to reappear in the last few decades, this argument works poorly for a thinking person. Screen doors do not work on submarines either. Let's cut to the bottom line: all the reparation cries are just a hustle. Much like what I call the Lyndon Johnson hustle. The $6 trillion spent toward the war on poverty. The demand for reparations is being made ironically enough in the form of a hustle — a stimulus hustle. The money in a stimulus fund will be ready for attorneys to dip into at any time as they decide who gets paid on any day. It is an all too familiar sound similar to the late Reverend Ike's call for people to send him money. "Send me $20; I will send you $20 worth of blessings." Not all that far removed from "Give us $1 Trillion. We will not cry for more until it is spent."

Tell me how "all races, ethnicity and national origins" are going to benefit from this shakedown. You may not agree, and I am sure many do not, but no apology and certainly no reparations are going to make a bit of difference in the lives of those they are supposedly supporting. The answer is to put racial animus aside which many blacks are seeking. It would then be best to adopt what the ancient writer Paul once said, consider that there is no longer " Jew or Greek, slave or free, nor is there male or female . . . [or black or white] . . . you are all one . . . " Said differently, seeking an egalitarian society where we are all Americans, no separate race distinctions or designations, is preferable.

Today, instead of creating disturbances because someone in one ethnic group has more than someone in another, the real disturbance should be made over what Americans have been taught the last century by so-called "leaders." Imagine a father with four teenagers: two with part-time jobs after school and weekends, one with a full-time job, and one who does not work at all. He requires his three children to give him their earnings each Sunday evening so he can divide the cash into four equal amounts for each child! Dr. Phil would have week-long programs on Oprah Winfrey's network blasting any parent who would do such a thing, impacting a child's psyche for life. We have that scene going on nationally now. Should not there instead be demonstrations against what the socialized system has been teaching students, much like the father in the example above. There should be marches against government schools and teachers to provide real education to help free students to be individuals, highly motivated to tackle the world once they graduate. No more poor education. No more dividing students into ethnic groups. Those who claim to be lifting up students are in reality robbing them of their future. They do so because they have robbed them of their true history.

You might want to ask yourself the question, "Why was I not taught these things?" Is it because the government schools are in essence mind control centers or re-education camps? Did they not know these facts themselves, or more likely, is it because they did not want you to know the truth at all?

"What is the meaning of a gold standard and a redeemable currency? It represents integrity; it ensures the people's control over the government's use of the public purse. It is the best guarantee against the socialization of a nation. It enables a people to keep the government and banks in check. It prevents currency expansion from getting ever further out of bounds until it becomes worthless. It tends to force standards of honesty on government and bank officials. It is the symbol of a free society and an honorable government. It is a necessary prerequisite to economic health. It is the first economic bulwark of free men."

— Walter E. Spahr

Professor of Economics, New York University

Chapter Seven

The History of Labor Unions Is Their Problem

"Those who tell you of trade-unions bent on raising wages by moral suasion alone are like people who tell you of tigers that live on oranges." — Henry George, 1891 1

THERE ARE MANY DEFINITIONS OR DESCRIPTIONS given for labor unions. One has been that they exist as "private combinations of workingmen" or "workingwomen" dedicated to increasing wages and improving working conditions for members. Through the years, negotiating tactics of labor unions has been questionable. As Henry George suggests, trade unionists are hardly known for their genteel ways or kindness to strangers.

From the very beginnings of this country in colonial America, trade unionists found their attempts to organize a path plagued with difficulties. For one thing, the solidarity of this "working class" possessed an ideology that went against the grain of everyday culture and was less than respectable. Theirs was a well-earned reputation for not only anti-social behavior, but outright criminal activity and law-breaking. Historically, some unions have been secret societies with secret oaths and passwords. Negotiation tactics used by its members first incorporated intimidation, threats, vandalism, and in particular, violence against any worker unwilling to cooperate or join their group. Second, if unsuccessful, witness the members openly and publicly denouncing any nonunion worker as being subhuman scabs or blacklegs. America was built upon the celebrated idea of private property ownership, freedom to contract work as a person desired, open competition, and the ultimate freedom to move from one job to another and across occupation lines. But at our founding, mercantilism with such monopolies and business cartels promoted by government (a relative of the term today for government picking winners and losers called crony capitalism) — all this was unpopular leading some to attempt to organize.

Rulings in courts of law also displayed their lack of affection for union methods. A majority of employers, consumers, and workers often resisted these "militant" unions. The competition from imported goods made union life difficult too. Witnessing ill treatment of fellow nonunion peers, some workers became fiercely anti-union. It was not just the employers. America was an open society, frontier communities, farm-dominated, expansive, and free, and wages often were double those paid in England because good labor was so scarce here. There exists only scarce reports in those days about union membership. Therefore, membership in unions probably remained low, less than one percent of the total workforce most of the years from colonial days into the 1870s.

Most unions that went on and later "lost" a strike typically collapsed and vanished. In business downturns, many unions failed because jobs went away, as well as the membership and the revenue made through dues. Add to these scenes the "wage rigidity", a response by union management to wage rate depression insisting that their wages stay unchanged and high. Companies would hire more nonunion workers with lower wages; that made production costs fall and unemployment drop. These wage-price fluctuations acted as shock absorbers within the economy; they eased the pain of business recession, shortened their cycles, help an ever expanding manufacturing output, and raised employment in the communities. In reality, all this were threats to the unions.

In the early American economy, the story of the labor unions is more of a peculiarity than any prominent feature of the business picture. Unions were usually confined to big city manufacturing plants, factories, and railroads where skilled labor was required. Not until the prosperous 1880s in the heart of the industrial revolution, when the philosophy of collectivism and Marxism started forming a sizeable or meaningful shift in the politics of the day, did trade unions start gaining a real foothold in America.

Unions in Colonial Days

This early modern era provides evidence that the European guild system, which consisted of local occupational and product monopolies that were tightly regulated, never gained a solid foothold in North America. A smattering of guilds with apprenticeships did exist in the major cities during the 18th century. Those were usually those of carpenters, printers, shoemakers, tailors, and hat makers. The 19th century unions were made up of "Journeymen" from these guilds plus workers' "benevolent societies". The labor protests were not planned but were spontaneous, a microcosm of which was reported in 1763, in the *Charleston Gazette*, when Negro chimney sweeps "had the insolence, by a combination among themselves, to raise the usual prices, and to refuse doing their work."

Before 1800, printers and shoemakers organized in Philadelphia and New York. Philadelphia printers conducted the first recorded strike for higher wages in 1786, opposing a wage cut and demanding a minimum wage of $6 per week.[2] Employers quickly acquiesced, confirming the generalization in industrial relations that unions win short strikes and lose long ones. Because the average daily wage rate for laborers was $0.53 and $1.00 for artisans in the Philadelphia area, it is not clear that the strike boosted wages for a majority of printers, but a cut was thwarted.[3]

Union activities were centered in the cities, developing subcultures in each community. Philadelphia, an example, has the reputation of being the city of labor union firsts. It was the place where the first union strike happened; it had the first labor newspaper, first city central body of unions, and the place of the first labor-union political activity. The subculture developed by unions in this City of Brotherly Love, was the city of hostilities.

Tactics Used by Unions

Reaching a monopoly and total control of the local labor supply making it a "closed shop" environment where companies could only hire union members was the goal of the trade unions in the early Republic. Apprenticeships to train new workers were choked down as if in a funnel restricting membership. This artificial limitation in the supply of skilled labor for hire put an upward pressure on wages.

The trademark of unions was strikes, accompanied by the typical threats, bullying and violence in various forms, just like in England and as seen today. The typical strike was called to force employers to pay more than necessary for talent on the open market. The silent message to workers was that everyone, union or not, willing or not, must strike, refusing to work for any less than that demanded by the strikers. Employers were intimidated and intentionally discouraged from hiring replacements, called strikebreakers. A union warning from the 1830s suggests how unions discouraged interlopers: "We would caution all strangers and others who profess the art of horseshoeing, that if they go work for any employer under the above prices, they must abide by the consequences."[4]

The stronger the union, the more secure it is in its power acting like a unilateral and independent force, means the less overt threats and violence it creates. Elements of the local culture and its ideology play a huge role in the violence of unions which has been typically limited by the responsiveness of the police, courts, and local politicians. Union tactics that we see today were fixed and in place by 1810: the "collective bargaining," the demand for fixed minimum pay rates, the enforcing of closed shops, stage strikes with picket lines, scab lists, strike funds, and traveling cards, and promoting unity among skilled and unskilled workers and solidarity among locals of the same trade.

Union activities such as their coercion and violence waged against non-members, run in contrast to and is incompatible with any individual seeking his or her own independent freedom in employment. This is an ugly truth ignored by most supporters and writers of union activity. As Ludwig von Mesis has written, "Actually labor union violence is tolerated within broad limits . . . the authorities, with the approval of public opinion, condone such acts."[5]

Legal Restraints

From the very beginning, the courts in America have struggled with the legal status of labor unions. The question bandied about asks whether combinations or "labor cartels" are lawful or not. Legal advice varies, but according to some legal doctrines, unions were "criminal conspiracies in restraint of trade" and illegal combinations to fix prices for labor.

These issues were tested in the state courts from 1806 through 1842. In the famous 1806 criminal prosecution of the Philadelphia cordwainers (shoemakers), *Commonwealth v. Pullis*, a three-day trial led the jury to convict the accused unionists of a criminal conspiracy to fix prices, and eight defendants were each fined $8, slightly more than a week's wages. Only 18 unionists were convicted on conspiracy charges when this doctrine was at its peak.[6] In 1842, Massachusetts Supreme Judicial Court Chief Justice Lemuel Shaw, in the influential decision of *Commonwealth v. Hunt*, ruled the bootmakers' union a lawful association with a lawful right to organize and collectively could withhold labor, or "strike". The courts stopped short of authorizing threats and violence by unions as legitimate "weapons of labor" during strikes. The problem, as pointed out by Ludwig von Mises, is that law enforcement was and is careless and delayed in many labor disputes. The state thereby fails in its alleged basic purpose, to protect life, property, and individual liberty against (private) aggression.

Unions from 1850–1900

Nearly everything was tried in some form or other during this era: socialism, syndicalism, anarchism, cooperatives, political unionism, and, the most seductive idea of all, the welding of everybody (barring bartenders and bankers!) into one gigantic union. Some were unions and some were secret societies, or even thug mob groups, with interesting names. Names familiar to many are those, such as the Knights of St. Crispin, a shoemaker's union, and the Molly Maguires, a secret society in the coal mining industry. Yet the main adhesive of British and European unions, easily aroused class antagonisms, was absent in America, and Marxist-style sentiments about the plight of the working class never became the dominant mood, contrary to some historical accounts. More often, American public opinion was horrified and disgusted by outbreaks of labor violence and union disruption of production, especially if the outbursts had revolutionary overtones.

Following a few decades of attempts with many forms of organized labor, eventually, one form of unionism emerged as the survivor in this unfavorable environment. Experiments with political radicalism gave way to so-called "business unionism," which said that unions must pursue immediate, material gain for members "within" capitalism and the free-enterprise system. The concept acquiesced to accept the capitalist wage, price, and political system and achieve marginal gains for members within it. Consequently, all the ambitions of socialistic visionaries and leftist radicals who saw unions as a vehicle for radical change to usher in Marxism gradually were kicked to the edge of the curb.

History should show that the traditional 20th-century U.S. unions many of us remember ware largely the result of the work of the American Federation of Labor (AFL) and its leader, Samuel Gompers. Founded in 1881, it was a federation of national trade unions, each composed of members of a particular craft such as locomotive engineers or carpenters. Union membership has been all over the map; in the early 1890s was barely 200,000, but as the economy expanded after the Panic of 1893 unions found more effective methods of organization, and membership hit 447,000 in 1897. Given the formula for national craft unionism, unions grew to a modest share of the labor force without enormous government intervention, aside from the laxity toward union threats and the actual use of violence.

By 1900, the end of a long century of membership drives for union labor came to an end in the United States with only 500,000 members. That amounted to less than two percent of the nation's labor force with only twelve unions claiming at least 10,000 members each. The Locomotive Engineers with its 30,000 members was the largest of the unions; the second largest, the Cigar makers with 28,300. Home of the most famous president of the AF, Samuel Gompers, and Cigar makers union lasted until the 1970s, being swallowed up then in a merger with the Retail, Wholesale, and Department Store Union. Though a small part of the total workers in America, unions made up a substantial percentage of certain occupations in construction, railroad, printing and postal service trades.

Pro-union federal legislation benefited only two of the unions; the railroad and postal unions. However, during the 1880s and 1890s there were 17 state legislatures that passed laws prohibiting employers from firing employees for belonging to or joining unions. These actions were a preface for the "Progressive Era", announcing a new pro-union political climate just on the horizon.

20th Century Unionization

In the early 20th century, union membership rose to 6% of the labor force. There were 2.7 million members by 1913, and the share stayed around 6–7% until 1917. "This was the "Progressive Era" of 1900 through 1918 which fastened a welfare-warfare state on America which has set the mold for the rest of the twentieth century... a unique set of conditions had destroyed the Democrats as a laissez-faire party and left a power vacuum for the triumph of the new ideology of compulsory cartelization through a partnership of big government, business, unions, technocrats, and intellectuals."[7] By the way, "progressive" does not infer moving forward as some people think, but is a more palatable name for collectivism, or Communism. A Progressive is simply a patient communist.

Unions during World War I

Union membership was held down by both general public mood and politics up until World War I. Specifically from 1842 moving forward unions were allowed the legal right to exist, workers could join them if they wanted, but employers were under no obligation to hire union workers, or "bargain" with the unions as it was called. Specifically, the courts by their rulings had tended to condemn and restrict union tactics such as threats of violence, mob actions, violence in any form, attacks, and any interference with non-union production. Furthermore, court opinions were written making little distinction between business union "restraints on competition." For example, individual union members were fined being found responsible for actions in a boycott organized by United Hatters of Danbury, CT, when they acted against the products of D.E. Loewe and Company in 1908. The courts said they were "in restraint of trade" as declared under the Sherman Anti-Trust Act of 1890. Anytime unions had incorporated they were held liable as an organization for damages they caused. "Unionists therefore prominently demanded governmental privilege and mounted persistent and intensive campaigns for favorable legislation."[7]

Another action taken to support unions happened in 1912, when Congress passed the Lloyd-LaFollette Act compelling collective bargaining by the US Post Office and encouraging postal-union membership. The Clayton Act followed in 1914, with Congress passing these antitrust provisions to prevent anticompetitive business activities. This act "put more teeth" into antitrust that started with the 1890 Sherman Anti-Trust Act. The Clayton Act exempted or provided a safe harbor for union activities restricting the use of court injunctions in labor disputes. It also reversed earlier rulings declaring picketing and similar union tactics as not being unlawful. Union members celebrated this passage in a kindred spirit like Mardi Gras. Samuel Gompers was ecstatic praising the Clayton Act as being labor unions' Magna Carta. However future court rulings and interpretations would neuter the pro-union provisions.

World War I and the entry of the U.S. into the war opened the door for skilled workers and provided for subsequent intervention on behalf of labor unions to move into industry with a larger footprint. Union membership shoot up to 12 percent of the labor force from the pressure of World War I and the government's intervention. Historian William E. Leuchtenburg, for instance, points out, "The panoply of procedures developed by the War Labor Board and the War Labor Policies Board provided the basis in later years for a series of enactments culminating in the Wagner National Labor Relations Act of 1935."[8]

Further strengthening unions were the War Labor Board and the War Labor Policies Board. Felix Frankfurter led the latter which was modeled after Franklin D. Roosevelt's directive. Representing the United States Navy, Roosevelt proclaimed absolute governmental support of unions, enforcing pro-union measures on industry. An example of their work, the boards established "work councils" composed of various employee representatives who infiltrated industries defiant to unions.

The pro-union influence of Roosevelt and his policies board during this time can be seen in that even the government created a union, the Loyal Legion of Loggers and Lumbermen (aka, "Loyal Region"), and forced lumbermen to join in its battle against the radical leftist Industrial Workers of the World. or IWW, aka, the "Wobblies". After the war, The Loyal Legion collapsed despite all the government efforts and money to keep it alive, while other labor groups became so-called local company or independent unions that were eventually banned by The 1935 Wagner Act, or National Labor Relations Act.

The War Industries Board dually led by Bernard M. Baruch and Army General Hugh S. Johnson was the harbinger for the 1933-35 cartelizing steps under the National Industrial Recovery Act (NIRA) administered by Johnson. Similarly, the War Labor Boards were forerunners to the federal labor boards used to administer NIRA's Section 7(a) and the subsequent National Labor Relations Board (NLRB); this was the creation of the National Labor Relations (Wagner) Act of 1935.

Unions in the Roaring 20s

The end of WW I brought the end of union's growth and infiltration of the American workforce and the 1920s saw a further receding of its part of employment. By 1924, union's share of employment was down to 8 percent. By 1933, it had slipped to 6 percent, the same as it had been thirty years earlier. While wartime had smiled on unions for obvious reasons, the end of "The war to end all wars" eroded the gains made earlier.

However, the "Progressive" political movement in peacetime was soon to provide resuscitation for unions. The Railway Labor Act of 1926 was the first help for private sector unions. Highly visible labor disputes had been erupting periodically on the railroads: they were violent, unpopular, and politically embarrassing. As interpreted then, the interstate commerce clause of the United States Constitution, restricted the ability of the federal government to intervene in most economic affairs, and Congress had the unchallenged power to regulate interstate commerce. A sequence of federal laws beginning in 1888 regulated railway labor matters, and Congress passed the 1926 law in almost the identical form agreed on by the major railroads and unions. As amended in 1934, the act essentially dictated collective bargaining for all interstate railroads and set up machinery for governmental intervention in labor disputes.

This was the first of many examples of monopoly intervention that government would tackle in the years to come. Those railroads which were unionized found it easy, with legislation standing behind them to pressure other non-unionized railroads to join labor. The Interstate Commerce Commission (ICC), helped in turn, by fixing freight rates for railroads based on "costs," which were now much higher because of unions. In this way, railroad wage and price determination was transferred from the marketplace to the political arena in Washington, D.C., all of which started by the interstate commerce clause.

Unions in the Depressed 1930s

At the behest of FDR, now President of the United States, during the Great Depression, Congress worked quickly to deliver a series of six pieces of major labor legislation which brought on a revolution of sorts for pro-unionists. They were: "the Davis-Bacon (1931), Norris-LaGuardia (1932), National Industrial Recovery Act (1933), Wagner National Labor Relations Act (1935), Walsh-Healey (1936), and the Fair Labor Standards Act (1938), popularly known as the minimum wage law. This avalanche of legislation to entrench unions was hastened by the prevailing doctrine of 1920s business leaders, that "high and rising wages were necessary to a full flow of purchasing power and, therefore, to good business," which was followed by its corollary, that "'reducing the income of labor is not a remedy for business depression, it is a direct and contributory cause.'"[9] This statement was made in ignorance, in not being able to identify cause and effect. Any reasonable economist or project manager will identify that higher wages are an effect caused by high levels of productivity and profits. High wages do not cause high productivity and profits; if they did, businesses and nations would simply lower the price of goods, raise wages across the board, then stand back and watch poverty disappear, all on the wings of hopes, prayer and little work.

The Davis-Bacon Act: Following the rapid decline in construction activity at the beginning of the Great Depression, this bill was passed in 1931. Construction spending had dropped an amazing $8 billion a year, going from $11 billion annually to only $3 billion, with half of this financed by the government. The competition of companies and contractors bidding on work was fierce, with many of the bidders hiring cheap migrant labor to underbid their competitors. Many contractors and building trade unions welcomed the law to protect themselves from the competition of what one congressman called "carpet bagging sharpie contractors."[10]

The law was designed to protect local workers from the competition of outside workers, especially migrant workers, by requiring that all workers on federally financed construction be paid wages at "local prevailing rates" for comparable construction work. There was an ambiguity about these "prevailing wages" which provided the United States Department of Labor (DOL) scope to set minimum wage rates at the level of union wages in about half of its wage determinations. These actions have cost taxpayers at least a billion dollars per year in higher construction and administrative costs.

Since 1931, Congress has worked to extend the prevailing wage provision to include most federally assisted construction, whether state, local, or national government is the direct purchaser. In 1964, additional amendments were adopted to add fringe benefits to prevailing wage calculations. The effect of the Labor Department's oversight and administration of the law is to dish out government work to higher cost contractors and the building trades unions, not to protect local contractors from competitors. Currently Davis-Bacon regulates about 20 percent of all construction, with the workers being among the highest paid in America, earning over double the hourly rate of employees in retail trade. Most states passed "little Davis-Bacon" Acts to continue the trend of unionizing the construction industry.

The Norris-LaGuardia Anti-Injunction Act: This legislation was signed by President Herbert Hoover on March 23, 1932. An interesting footnote; the bill passed the House 363-13 and the Senate 75-5. It was the culmination of a 50-year campaign by labor unions against "government by injunction."

The threefold purpose of the act was to:

- declare nonunion employment agreements ("yellow-dog contracts") unenforceable in federal courts (in section 3);
- grant labor organizations immunity from liability for wrongful acts under antitrust law (in sections 4 and 5); and
- Give unions immunity from private damage suits and nullify the equity powers (injunctive relief) of federal courts in labor disputes (in sections 7–12).

The acts' dominant objective was to unshackle organized labor from the typical constraints that bind the typical and non-unionized private sector businessmen and others; it allowed unions a broader scope to use their aggressive and violent tactics to get their way. Immediately, between 1932 and 1933, the number of strikes doubled to a then record 1,695 and just continued climbing to record highs throughout the 1930s. The peak was reached with a total of 4,740 separate strikes in 1937. The rules had suddenly changed in business; previous economic downturns had typically diminished strike activity — now with the deep depression having set in with massive unemployment unions were holding communities as economic hostages. As Hayek summed it up, "We have now reached a state where [unions] have become uniquely privileged institutions to which the general rules of law do not apply."[11]

The National Industrial Recovery Act; NIRA was just one of the inventions of Roosevelt (FDR) made to deliberately boost prices and wage rates, based on the horrible theory that the depression falling wages and prices were causing the depression. The administration could not see what was truly needed. That is for government to get out of the way with regulations and taxes and allow market-driven adjustments to re-coordinate the economy and restore production and employment. The NIRA, which was part of the New Deal fascist system of codes to cartelize both industry and labor markets and push up prices throughout the economy, was struck down in 1935 by the Supreme Court in the famous *Schechter Poultry* case. They opined that the act delegated virtually unlimited legislative power to the president. For example, section 7(a) of the NIRA promoted unions and the practices of collective bargaining. Congress then re-packaged similar labor regulations and new interventions piece by piece in surviving legislation like the Wagner, Walsh-Healey, and Fair Labor Standards Acts.

The National Labor Relations Act (NLRA): Also known as the Wagner Act, the NLRA was actually a rewrite of the NIRA's section 7a. The act passed the Senate 63-12 and an unrecorded voice vote in the House, which Roosevelt signed on July 5, 1935.

The NLRA still remains as the foundational structure for labor unions framework in the America to the current day. Its declarations? The federal government encourages the practice and procedure of collective bargaining. It also protects the worker designation of representatives in negotiating terms and conditions of employment. It uses It declares that the labor policy of the federal government is encouragement of the practice and procedure of collective bargaining, as well as protection of worker designation of representatives to negotiate terms and conditions of employment. It uses the bullying power of the federal government to make it easier to unionize private sector enterprises and employees who otherwise would not actively participate in becoming unionized. The main regulatory features of the act were as follows:

- Creation of a politically appointed board, the National Labor Relations Board, to enforce the act, thereby the courts, viewed as apolitical and often "anti-union" in their rulings.
- Identification of multiple "unfair labor practices" by enterprises to hamper their resistance to organized labor.
- NLRB enforcement of majority elections for union representation.
- NLRB determination of eligibility to vote.
- NLRB enforcement of "monopoly", or exclusive, bargaining for all employees in a bargaining "unit" by NLRB-certified unionists only.
- NLRB enforcement of union pay rates for all employees represented, whether union members or not.

Roosevelt had famously threatened to "pack the court" if the Supreme Court did not start passing his desired legislation carte blanche. Standing against FDR were many in Congress who wanted the Supreme Court to reject NLRA in April 1937 has they had done with NIRA in the past. But, with the overriding pressure from the Oval Office, by a vote of 5-4, the court declared the Wagner Act constitutional in the midst of FDR's threats. Their vote put a stake in the sand, marking the judiciary's general abandonment of constitutional protection against federal encroachment on economic rights and due process.

It would take several years, after the public had reached a point of national nausea with and repulsion for the adversarial unions and their gangland corruption, before further federal legislation was produced modifying the Wagner Act. The legislation was: the **Labor-Management Relations (Taft-Hartley) Act** in 1947 and the **Labor-Management Reporting and Disclosure (Landrum-Griffin) Act** in 1959. The legislation became less favorable to unions, though many will argue this. Neither law tampered with the basic privileges and immunities previously granted to organized labor. As legal scholar Richard Epstein says, Taft-Hartley was a partial union victory because it maintained the original structure of the statutes, making it more difficult to return to common law.[12]

One most notable section (602A) in Landrum-Griffin, although intended to rein in union officials' abuse of members' rights, highlights the immunities the state grants to unions:

It shall be unlawful to carry on picketing on or about the premises of any employer for the purpose of, or as part of any conspiracy or in furtherance of any plan or purpose for, the personal profit or enrichment of any individual (*except a bona fide increase in wages or other employee benefits*) by taking or obtaining any money or other thing of value from such employer against his will or without his consent.

Notice the italicized exclusion. It is astonishing. These openly blatant exceptions, aka privileges and immunities from the law, for unions if the objective is really to promote the national labor law of the 1930s are to be promoted. Specifically, this is nothing more freeing unions from the constraints that the rest of civilization must live under, so that they can extract more money from unwilling employers, all in the name of the law. It is usually paid in the form of higher wages and benefits to union members.

The Walsh-Healey (Public Contracts) Act: Congress passed this legislation in 1936. It was relatively ineffective, though its purpose was to accomplish for unions what Davis-Bacon did for the building-trades unions. Walsh-Healey targeted bureaucracy on all government contracts over $10,000 in value, specifically the poor administrative governance of employment conditions. Separate and legal minimum wage scales were allowed to be set by the Secretary of Labor in order to "fix" wages issues when contracting with the government. Unionized employers were considered "responsible" businesses, since they generally urged that standards be imposed to discipline "unscrupulous" (aka, the low-cost, nonunion) competitors. The reason the act was ineffective was that the Department of Labor never could settle on a consistent method of determining the "prevailing wage" for such a bewildering array of jobs, individual skills, and pay systems. The Walsh-Healey is dead, with its "wage and hour fixing", evidenced by the fact it no longer stimulates any controversy in the business community while Davis-Bacon still does.

The Fair Labor Standards Act: Congress passed it in 1938, setting a national minimum wage rate of 25 cents per hour. It applied to an estimated 43 percent of employees in private, nonagricultural work and gradually grew to cover nearly 90 percent. State minimum wage laws cover most remaining employees. Effective July 24, 2008, the federal minimum was $6.55 per hour and becomes $7.25 per hour effective July 24, 2009, a 29-fold increase over the first minimum wage in 1938.[13] A 90-day beginners' minimum of $4.25 per hour applies to workers under age 20.

Covered "nonexempt" employees must be paid overtime rates of one-and-a-half times the regular pay rate for any hours over 40 in a seven-day period, as specified by the Wage and Hour Board regulations. Over the years, the minimum wage in manufacturing has fluctuated between 35 and 50 percent of the average hourly wage in the nation.

There is much excitement and political talk about raising minimum wages, periodically every few years. While less than 10 percent of wage and salary employees have pay rates low enough to be directly impacted by the minimum wage, unions will consistently campaign for increasing that minimum wage. The reason? There are two. First, it will impact the other pay grades within collective bargaining, meaning more money. Second, it benefits unions by pricing competitors and potential nonunion entrants out of business. That too spells more money for unions, for without competition, rates are generally raised.

But raising minimum wages actually has a negative impact. Many young people, women, older people, and members of minority groups such as inner-city blacks find it more difficult to find beginners' jobs because minimum-wage and union wage rates price them out of the market. But by logic and reason, accepting a low-paying job for its on-the-job training is no different in principle from that of paying to go to school to get trained for a job there. Economic studies show that about half of the training in the US economy occurs on the job rather than in school.[14] Work opportunities and the number of jobs have shrunk, caused by the minimum-wage law, raising the minimum wage. Said differently, management in charge of making a delivering a product, when faced with paying higher wages to make said product, will trim jobs in order to keep costs low enough to make a profit. Many careers have been stopped before they got started, most visibly among black teens in the ongoing tragedy of inner cities. Milton Friedman called the minimum wage law the most anti-black law on the books.[15] Turns out it is not an anti-poverty device after all.

Unions during World War II

With fears that the European was would spread to members of the Western Hemisphere, in 1940, Congress passed the first peacetime draft compelling conscripts to serve in the military, a prelude to the command economy of World War II.[16] This draft accounted for over 10 million of the 16 million military members who served during World War II, creating a depressed labor market and shortage of workers. In response, government policy shifted from promoting artificially inflated high prices for labor services to keeping prices artificially low during wartime. There were a series of temporary boards and commissions given charge over planning, presenting, and coordinating economic mobilization. They took steps to fix prices and wages below previous market levels among other initiatives. It was in effect, full blown socialism.

In order to respond to the nagging chaos caused by lingering disputes, in

January 1942, Roosevelt created the National War Labor Board, patterned after the War Labor Board of World War I. Given wide latitude, the board could and did seize private sector plants in accord with the draft act of 1940. Also in early 1942, the president created the War Manpower Commission. By late in the war Roosevelt tried to transform the commission into an authoritative "work or fight" agency, forcing compulsive membership. However, Congress never approved such a national service law.

In order to keep "labor" from raising wages artificially and rapidly in the midst of a price-controlled market, which would have squeezed businesses, putting many of them out of business, the government came to the rescue. In October 1942, FDR received total unilateral authority over all prices and wages in the country. For the most part, the War Labor Board placated and appeased unions with security arrangements and administratively "looked the other way" as to wage controls and other privileges unions were barred from having. The government and more importantly the American people got nothing in trade for these moves in the realm of "labor peace." Despite all the promises made by labor to end work stoppages, they rose to their worst in 1943.

Post World War II Unionism

The Labor-Management Relations (Taft-Hartley) Act: A Republican majority Congress passed this act over President Truman's veto in 1947. More Democrats joined Republicans in voting for the bill and the override than those who voted against it. Taft-Hartley was unfortunately not an outright repeal of the pro-union Wagner Act; rather it added a list of prohibited union actions, or "unfair labor practices," which would supposedly "balance" the NLRA, which had previously only banned "unfair" labor practices for employers. Also outlawed were the union practices such as jurisdictional strikes, wildcat strikes, solidarity (political) strikes, secondary boycotts, "common situs" picketing, closed shops, and money donations by unions to federal political campaigns. Ironically, union officers were to sign non-communist affidavits with the government, in compliance with the anti-communist activities which were proceeding nationally. "Right to work" laws were created in 22 states, all in the south and west at this time, in response to union shops, which were compelling union membership and/or dues payments as a condition to retain a job. This finally gave the executive branch of the government the power to obtain injunctions in federal courts if an impending or current strike might "imperil the national health or safety," a test that has been interpreted generously by the courts.[17] President George W. Bush invoked the law most recently in connection with the employer lockout of the International Longshoremen's and Warehouse Union during negotiations with west-coast shipping and stevedoring companies in 2002. President Obama was urged by congressional members and company management to invoke Taft-Hartley to avoid a strike by the International Longshoreman's Association in December 2012.

The Labor Management Reporting and Disclosure (Landrum-Griffin) Act (or LMRDA): This 1959 act was named for its sponsors Democrat Phil Landrum and Republican Robert P. Griffin. The LMRDA is tasked with regulating the internal affairs of labor unions and union officials' relationships with employers. The legislation came about because of well-publicized revelations of corruption and undemocratic practices in the Teamsters, the Longshoremen's Association and United Mine Workers. It required secret elections on a regular basis for local union officers followed by authoritative reviews by the Department of Labor, all to silence union members' claims of improper election activity.

Other provisions:

- Required unions to submit annual financial reports to the Department of Labor.
- Declared that every union officer must act as a fiduciary in handling the assets and conducting the affairs of the union.
- Limited the power of unions to put subordinate bodies in trusteeship, a temporary suspension of democratic processes within a union.
- Specified minimum standards before a union may expel or take other disciplinary action against a member of the union.
- Barred members of the Communist Party and convicted felons from holding union office.[18]

More on Union Membership

With withdrawal of World War I federal intervention, dues-paying union membership fell throughout the 1920s from a reported peak of 5 million in 1920 to fewer than 3 million by 1933. According to NBER figures, membership then turned around to more than double to 7.2 million by 1940, doubled again to a staggering 13.2 million by 1945, and increased more slowly to 14.8 million by 1950. There was no such postwar slump in membership after World War I because the pro-union legal framework empowering unions remained in place.

Unions prospered again during the war in the 1940s. WW II government labor boards operated as if their entire purpose for existence was to advance union membership, regaining losses since WW I, and the FDR, New Deal interventions. The labor boards worked hard and between 1933 and 1945 the unionized portion of the civilian labor force rose fourfold from 5.7 percent to 22.4 percent. Following the end of the war, membership eroded to just above 20 percent, but remained above 20 percent through the 1950s.

The trend in membership has changed since 1960 in all Western countries, having a sharp decline through the following years. According to OECD data, the decline has been as follows: estimated density was 30.9 percent in 1960, 22.3 percent in 1980, 12.8 percent in 2000 and 11.6 percent in 2007. The rate of decline in recent years has slowed, mostly because of the concealed union growth in the public sector.

Since 2000, BLS data show a decline in union membership. For example, unions having privately employed wage and salary workers moved from 9.2 million to 8.3 million with an eroded percentage from 9.0 to 7.6 percent. Membership in private-sector unions reached a peak in 1970 of 17 million. Since that time total membership has fallen to less than half that number. Conversely, membership among government-employed wage and salary workers grew modestly from 7.1 million to 7.8 million since 2000, with a stable density of 36.9 percent in 2000 and 36.8 percent in 2008. Since then the population has exploded under the Obama Administration.

Union density in the private sector now is not much higher than it was in the early 1900s despite massive federal intervention on behalf of unionism since World War I. The wage-boosting success of private-sector unions has gone hand in hand with their decline in membership (nothing fails like success), as the silent, steady forces of the competitive marketplace continually undermine government-sanctioned labor cartels.

Public-Sector Unions

The rapid growth of federal government in the past few years translated into the great numbers of employees being hired into public-sector unions puts public sector unions on pace to be the dominant or absolute majority of all union members in the near future. Said differently, private sector unions, traditionally much larger than public-sector unions, will soon be eclipsed by government. That are on pace to claim an absolute majority of all union members in a traditionally private-sector-dominated labor movement within a few years. Government jobs constitute the "healthy" part of organized labor. Government has grown so much with unilateral authority that external competition is not even a major factor against the poorly disciplined union inefficiency, high costs, and perceived special privileges. From 900,000 union members in 1960, government membership rocketed to 4 million by 1970, nearly 6 million by 1976, and 7 million by 1993, with a slowdown in growth to 7.8 million by 2008. Currently it is growing exponentially that it threatens even the economic security of the nation.

The explanation for the sudden burst of government unionization is another intervention, namely, President John F. Kennedy's Executive Order 10988 promoting unionism in the federal bureaucracy, which he signed in January 1962. Kennedy had received considerable campaign support from unions and his executive order declared that "the efficient administration of the government and the well-being of employees require that orderly and constructive relationships be maintained between employee organizations and management." The language does not say "orderly relationships between employees and managers" but "between employee organizations and management." The order set up procedures for determination of collective bargaining units and recognition of unions, compelled agency heads to bargain in good faith, and specified unfair labor practices for unions and management. The order was less generous than the NLRA to unions as it prohibited strikes and established no separate NLRB-type bureaucracy — but it was a beginning.[18]

Kennedy's executive order triggered collective-bargaining laws in states such as Michigan, New York, Washington, and Pennsylvania, all of which had substantial private-sector unionism. Only half-dozen states in the south and west are completely free of such laws promoting public-sector unionism. The National Education Association (NEA), headquartered in Washington, DC (an unsurprising location), is the largest public-sector labor union in the United States with 3.2 million members, although it is not part of the AFL-CIO federation of unions.[19]

Opposition Both Ways

Unions bitterly complain that uniquely American management resistance, legal as well as illegal, has thwarted employees' desire to unionize. If true, stronger government controls to hamper business opposition and allow open expression of employees' desire to unionize might reverse the decline of private-sector unionism. That is the rationale for the **Employee Free Choice Act (EFCA)** backed by the AFL-CIO and the Obama administration.[20] The Employee Free Choice Act would amend the National Labor Relations Act to certify a union as the exclusive bargaining agent (called monopoly) for all employees in a unit appropriate for bargaining given that the members have voted in valid authorizations designating the agent as their official representative. There are three significant parts to the legislation. That is: (1) It would eliminate the need for an additional ballot to require an employer recognize a union, if a majority of workers had earlier signed cards expressing their wish to have a union; (2) It would require that an employer begin negotiating with a union with the purpose of reaching a collective agreement within 90 days, and if not, it will be referred to mediation, and if that fails, to binding arbitration; and (3) It increases the penalties on employers treat workers detrimentally for being in a union. Reviewing the legislation, it seems surreal that industrial democracy has gravitated this far to the left.

Free choice laws will most likely not help unions to change their trend and grow again. They are a relic of the past, subject to competition in the marketplace. Shifts from goods toward services and from the Northeast and upper Midwest to the South and West, a trend toward smaller companies, higher-tech products, and more professional and technical personnel continue to erode the demand for private-union membership. Further, American workers, like the general public, have a low opinion of unions and union leaders, and surveys consistently show that only one in three US employees would vote for union representation in a secret-ballot election. Organizing drives and dramatic confrontations play a small numerical role compared to quiet reductions in the number and size of union establishments and growth in number and size of nonunion establishments.[21]

An Economic Conclusion

Historians and human resources professionals trained in industrial relations are well versed in industrial relations laws, and especially the jargon; the problem is for the most part, very few can interpret them properly. The view among man labor historical writers is this: they believe that what is good for unions is good for all workers and the country. Most come from a pro-union statist background in various markets. But the view is faulty as economic reasoning and data-driven evidence will prove.

First, whenever unions move in and drive wages up, the number of jobs available in the companies and industries declines. This is the simple result of the law of demand: when unions raise the price of labor, employers purchase less of it. Also, prices go up for the consumer. Fewer products are typically purchased putting a backward pressure on the employer and the market. Unions are clearly an anticompetitive force in labor markets.

Second, workers priced out of work by unions remain unemployed or obtain jobs at nonunion companies. A larger labor supply depresses wage rates there, so union wage rates come partially at the expense of lower nonunion wages.

Third, cartels flourish only where rewards are high and organizational costs low. Historically, highly paid craft workers (known as the "aristocrats of labor") organized instead of "downtrodden," low-wage workers because they met two conditions:

- Union wage rates often decreased employment relatively little because demand for skilled workers was "inelastic," that is, employment levels were relatively "insensitive" to changes in wage rates, at least in the short run.
- Craft workers also could organize at low cost because they were few in number, had a common mindset, low turnover, and few or geographically concentrated employers.

Many early economists who sympathized with unions knew unionization could succeed only if restricted to a minority of workers, but they endorsed unions as a device to benefit a visible group and ignored the consequences for everybody else, especially wage earners outside the unions. These economists probably wanted to gain a hearing rather than being dismissed as "mean-spirited." That left the field to a handful of truth-tellers like W. H. Hutt and Sylvester Petro. Mises set the standard for advocating the blunt truth with no bow toward labor mythology: "No one has ever succeeded in the effort to demonstrate that unionism could improve the conditions and raise the standard of living of all those eager to earn wages."[22]

The most astounding phenomenon revealed by this history of American unions is that U.S. business and labor markets continue to work as well as they do. Despite all the union privileges and immunities granted and a never-ending stream of federal labor interventions, the famous flexibility of U.S. labor markets remains. But there have been bailouts, especially by the Obama Administration, all at taxpayer expense. For this and other reasons, the vast majority of American workers remain stubbornly nonunion despite the best efforts of labor unions, the federal government, its court intellectuals, and the mass media to put every worker in a union.

To see the tainted trail of organized workers, please see a *Chronology of Labor Union* below:

> 1684 – New York City government suspends and discharges striking truck men
>
> 1746 – Savannah carpenters strike
>
> 1763 – Negro chimney sweeps in Charleston, South Carolina, institute a work stoppage to get higher prices.
>
> 1770 – New York coopers convicted of conspiracy in restraint of trade by striking for higher rates
>
> 1779 – Sailors strike for higher wages in Philadelphia; troops used and some strikers jailed
>
> 1785 – New York City shoemakers strike for three weeks
>
> 1786 – Philadelphia printers strike successfully for a minimum wage of $6/week
>
> 1790s – Labor "mutual aid" and benevolent societies formed
>
> 1792 – Philadelphia carpenters fail in strike for 10-hour day and overtime pay
>
> 1792 – Shoemakers form first permanent labor union in Philadelphia
>
> 1799 – First strike by a permanent union — Philadelphia shoemakers — in opposition to a wage cut, fails after 10 weeks
>
> 1806 – In Commonwealth v. Pullis, jury convicts eight cordwainers of criminal conspiracy to raise rates, fines levied, union disbands
>
> 1819 – Financial Panic, most unions pass out of existence
>
> 1823 – New York City hatters convicted of conspiracy
>
> 1825 – United Tailoresses of New York City conduct first all-female strike
>
> 1829 – Workingmen's Party of New York formed
>
> 1820s–1930s – Attempts to form local unions into national unions fail
>
> 1834 – First attempt at a national federation, the National Trades Union, formed in New York City
>
> 1834 – Factory Girls' Association at Lowell, Massachusetts, strikes
>
> 1837 – Panic ends National Trades Union and most unions
>
> 1840 – 10-hour day without reduction in pay for federal government employees
>
> 1842 – Massachusetts Supreme Court rules bootmakers' union and its threatened strike are not unlawful
>
> 1842 – Connecticut and Massachusetts pass laws prohibiting children from working over 10-hour days

CHAPTER SEVEN — THE HISTORY OF LABOR UNIONS IS THEIR TROUBLE

1845 – First teachers' association formed in Massachusetts

1847 – New Hampshire first state to pass a 10-hour workday

1850 – Delegates from 43 unions attend workingmen's convention in New York City

1857 – Depression, many unions fail

1852 – Typographical Union ("printers") founded, become the oldest surviving trade union at its dissolution in 1986

1860 – Successful strike of estimated 20,000 shoemakers in New England; Abraham Lincoln comments, "Thank God we have a system of labor where there can be a strike"

1861–65 – Civil War, unions expand from 79 to 300

1863 – Brotherhood of Locomotive Engineers founded

1866–86 – Many local trade unions ally into dozen national unions

1867 – Knights of St. Crispin founded as union open to all factory workers in shoe industry

1868 – 8-hour day for blue-collar federal employees

1868 – First state labor bureau founded in Massachusetts

1869 – Formation of Knights of Labor, ultimately superseded by American Federation of Labor (AFL), formed in 1881

1870s – Strikes defeated in textiles and mines

1873–78 – Panic of 1873; during postwar deflation national unions resist wage cuts and shrink from 30 to fewer than 10; three-quarters of membership lost

1873–74 – Molly Maguires, a secret Irish terrorist group, scorn conventional unions and commit wave of murders; bosses come to work armed

1874 – Union label first used by Cigar Makers International Union, tells customers product made by white hands

1876 – Forerunner of Socialist Labor party organized

1877 – Four Molly Maguires convicted and hung in Pennsylvania for murder

1877 – First nationwide strike on railroads ("Great Railroad Strike of 1877") in opposition to wage cuts, freight trains obstructed, some state militias side with strikers, federal troops used for first time

1881 – Forerunner of American Federation of Labor (AFL) formed in Pittsburgh

1881 – First Labor Day celebrated in New York City

1882 – Chinese Exclusion Act prohibited citizenship for Chinese immigrants, supported by union leaders, immigration controls reinforced by acts passed in 1884, 1886 and 1888

1884 – Federal Bureau of Labor established within Department of the Interior

1885 – Foran (Alien Contract Labor) Act bans employers from recruiting and paying passage for foreign workers; unions endorse limiting supply of labor, some employed as strikebreakers

1886 – Chicago Haymarket Square riot (May 4), 8 police officers killed and an unknown number of civilians, five convicted and executed, inspires May Day observances for workers

1888 – First federal labor-relations law applied to railroads

1890 – United Mine Workers of America formed

1892 – Homestead strike (Carnegie Steel) in Pennsylvania results in pitched battle between Pinkertons and strikers, 7 die, 2 dozen wounded; Pinkertons lose battle but union loses in long run as Carnegie/US Steel stays nonunion for 45 years

1893 – Business panic and depression eliminates many unions again

1894 – Strike against Pullman Car Company led by Eugene Debs spreads to railroads, injunction defied, federal troops called out on grounds of striker interference with mail delivery, 13 strikers killed, and widespread property damage

1898 – Erdman Act provides mediation and arbitration for rail disputes, succeeds 1888 law

1901 – US Steel defeats steel union again after 3-month strike

1901 – United Textile Workers founded

1902 – Coal miners agree to arbitration by presidential committee to end 5-month strike

1903 – US Department of Commerce and Labor established

1903 – Mother Jones (Mary Harris Jones) leads "March of the Mill Children" to President Theodore Roosevelt's home in New York

1905 – Industrial Workers of the World ("Wobblies") formed in Chicago

1905 – In Lochner v. New York Supreme Court declares a New York maximum-hours law unconstitutional

1906 – Typographical Union successfully strikes for 8-hour day

1906 – Upton Sinclair publishes The Jungle exposing sanitary and safety problems in Chicago meat packing

1908 – In Muller v. Oregon Supreme Court rules female maximum-hours laws constitutional due to a woman's "physical structure and . . . maternal functions"

1908 – United States v. Adair decision declares so-called yellow dog contracts (employment agreement to not join a union) constitutional on interstate railroads, overturning the Erdman Act

1910 – In the "crime of the century," the downtown plant of the Los Angeles Times is bombed, killing 21; the newspaper is a powerful opponent of organized labor, leaders of the Iron Workers Union are convicted of the crime; the union had conducted a nationwide bombing campaign since 1905

1911 – Gompers v. Bucks Stove and Range ruling orders AFL to cease an unlawful boycott

1912 – Massachusetts enacts first minimum-wage law for women and minors

1913 – US Department of Labor established, secretary of labor has power to "act as a mediator and to appoint commissioners of conciliation in labor disputes"

1914 – Clayton Act limits labor injunctions and endorses picketing and related union tactics but court nullifies in 1921

1914 – In Ludlow Massacre in Colorado, day-long battle between strikers and

Chapter Seven — The History of Labor Unions Is Their Trouble

National Guard culminates in Guard attack on tent colony of 1,200 strikers and their families; death toll is 20 including 11 children

1915 – LaFollette Seamen's Act regulates seamens' working conditions

1916 – Adamson Act imposes 8-hour day on railroads to avert rail strike

1916 – Federal child-labor law later declared unconstitutional

1917 – Wartime mediation commission headed by labor secretary

1917 – Federal government seizes railroads

1918 – President Wilson establishes National War Labor Board

1919 – Unions lose nationwide "Great Steel Strike"

1919 – Labor leaders recommend labor clauses to create International Labor Organization in Versailles Treaty

1919 – First police strike occurred in Boston but broken by then-governor Coolidge, bringing him national fame

1920 – Women's suffrage amendment ratified

1921 – Supreme Court nullifies pro-union features of Clayton Act

1921 – In Truax v. Corrigan Supreme Court strikes down Arizona law forbidding labor injunctions and permitting picketing

1921 – Emergency Quota Act restricts southern- and eastern-European immigration

1922 – In "Herrin Massacre" coal strikers in southern Illinois murder 19 strikebreakers and two union members

1924 – Immigration (Johnson-Reed) Act limits number of immigrants to 2% of number of people from that country already living in United States in 1890, aimed especially at limiting Japanese immigration

1924 – William Green succeeds Samuel Gompers as AFL president

1926 – Railway Labor Act enacted as drafted by interstate railroads and unions

1929 – Hayes-Cooper Act restricts interstate shipment of goods produced by prison labor

1929 – October stock market crash "begins" Great Depression

1930 – Supreme Court upholds Railway Labor Act in Texas and NOR v. Brotherhood of Railway Clerks

1930 – President Hoover effectively bans immigration by decree

1931 – Davis-Bacon Act

1932 – Norris-LaGuardia Act

1932 – Wisconsin passes first unemployment insurance program

1933 – NIRA section 7(a) promotes unions and collective bargaining

1933 – Francis Perkins appointed secretary of labor, first female cabinet officer

1933 – Wagner-Peyser establishes US Employment Service at Department of Labor

1934 – Southern mill workers walk off job in "Great Uprising of '34"

1934 – United States joins ILO

1935 – Supreme Court strikes down NIRA in Schechter Poultry v. United States

1935 – Wagner Act (NLRA) passes

1935 – Committee for Industrial Organization (CIO) formed within AFL to promote industrial-style unions

1935 – Social Security Act effectively coerces states into adopting unemployment-benefits programs

1936 – United Rubber Workers (CIO) use first large "sit-down strike" to win recognition at Goodyear Tire

1936 – United Automobile Workers use sit-down strike at GM plant

1936 – Byrnes Act prohibits interstate transport of strikebreakers

1936 – Walsh-Healey Public Contracts Act

1936 – Railway Labor Act amended to cover airline employees

1937 – NLRB v. Jones & Laughlin Steel, Supreme Court finds NLRA (Wagner) Act constitutional

1937 – GM and US Steel recognize unions as exclusive bargaining agents

1937 – In "Memorial Day Massacre," smaller steel producers refuse to unionize, union protesters in Chicago take to the streets, police block their path and fire on the crowd, killing 10

1937 – AFL expels CIO for "dual unionism"

1938 – Fair Labor Standards Act

1938 – Federal Maritime Labor Board established

1938 – CIO changes name to Congress of Industrial Organizations, John L. Lewis made president

1938 – In NLRB v. Mackay Radio & Telegraph Supreme Court rules striking employees remain "employees"

1940 – In Apex Hosiery v. Leader Supreme Court rules sit-down strike — actually a plant seizure by unionists few of whom were employed at the plant — was not an illegal restraint of trade in interstate commerce

1941 – Ford Motor Co. recognizes the UAW, signs a union-shop agreement

1941 – United States enters WWII (December 8), long sought by FDR, and AFL and CIO announce no-strike pledges and then freely violate them

1941 – Executive Order 8802 or Fair Employment Act prohibits racial discrimination in defense industry

1942 – National War Labor Board established, Stabilization Act gives Roosevelt the authority to "stabilize" wages

1943 – Roosevelt issues executive order establishing Committee on Fair Employment Practices to eliminate "employment discrimination" in war industries

1943 – Smith Connally (War Labor Disputes) Act authorizes plant seizures to "avoid interference with the war effort" 23

1945 – WWII ends

1946 – Largest wave of strikes as wartime controls relaxed

1947 – Taft-Hartley Act (LMRA)

1947 – United States v. John L. Lewis holds that Norris-LaGuardia prohibition against labor injunctions does not apply to the federal government

1948 – GM and UAW agree on first wage-escalator clause based on Consumer Price Index

1948 – United States v. CIO holds that union advocacy that members vote for particular congressional candidates does not violate Federal Corrupt Practices Act as amended

1949 – FSLA amendment directly prohibits child labor

1949 – CIO begins expelling communist-controlled unions

1950 – GM and UAW agree on 5-year deal with pension plan, automatic cost-of-living wage escalators, and quasi-union-shop

1952 – President Harry Truman seizes steel industry after it rejects Wage Stabilization Board recommendations, 8-week strike follows after Supreme Court declares Truman's action unconstitutional

1952 – George Meany (aptly named) becomes president of AFL and Walter Reuther becomes president of CIO

1955 – AFL and CIO reunite with Meany as president

1955 – Ford Motor Co. and UAW agree to a supplementary unemployment compensation financed by the company

1957 – AFL-CIO expels Teamsters, Bakery Workers, and Laundry Workers for corruption

1959 – Landrum-Griffin Act (LMRDA)

1962 – President John F. Kennedy issues Executive Order 10988 to promote unionism and collective bargaining in federal employment

1963 – Equal Pay Act prohibits wages differences based on sex

1964 – Civil Rights Act Title VII bans employment discrimination

1965 – Immigrant Act eliminates national origin quotas in favor of new criteria of control

1967 – Age Discrimination in Employment Act makes it illegal to hire and fire persons age 40–65 based on age

1968 – UAW leaves AFL-CIO to join Teamsters in new Alliance for Labor Action (ALA)

1969 – Department of Labor intervenes on behalf of minority employment in Philadelphia construction industry

1970 – First nationwide postal strike

1970 – Occupational Safety and Health Act (OSHA)

1973 – Washington first state government to allow union shop for state employees (compulsory membership)

1974 – Employee Retirement Income Security Act (ERISA) regulates and subsidizes bankrupt pension plans

1974 – AFL establishes public-employee department

1981 – President Reagan fires striking air-traffic controllers for illegal strike

1986 – Immigration and Control Act

1989 – Worker Adjustment and Retraining Notification (WARN) Act requires employers with 100+ employees to provide 60-day notice of plant closings and mass layoffs

1990 – Immigration Act

1990 – Americans with Disabilities Act (ADA) is viewed as a civil-rights law that prohibits discrimination based on disability, defined as a "physical or mental impairment that substantially limits a major life activity"

1991 – Civil Rights Act attempts to overturn Supreme Court restrictions on employees' job "rights" under federal labor law

1993 – Federal Family and Medical Leave Act

1994 – California voters approve Proposition 187 to deny illegal immigrants access to government-subsidized schooling, social services, and medical care; a federal court strikes it down as unconstitutional

2009 – Ludlow Massacre site (ghost town 12 miles northwest of Trinidad, Colorado), owned by United Mine Workers of America, dedicated as a National Historic Landmark (June 28)

2009 – Federal minimum wage increases from $6.55 to $7.25 per hour (July 24)

2009 – Employee Free Choice Act (EFCA) gathers political momentum, would substitute union "card checks" for NLRB secret-ballot elections for a union to obtain NLRB certification as exclusive bargaining agent

2014 – President Obama pushes for increase of minimum wage from $7.25 to $10.10 per hour

The events shown on the organized labor timeline above has been substantially negative to American commerce, its outputs and many times its quality. The socialist platform on which they perform drags down the production of the nation. Labor unions played a positive role in breaking abusive child labor in the 19th century. However, they have by their actions mostly served to eliminate some categories of jobs. They have accomplished this negativity by hourly demands raising production costs, and destroying some industries by only their pensions which cannot be maintained without taxpayer assistance. One feature about unions that disturbs many Americans is that they protect poor performers from discipline and termination, they hold back exceptional workers who could be more productive and earn more outside of a union, and they send industry off-shore due to the costs. If time goes on, hopefully historians and media will be more honest about unions in the future than they are now.

"When a plane crashes and some die while others live, a skeptic calls into question God's moral character, saying that he has chosen some to live and others to die on a whim; yet you say it is your moral right to choose whether the child within you should live or die. Does that not sound odd to you? When God decides who should live or die, he is immoral. When you decide who should live or die, it's your moral right."

— Ravi Zacharias

Chapter Eight

The Problem with the Church

THERE IS A HEBREW MYTH WHICH says that when God formed man of the dust and breathed into him the breath of life, He gave man every treasure except one. He withheld from him satisfaction on this earthly stage, condemned him to perpetual restlessness, dissatisfaction and discontent with all things temporal and transient. The writer of Ecclesiastes had a shorter word for it: "God has set eternity in his heart."[1]

It is not easy to come back. Ask any beaten athlete, from blind Samson to Joe Louis; talk with an ex-convict as he looks for decent work with the hands of all society against him; or follow Arnold Toynbee's *Study of History* tracing the descent of civilizations. It is an axiom in the sports world that "they never come back." Long ago the Greek critic of Christianity Celsus said, "Everybody knows from long experience with actual life that once a man has gone a certain length in sin and folly, there is no smallest prospect of reclaiming him, because inevitably the man is carried downhill faster and faster by his own impetus."[2]

America's decline over the past 20 years has been nothing short of spectacular, like a meteor crashing to earth. The decline has been going on for 75 years to a century, but the exponential speed toward the crash ahead within the last couple of decades is easily observed. Politically, culturally, economically, and spiritually, we are hardly a shadow of our once-great selves. Today we try to sustain a pipe dream of being a "Disney Land" type of culture with Federal Reserve funny money used to bail out bankruptcies of auto makers, union pension plans, and trillions in relief programs like welfare and a load of other government spending. In truth, we devolved and resemble little more than a Potemkin village.

Just as America started as a protest, the Reformation movement too first saw life with a banner of protest against the corruption, rituals, doctrines, and ceremonies in the Medieval Church, when Martin Luther nailed "his 95 theses" on the Court Church door on the eve of All Saints Day, Wittenberg, Germany, October 31, 1517. Contrasting the permissiveness of that Roman Catholic Church, the Reformation led down another path with disciples like Luther. Luther meritoriously began focusing on exalting personal virtues again in the Christian walk: graciousness, honesty, integrity, holiness, sobriety and purity. Having a renewed emphasis on individual worth, it became the ideal faith for the common man, and it was this faith that gave the foundational contributions to the building of this nation.

R. H. Tawny, in his book, *Religion and The Rise of Capitalism*, traced the influence of the Reformation on the thinking of the Puritan forefathers. It was this Protestantism, by stressing its virtues of hard work, temperance in all things, individual responsibilities, free enterprise, and an uncompromising conscience that developed precisely the kind of economic push our stern Forefathers needed in their minds so they could grapple with the wilderness. As my grandpa used to say, "They were a solid stock and breed, they weren't much for jocularity; they were stoic, earnest men who kept the Commandments, and saw that others kept them too."

Churches are supposed to be about the business of changing the world! "Go into all the world and make disciples . . . ," is the way Jesus put it. The real trouble with the Reformation is that it stopped too soon, short of the goal. It did not crash through the tape at the end of the race. A few exceptions are found among denominations or congregations where true disciples are made. The church "at large" did follow through early on in our history to develop a social conscience. Chronically the anti-slavery movement started by the Quakers was one. Another was the Sabbath School movement to teach children to read and write. Then there was the Temperance Movement started by southern ladies in the Methodist Churches to fight the effect of alcoholism and public drunkenness and its effect on the American families. Martin Luther King led a movement among Baptist and other evangelical congregations for civil rights for all citizens. These were wonderful efforts for a cause, but each of these were initiated 50 to 250 years ago. The numbers of congregations who are fighting the fight today have been on the decline since that point, especially over the past half century. While pastors focus on keeping those on the inside of the church building walls happy and occupied, there has to also be a focus on challenging the prince of the power of the air in charge of the culture outside the walls.

Like America, the church in general is seen in the light of a rapid decline over the past 40 years, like a shooting star. Many entities have facilitated this fall. The World Council of Churches (WCC) has been one such group.

The WCC became a strong political force changing the face of the church today starting back in the 1950s, nearly to its inception in 1948. It was the organization through which groups like the Communists, Fascists, Progressives have been able to infiltrate the church. What shocks many people who know something of this organization, near its founding date there was some good which came out of the group. For example, in 1949, major denominations, most from the WCC, met challenging the clergy in attendance to study several passages of Scripture using laws of hermeneutics. The passages had historically been interpreted differently by the various denominations, thus they were the declared reasons for having denominations in Christendom. Those passages covered such issues as baptism, the Holy

CHAPTER EIGHT — THE TROUBLE WITH THE CHURCH

Spirit, how to become a Christian, and others. During the conference, leaders broke up into small groups to study the passages using one particular lens, leaving their denominational beliefs behind for the time. Following this lens of hermeneutics, each group did something they had not been able to do for centuries: completely agree on the interpretations of the various sections of Scripture. That was a true milestone moment.

Shortly after that time the WCC was infiltrated by political forces, Leftists all, and within a decade the declared purpose of the organization was to bring social justice to America. The themes were more caustic, like "Let's disarm America!" Other campaigns included the general themes of welcoming homosexuals, or at least not judging them; bring social justice to the Negro population. Note the name at that time, which now has become African American. It was not long until abortion and women's rights became one of the strongest proponents for the church. Gun control soon followed. Slowly, changes at the top were made, and the organization took on the mask of a political force for the Progressives in America, much to the joy of Communists, Fascists, Collectivists, and Marxists, whose organizations had contributed lots of cash, pushing to get this planned change to become reality. Today, the WCC is still a political machine, with no emphasis on spiritual growth but having a focus on social justice.

Further facilitating mission failure for the church has been getting cozy with cultural standards of society, rather than separation from it. With this stance the message presented to audiences and to the community was one of teamwork to make a difference in the world against drugs, against crime, against racism, etc. Scriptures began to be viewed through an allegorical lens, meaning of course that many characters in the Bible were not viewed as real people. They were fictional characters teaching us lessons about life. While it may seem attractive at first, the foundation of such a faith soon crumbles away with many people doubting whether their faith is real or if faith is even necessary. The end result is that many liberal churches bought into this plan, have witnessed large losses of membership over time, then doubling down on the allegorical methodology, meaning people are looking for the reality of God's story.

The overall impact on society, some observe we live in a post-Christian society today, A Christian society is one where people are compelled to meet the Savior, making a decision of participation of sacrificial living and sacrificial loving. These activities come from being introduced to and involved with spiritual reality, becoming a disciple of Him, convicted to do unto others as you would have them . . . and to love your neighbor as yourself, which is the royal law according to scripture, James 2:8. It also means denying oneself for the sake of others. You do not see much of that anymore. Some will say, "What about my needs?" In a society where people are living to serve one another, everyone's needs are met. See James 3:13-15. . . . there is wisdom of the world, bitter jealousy and selfish ambition; self-absorbed, and consumed with nothing but self — earthly, natural, demonic. Bernie Madoff was a prime example. Marriages are falling apart. You cannot have two gods living in the same universe expecting to be worshipped.

In opposition and contrast to this is the post-Christian. Once everything has been abandoned, it is all about experiencing and feeding the senses. So it is about sex, about sex, about making money, drugs, alcohol.

How far have we come to just feed the screaming desires of our senses? A man and woman will go have sex just to feed the desires. That is just the beginning. Now they have a child. So they will go abort the child since the child gets in the way of their pursuit of the lust of the flesh, the lust of the eyes and their boastful pride of life. We are willing to kill our young so that we can feed the **screaming desires of our senses**.

There are 300 million people living in America now. We have aborted nearly 56 million, which is 1/6 of our population, since 1973.[3] The writing was on the wall 2,000 years ago when humans were taught in person what is right and what is wrong, but we do not want God instructing us. The things of God are foolishness for a society that is perishing. Listen! Do not love the world or the things of the world. Why is America passing away? Because all the things this society loves is passing away, 1 John 2:15-17. Such a lifestyle does not sustain itself. The church has abandoned worshipping God for the sake of worshipping self.

Congregations, or rather ministers, who will not "disciple" new Christians past the initial messages of grace, peace, and joy, are a problem. They are sometimes referred to as "seeker friendly" churches, making the Gospel appear almost out of character; having few lessons on discipline, obedience, and sacrifice. Normally, these pulpits have a total hands-off policy when it comes to speaking about tyrants of the day. The Nazi church is a good example. It embraced Hitler during his day, or at least did not "rock the boat" looking the other way when people were being murdered. The result of all this was that while the Church sat in judgment on its own members about whether they smoked, drank, cursed, gambled, or kept the Sabbath (or in the Pilgrim day, wore buttons on their coats). Simultaneous, it permitted antisocial systems to take root and grow in America. Slavery was one of them. It was deemed unchristian to gamble, but at the time, not unchristian to own slaves. During the industrial revolution, many congregations and denominations did not take a stand against the piling up of huge fortunes by robber barons who, as Dr. Ralph W. Sockman said years ago, " . . . they kept the Sabbath and they kept the Commandments, and about everything else they could get their hands on."[4] This type of thinking, now in the DNA of some churches in our time has led to a message separating salvation and daily life. It would not be uncommon to hear one of the in a congregation say something like, "Well, my Jesus is not upset if I go to the casino and have some drinks, but it sounds like your Jesus won't let you have the freedom to go wild once in a while." With that statement, the Gospel has gone on sale. It is said to be less costly in some churches than in others. The simple fact is that Jesus

CHAPTER EIGHT — THE TROUBLE WITH THE CHURCH

is not inconsistent. He despises sin; He loves us. His message to us in the modern vernacular would be, "Stop sinning! Follow My example."

Within the some segments churches coming out of the Reformation, there are some pastors and members who have in large portion forgotten how to rightly divide the Word; what it means to study Scripture using a grammatical-historical-contextual exegesis. In other words, what it means to understand the original intended meaning. And what it means to be a disciple. It has sometimes been cheapened. It is not my intention to infuriate anyone but simply expose a problem.

In many locations, the real work the church has been assigned to do or manage, has been left sitting by the road; traded for trendy, politically correct talk about gun control, women's rights, welcoming homosexuals, restricting free speech and gun control. Meaning that a portion of this movement labeled, "The Reformation" that started 600 years ago is stalled.

As that has happened, it has created a domino effect, resulting in some of the greatest of all the collapses in America; the loss of morality in the culture and the loss of spiritual vision to make appropriate decisions at all times, especially in times of trouble. That has been brought on because one entity did not do its job. That is the church. It has failed to be the lighthouse for those loads of lost souls caught in life's storms that have been crashing on the rocks. Many will say, "The church is not to blame. It's easy to see that Satan, the spiritual enemy of us all, he is the one responsible for America's downfall. Isn't he? I mean, here we were, just minding our own business, having fellowship meals and bowling for blessings tournaments, keeping ourselves unstained from the world, and wham! Who else could bring about the dramatic downfall of such a rich and powerful nation as America?"

To represent Heaven, the church cannot be a bland Potemkin village at least that is the view point from where the world sits. People are for the most part lost, looking for answers. They want the real thing, not a hollow shell. Operating out of fear, or pretense, or being a pal to the political left, or just adopting an "emerging" style so as not to make anyone from outside uncomfortable, it has set up a shell of the end result leaves it at the end of the day a passive but complicit partner in the collapse of our country's culture.

Put this "village" of modern day disciples against the backdrop of our earlier ancestry who when beaten and arrested for their statements of faith in public, stood against those magistrates and authorities and famously said, "We cannot but speak of the things we have seen and heard." [4]

What makes the church weak? Division. In Mark 3:25 Jesus states, "And if a house is divided against itself, that house will not be able to stand." This is the church today; divided on something that weakens it greatly, serving and loving its neighbor. Every generation or so will go through circumstances, such as rowdy and bloody wars which will rudely awaken the church contemporaries to the realization that personal virtue is simply not enough, we have to have an effect on the culture.

Segments of the Church Are like a Prodigal

Every congregation or church should realize that with the attitude that we will follow some directives of Scripture and ignore others, brings on the countenance of what the prodigal son had in Jesus story. The prodigal did not like things at home, did not want to follow all the rules, and wanted more freedom. So he just decided to leave once he received his share of the inheritance. He decided he just could not do what was required any longer. He was not willing to be the disciple that he needed to be any longer. A segment of what is commonly known as the church has become lazy, impotent, ignorant and arrogant; actually at times refusing to allow true disciples to be associated with it. It then fits well within the Master's story of the prodigal son.

It is a marvelous story Jesus had told; Dickens called it, "the most divinely tender and humanly poignant story ever told on earth." Even the stiff-necked Pharisees softened under its spell. Everybody does. It takes hold of us too. Just read it without making any comment and you will find every line of it making for your heart. A boy saying, "Give me. . . . " to his father, chafing under the home restraint, wanting to get away from it all. Life is calling with laughter, music, dancing, the lure of the far country. How human it is!

But then there is a Law, an eternal inescapable law. It's God's Law, "There arose a famine in the land." An empty stomach becomes a preacher of righteousness. "I'll get up and go home." Trudging the homeward path, between sobs he made up a speech. He had made such a sorry mess of freedom. He was willing now to trade it for bread or a job. "Make me a hired servant." And the father who is the real hero of the story, with a love the boy never understood, sitting on the roof-top, watching the road, and then running to meet him. The speech was smothered in a choking sob. Get some decent clothes for him. The boy is home again. "They began to be merry."

A Segment of the Church Is the Older Brother, Respectably at Home

There is a good place to stop in the story of the prodigal; when he came home. But we cannot stop there. There is the rest of the story about another sinner: the brother who stayed home. It is really surprising how little attention we have given this elder brother. We nearly always think of him as some sort of an anticlimax. We nearly always stop with the return of the prodigal, with the vague idea in the back of our minds that when we have reached that place we have seen the entirety of the Gospel. And that if we could persuade all the prodigals in the world to repent and just come home, our obligation would be fulfilled. All of which reveals how totally inadequate is our conception of the range and the depth of the Christian message. We have not stopped to think that Christianity is much bigger than we have made it or imagined it. Consequently we have never seen the elder brother

Chapter Eight — The Trouble with the Church

for the downright sinner he really is; how far short he, and we, have come by the test of the real Christian standard.

We usually think of him as a good guy who did pretty well, certainly in contrast with his sibling. He was at least respectable. He stayed home and behaved decently. He had some virtues which our churches of today admire very much. He was thrifty, industrious, and dependable. In today's society he would be eligible for membership in Kiwanis, the Rotary Club or a member of the Church Board. I mean he was generally always in attendance. That is what a low estimate of Christianity does. It sees people through a different lens, the wrong lens. We see many people in the fold who are not in but shut out by sins. There are sins which we have not been morally sensitive enough to call sins. At any rate, we make a big mistake when we set up the respectable elder brother as a bright background against which the prodigal's blackness is painted. We are nearer the truth when we regard him as another type of sinner in need of salvation. He is someone who may be in church services most every week, but he is sorely lacking when it really comes to the love of God and discipleship.

The story being told is similar to a segment of the church today. We have sinned and need to come home. Or we have sinned while we stayed home. Either the congregation can be the prodigal who has run away from home, or it can live the older brother's kind of life, staying home sinning, with prejudice and social callousness. This kind of life is what put so much chaos in the world. The real sin of both is that they turn out being like the rest of the world. They are not a conscience for the world. When you boil down the sins of the bad-tempered older brother, you can label him with one word: 'lovelessness'. That is the church in many respects. Respectable as it is, it has lost the love it once had. It seems to lack that one thing without which all other virtues are worthless. And sad to say the world sees that when the church has deluded them. And so fitting is Paul's statement to a Corinthian church long ago, being, "only a resounding gong, or a clanging cymbal — I gain nothing." 1 Cor. 13:1 The New Testament emphasizes love over and over as being the mark of a Christian and the test of sonship. "How can we love God whom we have not seen if we don't love our brother whom we have seen?" The elder brother had no love of truth or anyone but himself. Much of what is called the church fits that scenario.

If you are familiar with that timeless story, you will remember that the home-coming that gladdened his father's heart stirred this older brother to jealousy and anger. "He was angry and would not go in." He stood outside hearing the music, sulking about the fuss being made over a wastrel, deep in his callous heart resenting his father's happiness and his brother's return. And when his father remonstrated with him, he blew up. "I stay at home. I do the work. I obey you. I keep myself respectable. You make no fuss over me. But when this, your son, is come home . . . " Listen to that! Your son; he could not say 'brother'. And it shut him out. The curtain closes on the story with the younger prodigal finally come home and in the father's house and the elder brother outside. This is a real picture of the church not showing the way for the world.

That is why I let my mind dwell on this story here, because we all wonder about some people who stay at home, go through the motions of keeping the rules, and feel pretty darned satisfied with themselves. It is so like the church for the last century in at least some aspects. "We are decent people here: well fed, thrifty. We watch for bargains, industrious, respectable, yet we are somewhat calloused to the catastrophe, not wanting to be disturbed too much, not caring too much about the people the trouble is hurting, just so long as the trouble does not reach us. Far too long, we have said do not bother us with that. Do not keep passing a collection plate in front of us. Do not irritate us with their troubles." And the world has not been impressed with our witness.

A Problem: The Church Wants To Be Left Alone

Given the directive to "go into the world" by the Lord, it seems odd that a major part of the church has come to a point in time where it prefers to stay in the building and not get involved in the touchy issues of the discussions of the (like homosexuality, abortion, marriage rights) that are front and center in the nation. Encounter groups are good but getting out in the deep water in taking a stand against those hot issues is foundational to making disciples. So while the church has been respectable, she has been also shiftless, occasionally loveless. What a church wins a convert with is what they win them to. Staying inside the walls just to keep singing songs on Sundays is one thing, but there is so much in the recipe to change the world of its habits.

The churches upon whose faith America was built resisted the culture in some cases just a little. That is, a little in a few spoken words. Usually this was done before lunch on Sundays. They spoke with almost a united voice across denominational lines about the evils of abortion, euthanasia, sexual decadence, re-defined marriage, addiction to welfare, fatherless children, inner-city gang violence and undeclared wars abroad. And they suggested that Christians strongly consider the statements of those they elected to office regarding these evils.

They did all that, didn't they? I mean they were, ah, um, I mean we were faithful weren't we? Well, not really. Possibly, the answer can be found in *the Bible in Revelation* 3:14-17:

"To the church in Laodicea write:

These are the words of the Amen, the faithful and true witness, the ruler of God's creation. [15] I know your deeds, that you are neither cold nor hot. I wish you were either one or the other! [16] So, because you are lukewarm—neither hot nor cold—I am about to spit you out of my mouth. [17] You say, 'I am rich; I have acquired wealth and do not need a thing.' But you do not realize that you are wretched, pitiful, poor, blind and naked."[5]

If this is a judgment on the decline of the American church, it is likely because its people subtly "drifted" away from the power of the Gospel blending itself into the rest of American culture — becoming unaware of their decline of spiritual acuity and potency like in Laodicea. The Laodicean's decline was because "he" enjoyed his life in his culture so much. He began to assimilate his feeling of wellness in society with spiritual security that is when the sin of presumption entered the scene. The trail to this conclusion is simple. They didn't walk the talk. They developed a lackadaisical approach to spiritual life. Rituals and liturgy likely were substituted for a true discipleship to their Savior, and thus received His reprimand.

> "I also will choose their delusions, and will bring their fears upon them; because when I called, none did answer; when I spake, they did not hear: but they did evil before mine eyes, and chose that in which I delighted not" (Isaiah 66:4).

Guess what, America? Guess what, American Church? Potemkin Villages are sickening to God because they are a pretense. Your demise is being orchestrated by yourselves since it was none other than God Himself who prepared punishment for pretenders, as indicated in Scripture. You were called to do the right thing and make disciples. You chose to do lesser, ignoring God in the process and have in effect robbed yourself through your own hoax.

Segments of the Church Are Also a Turncoat

Fundamentally, the problem is the overall silence and inactivity of the American Church. And this lack of speaking out against government's scandalous overreach is across most denominational lines. If the church is going to strive for a culture like that of the world, the culture will disdain it. Those who are seeking answers to life's ultimate questions do not need, nor do they desire, a culture that has little difference to the one where they live.

Changing names and changing pastors may be a diversion for a time. But while the church lost its way, many times it has lost its message; it didn't turn to God for guidance. Rather it has turned to the world for acceptance and a warm fuzzy. Instead of preaching the old true Gospel and being on the front lines in the fight to be a conscience to the world, it has stood on the sidelines trying to get the world to accept it as a business partner in the business of "cheap grace," as Dietrich Bonhoeffer said to Hitler and the Third Reich.[6] The church has to stand for relevant truth, for the truth of the Gospel and boldly go into the dark and danger of this world to hold His banner high. To force the world to remember, if only for a moment, sin is sin and death follows to those who do not heed. It's worth living for. It's worth dying for. The world notices when we are those who don't stand for much of the truth it was assigned to preach. I heard it best described by the late

Don DeWelt, author, pastor, and writer. He said, "The church is trying to make the world churchy, and the church worldly, and that dog just won't hunt."

The dog won't hunt, because the "emerging church" is worth as much as a cheap umbrella in a hurricane. While the church complains that our government is not operating anything like our founders' government, don't look now, but neither is the church. We have become politically correct, afraid to stand against the obvious wrongs as spelled out in the Bible. Following Robert's Rules of Order, or saying the Lord's Prayer, both very good things, are still not enough to lay claim to the message that the church is operating correctly. Guess you would say the emerging church has wandered off the reservation just like those happy wanderers at Laodicea. Guess fear of government can buckle the knees of a disobedient church or even an obedient one at times just like it did to Christians in Nazi Germany 80 years ago.

Many years ago before television was born, a well-known comedienne on the radio dramatized the Garden of Eden story. She basically performed a burlesque show of Eve and the forbidden fruit. From all sections of the nation arose a profound moral protest to her sponsors, and to NBC radio. The company in turn, banned her program from the air on the grounds that it was obscene and profane. (Wouldn't it be nice if they would do that with some programs today? I know it is a pipe dream, but . . .) The buxom lady hearing what they did, protested. "Profane?" she snorted. "There wasn't a word of profanity in it." She was right. There were no cuss words. What she lacked was the moral insight to see that the whole skit was obscene and profane in its theme, its spirit and its central purpose. God's people having moral character must stand up against these events outside the church walls. The sad commentary is — they often don't anymore.

She is like many today within churches who stay at home and keep the rules, and sometimes get elected to church boards. They don't drink or curse, or gamble much, or participate in lewd "sex-capades." But so far as their insight into the larger purpose for which Christ died is concerned, they seem almost blind, and often repeat in their social attitude the same sins that conspired to put Him on the cross.

So when you study that parable of the prodigal son, what you have is not one prodigal, but rather two, one who sinned by leaving; one who sinned by not going, but by being loveless while staying home. Many members of Christianity are like those two brothers. Both are wrong. One group is respectable though they are empty of spiritual attributes. The others are just rebels.

What the Church Has Not Done Lately

One of the great criminal acts of the church in the last quarter of the 20th Century to date has been to remain silent while the criminal activity of the government has gone on. The church as a whole hasn't stood up against the crimes of the government such as those now with the Obama Administration. With the scandals of Benghazi, the IRS, Obamacare, Fast and Furious, NSA spying on citizens, voter

Chapter Eight — The Trouble with the Church

intimidation, etc., it would be hard to imagine a preacher like Dietrich Bonhoeffer being silent during all this. Where are the saints with their pitchforks and the screams of anger at the sin?! Fear has been a wicked paralyzer for the current age of disciples. Rather than rally and take on the enemy here at home, the church has tried to cuddle close and hold onto the enemy or they have run in fear like chickens in a storm. They have forgotten the message from their leader, "Perfect love casts out fear." (1 John 5:7)

Commentary from a modern day Alexis de Tocqueville would most likely only report the deafening silence from the pulpits of America. It is past time to speak.

Abandoned by God because of his sins. That was the message of God to the sons of Israel, given in Judges 10, "You have forsaken Me and served other gods, therefore I will deliver you no more. Go and cry out to the gods which you have chosen, let them deliver you in the time of your distress." Not only was Samson abandoned by God but so was Israel. What a tragedy!

Proverbs 1:24-31 records a similar sentiment. "Because I called and you refused, I stretched out My hand and no one paid attention and you neglected all My counsel and did not want my reproof. I will even laugh at your calamity, I will mock when your dread comes. When your dread comes like a storm and your calamity comes on like a whirlwind, when distress and anguish come on you, then they will call on Me but I will not answer, they will seek Me diligently but they shall not find Me because they hated knowledge and did not choose the fear of the Lord, they would not accept My counsel, they spurned all my reproof, so they shall eat of the fruit of their own way and be satiated with their own desires."

Samson must have longed for the days gone by, in his youthfulness when he was both faithful and happy, remembering the contentment that came from having a clear conscience and a clean heart. He was living within God's will and things were good. The culture of the world calls it good karma. And now, all, not only Samson, not only Israel, but to all who turned their back on the wisdom of God, they are left abandoned by God to eat the fruit of their own ways. In Hosea 4:17 it is recorded that God said this frightening sentence, "The people of Ephraim has chosen to worship idols; let them alone." One translation says, "Let them go." Abandoned by God was Ephraim. Ephraim made its choice, God said let them go. Do we have to spell this out? The message for those who won't follow within the Church is basically the same. Let them go.

The Church Is Often Biblically Illiterate

Most tragically, American Church members may know how to raise their hands when they sing a hymn, or chant or say "Amen" when the name of Jesus is called out in a church service, but sadly they do not have Biblical literacy increases among younger generations. Said differently, they may be wonderful people, but they can't prove their faith through their knowledge of Scripture. They let their fingers do the walking through Scripture. Gone seem to be the days when Bible studies were held to seriously teach members not just verses, but concepts and doctrine. That's not to say that no good teaching is taking place anywhere within Christendom or that all teaching or preaching is worthless. There are those scattered around who are faithful to still perform a grammatical, historical, and contextual approach in their approach to study and teach the truth, even including the laws of hermeneutics in their study and teaching, but they are few and far between.

Over time, the church in general has allowed a mysticism or superstition to creep into the faith in the absence of solid learning and/or teaching. Mysticism is a substitution of how one thinks over what they know from God. Mysticism and superstition are a huge problem, for they come with a boatload of emotionalism, chanting, spiritual highs and "lite thinking," some or all have replaced knowing God. The drive to get "that special knowledge" can actually be a part of the modern 'Gnostic' that has replaced the age old message of truth, which is God's story. Some are taught to reach into themselves, to that part of themselves which is really divine — that's believing the lie that the serpent told Eve; "You too can become god." It is not uncommon to witness members of some congregations, go through "liturgical séances," rituals which over time become a superstition that replaces both relationships with God and solid knowledge of God. Knowing "the truth that will set you free" has often been replaced by a feeling that becomes the rabbit's foot for the week.

Some Preachers Share in the Problem

A brief history of the problem in today's pulpit is divided into two general categories, with individual reasons for each.

Category 1 – The Pulpit Is Too Often Weak

Evangelical Christians vote in less than great numbers and polls indicate they don't vote significantly different than the population in general. Polls show for example that some Christians vote for "homosexual marriage" and post-birth abortions. The U.S. currently has a president who asked God to bless Planned Parenthood, the nation's largest abortion provider. These stances have to be due at least in part to the weakness of a sizable percentage of persons in the pulpits. Often, they have not been directing their congregations to think. Lessons, sermons, and messages should be based on logical, critical thought from an expository approach to Scripture.

Much of the blame rests on the study habits of ministers — often not studying, working through concepts, or reading good books. An average pastor today can access the Internet and within 20 minutes has a "Dump Dinner" or "Dump Desert" sermon ready to present to the people. Good preaching requires time — based on grammatical, historical, exegetical work to "feed the flock" with the message from

Scripture. I know of a couple of pastors have been heard to proudly advertise that "you will hear at least 30 Scriptures quoted in each Sunday's sermon." The problem is their case at least 29 of those text quotations are being made out of context, therefore their original meaning for us is missed.

Information gained from the Center for the Study of American Culture and Faith (CSACF) over the years has proven helpful in gauging the direction of evangelical congregations by identifying and providing targeted data.[7]

The CSACF identifies churches that are considered to a "culturally-impacting church." — Those congregations are those that:

- Believe the Bible is God's holy infallible Word
- Preach and teach the Bible
- Believe life is sacred
- Believe marriage is only between one man and one woman
- Encourage the congregation to vote Biblical values
- Believe that prayer is key
- Believe that the church is responsible to be actively engaged in helping the community.

Significantly, <u>each day</u> the Center individually contacts some 500 of America's more than 350,000 churches to identify those which hold these seven beliefs. Of the tens of thousands of churches they have thus far contacted, only about ten percent embrace these positions. Having currently identified over 6,000 of these Biblically-conservative churches, noted national pollster George Barna conducts surveys solely among this group. More individual pastors and their respective congregations need to get involved in helping to actively point out and fix social ills in our society. As an example, in 2012, with an ideologically charged election, there were four issues which should have dominated the thoughts of Christians as they prepared to vote at the polls. The issues were:

- Abortion – 97 percent of theologically conservative pastors believe that the Bible provides principles that relate to the morality of abortion;
- Same sex marriage – 95 percent say that the Scriptures offer moral principles related to same-sex marriage;
- Care for the environment – 92 percent argue that the Bible describes principles regarding the morality of environmental care;
- Illegal immigration – 71 percent say that there are moral principles related to immigration policy in God's Word.[8]

In spite of their critical review by membership, none of the four issues were preached on by even half of the theologically conservative pastors, according to one survey.[9]

So in spite of the fact that pastors say they believe the Bible speaks to these issues, in large part, they refused to preach about them. The survey explained findings that of the four issues, abortion was most often the subject of a sermon in a theologically-conservative church in 2012. Overall, 42 percent of the surveyed pastors preached about abortion, which was higher than the numbers who preached about same-sex marriage (36 percent), environmental care (21 percent), or immigration issues (10 percent). While 42 percent of those pastors preached on abortion in 2012, pastors' responses suggest that the figure is likely to drop to 34 percent in future years. Same-sex marriage was taught about from 36% of these pulpits in 2012, but will likely drop to 26 percent in the future. The frequency of preaching about environmental care is expected to drop almost by half (from 21 percent to 12 percent). Only immigration is anticipated to hold steady (10 percent in 2012, 10 percent planned for later).[10]

The Center has discovered through its survey that only around ten percent of America's churches believe that the Bible is true and provides guidance on such issues, and only about one-third of that ten percent — or only about 3-4 percent of total churches nationally — will speak publicly about these issues. The CEO of the Center conducting the polling accurately observed, "Without such guidance [from pastors], the mass media takes the lead on providing the worldview that shapes cultural choices, producing lowest common denominator lifestyles and spineless leadership."[11]

Said differently, the research reports that the lion's share of pastors do not believe in the Word enough to preach sermons often on some of the most critical social problems in America. Some of our pastors, perhaps more interested in building their own following than God's church, would prefer to preach "seeker sensitive" messages. Or there could be the message on unity, which is good but regretfully bland when not the solid calls for the people to "stand up" for biblical truth. Bottom line, sermons can be off target or weak where there's a lack of study and lack of attention.

Category 2 – The Pulpit Can Avoid Issues

There are several reasons why pastors avoid tough issues, even those that are political / cultural.

Money is a big one. Most ministers talk a good game in minster's meetings but the truth is they lack courage or have an unwillingness to give political offense when offense is needed. Taking a Biblical stance on a political issue can cost them big in offerings. Because offerings have been threatened in the past in some churches — that news travels fast — and lifestyles have to be maintained. Most feel from peer pressure it is better to keep the offering plate filled. There's not a big difference between this stance and that of a prostitute. Both are done to please the client and to get the cash.

Fear of people in and out of the congregation. Anytime a pastor takes a sturdy stand on a substantial issue, it usually ends up offending some people. But pastors should remember that when they speak of soft issues, that offends others too. If a congregant gets angry because you have just barbequed his favorite ideological golden calf, cash can leave early with the angry member, plus there can be other threats, like withholding fellowship from the minister, which many ministers are not ready to face. Men "of the cloth" should regard God and his opinion as "the trump card" to what a person with feet of clay might do.

The remedy is of course to get the minister to lead, not follow — to fear God! Declare his will and his way and let the chips fall where they may. Within both the Old and New Testaments there are very un-muddled, eternal opinions on current political issues. These opinions should be embraced and shouldn't be publicly curbed and bridled because some deacon, a congregant or a politician doesn't agree with the scripture and might get over a particular political issue.

Pastors don't want to anger those who fill the offering plates. When one minster was finally being run off because of his ministry, he said, "You may be getting rid of me, but you're not getting rid of yourself."

Then there's the tax-exempt status. The government has threatened and many pastors, priests and parishioners have been cowed into inactivity by the supposed loss of their tax-exempt status if saying anything remotely political — makes folks fold up like a tent in a storm; but shouldn't.

First of all, there's no need to have an IRS 501[c][3] tax-exempt charitable status to assemble and be a proper church. The church has been around a little bit longer than the 501 [c][3] statutes. What about a house church? We are afforded the right to assemble, by God and by the Constitution. Not having the tax exempt status simply means you pay taxes at the store when purchasing hamburgers for the church picnic.

Second, 501[c][3] or not, we are called to obey God rather than men, and God has called his leaders to be involved in civic affairs, and to represent Christ and his word in all areas of society. And that entails expounding the biblical worldview all the time, including election time. Sometimes you have to rebel against unrighteous, limiting laws. There's nothing wrong with proper civil disobedience when the need arises, especially if the government tries to stifle your scriptural rights and obligations. I refer to Peter, John, Stephen, and Paul, as well as others.

Off the clock, in his personal capacity, the pastor or priest can endorse and support — or oppose — whoever or whatever he wishes, like any other citizen. There are no limitations to the individual; the ones which do exist under the 501[c][3] statute are only for the church entity and/or the pastor in his official capacity, not for the pastor or the members who make up the church.

Sometimes there is the age old laziness/sloth. Classically defined, sloth is lethargy stemming from a sense of hopelessness. Viewing our nation and the world as an irreparable disaster, AKA, going to hell in a hand basket, where our exhortations, prayers, votes and labors may seem not to produce much visible result, can leave one with the fervor equal to kissing your sister.

Don't be so grim, because you knew when starting this job how it was going to turn out. The book of Revelation told you that. If you read to the end, we win. Don't pump doom and gloom into your message, but stand up to the evil that most think will triumph on our terra firma. Speak like a warrior against the "big anti-Christ," stand toe to toe with the foe, because it is Jesus who lives in you. That will help give your parishioners some of their passion back.

Then there is discord or division. I hate the current non-essential divisions in the church as much as the next acerbic Christian columnist. Squabbling over the color of the carpet, who'll play the organ next Sunday or who the Beast of Revelation is! Dial down on the focus on inconsequential things that don't matter. Relax. Go sit under a fig tree in the desert if need be and get focused. The church is currently so divided and defeated with such minutiae that we can't agree on which shade of white to use for our surrender flag to the culture.

Fake or pretend righteousness, demonstrated by one claiming to be a Christian, is identifiable almost immediately upon sight by a non-Christian. Any Christian needs to remember that sanctimonious trappings are not a mark of spiritual nature. We are to be "in" the world, but not "of" the world. Pastors and priests many times will avoid the subject of politics for example because some of them say, we should be discussing spiritual things, not be discussing politics. Make no mistake about it — the church should be discussing politics. The trail of carnage in schools, our government, and our institutions because of the liberal humanism and its impact are a visible sign that the church and its leaders have not been trumpeting the right messages about integrity, morality, and ethics in our land. The Christian and the church are to be salt in this world, e.g., adding flavor and a preservative for that which is right.

When you explore many of the church programs at the mega-churches, you begin to see behind the flashes of action, a liberal theology, which is running in tandem with the culture, not the Bible. What drives this type of clergy and Christian? Well, this brand of believer desires a "personal relationship with Jesus only" type of religion. This bunch is primarily into heavenly emotions and personal Bible study, tucked away from society and its complicated issues. Being preoccupied with looking inward and upward, such solipsistic saints inadvertently chain themselves to the never ending treadmill of spiritual introspection. They forget that they are commanded to be seriously engaged with our culture. The effects of this type of "Christian" separatism/pietism proved disastrous in pre-Nazi Germany, and aided and abetted Hitler in mounting his hellish warhorse.

Palace Propaganda. Ministers can't get involved in studying or speaking out regarding political issues simply because of the ten tons of minutiae they are forced to field. Spending time wet nursing 30-year-olds without a life and being bogged down in committee meetings over which shade of pink paint should be used for the women's restroom, and the color of curtains to use in the windows of the class rooms of their church. Ministers are lucky if they get to study the scripture nowadays, much less anything else.

In the unending, need-driven narcissistic American church, pastors work overtime for parishioners who are spiritually overweight; i.e., many parishioners live on spiritual junk food. Ultimately, whatever they believe or don't believe about a subject is for all intents and purposes inconsequential. Said differently, many modern day church members, due to their lack of spiritual maturity, do not have the depth to make intelligent decisions, nor the courage to make some tough, righteous decisions. This is both the fault of pastors and their congregants; both need some deep changes if the church is going to tackle pressing cultural issues and become a credible voice in the community.

1984 is here with the Thought Police. Pastors and priests have muffled their political voice because they fear being lumped in with the radical Muslim extremists by the politically correct thought police. The correlation made between Christians' non-violent attempts at policy persuasion and Taliban's kill-you-in-your-sleep campaigns is nothing more than pure uncut garbage. Here's what I'm talking about: A minister who wants to protect the unborn, preserve the Biblical and traditional view of marriage, maintain our nation's basis in some semblance of Biblical righteousness all of the sudden gets grouped up with Osama and his nuclear-suitcase-carrying cabal.

Ignorance of the world. Most people are not bold in areas where they are ignorant; except for those like Alec Baldwin, Sean Penn, or Michael Moore. A good preacher should have his feet both in the culture of the world and in the Bible. Knowledge of both is vital in order to communicate the message effectively. The medium of communication may change through the years, but the message should stay the same, consistently on target with the context of Scripture. Know the urgent issues of the day, keeping up with all the pressing political issues is maddening but that's life. Brief yourselves with the *Wall Street Journal* Editorial section for the running issues globally. You can run through the gauntlet of the scripture determining God's mind on a certain subject, but it helps to know what the society is thinking.

God will send you better soldiers of the cross who have been so faithful.

The Church — She's Become a Compromiser

The church has not been attracting the generation of the millennials in any credible amount, so to answer that, she has started courting the liberal side of society to attract them. At least one notable person says that.

Rachel Held Evans, according to her own statements, some on her blog site (Rachaelheldevans.com) offers what I think is a ridiculous answer to the church's need to draw young members. "Go liberal," she says. Of course she would say that since she weekly if not daily rails another polemic against conservative evangelicals, whom she has been battling for years. In her post, "Why millennials are leaving the church," she gives her unsavory advice.

Evans explains that young people are rejecting evangelical Christianity because it's "too political, too exclusive, old-fashioned, unconcerned with social justice and hostile to lesbian, gay, bisexual and transgender people." When she says "too political," she means too conservative but Evans is just as political as she's always been. She has just switched teams. "Too political" comes down a desire to see evangelicalism embrace the progressive views of the day as she has done.

Specifically, Evans explains that "young evangelicals often feel they have to choose between their intellectual integrity and their faith, between science and Christianity." Read: evolution. Evans has rejected her past views on creation and now embraces evolution so the church should too. "Evangelical obsession with sex can make Christian living seem like little more than sticking to a list of rules." Who is obsessed with sex in the LGBT debate? I would argue LGBT proponents, such as Evans, are much more obsessed with the issue than conservative evangelicals. Apparently, if you hold to a biblical view of marriage, family, and human sexuality, you are obsessed with sex.

"Millennials long for faith communities in which they are safe asking tough questions and wrestling with doubt." "Safe asking tough questions" sounds wonderful but what those like Evans often mean is a desire to hold any view on any issue no matter what Scripture has to say without being told they're wrong. If you don't believe all views are equally valid your church is not a safe place.

"The coming of the lawless one will be in accordance with the work of Satan displayed in all kinds of counterfeit miracles, signs and wonders, and in every sort of evil that deceives those who are perishing. They perish because they refused to love the truth and so be saved." (2 Thessalonians 2:9, 10).

"As the whole purpose of God in the ages has its consummation in the yet future coming of Christ, so Satan, in imitation of the program of God, has appointed a coming one (2 Thessalonians 2:9), who will be his greatest manifestation, and upon whom he will bestow his greatest wisdom, power and attractiveness. The study of this mighty and imposing character can only be suggested in the following pages." ("Satan," by Lewis Sperry Chafer, 1909. Available from Project Gutenberg.)

The truth of the matter is that there are times when culture and its influence ebbs and flows and there are also times when the church in its influence ebbs and flows. The church has indeed changed the culture in times past, only to have the culture try to change the church in other eras. We are in one of those periods when the culture wants to change the church drastically. Though there may be few who will stand by the church and the message of the Gospel during this time, remember there will still be a few. In times past when the culture was in a dictatorial mood as it is now, that's when from among the few, great leaders were raised up, leaders like Billy Graham, or "Raccoon" John Smith, or Jonathan Edwards, or John Wesley, or Martin Luther. Just remember that in Nazi Germany, at the height of Hitler's pathology, the church supported him, in spite of the fact that Dietrich Bonhoeffer was there. And Bonhoeffer, from a death camp called Buchenwald, taught the church how to change the culture by never being silenced.

One of the greatest problems of some Christians it seems, they have become too secular, not counting the cost of discipleship. "The expansion of Christianity and the increasing secularization of the church caused the awareness of costly grace to be gradually lost. . . . But the Roman church did keep a remnant of that original awareness. It was decisive that monasticism did not separate from the church and that the church had the good sense to tolerate monasticism. Here, on the boundary of the church, was the place where the awareness that grace is costly and that grace includes discipleship was preserved. . . . Monastic life thus became a living protest against the secularization of Christianity, against the cheapening of grace."[4]

Many of the church today do not get involved with the fight for their freedom. Some suggest the reason is that great voices from the past who mounted the pulpits every week to communicate the Gospel of liberating truth to remain free from secularism are no longer there. They seem to have been replaced by voices with messages of compromise, a death knell for true discipleship.

"Can there be any doubt, hearing those echoes from culture, that a great civil war of values is being waged on Western Nations, or that radical anti-family forces are making dramatic alterations in the way we think and act?"

— Dr. James Dobson

Former President of Focus on the Family

Chapter Nine

Where Do We Start?

THE KEN HARRELSON INTERVIEW WAS ON the MLB Channel during the fall of 2013. I watched it with great interest. If not the best interview I ever saw, it will do until the best one comes along! Tears came into and dropped from my eyes as Ken described being on the field that day for Mickey Mantle's entrance into his last game ever played. It was in Boston. Ken was a member of the Red Sox then, and had a great perspective since "the Mick" was both a close friend but he was close to him that day on the infield. He said Mickey hit a routine ground ball to second, a certain out, but with his almost miraculous speed still at his advanced age, turned it into a hit beating the throw to first. Because Mickey's knees and legs were so bad and fragile toward the end of his career, he could not stop quickly like other players running to first base, so he had to slow gradually as he went down the right field foul line. When he returned to the 1st base bag, Ken said, "You could see the tears streaming down Mickey's face because of the pain in his legs. It hurt me and many of my team mates to see him suffer so. We had tears in our eyes as we watched him."

Ken also recalled that on the first pitch to the next batter, Mickey was off racing toward second, sliding in with his patented hook slide, and swiped the base. "But when Mickey got up from his slide," Ken said, "We gasped, because we could see the red blood stain soaking through his uniform pants leg." In sliding, Mickey had torn the stitches and the bandages loose that were helping to hold his leg together, and the blood was running out. Ken said, "My teammates and I cried; we had tears streaming down our faces as we witnessed this legend in all his dedication; seeing the torture he endured as he continued to do what he loved to do, pour his best out on the field, here at the very end of his fabulous career. "Mickey just did not know how much I and the rest of my Red Sox teammates loved him for who he was and what he had given to all of us in the game," Ken added with tears in his eyes.

Later in life, Ken said he sat and reminisced with Mickey about their careers and asked him what he thought was the biggest mistake he felt he had made in his own life. To which Mick replied, "I think there's many. But probably the biggest was in naming my son Mickey." "Why in the world would you say that?" Ken retorted. Mickey humbly said, "Because I didn't know I was going to grow up someday and become Mickey Mantle."

The power of Ken's dissertation came after he spoke of Mickey and other greats from those glory days of the game, true giants like Sandy Koufax, Stan Musial, Bob Fellar, Willie Mays and others. That is where he did something you rarely witness in this venue. He opened his own life like a book, laid it almost completely bare, and shared intimate details of the ghosts from his past; his own failures, his sins, his extreme disappointments and his steps he took to change. It was revealing and so refreshing, because Ken "Hawk" Harrelson was blatantly honest in laying open his life, about his own drinking for example, how he said he broke his wife's heart, and then his pause with quivering lower lip. He was forced to make the tough decision to quit drinking or else lose his wife. The emotion welled in my throat and even laughter spilled out several times as I heard Ken speak of the boyish pranks played on each other, seeing his reflection on the good, the humorous and the bad during which he saw himself as he really was; a spoiled brat that had spent his life focusing on himself; then he started doing the work of looking into the mirror, seeing himself as being the bankrupt person he was. He began focusing on his sins, seeking forgiveness and that started the process of maturing into a man.

What a hard-hitting and courageous interview! Prodigious interview!! It is the kind of interview an individual needs to see. It is a facilitator that leads to the deep dark long look into their own life and heart. It is the soil where seeds of change and individual revolution germinate and take root for change.

Keep the Harrelson interview as a backdrop transitioning to our current national predicament. We as Americans need to begin is to take a long look into our national soul. Realizing that look will somehow vary from mirror to mirror across the country, we still need to look as we see the darkness and emptiness that can rest within the lives and hearts of what secular humanists describe as the "human animal." The problem is we have begun to see ourselves as animals — we have forgotten our history. However, there is one sentence in all of the books of the Bible which describes the starting place for America today in 2014. Actually it is for any people who used to love truth and follow the statutes of God. 2 Chronicles 7:14 contains the real "restart" button for health, prosperity, and happiness: "If my people, who are called by my name, will humble themselves and pray and seek my face and turn from their wicked ways, then will I hear from heaven and will forgive their sins and will heal their land."

That's the place to start. It can be a lonely place, or at least can seem that way. Many of our society react with violence at such thought. Some balk, other chuckle calling the thought "jest." Nonetheless, it's the genuine starting point for all people, especially those within churches, synagogues. For obvious reasons that is true since they must lead the way in repentance for the balance of the nation. It is the starting point for the balance of citizens who want to get their nation back because it is the one place from which we are forced to look deeply into our own lives. For it is there that we will see the emptiness when we attempt to stand on our own. But our look must be more than a surface view. We must begin to look inside ourselves, our homes, our businesses, our social clubs, our government, our churches and synagogues; to begin the process of coming clean, first with ourselves, with our loved ones, and then our Creator in admitting what is wrong. I am not so naïve as to think we can sit around like kids hand-in-hand warming by a campfire singing Kumbaya" making all this problems of our nation simply disappear because of some chants and statements of recommitments. Because part of the delinquency is not in us, but part of it is in us. There are so many warning signs of our problems, as we have seen. It seems like all is lost and maybe it is. God has lifted His hedge that has encircled this nation as a protection, all because we abandoned His leadership and will. But possibly He will put it restore it again, like He did for Israel before. Unashamedly I am one who believes in God, His mercy, His grace, His justice, and His Word. I believe the cure for all our woes is not some magic wand, nor a prayer, nor a set of prayer beads or a prayer wheel, but a genuine return to God, to honor Him and His goodness, what He has established as "rightness" in life. If we don't, all will be lost for certain.

People who have Judeo-Christian beliefs as their foundation should not apologize for their stance. If for no other reason, look at how the Liberal Progressive Left has worked boldly on their faith principles for decades. Our schools have been converted into centers that have taught secular humanism, a tired and old religion, for over 50 years now and have garnered more than a few disciples for that belief. They have at the same time been taught to hate those of Christian and Jewish beliefs. Despite the so-called "education" of these secular humanists, Progressive Liberals, atheists, or anyone else on the Left, do not apologize for their capaciously proud, arrogant, and in many cases self-diluted beliefs. Why in the world should we? We choose to believe in God who through grace can save those who follow Him; it seems wise just as our Forefathers were wise. Though we are weak and inconsistent, He is not. While this current culture chooses to hold onto opposing practices, just reason within yourself. They fight moral absolutes, ethical standards which alone is opposed to rational behavior for any group which wants to survive.

That beginning is always the hardest step in personal or national repentance. For it exposes an emptiness and bankruptcy of our current culture. We long had such pride in our culture and never saw the attribute becoming our greatest weakness. It is to look deep within ourselves and realize the moral and spiritual bankruptcy that exists there when we are left to our own devices. We must start there with our own shortcomings, just like Ken Harrelson did in his interview.

This is also the first step especially for the church to take in America. For it to become the church as it was 200 years ago, it must collectively look in the mirror and admit the sins and shortcomings. A people of conviction, of leadership, of moral authority, of truth telling, engaging in politics and holding themselves, their families, their churches, their communities and their elected representatives to their word. We need to be a people of warfare, being equipped because war has been declared on us, who will carry the mantra against, and the battle to the villains. The church has been sidetracked far too long, not willing to enjoin the battle, with the appropriate armor. It seems only a shadow of its former self.

Many are writing books suggesting that the need of our country is to repeal certain amendments to the constitution. Mark Levine has written an exciting book entitled "Liberty Amendments." It is a genius work proposing the repeal of the 17th amendment plus enacting eleven new amendments. He has some exceptional offerings for our nation. Mark is indeed a genius and we should absolutely listen to him. I agree with his offering of having term limits for congress. I agree with much of what he wrote in this volume, not all but most. You noticed my suggestions that we agree on a few action steps as stated earlier.

Start at the Beginning

Mark Stein has some wonderful ideas. My ideas differ in only one critical area: return to a stated reliance on the Judeo-Christian God, in other words, where we were from our founding to a point prior to the War Between the States. Largely, during this time period, it was given that our nation was reliant on God. There were large numbers of people who did not follow the faith beliefs, but at least three times historically, our nation has undergone a revival when it reached a critical point and needed to get back on its feet. Not all people want to honor God; Individuals can live their lives the way they want. That is freedom. It is even alright if any person wants to be or claims to be a liberal. 'Liberals' want to live their lives in peace and do not place demands that I follow in their footsteps. The problem is with Progressives who not only insist on being liberals. They also insist that the rest of society live by the same restraints duck step to their leaders too. They can build shrines to themselves in their own homes for self-worship as far as I am concerned. If some want to be secular humanists, what difference could that make as long as they do so privately? It is fine if they want to have that faith in their own lives, bow to Satan as Saul Alinsky suggested, or worship some extra-terrestrial being which they may wish to name as their personal god. It is their home. I do not want to live that way but do not want legislators telling any of us what we must believe in order to make others feel comfortable. But nationally, for the bulk of persons who wish to honor God and preserve our nation, they should continue openly with honoring God and His protection for this great nation. This is the only avenue for us to begin to recover our nation and watch it become great once again.

We must be bold in reclaiming a portion of our past one step at a time, using the Chronicles platform on which to stand. I like to think we can do that in every season of the year, reclaiming old territories. For example, we can be bold about celebrating Christmas each year. A little thing to some, but I am happy to irritate some when they want me to call my decorated tree in my home a holiday tree instead of a Christmas tree. But I refuse to do that. It is a Christmas party, not a holiday party. I will not be quiet about that. Then we can advance the ball forward within each or the sacred holidays that Progressives hate and have tried to take away from us. No more. Stand your ground.

Peer into the world of liberals and progressives from a little different angle to show the difference in their beliefs. A liberal wants to have a separate lifestyle; unique from others in the nation who wishes to honor God, who have established faith principles, etc. They want liberalism for their own life, and here is a key difference, but do not try to force everyone else to follow their lead. A liberal, in a pure form, is not a danger to the rest of the nation because they do not try to evangelize their faith system to others. Ah, but the Progressive is different. They not only want to rid their own lives of Christian and moral influence, practice Marxist Collectivism, they insist that everyone else do the same. Therein lies the difference.

We need clarity in an established moral code, established reliance as a nation on God, and therefore an established identity; what we possessed shortly after the founding of our country. Said differently, let us go back to our Christian roots and heritage. I believe nothing else will allow us to survive as a country or once again prosper.

Take for example a report which the *Los Angeles Times* provided in January, 2014. *The Times* reported that as of October, 2013, 50 percent of Californians were "in desperate financial condition, at or past the point of bankruptcy. Of the remaining 50 percent, 4 in 10 of those were just 2-3 weeks away from total financial failure." While the percentages differ slightly for other states, that is a fair overall picture of life in the great United States for most people. Translation: we are headed in the wrong direction. Add to this the climate of government or public schools, the emptiness of our current politicians and political system, the moral decay of our universities, public institutions, as we did in earlier chapters, and all speaks of the same downward spiral.

The evidence points to a common thread which runs through all these factors. This is our society being moved off its bedrock of Judeo-Christian moral code, that common faith, and the common vocal adherence to them. There are many who oppose this notion. Some think we are crippled if we lean on some god out there someplace. Some think it impossible to go back. Some want no mention of God whatsoever. Some only want the god of Islam, Allah. That would be a horrible, satanic move. I am way past the point of caring what liberal progressives, the liberals, the Muslims, or the 'I don't believe anything" person wants. I know what has been destroying our nation. It is been the abandoning of our spiritual moorings. If they cannot see that common evidentiary thread, they have no business telling anyone what to do.

Steps for People of Synagogues and Churches

Meanwhile, American Christians who understand the genius of the Founders, knowing the future of the country depends on a return to first principles. We must organize around God's promise in 2 Chronicles, unify and activate daily engagement in taking the specified steps, talking seriously about following God's directive. Then we need to rally around solutions, and finding ways to implement them through upcoming rallies, events, and elections at all levels of government. It starts with the church.

Then, given the convergence of evil and negative events, it appears we have few windows of opportunity left to turn our country around. The good news is we have those opportunities. If we do not take advantage of them, shame on us. All who gave their lives for this country are watching, waiting, and praying.

EDUCATION REFORM: The absolute first priority for reforming our nation is to change several features about public education: The first step: fire the Federal Government from educating our children; States will take over the task. Constitutionally, the states have had their authority to teach children usurped by the federal government in the first place. That has been done by funding. What this all means is that the Department of Education in Washington, D. C., is to be closed, doors locked, and all those thousands of people who are provided paychecks through that department are laid off or have their "jobs" terminated. Before the lights are turned out however, all money within that department, having been sequestered from taxpayers, would be sent back to the appropriate states.

Each state would oversee the school system within its borders. <u>This means they determine the curriculum</u> for those schools, as well as the credentialing for their teachers. The State of Kansas then could as an example start teaching creationism in science classes. A teacher in a civics class, another example, could have no more than an associate's degrees. There is a reason for emphasizing this; here it is. Many teachers chose to teach in school because they enjoyed and were successful in their own school experience. But they often cannot identify with the child who does not like school because that was not their own experience while they, the teacher, was in school. So hiring some teachers who did not have a good school experience, but were very successful in their own path in life, can provide much in the classroom; e.g., they can reach a large segment of the population. <u>Teachers could actually be selected on their ability to teach and reach children, rather than by having jumped through hoops to keep standing in a union.</u> What this means for a Progressive Liberal family who does not like the new curriculum of creationism for example, is that they have choices. They can send their children to a private school, home school their children, or get the heck out of the state, moving to one where their secular humanism, including Darwinism, is taught. In other words they can remain quiet and put up with it similarly to how they have instructed conservative families to do for the past 40 years. When the states are in control of education, you would find the curriculum focusing on the 3 R's and other critical basics that will equip students for the job market ahead to support business within their state. This is something humanists hate. Business could actually co-op so much better with these school districts than is now possible, since most of the ridiculous red tape would be eliminated. As for the use of technology in the classrooms by students . . . it can be nice and sometimes productive, but it can also be very counter-productive as we are seeing in the Orwellian world. Children should be taught to use the calculator in their brain for many math problems. Oh and by the way, no smart phones or texting in class. Amazing what might be learned.

To a great extent, Americans today are ignorant about the real status of our nation's education programs and schools as operated today. Sadly, most citizens are ignorant about most everything that matters to patriotism, especially those ideals that are core values, which were all integral in our founding. The principles which our Forefathers held dear for personal life, government, foreign policy and especially for education were ideals that served this nation well for over 200 years. Informing uninformed citizens about these incredible truths is a huge challenge, but it is an absolutely essential if we are ever to restore our country. And it is absolutely essential to get control of education to once again restore faith and consistency in the training of our young people. In many ways, students have been uncoupled from truth by the education which Dewey's plans have put in place over the past century. Liberal Progressives have been able to reform our nation in a very negative manner by taking hold of education over time. A conservative movement needs to take hold of education, reversing the trend and retracing our path back to credible education, no matter what liberals may say.

Other than the obvious, teaching creationism in school would have some terrific side benefits. First of all, it would replace teaching theories like natural selection as a part of evolution. Talk about a fairy tale. Most of the true intellectual community and scientists have moved way past that, knowing that Darwinism cannot be proven. It just does not hold water when taught as a fact. Unfortunately, the only places where you see Darwinism held tightly is by Progressive Liberal teachers in high schools and universities. However when Creationism is taught, there are side benefits, such as fixed morals, better reading skills, less violence in school just to name a few. Remember, this theory is Bible-based. Oops, that means also having the Bible and prayer back in the classroom. There should not be too much complaining; the liberals and progressives have already been fired from working in the classroom. Oh, and if you do not want your children learning good moral platitudes, and discipline, then take them out of school. That is what we conservatives had to do with our children for 50 years when he government pumped secular humanism, alternative lifestyles, progressive and "common core" lessons; all filth, to cloud the minds of young children. The current trends in "public education" are nothing less than a liberal attempt at brainwashing. In response, it would seem best for the liberals to try alternative education for a while, if they do not like the direction conservatives take in restoring a credible education for children in America.

SEEK A NEW KIND OF POLITICAL LEADERSHIP: First, this simply means no more career politicians. I agree with our Framers who held that politicians would come from industry, the factories, the farms, the offices where people worked and "produced" some sort of product, e.g., those who had a real job in life, and understood at least in part how a business ran. Second, there must be an emphasis on morals, ethics, and Biblically-oriented leadership or else we will face the same dilemma we currently face with Washingtonians. Without strong, morality-driven and Biblically oriented leadership, no good thing will be accomplished in our nation.

Conservatives and Biblical conservatives cannot shy away from the social and political issues. Pastors are going to need to quit standing behind the skirts of little ladies in their congregations and find the courage to preach expository messages from the Word on hard, tough, issues, such as the leadership, and the need for repentance in our nation. That is the best way for them to influence their followers and communities. When pastors preach Biblically, they will preach on the tough subjects that face our society today. You know, let the chips fall where they may!

Third, leadership means being out front, not behind, setting the example, showing the way. And as a whole, leaders must take a strong stand for family values, such as those found in Judeo-Christian teachings. Support for pure home life where children are nurtured is essential. That also means standing opposed to abortion, partial-birth abortion, the feminine movement of today, all crucial. **When immorality reigns, society dies.** That is why fixed moral standards are essential. A fluidity in moral standards produces anarchy. We have been watching the rerun of that movie for decades. Our banner should echo the challenge laid down by Frederick Douglass in 1852: *"Righteousness exalts a nation. Sin is a reproach to any nation."*

From my point of view, any political candidate who won't commit to protecting citizen's lives should not be in public office. Any candidate who will not put forth legislation to protect children in our society should not be in public office. That same principle stretches into the realm of children who are not yet born. In other words, we need to have candidates who have a strong moral base and will be Pro-Life. "Reaching across the aisle" cannot be tolerated as a political position. Bible-based morality has to be the cornerstone for governance of this nation; therefore candidates must have the same. Progressivism has built the swamp existing in Washington. It is time to drain the swamp. The death camps of killing the unborn have to be stopped, firmly, finally, and with no negotiation. Saving a nation means getting progressives, liberal elites and their cronies out of power. They can believe whatever they want in their own living rooms, but not in our House of Representatives and Senate. Certainly not in the Oval Office.

The modern mantra is to scream that good leadership is one which negotiates. That is total idiocy. Just listen to the press interrogate a newly elected conservative. Usually the first question they ask is, "What items are you willing to negotiate with the Democrats?" The correct answer to that question is, "Nothing!" Wouldn't it be refreshing to hear the press agent ask a liberal, "What are you willing to negotiate with conservatives to get something accomplished?" They won't ask that. We are way past that point in trying to save our nation anyway. Good leadership is one that makes courageous decisions, based on righteousness, no matter who is opposed to the decision at the time. We must have leaders who tell "the truth," not what some willy-nilly, politically correct toady from a news broadcast would say.

ECONOMY: The first action step here is a balanced budget amendment. Stop spending money we do not have. Second, unless we can grow and expand based on competitive free enterprise, which does provide economic freedom, the poorer classes of people in our country have absolutely no chance. Create tax-reduced zones for business in certain areas of the country, like the whole continent. Have it in place for at least 20 years. Stand back and watch the economy grow and the tax revenue grow! If government officials say they cannot afford the tax cut, then start firing government employees, from the top layers down within the departments until you get the budget down to the tax base. Close some departments.

PRIVATE PROPERTY RIGHTS: Then there is the right of the people to own private property. That is absolutely foundational to liberty. Economic revitalization is not all that complicated, once you get the government out of the way. Those bureaucrats do so much harm. They must be brought to heel according to the consent of the governed, not the other way around.

Reduce regulation. Lower the taxes. Provide support to enhance productivity. Free the entrepreneurial spirit. This will allow manufacturing to be rebuilt here in the country. You will start getting rid of debt. Free up investment capital to support creative endeavors that are firmly based on good business decisions. Let the market work. Dismantle crushing bureaucracies. Capitalism works when you promote it. Competition develops, which by the way means we cut out all the mercantilism which government practices today and has practiced feverishly ever since the Civil War.

A strong economy provides the avenues for people who want to work to be lifted out of poverty and is the greatest national security issue we confront. Without a strong economy, we have a weakened populace and military.

ACTION STEPS TO REFORM: Immediate reform measures must be taken at the Federal level.

Cut government drastically. Since Hollywood is so focused on having a steady diet of reality shows on television, it would be nice to build a reality show within the federal government. The platform would bring in Donald Trump or someone like him, give him a microphone to be used in our multiple bureaucracies and hear him say, "You're fired!!" Unless we cut spending, balance the budget, and get out of debt, we are done, we are dead, we are buried.

Oh, and no Czars. They are done! That means immediately. Demand a balanced budget amendment. Make this one of two goals of each senator and representative during their term. Refuse to raise the debt ceiling. Immediate across the board cuts (not just slower increases in spending) but real cuts in federal spending, shared equally within the departments of government. Everybody shoulders the wheel.

That means departments slashed. Force the government to do what a family has to do: live within their finances. We are talking about survival here people.

The presidential campaign of 2012 brought out some great ideas about economics and cutting federal departments. I know one candidate suggested cutting Education, Energy and Health & Human Services. Those can be handled at the state level. Milton Friedman's economics proposed cutting most of the current cabinet-level departments: Education, Commerce, Energy, Agriculture, half of Health & Human Services, Housing & Urban Development, Interior (return 90% of federally owned land to the People and the states), Labor, and Transportation. I am for that. It is a step in the right direction.

Next action step: voting reform. The Founders had a great system. Only land owners could vote. They believed anyone else would not be leveraged in to properly vote on important issues. Amazing what a good system that was. To have someone who is supported by welfare voting on important issues such as welfare reform makes no sense.

Summation

In summary, here are other intermediate action steps to take:

1. Impose term limits on Congress;
2. Enact a single-subject rule in Congress to prevent pork barrel spending from being inserted into bills, say, on disaster relief;
3. Limit all legislation to 100 pages; no more;
4. Enact a balanced budget amendment to the Constitution;
5. Scrap the current tax code in favor of a user tax, flat tax or fair tax;
6. Allow no bills to be introduced unless they qualified under the 10th Amendment as powers specifically reserved for the federal government. PERIOD!
7. Legislators can never exempt themselves from the laws they impose on us! Social Security, medical care, etc. This ensures they if they want to attempt an aristocratic move; if they pass a bill, they are in the omelet too;
8. No more death tax. This tax robs the future investment of our country, by sending money to the federal government, taking away future investment by small business and private citizens;
9. Civil liberties. In the reformed country, everyone who is a citizen will have equal but not greater civil liberties. Non-citizen, don't have the same rights;

10. New Energy Policy — Drill, baby drill. Oil is the blood of any economy in today's world. It will be in ours too. No need to depend on Muslims for our oil;

11. National defense. No cutting of this department since the world is so dangerous and we have so many evils which can attack us;

12. Immigration. Enforce the border, no amnesty or citizenship for illegals, no matter what. "Me no speaka da English" NY Cartoon Poster Print by R. Van Buren. History has shown us that Mao had a simple plan to destroy his arch-enemy, the Soviet Union. It took five days total, no more. On day 1, he would send 1 million troops to and through the border, who would lay down their arms and surrender. Days 2-5 the same scenario. The Soviets would be forced to care for the prisoners, but by not having the required food, nor the bullets to kill all of the enemy, it would topple the nation. Simple plan. What we see happening on our southern border is the same plan.

Viewing the past twenty years, even a beginner student of history should see the need for digging deep into the past to see pitfalls and to establish trends for future decisions. It is simple. Learn the lessons from those nations which refused to learn from history and thus became dust. It is much easier to look upon those nations that did learn and follow solid lessons from their own past, so we can build a strong future for our children and children's children.

Refusing the lessons from the past (lessons on morality, unity, purpose, two generations losing sight of those things and the nation slides into the dust of history. Germany is an example. It was actually a total of forty-five years, from 1888 to 1933. It took only those few years for them to take their eyes off the ball. The result was Hitler. We can and must learn from the past to save the future. It takes hard work, but it can be done.

*"It is not the function of our government to keep
the citizens from falling into error;
it is the function of the citizens to keep
the government from falling into error."*

— Robert W. Jackson

U.S. Supreme Court Justice, 1950

Chapter Ten

Listen to the Past
Speak to the Future

"The democracy will cease to exist when you take away from those who are willing to work and give to those who would not." — Thomas Jefferson

"There is pleasure in viewing old things from a new viewpoint." — Feynman

MY MIND IS FLOODED AT TIMES with memories of my youth, when my mother was active in who I was and what I did. Mom died when I was in college, and my memories of her are extraordinary. In particular, I recall when preparing to go away to university, as a freshman on a basketball scholarship. Here I was the country boy going off to the big city. My mother was frail. She had been sick most of her life, with just about every childhood disease a person could have. Then she had two adult diseases: tuberculosis and cancer. I think through my teenage years when I was playing ball, her health endeared me to her even more than the typical son to his mother. Though she was in such terrific pain, she came to all my games. Mom had been my friend in life, because Dad was gone all the time. There we were, just she and I, as I was getting ready to go to the city that day in September, we both had lumps in our throats I am certain. After getting my luggage into the car, she stood there in front of me with her arms reaching high in the air to put her hands on my shoulders, wanting to say so many things, yet saying just one, though it was quite enough, "Dean, don't ever forget who you are." Worth more than a book of rules or an entire score of lectures on behavior was that one challenge to something deep in her boy's remembrance. "Never forget who you are," brought back all the lessons she had taught in my childhood on making wise choices. Wise teachers and parents have always known that the strongest defense the soul has is a determined estimate of one's self that will not let us fail. Moms know when their boys are far from home off in the bright lights of the city, we can be tempted so terribly to desert our better self. That image of my mom looking me in the eyes still brings back tender memories and wells up tears in my eyes as I still hear her soft, guiding voice from the past.

Voices from the past can be tender and soft, sometimes haunting, warm and friendly, or even nightmarish. But usually these voices from our remote past beckoning us to either recall a heritage or return to a higher walk. From time to time their messages are disturbing, speaking of national, or corporate, sins, as well as singular and private ones. They speak from the experience of knowing temptation comes to tell us that everything can be gained by sinning and everything lost by keeping true to ourselves. Hopefully, something deep inside will speak to those who have a moral compass; whispers will be heard calling us back to ourselves. "How could we have done these things?" Deep inside, we as conservatives and Christians need to know who we are, and in knowing that, know that some things are beneath what we were called to do, and should not be tried.

Times like this require we confess our wrongs both individually and corporately, as a nation. Corporate or community sins, refers to those we as humans commit collectively as a nation doing bad things or omitting the good from our lives. Sometimes however, their messages can be glorious thoughts or visions that will make the earth stop for a time because of the depth of spiritual truth contained in the message. The real problem is we get too busy with the mundane things in life, or in the chatter of what is happening, so much so that the voices, as I like to call them, get drowned out by all the "white noise" of life. And that is a horrible shame. Don't feel too badly about it. The same happens to me, but now that I am getting older, and hopefully just a little wiser, I am turning down the white noise so I can hear some of these great voices form the past as they speak to us, as well as see them with the picture tube in my mind.

There are four voices which you should hear. The messengers and their respective messages were all very real and urgent at the time they were made. And while the contexts of their respective messages were made initially to fit a different time and situation, our time it turns out is not all that different. Thus their words still carry heavy weight into our time in the world and our place in history. The voices may communicate several different messages to you, but to me they all speak of the need of a spiritual revival! To hear that, to achieve that, to do that, to have that, will require that we first awaken and attend to the messages, as they call on us to remember who we are, whose we are, and then rededicate ourselves to the purpose for which we were called to in the beginning.

Voice #1:

Listen! You can almost hear the shuffle of people's feet as they nervously gather closely around a makeshift stage and stare as a gaunt man climbs the steps and approaches a podium in the forefront. From his pocket he pulls an ordinary white envelope on which he has scratched only a few scant words from which he will make remarks. This is a very dark time in our nation's history; the timing is consequential to our day, since it was exactly 150 years ago today as I write about him, that he made his brief remarks that day. His name: Abraham Lincoln. He is preparing to give what we know now as one of the most significant messages ever delivered by a President. It has been memorized by school children for over a century

Chapter Ten — Listen to the Past Speak to the Future

because of how remarkable it was as it called for a national revival: The Gettysburg Address. As you focus, almost straining to hear what he says, you can almost feel and hear the rumblings of discord in our country in the background, a nation that is torn in two. His words are insightful as he called on this nation to look deep inside its collective soul for a revival of sorts during a time of extreme civil conflict: the War Between The States. As I said, it seems almost to fit for our time like few others, because our nation is once again torn in two by another great civil conflict. So his words are sturdy and they carry the freight as he speaks from the past to give deep meaning for even us today. Listen to his wonderful message:

> "Fourscore and seven years ago our fathers brought forth on this continent a new nation, conceived in liberty and dedicated to the proposition that all men are created equal. Now we are engaged in a great civil war, testing whether that nation or any nation so conceived and so dedicated can long endure. We are met on a great battlefield of that war. We have come to dedicate a portion of that field as a final resting-place for those who here gave their lives that that nation might live. It is altogether fitting and proper that we should do this. But in a larger sense, we cannot dedicate, we cannot consecrate, we cannot hallow this ground. The brave men, living and dead who struggled here have consecrated it far above our poor power to add or detract. The world will little note nor long remember what we say here, but it can never forget what they did here. It is for us the living rather to be dedicated here to the unfinished work which they who fought here have thus far so nobly advanced. It is rather for us to be here dedicated to the great task remaining before us — that from these honored dead we take increased devotion to that cause for which they gave the last full measure of devotion — that we here highly resolve that these dead shall not have died in vain, that this nation under God shall have a new birth of freedom, and that government of the people, by the people, for the people shall not perish from the earth."[1]

While many will contend various different interpretations from his text, I believe in my heart that President Lincoln was and is calling this country, then and now, to a national revival. In seeing the result of attacks on the heart of this nation by the progressive movement, by the slack attitudes, and the treason we now face by evil politicians and others who would poison our body politic, there is no human self-will which alone is strong enough to pull us from the brink of the disaster we collectively face. There is only left this one thing, Lincoln said it, divine intervention.

What was it that kept Lincoln going through those terrible years of war between our states, when nobody seemed to know what action to take? It was in those days when he carried the weight and burden of terrible choices in his heart and mind. Carl Sandburg, a devoted student of Lincoln, was called to give the commencement address to a graduating class at Harvard. It was in an hour when another war was shaping up and young college men were confused, baffled, and some of them bitter. In his quiet mystic way, Sandburg said, "Young gentlemen, I think you need the spirit of prayer and humility of Abraham Lincoln who in 'the divided house' of his day, knew what to do because he knew who he was." There is something there to ponder: a man who knows who he is will know what to do; the whisper is in his soul won't let him give in or run away.[2]

No amount of Keynesian economic studies of deficit spending, no amount of atheistic or secular humanism pursuits, no amount of self-improvement courses, nor any psychological "pull yourself up by your own bootstraps" training, will ever provide the answers to the need we have. Lincoln knew it for his day. We know it now. It is only the Author of our country who can reverse the results of our trek of betrayal. If America will really be given another chance, it will be because of God's Grace in that we avoid tumbling like other kingdoms of darkness that have fallen like dominoes. That can only happen if God chooses to show us the mercy we most assuredly do not deserve.

We cannot just restrain from further abuses; that is to quit doing what we have been doing. Sure, that is a start. I believe we must return to the dreams of our founders and recapture their intent in order to reestablish and preserve the dream and purpose of America; to once again be a shining city on a lofty hill.

And as you wait for some soul to take the lead in doing something, anything; know this: the revival must start with those throughout the country who claim to be followers of the Way. This revival is not going to be led by the occupant of the Oval Office, nor by those in the Senate, not even those in the House of Representatives are going to do this. Most of these are so out of touch, it could not happen from there. It cannot anyway: It must start and it must end with "we, the people...."

Voice #2:

He stood in front of the large crowd that day, a freckled-faced and sandy-haired man, rather tall, rather awkward. The crowd was gathered for the inaugural address of the new president and he was there to give the address. Most knew this man as a premiere correspondent, exceptionally sharp, but he was really no public speaker. In the Virginia House of Burgesses and in the Continental Congress, he contributed his pen rather than his voice to the patriot cause. He became known there as the "silent member" of Congress. His name: Thomas Jefferson. He was a remarkable man with a tremendous mind. At the age of 9, he studied Latin, Greek, and French. At 16, when he entered the College of William and Mary, his friends were spellbound by his ability to write a message in Greek with one hand while writing the same message in Latin with the other. At 25, he was elected to the Virginia House of Burgesses, and at 32, was a Delegate to the Second Continental Congress. At 33, he wrote the Declaration of Independence. And with many other major accomplishments to his credit, most notably, he wrote a bill establishing

Chapter Ten — Listen to the Past Speak to the Future

religious freedom, enacted in 1786. Now here he stood at age 57, elected the third president of the United States. Not a prophet, yet his words and actions below should be heeded as a great message from the past and a warning about this enemy. An excerpt of his words follows,

> "Called upon to undertake the duties of the first executive office of our country, I avail myself of the presence of that portion of my fellow-citizens which is here assembled to express my grateful thanks for the favor with which they have been pleased to look toward me, to declare a sincere consciousness that the task is above my talents . . . I approach it with those anxious and awful presentiments which the greatness of the charge and the weakness of my powers so justly inspire.
>
> . . . A rising nation, spread over a wide and fruitful land, traversing all the seas with the rich productions of their industry, engaged in commerce with nations who feel power and forget right . . . [we are] advancing rapidly to destinies beyond the reach of mortal eye — when I contemplate these transcendent objects, and see the honor, the happiness, and the hopes of this beloved country committed to the issue and the auspices of this day, I shrink from the contemplation, and humble myself before the magnitude of the undertaking . . . having banished from our land that religious intolerance under which mankind so long bled and suffered, we have yet gained little if we countenance a political intolerance as despotic, as wicked, and capable of as bitter and bloody persecutions.
>
> But every difference of opinion is not a difference of principle. We have called by different names brethren of the same principle. . . . but would the honest patriot, in the full tide of successful experiment, abandon a government which has so far kept us free and firm on the theoretic and visionary fear that this Government, the world's best hope, may by possibility want energy to preserve itself? I trust not. I believe this, on the contrary, the strongest Government on earth. I believe it the only one where every man, at the call of the law, would fly to the standard of the law, and would meet invasions of the public order as his own personal concern.
>
> . . . our fellow-citizens, resulting not from birth, but from our actions and their sense of them; enlightened by a benign religion, inculcating honesty, truth, temperance, gratitude, and the love of man; acknowledging and adoring an overruling Providence, its dispensations proves that it delights in the happiness of man here and his greater happiness hereafter — with all these blessings, what more is necessary to make us a happy and a prosperous people? Still one thing more, fellow-citizens — a wise and frugal Government, which shall restrain men from injuring one another, shall leave them otherwise free to regulate their own pur-

suits of industry and improvement, and shall not take from the mouth of labor the bread it has earned. This is the sum of good government, ...

... it is proper you should understand what I deem the essential principles of our Government ... Equal and exact justice to all men, of whatever state or persuasion, religious or political; peace, commerce, and honest friendship with all nations, entangling alliances with none; the support of the State governments in all their rights, as the most competent administrations for our domestic concerns and the surest bulwarks against anti-republican tendencies; the preservation of the General Government in its whole constitutional vigor, as the sheet anchor of our peace at home and safety abroad; a jealous care of the right of election by the people — a mild and safe corrective of abuses which are lopped by the sword of revolution where peaceable remedies are not provided; absolute acquiescence in the decisions of the majority ... a well-disciplined militia, our best reliance in peace and for the first moments of war till regulars may relieve them; the supremacy of the civil over the military authority; economy in the public expense, that labor may be lightly burdened; the honest payment of our debts and sacred preservation of the public faith; encouragement of agriculture, and of commerce as its handmaid ... freedom of religion; freedom of the press, and freedom of person under the protection of the habeas corpus, and trial by juries impartially selected. These principles form the bright constellation which has gone before us and guided our steps through an age of revolution and reformation.

The wisdom of our sages and blood of our heroes have been devoted to their attainment. They should be the creed of our political faith, the text of civic instruction, the touchstone by which to try the services of those we trust; and should we wander from them in moments of error or of alarm, let us hasten to retrace our steps and to regain the road which alone leads to peace, liberty, and safety.

I [go] to the post you have assigned me ... Without pretensions to that high confidence you reposed in our first and greatest revolutionary character, whose preeminent services had entitled him to the first place in his country's love and destined for him the fairest page in the volume of faithful history ...

When right, I shall often be thought wrong by those whose positions will not command a view of the whole ground. I ask your indulgence for my own errors, which will never be intentional, and your support against the errors of others, who may condemn what they would not if seen in all its parts. The approbation implied by your suffrage is a great consolation to me for the past, and my future solicitude will be to retain the good opinion of those who have bestowed it in advance ... concil-

CHAPTER TEN — LISTEN TO THE PAST SPEAK TO THE FUTURE

iate that of others by doing them all the good in my power, and to be instrumental to the happiness and freedom of all.

I advance with obedience to the work ... And may that Infinite Power which rules the destinies of the universe lead our councils to what is best ... for your peace and prosperity."

Thomas Jefferson would also teach us something from his own experiences and history of which the majority of Americans are unaware — specifically what happened just over 200 years ago; the United States declared war on Islam. The reason? During the late 18th century, Muslim pirates representing the nations of Tripoli, Tunis, Morocco, and Algiers (aka, the Barbary Coast) had become the terror of the North Atlantic and Mediterranean seas. Attacking every ship in sight, they held the crews for ridiculous and extortionate ransoms. At the same time, the pirates terrorized the hostages with barbaric beatings, all spelled out in heart breaking letters written home to family begging for help by the hostages. Jefferson described these thugs as a dangerous and unprovoked threat to the very young Republic of America.

Our ships had been safe up to this point in time, being protected before the American Revolution by England During the war, they were protected by France. But for over the three decades following the war, America was on her own in attempting to protect her own ships.

As far back as 1784, Thomas Jefferson expressed his anger with the Muslim pirates from his new post of America's Minster to France. The young American Congress had been following in the footsteps of Europe by trying to appease the Barbary States in paying their demands of ransom and extortion for captured ships. Jefferson wanted to take the Muslims to task in war. After Algerian pirates had captured more American ships in July 1785, the Dey of Algiers sent a ransom demand to American leaders for $60,000, a huge sum of money for the time. Upon hearing this, Jefferson angrily voiced to Congress his contempt for any extortion payment and made a proposal of an alliance between the U.S. and allies to forcibly make Muslims stop their piracy. A busy and distracted Congress did not act on that initiative; rather they acquiesced to the Muslims and paid the ransom.

A real turning point to this story and subsequent history was reached in 1786 when Jefferson and John Adams, both future presidents, met with Tripoli's ambassador to Great Britain, challenging him with a question about his nation's "so-called right" to attack American ships, a nation with which America had no previous contacts. Adams and Jefferson report that the Ambassador Sidi Haji Abdul Rahman Adja had responded that Islam "was founded on the Laws of their Prophet, that it was written in their Qur'an that all nations who should not have acknowledged their authority were sinners, that it was their (Islam's) right and duty to make war upon them wherever they could be found, and to make slaves of all they could take as prisoners, and that every Musselman [Muslim] who should be slain in Battle was sure to go to Paradise."

This admission out of the mouth of a diplomat from a so-called religion of peace in their premeditated violence on non-Muslim nations, given to two American Statesmen who were objecting to the treatment was absolutely stunning. Upon hearing this, George Washington warned Congress they should not cave in to Muslims saying it was both wrong and would only serve to embolden them to more acts of terror. But Congress did not follow wise counsel, caving in and continue to pay the ransom for their ships' safe passage and the return of hostages. Their actions had the result that Washington had warned them about. It indeed emboldened the Muslim nations to continue their piracy course for another 15 years. The payments in ransom and tribute climbed through the years reaching an amount equal to over 20 percent of the United States government annual revenue in 1800.

After being sworn in as the 3rd President of the United States in 1801, Jefferson received a note from the Pasha of Tripoli demanding the immediate payment of $225,000 plus an additional $25,000 each following year to allow ships through that region. Jefferson had all he could stand of the situation, sending a message to the Pasha that he (Jefferson) had a suggestion of what he could do with his demand. The Pasha, knowing the past cowardice and acquiescence of the new American nation, responded by cutting down the flagpole of the American consulate and declared war on the United States. He was immediately joined by the nations of Tunis, Morocco, and Algiers in their declarations of war.

Tired of watching our nation be cowed down by Muslim thugs, Jefferson said it was time to meet force with force. He declared that things would change. An American naval force would be put in place, not just to guard the United States coastline as had been the practice of the past, but to rule the sea against Muslim thugs. Dispatching a squadron of frigates to the Mediterranean, Jefferson was about to teach each of the Barbary Coast nations a lesson at war that would last in their memory. Congress finally authorized the action, empowering U.S. ships to seize all vessels and goods of the Pasha of Tripoli. As their closing words mentioned, to "cause to be done all other acts of precaution or hostility as the state of war would justify".

The new will and might of the Americans to strike back put fear into the leaders of Algiers and Tunis. They abandoned their alliance and allegiance to Tripoli. However the war with Tripoli lasted for four more years through 1805. In 1815 Tripoli started their piracy again, flaring up the war with the U.S. But the bravery of the American men, called the U.S. Marine Corps in these wars led to the line "to the shores of Tripoli" in the Marine Hymn. The U.S. Marines who wore heavy leather collars on their uniforms as they boarded enemy Muslim ships to prevent their heads from being cut off by Muslims using their scimitars (a lasting Muslim tradition to cut off heads), would become known as "leathernecks."

Jefferson had for his time driven a temporary stake in the heart of Muslim especially for those leaders on the Barbary Coast. However, he was deeply disturbed by what he witnessed in Islam and its disciples in these nations, who justified murder and extortion in the name of their prophet and god. America had a tradition of toler-

CHAPTER TEN — LISTEN TO THE PAST SPEAK TO THE FUTURE

ance of religions — Jefferson had helped himself in writing this principle in the Virginia Statute for Religious Freedom, but Islam was like no other religion the world had ever seen. Jefferson saw it as a religion of supremacism, with its holy book not only condoning by mandating violence against unbelievers who would not convert. Jefferson's greatest fear was that one day this brand of Islam would return again to our shores and be an even larger threat to our country than it was then.

Jefferson's words and actions petition us to look back, seeing the holy reminder of who we are and whose we are, as noted in our original heritage chiseled into monuments and inscribed upon our early national documents. He also uses his experience with this enemy, telling us to fight this sinister religion with its push for control of our nation, masked at times by political correctness, and with the countenance of terror at other moments. He warns us with advice to insist that immigrants adapt to our culture if they chose to be here, rather than having liberal politicians coerce us to adapt to theirs. America needs to heed this rather sober warning from a gentle voice from the past.

Voice #3:

Though accused by some modern liberals as not being a man of faith, a study of this gentleman's private and public statements demonstrates he believed that Christianity must be rooted in the nation's culture for the nation to survive. His voice, his words come on the occasion of March 6, 1799, when he called upon this nation, from his position of President of the United States, to have a National Day of Fasting in seeking forgiveness of sins. His name? John Adams. Listen carefully, as his words speak to a particular need we have today:

> "As no truth is more clearly taught in the Volume of Inspiration, nor any more fully demonstrated by the experience of all ages, than a deep sense and a due acknowledgement of the growing providence of a Supreme Being and of the accountableness of men to Him as the searcher of hearts and righteous distributer or rewards and punishments are conducive equally to the happiness of individuals and to the well-being of communities.... I have thought proper to recommend, and I hereby recommend accordingly, that Thursday, the twenty-fifth day of April next, be observed throughout the United States of America as a day of solemn humiliation, fasting, and prayer; that the citizens on that day abstain, as far as may be, from their secular occupation, and devote the time to the sacred duties of religion, in public and in private; that they call to mind our numerous offenses against the most high God, confess them before Him with the sincerest penitence, implore his pardoning mercy, through the Great Mediator and Redeemer, for our past transgressions, and that through the grace of the Holy Spirit, we may be disposed and enabled to yield a more suitable obedience to his righteous requisitions in time to come; that He would interpose to arrest the progress

of that impiety and licentiousness in principle and practice so offensive to Himself and so ruinous to mankind; that He would make us deeply sensible that "righteousness exalteth, a nation, but sin is a reproach to any people. (Proverbs 14:34)"

John Adams wrote letters expressing his faith in God. On one occasion, he wrote to Thomas Jefferson stating that "The general principles, on which the Fathers achieved independence, were.... the general principles of Christianity."[3] A few years later Adams wrote a letter to Jefferson in which he stated that "Without religion this world would be something not fit to be mentioned in polite society, I mean hell."[4]

Heed his words. Though removed by approximately 200 years, his words speak almost hauntingly as a ghost from the past to our need today. His is a voice of reason in an age of absolute anarchy. He knew from experience what happens when you cut out the Author of the Universe you welcome in the author of deception and destruction.

Voice #4:

While some might think the last voice will be some noteworthy person of the last thousand years. Some will guess it is Nostradamus who will speak dramatic words, but it is not. Long before this Frenchman lived the speaker we will hear ruled in the Western Orient. Nor is this person a traveling evangelist of the church, nor a former occupant of the White House or a member of the US Senate or House of Representatives. The third of three acts of the drama enlists the help of a king's voice, Solomon himself. Read 2 Chronicles 7:14 again with me and notice that Solomon recalls the words that the Lord shared with him and his people. Notice the key words:

> "If my people, who are called by my name, will humble themselves and pray and seek my face and turn from their wicked ways, then I will hear from heaven, and I will forgive their sin and will heal their land." (2 Chronicles 7:14)

That is the place to start. Notice the words, "if my people..." That is the church and the synagogue, the people of God. Not the building, the arches, the crosses, but the people who are disciples of God, of Jesus Christ. No Muslims here, just Christians and Jews. The reform and remaking of America has to start with God's people realizing their sins, humbling themselves, praying, seeking His face, His way, and then turning from our wicked and forlorn ways.

America has experienced three great periods of revival in the previous two centuries, during which our whole society was dramatically impacted. There was a widespread restoration of the people of God that resulted in tens of thousands of conversions greatly affecting the culture of the day. America started returning to its Christian roots. Bars and taverns were closed, families were reconciled, and young people became sober in their pursuit of God.

From our past, we learn the clear lesson that a genuine spiritual revival can do more to transform culture than all of our political and social activism put together. We need a renewal that can only be affected by widespread repentance before the Almighty whom we have so grievously offended. I have shared in earlier chapters the wrongs and sins we have committed which has separated us from the Almighty. The forces of evil are so deeply entrenched that any cultural shifts will only be cosmetic unless they are accompanied by a true heart-felt spiritual awakening that affects large segments of our churches and then the general population. And this can never be expected to come from a government office of any kind. Revival begins with the people of God!

When the people of God in ancient Ephesus experienced revival, it impacted first the non-believing people of that city who brought their occult books and artifacts, and publicly burned them (Acts 19:18-19). Can you imagine all the black smoke from the scrolls that were dedicated to false gods and to pornography forming huge clouds that blocked the sun and at night the stars?

What bonfires of pornography, rock music, artifacts, and books of occultism, books on Islam and all false religion we would have if God's presence was truly sought and then manifestly felt!

As bad as things are now, there is hope. Revival is possible as long as God is God. But it is going to take pastors who are willing to drop their fears long enough to stand up and preach the truth to their congregations. Jonathan Edwards, a leader during the First Great Awakening in America, argued that God grants light when the darkness is the greatest, and it was in just such times that the glorious periods of revival occurred in America's history. When there was disinterest in religion, gross immorality and rampant unbelief, God poured out His undeserved gracious blessing because the people sought His face while turning from their ways.

So why not dream about what could be as we start. Catch the vision of people treating neighbors as they would want to be treated, businesses taking an hour off for lunch as workers eat, study and pray. Imagine our legislators turning to God for true wisdom as they make decisions. The end goal being our nation returned to its ultimate place for people to see and witness the goodness of God, not socialism, communism or some other rank invention of the human heart. Think of how sporting events, school graduations, the nightly news and other events would have a different tenor to them as remarks would be make about thousands who have made changes in their lives to rebuild relationships, etc.

Dream of being in a fertile land where abortion would become so rare, not just through legislation but because mothers valued their children and immorality was on the decline. Imagine a country in which homosexuals repented and sought God for help in overcoming their lifestyles rather than imposing their values on society. Imagine a country where the courts would make decisions based on the reflection of America's Christian roots. Not the race bating we have today with the fake preachers such as Jesse Jackson, Al Sharpton et al.

Those in the church need to be demonstrating a deep commitment to God, showing their faith not by words they speak, but by deeds they do. We need to believe in Him for something more than just hoping to 'get things' from God, like a nice car, nice home, good vacation, etc. Bottom line, the church has to stop treating God as if he is a good luck charm. We can't pray just when we are in trouble. Or seek 'some of His advice' if things aren't working out for us on our own. Get serious. We need a national revival, and it starts with me; it starts with you. Stop waiting on someone else to do something. It starts with us now. What God has done in the past, He can do again!

The Church has to be the leader, meaning it cannot melt under persecution and hostility of our hedonistic culture. And that means it has to start with the pastor. Unfortunately, most pastors are frightened of threats coming from government, Muslims, news media. Everyone can have fear, especially when the enemy seems bigger than we are. But therein lieth the problem. God is bigger than all them. God and one person make a majority.

To have courage and to teach properly, every man of God has to have one foot in the Bible and one in the world. I believe this is also a requirement to help preachers to be bold when confronting the opposing culture. To assist with this, pastors would do their congregations much good if they were to get involved in projects with the local businesses and political culture of their cities. Learn how to get involved and take a stand. Gradually over time, they can learn how to lead outside of the church walls. And this means depending on personal power rather than position power. Now I know that not all pastors are this way. Some are very strong leaders. However, when you average the impact of all preachers across the land, it seems weak. To teach truth when truth is hated is an essential time for revival to start. It must start with the leaders. Our society has quickly become openly hostile to Christians and Christian values. The media trivializes and ridicules Christianity in the name of humanistic and pluralistic concerns, saying, "We live in a post-Christian nation."

American culture is dominated by television and movies. 30 years ago I told a group of parishioners "... you need to get ready for more sex, violence, and four-lettered words on TV shows and movies, because it is coming." Some of them laughed, though some were able to see the trend even at that time. Well look and listen if you want, those movies have profanity and lewdness over the top, they trample God's honor into the mud, laughing as they do so. And so now they ingrain non-Christian values from infancy. Public schools teach our children how to practice various forms of immorality. One school curriculum in America teaches acceptance of homosexuality in the first grade and mutual masturbation in junior high.

But my question is this, "Where is the church on this? Why is it not 'publicly' denouncing these activities? It seems at least a part of the problem is pastors and parishioners alike are busy getting through the sermon on Sunday, so they can race home and get into the latest episodes of their favorite happens to be full of the sex, violence and foul language on TV, the kind which was criticized in the morning sermon.

Billy Sunday, famed professional baseball player of the 1880's, was converted to Christ In 1886, and turned evangelist. Following the turn of the 20th century, he became the nation's most famous evangelist with his colloquial messages and frenetic delivery. He preached to over 100 million people, in person, mostly before the advent of electronic sound and microphones. He preached temperance, denounced drunkenness, the sex industry, and much of what we see on TV today. He was very conservative in his Biblical doctrine and actually thought the emotional preaching which had been common before the turn of the century was unnecessary. Billy would hold month long meetings in cities like Denver, Chicago, NYC, Boston, and Detroit. It is said that when he preached a revival in Chicago, more than 65 bars and taverns closed permanently.

While people today may laugh at such accounts, America needs a revival of similar proportions today. If it comes, it will need to come from the ranks of Christendom, the church. It will have to come from leaders who are not 'waiting' for the federal or state government to do something. America is reaping the dire consequences of rejecting God. Our society is morally bankrupt, and the problems are certainly resistant to any cure that would come from government. William J. Bennett, in his Index of Leading Cultural Indicators, provides the following statistics for the past 30 years;

> "Despite increased funding and stricter laws, violent crime has increased more than 500 percent. While sex education programs have proliferated, illegitimate births have increased over 400 percent, significantly among teenagers. The divorce rate has quadrupled, and single parent homes have become the majority. Our young people today exhibit a hopelessness, with a more than 200 percent increase in the teenage suicide rate. And America appears helpless before its great problems." (Source: Erwin Lutzer, http://articles.ochristian.com/article3157.shtml)

The verdict is in on the Church: It has been ineffective. It has become a non-issue in today's culture and especially in the area of fixing the nation. That is a sad position for the church. The American Church, despite its many televangelists, busy calendar of events, and reported successes, has made no measurable impact in reversing this downward spiral. When you look at just the sheer numbers, no nation in the world has the number of Churches, Christian organizations, religious radio stations, books, seminars, and Church Conventions and they seemingly have so little impact on society. We are confounded with the pollsters who tell us that religion is up but morality is down.

But I believe there is a reason for this. Sadly, the influence has been in the wrong direction, as we see evidence that our culture has begun to permeate our churches. The church is seduced by the social agenda of wealth and pleasure, and has condoned sinful compromises. There is moral decay within the church, with highly publicized scandals involving ministers, and divorce statistics which are not much better than those outside the church. Think of all that we and our churches would have to repent of if a spirit of holiness began to captivate us. How can America be influenced by an inconsistent and hypocritical church? The answer is, it can't! The church has to come alive spiritually and turn back to its source of life — God.

"We have no government armed with power capable of contending with human passions unbridled by morality and religion. Our Constitution was made only for a moral and religious people. It is wholly inadequate to the government of any other."

— John Adams

Signer of the Declaration of Independence; One of the two signers of the Bill of Rights; 2nd President of the United States)

"The further a society drifts from the truth, the more it will hate those who speak it."

— George Orwell

Chapter Eleven

Find the Servant-Driven Leaders

"To every man is given the key to the gates of heaven.
The same key opens the gates of hell." — Dr. Richard Feynman

WHILE THEIR CHILDHOOD WAS NOT OSTENTATIOUS, it was rich in culture and spiritual guidance. These two brothers grew up sons of a Presbyterian minister. When they were much smaller children, their parents were missionaries in Mexico and Latin America. In their formative years, the family moved to New York near Lake Ontario, where the boys' lives were filled with days of fishing trips with their father. These trips turned into great discussions and lessons on American history, world events, politics, and the inordinate issues facing America. These lessons influenced the boys more than the parents could even begin to fathom. In their adult years, the brothers both outshined their father in at least one respect. They each had a life of great influence in the world, impacting the lives of hundreds of millions of people with the work they did. When the older of the two brothers, John Foster Dulles, died on May 24, 1959, a heartbroken nation mourned the loss of this man, one of their favorite sons; they mourned even more passionately than they had since the death of FDR in 1945, a decade and a half before. The sidewalks outside the National Cathedral in Washington were lined up with thousands who gathered to pass by his coffin. Dignitaries from nations around the world, led by Chancellor Konrad Adenauer of West Germany and President Chiang Kai-shek of Taiwan, who came to the memorial. The funeral was broadcast on network television, ABC and CBS carried it live. Many who viewed that day agreed as President Eisenhower said in his tribute that, "the world has lost one of the truly great men of our time."[1]

In a tribute to this gigantic personality, President Eisenhower signed an executive order declaring that the new super-airport being constructed in the western suburbs of Washington, at Chantilly, Virginia, would be endowed with the name Dulles International. But when Ike left the White House in January 1961, the executive order all but died because John F. Kennedy, the new young Democrat president did not want to name a magnificent, modern, and massive part of America's transportation future named after a popular Republican Cold War veteran. Realizing his brother was going to lose this contest posthumously, Allen Dulles went to work with other political allies to pressure Kennedy to acquiesce and complete the previously planned dedication that the airport wears the name Dulles.

On November 17, 1962, with both former President Eisenhower and former Secretary of the CIA, Allen Dulles, watching, President Kennedy presided over the official opening of Dulles International Airport. In his remarks, he said among other things, "How appropriate it is that this should be named after Secretary Dulles." Kennedy also said in his speech, "He was a member of an extraordinary family: his brother, Allen Dulles, who served in a great many administrations, stretching back I believe to President Hoover, all the way to this one, John Foster Dulles, who at the age of 19 was, rather strangely, the secretary to the Chinese Delegation to the Hague, and who served nearly every Presidential administration, from that time forward to his death in 1959; their uncle, who was Secretary of State, Mr. Lansing; their grandfather, who was secretary of State, Mr. Foster. I know of few families and certainly few contemporaries who rendered more distinguished and dedicated service to their country."[2]

The dedication ceremony included what became a newsreel film clip for weeks to come, the one where Kennedy unveiled the airport's symbolic centerpiece: a larger-than life bust of John Foster Dulles. It was positioned so as to overlook a reminiscent reflecting pool that had been constructed at the airport's center designed by the architect to calm travelers' nerves. More than fifty years after Americans were saddened by Dulles's death, few are left alive who even remember him, let alone remember his name. Most only associate the family name with an airport. And during renovations to the airport in the 1990s, even his bust was removed during the work and was never returned. It disappeared and became a mystery to many in Virginia. The movement of the bust remained a mystery for many years until a worker with the Airports Authority revealed that it was still at the airport, but in a small private conference room next to baggage claim area number three, out of the public view. There, more or less stored with pictures and plaques on the wall that speak of local golf tournaments where workers sometimes eat lunch, the evidence spoke that the bust has been deliberately moved so that public consumption was no longer possible.

What a fate for the monument of this man. Dedicated by the President of the United States, unveiled by the shimmering pool while the world watched on television. Here was a bust of John Foster Dulles, a secretary so powerful that when he served no government in the Free World would have dared to make an international decision without consulting him first. Now his memory in the form of a bust shuffled off into a private employee conference room that seldom gets used. It is a microcosm of the real journey taken past conservative heroes, and therefore what history has done to the Dulles brothers. One biographer states that since a time immediately following his death of Dulles, memory of him has been politicized by the progressive left; he has been robbed of his rightful place in history. Another journalist in 1971 wrote about how quickly the Dulles memory has faded, saying that while the name is not completely forgotten, "certainly most of the éclat had gone out of it." Yet another biographer talked of his brother, Allen, naming him "the greatest intelligence officer who ever lived." These very unique and powerful brothers set in motion many of the practices that shape today's world. Understanding who they were, and what they did, is a key to uncovering the buried backgrounds of political upheaval even in Asia, Africa and Latin America.[3]

I share this account of the Dulles brothers for a few reasons: first, to show the picture of a good leader; second, to show how progressives work to destroy the reputation of conservative leaders and heroes, even after they are gone. There is no length they will not go to attempt to discredit an honorable person of their reputation. Third, I share this true account to offer advice, since any who would cherish a leadership role, be aware of what mud-slinging and character assassination that will go on trying to destroy the reputation of anyone who tries to do the right thing in this progressive culture today. Our political centers, the cities where politicians sit, have become vile, venomous cesspools — evil places. This is due to the dirty political tricks and psychological assassinations, done partially by an obliging media who openly lies and fabricates stories to fit an agenda, which fits into the progressive agenda. That agenda has been established for the sole purpose of destroying the liberty and the foundations of this nation. That is an absolute. Think of anyone who has come forward to tell a truth against the liberal regime — squads of attorneys have unleashed to dig up any dirt attempting to discredit. No matter how dangerous it is for honest leaders, we need courageous leaders who are willing to step forward, rise up and lead the people of this nation back to their rightful position; that is into the righteousness of God and His liberty. What we have in Washington and various state capitols right now, cannot do that job.

There are many mirages and illusions today about what leadership is and what it is not. Weird and fantastic are the stories about optical illusions, of which the mirage is one of many manifestations that infect many people. "Napoleon once crossed a desert on one of his long marches; the hot sun beat down on the long line of soldiers, tired, hungry, burning with fierce thirst, when out there just ahead of them they saw a beautiful lake, green palm trees, sparkling waters — a lovely oasis in the middle of the desert. The men shouted, broke ranks and ran for the water. But as they ran, the lake ran; the faster they went, the faster the lake receded, and then suddenly it wasn't there at all. It was a cheat, an illusion, a mirage ... a boy left home and found out all about mirages."[4]

What Makes a Good Leader

One thing we know for certain — from Jesus to John Wayne and prosperity to prowess, leaders and what attracts others to them might vary, but one constant remains the same: everything rises and falls on leadership, as Dr. John Maxwell has put it. Leadership has built the biggest empires. It has collapsed the greatest corporations. It can unify diversity or divide unity. It can cast visions, catalyze movements, it can coalesce people and revolutionize industries and culture. Or it can run an organization and country into the ground by hardly trying or making a few wrong moves.

It has been said you get what you pay for in leadership, not just monetarily but in quality of leader replication, organizational development, and succession planning. There is direct link between the health of an entity (e.g., nation) and the depth of its leaders. It translates on how far their subordinates and the nation can eventually soar. A nation will falter, pure and simple if it declines to select good leadership. Leaders can cause the morality, magnanimity and mistakes made to metastasize. We cannot grow greater, wider or deeper than the person and people at the top.

There is a mirage among many of the people of this country when it comes to good leadership, especially among young adults. The mirage, or confusion, is in 'what' people think constitutes a good leader, or leadership in general. People have historically fallen into two different camps when picking leaders: Form vs. Substance. It is amazing to see how many people are suckered by the shallowness of form: who looks good to them, or who appeals to people on television, or seems to be hip and "with it." Form is always appealing to the visually oriented TV crowd of today, but when leaned on as being the critical vote of who really is a good leader, it is a cheat, it is an illusion, it is an empty suit. Why do you think they call it a TV stage? Everything on it 'is dressed up' or "staged," to give the pretense or appearance of being something that it is not.

Substance or maturity is the stuff that seemed to characterize good leaders in earlier generations, especially my mother's and grandparents', which mark them as unique when compared to the young. In fact as you go back in time, it is amazing to see the amazing substance of character which was common in our Founding Fathers, as seen in their written communications. Not only was their education better, their vocabulary better, but their maturity seems to have been stronger too. That is partially due to the natural course of life; it takes time to mature. However, I fear the quality, as defined by earlier generations, is out of reach for most Millennials [???], Generation X and Y, and even some Boomers. The distractions of gaming, texting, and even the basic technology being around to soak up time, has taken a toll in personality, in ability to communicate, in ability to focus, and even at times, substance in character. Another signal within youth that maturity is still out of arm's reach, is the spoken need for instant gratification. Whatever happened to working toward a goal or saving money over a year or two in order to buy a new sofa? Instead, it must happen now. There is no tomorrow or next week with younger people.

Turn Weaknesses into Strengths

What to do about finding weakness in your life that needs to be a project of improvement? I suggest doing a bid tab. (Of course, the process of bid tab can be done for about anything.) That is an engineer's term used when bidding on a project or doing analysis of some application on a project. It does not take an engineer to do one. In fact most people have done this mentally at some point. It is a simple process, but challenging in all the analysis. Take a blank sheet of paper, 8 ½ X 11 is okay. Draw a line from top to bottom separating the paper into two halves. On the top of the left side place a "+", and on the left top place a "-." Now, let us say that our project today is "Buying a new motorcycle." As you list your positives under the "+" and the negatives under the "-," it will become noticeable quickly whether other things needs to be managed first or not. Possibly under the "—", it might become obvious that your wife or husband might need more important necessities, rather than a luxury like a motorcycle at the time. This would be seen because the "—" list is longer than the "+". This "data" should then be viewed as the most important criteria in making a decision rather than the emotion or felling of the moment. Thus begins the process of being data-driven and the choice of making decisions based on logic rather than "but, I want that." This is just an example of how to start thinking outside the box — Sorry, I dislike that term "outside the box"; I won't use it again.

Even under the best of conditions, maturity is such a difficult attribute to clench; it is a painful journey with most of us having multiple scars from lessons learned. Or in some cases, just scars, with nothing learned. We need all the allies we can get as we grow. Time can be a tremendous associate, if used appropriately. Time is needed to embed within us the learning of a new job, the how to's of just about everything. And no, work is not always fun things to do. That is why it is called a job.

Substance of character and maturity it seems are equal to opponents, especially very early in life, because they will only stand firm with experience. Forgive me for what you might think is talking down to you. The point is, substance is very difficult to find in someone touting themselves to be a leader, especially if you do not have wells of experience to examine. When I look back at the TV shows and televised political campaigns with which I have been familiar, they have had a major emphasis on covering up details of character and presenting a 'visual' of what the person wants you to see. So while technology has served us humans well in a few areas, it certainly becomes a cheat or at least a hurdle when you want to find a good leader.

The first thing many look for in a teacher, preacher, politician, etc. is typically style, polish, or "the look." What should be the first thing we seek is substance. It is best seen over a space of time in varying settings; some circumstances that are amiable and some that are stressful. As should be gained in an interview, an understanding must be gained of how a person reacts not only when things are good, but also when the pressure is on, when things are extremely difficult. That is why examining a candidate's "record" for accomplishments is a great place to start; to determine the substance and competencies to drive projects to successful completion.

When I talk of great leadership, or of finding a great leader, it is obviously dealing with the substance, character, backbone, intestinal fortitude, guts, etc., to which I refer. Not macho, not poise, not pretty, not staged. Those things look nice, but they cannot deliver. Being older, I can appreciate the temptation that comes with the TV, Internet generation. Meaning that I am old enough to remember what life was like without the I-pads, tablets, Smart phones, computers, hand-held devices, etc. Those tools of technology are nice, but they do not say a thing about the depth of a person at all. I have one foot in the substance driven world and one in the current, pretty world of what is visually attractive is good type world.

A Great Example of Leadership

He is arguably called the greatest coach in history. That is thanks to a long list of accomplishments, and many of the greatest players who ever put on a uniform, many of them consensus All-Americans who played for him. And this was capped off by winning 12 National Championships in NCAA Men's Basketball. And "7" of them were in a row! So many experts tend to agree. That is a feat completed by John Wooden that will never again be duplicated.

If you ever had the chance to hear Wooden speak, you would recall he said for him it was never about the number of wins or loses, but about how a person prepares and then plays the game to the best of his/her ability. His players testify that in all their practices or pep talks he gave, they never once heard him talk about winning a game. Rather it was about learning and doing the fundamentals over and over, building that into both their muscle memory and their mind.

In fact in his great book which is really about achieving success in life, *They Call Me Coach*, Wooden stressed that his coaching was not about playing a game, but rather all about teaching boys how to become men of character, responsibility, integrity and team-work. Wooden went on to say, "I never once talked to my guys about winning or losing because I think that is a byproduct of our preparation. I would much rather be focused on the process of becoming the best team we're capable of becoming."[5]

Coach Wooden's "Pyramid of Success" is a compilation of 14 years of work to build his famous philosophy on coaching, but mostly on life. "Once you saw it and it became ingrained in your mind, it became a part of you," his former players would say. But Coach did not create the pyramid with playing basketball games in mind; he worked on it over a 14-year period, aiming to create a new definition of success. He said that while he was teaching high school English, he witnessed parents criticizing their child for receiving less than an "A" or "B" in class. That's when he knew he needed to find a way to pass on his message that success is not just about making an "A", about how many possessions you have, or how powerful you have become. Rather, it is "all about finding peace of mind in knowing you have prepared and done the best you are capable of doing."[6]

Learning history is a lot like Coach's pyramid; it is one of the critical building blocks that will prepare an individual for a strong operating base in life and better decision-making. That at least is according to some of his players; ones like Bill

Walton, Andy Hill, Kareem Abdul-Jabbar, Keith Erickson, Keith Wilkes, Mike Warren, Kenny Washington and John Vallely.

Pretty or handsome is what we see first, what we expect, what we want. It is in our nature. Tell a young man that a young lady is interested in him, and his first question will invariably be, "What does she look like?" Everyone would like that, but it is not the most important attribute. Our nature is faulty and needs to be trained on identifying not what is good looking, but good. That is why corporations spend billions of dollars collectively annually on both teaching employees how to correctly interview candidates and then on resources and time interviewing them. Obviously, my concern is not with corporate entities and how they make decisions when selecting candidates for office. But with people who have not been trained or who do not have the experience in handling any of this. This is a concern, because one of those votes turns out to count as much as one that has done their homework.

Back in the television world, most TV commercials presents a person's looks, and how their product can make the appearance better, younger, tanner, or thinner looking and with more hair. It's for the visual. These ads have long since stopped targeting me, for the skin care, the rejuvenation, 'the look', about which the products speak. I smile and cringe too because most advertisers are targeting people under 25. My children tell me I was 25 just before fire was discovered. Oh, well.

Defining Leaders

There are many erroneous concepts about what makes a great leader. One infamous belief is that leaders are just born for the role. Some think a leader is great because of their superior size or presence in entering a room, or even their loud voices yelling four adjectives in a row all starting with the letter "F." Some think another is a great leader because they more or less trap their subordinates in a room, locking them in until they get their project work completed; and that completion is checked only when they reveal progress on their work by sticking it through an opening in the door. Some think yet another is a great leader because he is a blow hard huffing and puffing about how he will deconstruct inferior projects of subordinates by simply blowing on them. The world's stage has more than its share of people who have been placed in supervisory positions like these three. They are full of their own intimidating personality; getting subordinates to panic and surrender under his applied pressure. If these traits were all characteristics of true leaders, then characters like "The Giant" (From Jack and the Bean Stalk), "The Evil Witch" (From Hanzel and Gretel), and "The Big Bad Wolf" (From The Three Little Pigs), would all have been world renowned for their leadership skills.

Possibly the slight humor will help in uncovering the truth about leadership. True leaders establish traits and habits which are much more meaningful in their lives which are identifiable. Here are a few I like.

True Leaders are Students, or Disciples, First

Leaders should be in the business of learning and growing all their lives. That means that they are followers first, then they are leaders. Great leaders can never learn enough from those who have blazed trails and have been successful before them. They read, they study, they listen, they have a hunger for knowledge and wisdom that cannot be quenched. They develop focus, assertiveness, resourcefulness, diplomacy, steadiness, composure; in short they learn to keep their cool in tough times. Leaders are thirsty for knowledge and wisdom because they see within themselves the reality of shortcomings. They are brutally honest with themselves and with their people. What is really sad in our culture today is that most of our politicians and many of our leaders fail to pass the test of good leadership at this very first wicket. They do not see their own weaknesses and refuse to address them. Blaming someone else is not the brand of a good leader. Some individuals are promoted to a level and feel the exhilaration of having "made it." Having heard more than one pastor who has claimed he has enough sermons to last 7 years and when he has delivered them, it is time to go to the next congregation and deliver them again. That sounds like they believe they have "made it" too. True leaders never feel they "have arrived." There is always another lesson to learn, more data to crunch, more growing to be accomplished. We are so limited in our ability to see the realities of life, to understand the truth of God's Word and to meet the needs of others. Leaders know that and learn.

Leaders Have a Picture of What Needs To Be Done

The ancient seer said that where there is no vision, the people will perish. Sadly, most of us have witnessed leaders who have limited to no vision, and their organizations suffer because of it. Good leaders will give definition and direction to their followers that are certainly more than focused on the short-term, a few days or weeks. Guidance is a key word for quality leaders. They provide "the keys" to understanding the business, the opportunities, the challenges, the pitfalls, and the touch-points an organization must make in order to be successful, sort of a "Rosetta Stone." Leaders perceive the differences between assets, which need protecting, and commodities, which are used up in production, then tossed aside. One prime example of assets, are those precious people in an organization who must be provided for as they give their time and talent to the success of the organization. Too many leaders of companies treat employees like commodities, burning them up, and then throwing them out; only to replace them with more commodities, and then repeat the process. While this may seem to be the most tempting for short-term gains, leaders have a longer vision and will not use assets, but will prize them.

Leaders are "Principle-Driven"

Real leaders pursue principles for guiding their lives rather than popularity. They believe in showing power with employees, but not the type most people see.

They exhibit personal power rather than position power. That means they lead rather than bark out orders. They did not worry about getting elected; rather they believe in honesty, truth and integrity instead.

But picking leadership by visual characteristics results in weak to no leadership. When it comes to turning around a company, a city government, a church, or a nation, that has to all be driven by different characteristics of substance. I believe the more important ones are as follows:

First a leader must be able to see both the general features plus the specifics of their project work. It is the big picture trait. And not just any vision. We have been through that several times, especially lately where a leader wants hope and change. Turned out to be the hope for which he hoped and the change was what nobody who loves freedom wanted. A true leader needs to be able to envision where we should be, seeing the true promised land ahead. The vision needs to incorporate time-tested traits which have been proven from experience. Especially this is true for us now, since we are in need of a platform based on the morality and the spirituality on which we will stand as a nation. The vision is naturally driven by God's standards and principles. The vision needs to immediately incorporate those standards, principles and directives. What lawyers, politicians and activists want, may or may not play a part. They must agree with the vision. And this all takes experience in walking a particular type of life and having particular character traits. By the way, even when the culture calls these character traits extreme, the leader knows they are not; but rather are in line with what God and the Founders identified as being good.

Second, a leader must set an example by establishing goals which are solid and good for supporting the governing policies, or in the case of America, the Constitution. Because a goal is not a goal unless it is specific, quantitative, and measurable in time, all these must be established and communicated very well. And since this is to be done not in a unilateral action, the proper vetting must be done in an example setting mode. What a difference there would be now, if we and the media had properly vetted candidates.

Third, fourth, and fifth, are traits which are sometimes viewed together, for example in interviewing or interview training courses. They enable the discovery of the elements within a candidate to find a match between position and potential worker. That is one reason industry consultants have made fortunes on teaching variations of them, in name and practice.

Identifying skill sets is trait number three, and the easiest marker to identify in the hiring process. These are the basic "skills" to do the job. Through a series of questions over a period of approximately two minutes, an experienced interviewer (or journalist) can discern if someone has the skills to most jobs. In our case, of a job to lead a revival, a leader must have both the God-given talent and the skill sets to lead and then designate other leaders who in turn will work alongside to equip others who in turn will help in accomplishing the mission of directing our country back to a righteous path and to God.

Core Competencies: The fourth, on our overall list of traits. What is that you might ask? These are more difficult to discern immediately and usually take some time in an interview setting or more questions from a journalist. Basically, it is a question of seeing if someone fits culturally into the group, nation, etc. How do you go about making decisions about ____ when you are faced with _____? As you can see, they are best seen in an individual in how he/she works on projects, how he makes decisions, how he approaches problems or the general work. In other words does this person make a good cultural fit into the group or this the job? Situational problem questions are good, but not nearly as good as watching a person in the heat of work over a period of 5, 10 or even 20 years.

Motivation to do the job: Fifth, and the last trait on our short middle list. What motivates the leader? What is their moral compass? How is that compass grounded? How does that fit into the overall goal of our church, our community, projects, or our nation? You see, these are critical vetting points in selecting someone to lead, not just did they say they wanted to have the job. Motivational drive can be so difficult to see unless you observe how one makes decisions over time in some difficult situations. When I was in charge of hiring leaders for the company with which I was employed, these were the largest three questions I had in mind as I tried to find this "cultural fit."

Numbers three through five, are three very huge questions every church or synagogue should be asking themselves as they seek a leader, pastor, priest or rabbi. The same applies to a company as they seek an employee or leader for their firm. Or for a county, city, state or nation, the same questions should be asked as a sheriff, mayor, representative, senator, or president is sought. Interesting, how this type of vetting with certainly a business and a Biblical perspective can identify the best potential leadership candidates for a variety of work, all in getting this nation back on the right track toward healing, being economically sound, returning to God, and our first principles of the nation. If you doubt my thinking process, check most any corporate training program, including the motivational workshops and you will see that virtually every point in the process is based on some portion of Biblical literature.

Passionate, Hands-On, and Morally Driven

Sixth, a leader needs to be one that is hands on but also very 'strategic' in getting our job done. Rolling the sleeves up is good PR but being strategic is crucial in seeing the big picture.

Seventh, is the love or passion for the type or business sector. That is so critical, and note I did not say love for the power that goes with the job. Most leaders we see today have love, but it is a love for money, for self or power to do something not so good for the country or even for the church/synagogue of which they may be a member. This trait is also unique from the motivational trait in that there may be motivation to be a "Director" for a firm but there may be no love for the business segment or industry.

Eighth, and I suppose last on this short list of qualifications, is the question, "Does this person have the moral authority, or the moral baseline, to lead?" God has always picked people who had feet of clay (meaning they had human frailties and made mistakes), but they had a moral authority BECAUSE, in spite of their wretched mistakes and sins, they leaned on Him, or came back to Him for guidance.

So as we seek leaders for our nation, our states, our counties, our townships, our co-ops, our churches and synagogues, we should seek those having these traits. When these personae are present in an individual, we must put them to work on projects commensurate with their abilities, and let them work. To employ their talents, there must be a plan in place; an appropriate leader can tackle a project and usually bring it to a successful completion with even modest support.

So when the work starts, there is vision, then goal setting, then specific work objectives toward the goal(s). What follows are established perimeters of activity which will help keep focus, then monitoring, quantifying, measuring and tracking progress. All this should be done from a simple platform of succinct national, regional, or local business meetings using PowerPoint® slides and spreadsheets having graphs, data, and bar charts to show progress. Obviously a new element to today's culture would be introduced; that would be truth and honesty. Remember the truth is the truth, let the facts speak.

The elites in Washington need to hear a new message, "There's a new sheriff in town. We're going to clean up our communities, towns, states, and nation." And the badge he wears in our community needs simply to be the heart of the leader out front helping to lead and facilitate a revival among the people. And the characteristics identified possibly could be utilized as a pattern for finding and training upcoming leaders to replace newly selected leaders. That is called succession planning. That is number nine in the steps to take.

Examine all nine traits again:

    First – Disciples or learners,
    Second – Having the big picture in mind,
    Third – Principle-driven,
    Fourth – Possessing appropriate skill sets,
    Fifth – Possessing appropriate "core competencies,"
    Sixth – Possessing the motivation to do the job,
    Seventh – Passion for the business sector,
    Eighth – The moral authority to lead,
    Nine – Ability to do succession planning.

As you examine each of these nine traits in brief or in more detail, hold them up as a template to our founders and their resumes or profiles, our early national leaders, some of the great pastors and preachers of our storied past, and I believe you will see these as a common thread run through the good ones. They were great leaders having these 8 or 9 traits.

Our First Lady, Michelle Obama, has been saying over the term of the president that many of our people live in or near "food deserts." I will not argue that here. But I will say this, we definitely are living in a nation, whose entire territory appears to be a leadership desert. Use the template of nine qualities above this time with current "leaders" and other politicians in various locations, and in particular Washington, D.C.; then recognize who is and who is not a great leader according to their "deeds" not just their "words" in speeches. Suddenly, many of those who seemed at first blush to be so great and wonderful will be seen through an entirely new lens — the correct lens. That will form an early view for us in seeing what needs to be done today to turn our nation around.

"We have rebelled against God. We have lost the true spirit of Christianity, though we retain the outward profession and form of it . . . By many, the Gospel is corrupted into a superficial system of moral philosophy, little better than ancient Platonism. . . .

My brethren, let us repent and implore the Divine mercy. Let us amend our ways and our doings, reform everything that has been provoking the Most High, and thus endeavor to obtain the gracious interpositions of providence for our deliverance. . . .

May the Lord hear us in this day of trouble. . . . We will rejoice in His salvation and in the name of our God, we will set up our banners!"

— Samuel Langdon

President of Harvard:
May 31, 1775 in speech to Massachusetts Congress

Chapter Twelve

Reforming and Starting Over

"Ah, and when to the heart of a man was it ever less than a treason,
to go with the drift of things, to yield with a grace to reason,
and bow and accept at the end of love or a season" — Robert Frost

HELLENISTIC, OR "KOINE," GREEK WAS THE most finite language I know. It had fewer than 10,000 total words in the entire vocabulary. Compare that to our current 225,000 plus words in American English, which also is exponentially growing daily. If a Martian were to visit in one or more of our towns within our society, and then listen to young people speak, our alien friend might be tempted to believe four-lettered words make up the bulk of our vocabulary. That is a reflection of the heart of people in this new culture about which we need to change; the heart needs to be reformed — when it is a basis necessary to reconstruct our society and begin to salvage what good remains. We have challenges that lie ahead dealing with reform and starting over — it requires deep channels of change.

Back to Greek for a minute. Differences in word meanings and tenses of verbs are referred to as a 'phenomenon' by using different and unique word endings, much like changing a caboose on a train, to change declensions, cases, etc. English is similar in limited ways, but not as consistent.

Because of their very concise language, the Greeks used common words for actions, as an example, in using the word for the bone in the pointing finger as their word for "teach." To teach was to point at something. There are many things to which we need to point as we lead and teach our people the truth — truth about accountability in moral, physical and spiritual realms. And we will do it by leading the way and making smart choices and putting first things first in our own lives, then in the election processes for those who we select to serve.

Viewing our current national situation, some will say it is good intentions that has brought us to the brink of disaster of these results: Pollution, inflation, statism, disorder, and without knowing the right words to halt our headlong plunge. That may be part of the visual problem, but there is a deeper cause as identified by an ancient prophet, "The heart is deceitful above all things, and beyond cure; who can understand it?" Jeremiah 17:9

Where are the answers to be found!? Not in governmental management of creative activities! They are not to be found in a collectivist economy or welfare state, but in the absence of these arrangements — they'll be found in the practice of freedom to do what we ought, not what we want. For it is only in an essentially free society that has a Judeo-Christian ethic and morality that provides the soil where unknown answers to problems emerge from the minds of men and become known. Such freedom allows answers to be found and allows them to be performed, while coercion stifles answers — never allows working solutions a performance.

The wisdom of self-rule through the discipline of free-enterprise has made our lives so rich and through which we now exist is an enlightenment that emerged from free men — not Socialists, not Communists, not Progressives, not radical liberals. Were they the geniuses they claim, we would be forced to confess that all progress sprang from collectivist supermen, but the truth is, none ever existed.

Despite freedom's overwhelming case in building all provisions in our land, it is cruelly mocked, assaulted, and ridiculed from every angle in our current, revolting statist culture. Reasons and excuses are endlessly massaged for our ears. "I like freedom but . . . " is a shrill loud, persistent, repelling chorus, bedeviling any soul daring to champion the cause for independence in a Christian nation.

Social statist theorists announce almost daily that humans have gotten smarter through the centuries. At best that's laughable. At worst within our culture and time, it's a fabrication or pretense. We are not smarter. We are not because we have removed the underpinnings beneath our foundation of knowledge. Those underpinnings make learning meaningful and fun. History, that is a wonderful mentor and teacher, provides us a benchmark against which we can size up the current trends in America. If there is a lesson we can learn from just the low-hanging fruit, it is that we need to put into practice the basics of English, math, history, civics, and science in teaching our young people in school. What they receive today is eons from what was taught generations ago, when they knew how to read and write. Our nation has a leaky bucket in our education system today — we must patch it up and start practicing the same principles the adults of our early nation taught. A patchwork with Common Core is a tragic mistake taking us further from the goal we seek.

Another huge mistake we've made is in believing that our knowledge in and use of technological devices, are all in some way an ingenious replacement for learning how to speak, write, or read — it is not! To push buttons on a computer game, to use keys in texting a friend, forward emails containing jokes, to transfer music to an MP3 player, or to photo shopping pictures are not a replacement for a real education. There are huge gaps in the learning process and curriculum from a past day that must be recovered — current technology can only be an assistant, certainly not a replacement for learning. Math, history, English composition, science, civics, and others need to be resurrected. Math should be taught without the use of calculators so as to ensure we have engrained our minds with data necessary to excel in society. Old fashioned ciphering matches in math classes using only the computer in the brain are a great example of training that will only help in careers outside the classroom down the road. Using hand-held calculators every day in math in similar to being tongue-tied in speech — learning is not as complete.

The first scene that comes to mind is watching a young cashier in a restaurant trying to grapple with making change out of a $20 bill when the total check is $13.57. The calculator has made this process easy, but in some ways it has robbed our youth of learning the hard math skills and having the formulas live in their brains so they can function without technology if necessary. There's an item to reform.

Challenge a young people with that project and you might very well hear them say, "Why would I want to learn that? We will always have calculators." That statement is quite a statement of faith, and hopefully one that will be true. But it could turn out to be crippling. A person limits himself by following such advice and not learning everything they can, especially when it comes to math. The future is too uncertain. Too many potential disasters loom out just ahead that could destroy much of the technology that exists on earth. A person would be wise to prepare themselves to be able to do some challenging calculations in their mind. It is good preparation just in case.

Going further with a similar illustration, some young students and adults think texting using the "new English" is the best avenue to learn communication skills, such as English and spelling. (Laughter, loud laughter here.) Again, it is not. At least allow me to say, it is sad to see civilization start to devolve into a death spiral, where normal communications are impossible. The only thing missing in your hand is a gun, and the dialogue from the ridiculous game of Russian roulette you play in doing this. Dumb and dumber. Some English teachers are actually teaching students to spell as they are texting. Just as I say that, some English teachers are telling students to spell just like they text. There we have change #2 in the classroom. If we do not stop the devolution, the human race might well become hampered in writing and speech much like Eloi the Morlocks in the movie The Time Machine with Rod Taylor. You might recall, the Eloi could not read books, or anything else. They had difficulty understanding English; the Morlocks could only grunt and growl when they were hungry. Both had lost the ability to communicate.

Having said that, I am a proponent of educational psychology; that is the science behind "how students learn." Math as it is being taught in "some" of the current class rooms excites me.

There is a pattern to the transformation of education which would make radically good changes for our students. As we approach education reform in our country, there must be serious changes at several levels and in several directions. Where to start?

First, there must be eradication of the secular humanist doctrines; real education must take place. That is an essential step. Not only must the federal government be cut out of education, but a curriculum must be built which promotes the American way of life, rather than one that tears it down. Many people have listened to the continual drumbeat of liberals against the American free-enterprise system so long that they seem to want to apologize for it. Go to any university or high school and ask teachers what students want to learn. They will tell you that they are only interested in learning the answers that will be asked on tests. Students have been indoctrinated by both technology and the government and have reached a point they cannot think on their own nor do critical thinking. We must teach solid business methodologies accompanied with the morals and ethics demanding uprightness in our society. So along with the 3-Rs and basic curriculum mentioned earlier, No more one size fits all for all the children.

Once education is back in the state's court where it belongs, each state may add to its learning structure each day, so students will study and memorize things important to America. Among these are:

- Say the Pledge of Allegiance every morning;
- Memorize the Gettysburg Address;
- Memorize George Washington's Farewell Address;
- Bible passages should be read in primary and secondary schools on a regular basis;
- School assemblies should be held periodically focusing on American historical events presented by college professors;
- Career fairs will be held regionally for high school students giving them glimpses of business.

As you follow along with these thoughts, most people can see where my mind is leading. We want to establish a process in schools that promote thinking about American democracy and ideals, moral absolutes, free-enterprise, all built on the underpinnings of morality as taught in Judeo-Christian beliefs.

When local residents within their states have control of education, pride of ownership within a state to equip local the labor market with superior talent which is educated will drive the schools to excellence. Frankly, I'd like to see some schools which focus on Biblical literature for at least a portion of the required reading material. Over time the tenor on campuses would change since the morality children would read will seep into the brains and change the atmosphere on campuses, plus the reading scores would excel; resulting in smarter, safer, more civilized places of learning, rather than the jungles that exist in many areas now operating under the "federal banner of learning."

Math would be done with the calculators in the head. No other calculators would be available for the students during general class time. I would also reintroduce the ciphering matches of old, games of challenge to train the mind in using numbers, which by the way helps later on in a career and life in general. This is called "learning," — children are often opposed to it because it involves using or exercising the brain, however, it really works when used appropriately.

There would be discipline in the classroom and on campus. Real punishment would be handed out, rather than the "three-days off with pay" program that exists now. Students would be allowed to excel in classes in this setting. But the appearance of classroom activity and the demeanor of students would change — there would be just the glimpse of yesteryear, with morals, common courtesies taught, and higher GPAs with students more prepared to deal with life than they are now.

Second, a Balanced Budget Amendment is absolutely essential. The government must be operated like a typical family at least from a fiscal standpoint. If my household does not have the money, the household cuts back on many different things in different areas. Government should run the same way. It's time to start cutting departments at the national level and send the employees (government) packing. Let them find a job like the rest of us when we get laid off. No more life time employment. States should require their candidates to pay allegiance to a balanced budget amendment and stick to it. The solution to the government's fiscal crisis is to cut drastically in every area, especially the pork barrel legislation. We're in a crisis mode, cutting the fat and some of the lean, just like the family does, which has lost a revenue stream. The first year's budget would be approximately 50 percent of what it is currently, meaning layoffs in federal government offices, starting now. Next year, it might be cut another 50 percent to get spending under control. Obviously, this means some programs would be cut or trimmed severely. The federal government has no business being in the business of running every part of a family's life. This has to stop immediately. Freedom to operate at home is a wonderful thing when the eyes of "Big Brother" are not watching.

Third, the Constitution will be our governing document for civil liberties. The Bible will be a companion volume for guidance as it was in the beginning of our nation. No questions asked. If you do not like that plan, move to a country that follows a plan more to your liking. The Founding Fathers warned of a Federal Government that would usurp the power, rights, freedoms, and privacy away from both the States and citizens. Our federal government is out of control and has to have the gas, electricity, water, and oxygen cut off (basic services) for a time to get their attention. For twenty-six years, the Federal Government has expanded the scope of its power at an alarming rate, just ignoring the Constitution. Civil liberties are critical. By the way, they are not just a racial issue for one ethnic group. It is an issue for every American during this current reign of government. That means there are no more African Americans, Spanish Americans, European Americans, and so on. There are simply Americans. I don't care if your skin is green in color. No special privileges should ever be based on any color. To work this plan, we should start the process at the local election level and work up. Sure if we can elect a president who shares this opinion, that's great. Get him or her in the office. If a candidate does not want to follow Christian morality or the Constitution, move on to the next candidate. We need to get radical, folks. It is late in the game if we are going to save this nation.

Fourth, our tax codes should be revised. All these pages of tax codes have to go. No one understands them, not even the people who passed the legislation. It's mass confusion. Recognizing this will cut an entire department of the treasury and their revenue department by 90 percent — Irrational Retreat Socialists (IRS) — let them go get a real job like the rest of the nation following school. I'm for a user tax: Put a tax on anything sold, nothing else — computer systems are set up to deal with those taxes already, so there would not be any major infrastructure investment. No income tax — you keep your money. Just pay a higher tax when you buy something. No more estate tax, or death tax as it is commonly called. This robs businesses and families and sends money to professional politicians to hire more, pass more, do more, all to cost more and require new taxes. By the way at the same time, outsource lots of things done in government, reduce the size of some government department payrolls by 50 percent or more. Let states do much of what the Feds do. Let private companies handle much of the work. Non-taxable money will be automatically invested back in the economy by smart capitalists resulting in much more tax revenue than liberals dreamed possible because the economy will boom and roll past every other nation. That is what made us great to begin with, so we must return to what really works. What is happening now is not working.

Fifth, we should have debt limits for the nation. Families do, why not these crazy politicians? National debt is over $20 trillion now and rising. We cannot afford to mortgage our future away to foreign nations or our grandchildren or anyone else. This has to stop. Present a budget to work that is $750 Billion; keep it at that level for 5 years. Departments must fire employees to get under their particular budgets. Companies have to work that way. So should the government. If offices have to close, let them close. If states do not want to elect senators or representatives that will support that idea let those states lose any appropriations for projects — they'll end up paying their own bills. We don't need to be carrying the debt of Californians on the backs of other states, for example. The key is to cut spending, cut costs, streamline activities for better service, just like in a corporation.

Sixth, as to an energy policy — it's simple: drill, baby, drill! Economies of the world run on oil — ours should too. Immediately, America should start getting as much of the coal, oil, and natural gas we can to reduce prices, at the pump, which will reduce prices at the grocery counter also — get our economy rolling again. Look what is happening in North Dakota. That is a microcosm of what can happen in every state if we have such a policy. No more of these thousands of Washington bureaucratic regulations, corporate subsidies, and excessive taxation

Chapter Twelve — Reforming and Starting Over

that makes in nearly impossible to produce new forms of clean, cheap energy. Companies are more concerned about hiring lobbyists than they are with hiring scientists and engineers to drive technology. We are being robbed at the gas pump, and with all that oil and gas right beneath our feet. Besides when we follow this policy, we cut off the Muslim Brotherhood at the pass, and put them in a Hugo instead of the Mercedes they drive today. By the way, cut the Bureau of Land Management out of the Federal budget immediately. If the states want to have a similar department, let them. There will be much better control at the state and local level. Currently the monstrosity being run from Washington, D.C., is destroying family businesses and ruining individual's lives. If states like California want to run businesses out of their states by some state-wide environmental and land management program, let them. The other states will be happy to take those businesses and develop job opportunities for their people in the cities and counties.

Seventh, we need to dispense with, change the structure of, or put a short leash on the Creature from Jekyll Island, named the Federal Reserve. It starts with an audit of their activities. This will produce a report that every American can read as to how their money is really being spent in Washington. By the way, if one is interested in reading about the treasonous actions taken by the Federal Reserve, truthful reading material and a place to start would be to obtain a copy of the book, The Creature from Jekyll Island. There are over 50,000 law suits filed against the Federal Reserve every year. All are thrown out by the DOJ each year. Of course if we did even one of the things the Fed does, we would be arrested and prosecuted and thrown into the worst prison one could imagine. Next time you wait for money deposited into your bank account to become available to you, just know that it is being loaned to Middle Eastern interests so that the families who own the Federal Reserve can make money on your money while you wait to get access to it.

Eighth, there is a consistent and loving foreign policy. Couple with that a strong defense department. The current handling of both those departments is the worst in our history. Wrong people in the wrong jobs, weak people where strong people should be, etc. We have in effect done to our military what we won't do to our worst enemies — that is declare war on them. The military retirement, benefits, and pay have taken every cut imaginable. How disgraceful. Those who have voted for cutting the pay of these individuals should be removed from office. That is nothing less than treason, in my opinion. The world is more dangerous now than it was during the Cold War. Just supporting the Muslim Brotherhood to conquer another nation is not justifiable use of our money, our policy or our American service personnel.

Ninth, comes Healthcare, not the substitute called Obamacare. During the 111th Congress, the Congress passed and President Obama signed into law the Patient Protection and Affordable Care Act (PPACA) — commonly known as "Obamacare" (P.L. 111-148). This is absolutely the worst train wreck in our national history. It appears in many ways it was never intended to work, rather it was intended to be just another tax, a health tax. Go back to a plan and let companies and states run their own programs within a framework of competition. Services will go up and costs will go down — the exact opposite of what is happening now with this Affordable Care Act. Since the implementation of Obamacare, many states have filed Constitutional challenges based upon the mandatory purchase of insurance policies, and several courts have ruled the law unconstitutional. The Supreme Court will continue to uphold this terrible law, since it was, is and always will be viewed as a tax, with or without any medical allowances. There is a very serious plot against the American people in the bill or law, each day a new discovery seems to be in the offing about what madness it contains.

Tenth is immigration. Amnesty should not even be discussed in the current political climate. Take it off the table. If anyone wants to come into this country, they should do so legally. We must close our borders and enforce immigration laws, if we want to have a country. If you want to be just in a pot of stew, then keep the borders open. By the way, give the Border Patrol back their guns — what stupid idea to take their guns away. Either that, or take the guns away from the security patrols who surround our politicians and resident of the Oval Office. All of us immigrated here from someplace — or our families did — we have been made a wealthy people because legal immigration. Securing the border is the utmost issue here.

Eleventh — First and Second Amendment adherence. The idiocy of wanting to have gun-free zones does nothing but create traps for helpless citizens when you have a godless people running the streets – which by the way was caused when you took morality out of the classroom by removing the Bible and Prayer. What idiots. Fort Hood type shootings will continue to happen both there and many other places as long as we continue to take away guns from God-fearing people while allowing irresponsible people to run free with their guns. Gun control laws only restrict access to responsible gun ownership. High risk individuals will still be able to acquire firearms even with an increase in prevention. I do not support any proposed gun control law which would limit the right to gun ownership by those who are responsible, law-abiding citizens. Wherever Concealed Carry Weapons (CCW) permits are allowed to flourish, violent crime drops. Have you noticed Chicago lately? Amazing what happens when the threat is made to criminals that you might just have a gun underneath that shirt. More responsible gun owners = less crime. Don't question that again!! Freedom of speech is guaranteed under the Constitution. Since we are going to follow it, practice all the free speech you want. Be courteous, be gentle, be kind, but be firm. Use words wisely — they are powerful tools. And while you are at it, get some education and grow your vocabulary — it will be good for you to use some words other than 4-lettered ones all the time. Refuse to do business with people who cannot communicate. Force them to learn how to enunciate the language. Oh, by the way, learn English.

Twelfth is term limits on politicians — The gig that representatives and senators pull off was never intended to be a lifetime appointment or a career path. No more career politicians. Legislation has been submitted to limit the time any member of the House or Senate can work there to 12 years total. That is probably 6 years too many, but it is a good start in the right direction. It was originally envisioned by the Framers that men and women would go serve their fellow citizens for a short time and then return home to their business or life in the private sector. Instead, we now have monstrosities that not only stay in politics for life, but they build in defenses to their legislation so they do not even have to participate in the laws they pass downhill to us. The path forward should include a very simple rule — for example, if the legislators want to cut social security, they do so to themselves since their retirement will also be SS. No more exceptions for them or any politician on anything they put into law for the rest of us — in my example, they will be cutting their own pay too — because they will be in the omelet. Absolutely nothing should pass that they don't participate in themselves. Just imagine the sensible legislation that would start to be passed down to us when that would happen.

And finally, thirteenth, and last on this list, but certainly not last in importance — **We should be 100% pro-life.** Abortion is taking a human life. If you disagree look at the percentage of Americans who now agree with me. It's over 58 percent. There's too much medical evidence to think otherwise. I believe life begins at conception and it is the duty of our government to protect this life. You may want to argue that life starts at birth, but it is terribly obvious that is wrong. With some individuals, life has not started even at the age of 55 years. Life hasn't started yet since they are in all ways brain dead. Look at the US Senate — there is plenty of proof in that location. Seriously, Americans favor ending of the current abortion tactics which liberals and their media push often. And, no, I am not against a woman's rights. Listen very carefully. I value a woman's rights to make the right decisions about choosing what actions she takes with her body; that includes those which could cause pregnancy. It takes two biological organisms to make a pregnancy occur, both parties must take precaution. Under no circumstances should any Federal money be used to pay for abortions. In a real sense, when it comes to a woman's rights, it could be said I am pro-choice. I choose a child's life over death. That is the true pro-life stance. When someone argues that they don't want my morality being pushed onto them, I understand. But I don't want you or the government to push another morality on me to make me pay for abortions through tax dollars. No matter how you want to see it, insisting on government money to pay for abortions, is pushing an unwanted morality on me.

A Change of Heart Is Needed in America

In a 2013 interview, Senator Ted Cruz spoke about the plight America is facing — he said a spiritual revival is needed in America. Without a doubt he is correct. He went on to say, "I think we're at the edge of a precipice. If we keep going down this path we're risking losing our nation. We're risking losing the incredible oasis of liberty."[1] This sounds very familiar to Harvard President Langdon's message in May of 1775.

One of my purposes in writing about America now, is because it is obvious we have lost our way. The moral compass in the country appears to be unplugged. We have a tired, depressed, and misled leadership. We have huddled masses that are broke and hungry. The only thing that binds most of us together is that we are subjects of the current regime, rather than citizens of a wonderful country. Younger adults had a loyalty, love, and admiration for the promise of hope and change — but had no benchmark against which to measure it, or test it, or realize it as falsehood. Those of us who are older, may seem lethargic, but some of us have the keen eyes of experience, a great benchmark against which to evaluate activities, regimes, and their results. The same is true for seeing our depths of depravity and need for a true gut-wrenching revival. The mind can paint a picture that is not real. Our minds are constantly painting pictures for us that have no basis in fact — they paint pictures that cannot be real. It can fool us into believing that what we are thinking is achievable, when it is in no way possible. The mind keeps working, dreaming of great achievements, when often those achievements may not be honorable or good. A moral compass is so essential to balance the dreams that come our way, keeping us focused on realities when thinking about accomplishments, rather than impossible, or even lurid thoughts.

That is the underlying purpose in this book — to help people not only see the need for a revival, but also see the characteristics of what a revival should bring — the results that must accompany such a national awakening.

So what should be the results of such a revival? It should take us back to our roots — to truth as we have been reading about up to now — avoiding the pitfalls in further journeys like have plagued us to date — to secure blessings from God and keep our nation a special place for our children and children's children. The result: a great life that existed in this nation for so many years.

What Would a Revival Do?

A revival should produce results much like what the early spiritual awakening, or first Great Awakening produced in America. The revival spirit of the First Great Awakening was a forerunner to the American Revolution. The evangelical movement of the 1740s played an instrumental role in the development of democratic thought, as well as the belief of the free press, free ideas, and the belief that information should be shared in a completely unbiased and uncontrolled manner. These concepts ushered in the period of the American Revolution, which had as its bedrock the idea of religious freedom.[2] It was also during this time period that blacks, or African Americans, began to embrace Christianity in large numbers in Colonial America. Great preachers like the flamboyant George Whitefield, and the magnificent Jonathan Edwards were cornerstones in the revival spirit of this time, with possibly the single sermon delivered by Edwards entitled, "Sinners in the Hands of an Angry God," being the unofficial beginning of this Great Awakening.

This time facilitated the personal repentance, faith, devotion, piety, and obedience of individuals which began to pull the national conscience back to a solid platform of obedience and adherence of God and the Bible. Bottom line, it began to bring people to their senses, uniting the bulk of the nation toward a common goal. There was a new and fresh direction. People began to collectively look into their own lives, striving to produce results in their personal and professional lives to Christian service. Like then, this same change of the heart is needed now, followed by actions toward godliness and truth. This revivalist spirit when coupled with the Puritan spirit which was established going all the way back to John Calvin in his Geneva School of Preaching. It brought forth a hall of heroes in this country who felt up to the challenge of toppling kings and queens, as well as other tyrants in the world. It was key in establishing a new nation carved out of this wilderness on the eastern seaboard. The result was America was a place where God's truth would reign through a people who would be different than any other country ever founded in the world. The Colonists during this time believed they could be bold in confronting the authorities in the world — to break away when necessary in order to keep serving God freely. This is the kind of revival our nation needs again.

The same spiritual principles provided a solid work ethic and moral compass for an individual's personal life. As in Colonial days, there needs to be an emphasis on what the purpose of this country is. It is a place where the message of Christianity should ring out, where God is honored. Sanctification is needed in turning our lives around — clinging to truth. It is comforting to deal in business or just in personal arrangements with anyone where the spoken and certainly the unspoken message is, "What you see is what you get."

There needs to be, in my opinion, a return to the message of Christianity in our presence wherever we go. Our Founders knew this, our leaders of just 2-3 generations ago knew this. "In God we trust" is not to be just a motto on our money, it is to be a way of life; how we are self-governed.

We also would see a revival bringing about a consecration toward piety in our lives. We especially need leaders who have a gracious mind trained in a high form of spiritual life. We acquire inner strength from meeting God and godly people in those quiet times of self-reflection.

There should be a passion for doing what is right: no more complacency; no more instability; no more 'not knowing' the direction our nation is headed. To be the best we can be for our families, our neighbors, our communities and our nation — that all should start with the individual making commitments to God, as our Founders did, seeking the wisdom from on high in addressing daily needs.

Courtesy: CBN News/The Brody File

David Brody: *Do you believe that spiritual revival is needed in this country?*

Sen. Ted Cruz: *Without a doubt. I think we're at the edge of a precipice. If we keep going down this path we're risking losing our nation. We're risking losing the incredible oasis of liberty.*[3]

Even the finest of words and the best of intentions can sometimes lead to disaster. We are in the midst of a disaster now, which has all been set up with some very fine words that too many people believed and accepted as truth. What we need now is not words but actions — actions in the right direction to revive and restore our great nation.

"And can the liberties of a nation be thought secure when we have removed their only firm basis, a conviction in the minds of the people that these liberties are of the gift of God? That they are not to be violated but with His wrath? Indeed I tremble for my country when I reflect that God is just; that His justice cannot sleep forever."

— Thomas Jefferson

*Signer and Principal Author of the Declaration of Independence
Third President of the United States*

Chapter Thirteen

Defending Our "Shining City on a Hill"

"There can be only one end to the war we are in. It won't go away if we simply try to outwait it. Wars end in victory or defeat. One of the foremost authorities on Communism today has said that we have ten years. Not ten years to make up our minds, but ten years to win or lose... the world will all be slave or all be free." — Ronald Reagan

ON MAY 2, 2009, I WATCHED THE KENTUCKY Derby from Louisville on TV. I love the Derby for several reasons. One is that warm weather is usually here to stay in Middle America, meaning no more serious cold weather. But I also have a great interest in horses and in horse racing that goes all the way back to my early childhood. As a small boy in Los Angeles, my father would occasionally take me along as he went to Hollywood Park or Santa Anita to watch the horses run. Dad loved to bet on the ponies, and I loved to watch those powerful legs on those graceful animals trigger the speed for them to circle the track so fast, yet do it with such beauty and grace. I loved to pick up the colored tickets which most of the betters would throw on the ground following a race they had lost. It was fun to get home, bundle them up in a cigar box and look at them later; I actually took home a winner one time, which someone had thrown down too early.

When I was an older boy, then living in southern Missouri, I had a horse that I rode on a regular basis. Her name was Ribbon; she was graceful, powerful and fast; she and I formed a bond while I was in high school, which in my memory will last forever. I used to teach her tricks, imagining someday that we would ride in a rodeo together. One of the tricks was to get her to pull a handkerchief from my hip pocket as I bent over. To train her, we rehearsed with molasses on a handkerchief, placing it in my hip pocket and bending over. She did the rest. Her antics led her to start biting me softly on my derriere. This was her way of getting some personal enjoyment and attention from our time together. I could see it in her eyes when I jumped to a straight up position, yelling, "Hey, watch it!" What sweet memories of a wonderful animal.

Watching the Derby that day, I noticed a horse that reminded me a little of home. He brought back memories of Ribbon, my horse from some forty years earlier.

He had a similar gate and stride. Folks said Ribbon was plain looking, as was this horse at the Derby. But I recalled that as a boy of 16, filled with all my naiveté, she was equal to any Kentucky thoroughbred in my heart. The horse in the Derby that day was like Ribbon, plain looking but assured, full of energy. His name was "Mine That Bird." "Mine," had a good blood line, but absolutely no reputation.

A cowboy, along with some friends, had purchased him for $9,500. In Derby lore, that is peanuts, since the stables there are usually filled with horses, some of which cost millions of dollars each. More than one horse that year had been flown in from Dubai to run the race. The trainer of "Mine that Bird," Bennie Wooley, Jr. (the cowboy) had brought his horse to Louisville in an old trailer pulled by an old pick-up truck. It took him 21 hours of driving the road from New Mexico to get there. And with these two was a toothless jockey, Calvin Borel, who would take this so-called scrub into the starting gate. But what the crowds did not know was that underneath the skin of that scrub "Mine that Bird" beat the heart of a determined thoroughbred. Odds makers posted him at 50-1, the longest long shot in the history of the Derby.[1]

The announced attendance that day for the Derby was 153,563. The rich and the famous were gathered, all expecting to see one of the expensive horses from a major stable to race home with the purse and the roses. Of course the Derby is also a style show for the women who attend. The hats worn by many of the ladies are usually large, colorful and speak of plantation life. It is a money place, with most of the attendees dripping with the filthy lucre. The only little people present were the stable boys, along with this cowboy trainer, Bennie Wooley, Jr. He was way out of his league that day; his look, his demeanor, and his clothing spoke it. Making matters worse is that Bennie rode motorcycles at rodeos, and he arrived at the Derby on crutches, having broken his leg in a recent motorcycle crash in a dusty western rodeo. They just did not belong in this crowd or the Derby. Nonetheless, "Mine that Bird" a 50 to 1 runner, a crippled cowboy, and a toothless jockey were there, when it appeared they fit the scenery of some dog and pony race at a small county fair. And when the announcer yelled "And they're off," everyone knew "Mine" would come in last. He did stumble out of the gate that afternoon at Churchill Downs, looking clumsy and starting out the first quarter dead last. But the thoroughbred had another idea and it was going to be his day. He came from behind to win by some eight lengths when he crossed the wire.

Surprises and long shots have always been around. History tells us things seldom are what they appear to be.

A shepherd boy named David, the runt of his family, was sent on an errand by his father only to show up in the valley where his nation's army was. They were hiding, paralyzed in fear at the site of a mighty giant from Philistia. The scene was surreal; this small boy, mentored in solitude, having hatched only secret acts of bravery alongside his tiny flock of sheep could not believe what he was witnessing. The fear his siblings must have had, became apparent to him in their cringing, hid-

CHAPTER THIRTEEN — DEFENDING OUR "SHINING CITY ON THE HILL"

ing, and shaking behind rocks. The reason? Just across the small stream, the giant Goliath shook the ground with his basso-profundo voice challenging someone to come face him. Not only ugly, Goliath was huge, well over nine feet tall in his bare feet. We are told his armor included a bronze coat of mail, that alone weighing over two hundred pounds, a solid-iron spear (the head alone weighed twenty-five pounds), and a heavy, huge bronze helmet to cover his oversized head. Little David volunteered to go fight because everyone else was frozen in terror at the surrealistic image. His brothers pleaded with him, saying he would be pulverized. They finally acquiesced, putting heavy armor on their brother. But he could not move, so taking it all off, he insisted on going into battle as he had been mentored when he was alone with God; he went with his faith that God could deal with any giant, any threat. With only his simple leather slingshot, he picked up five small and smooth stones. Walking out into the clearing, David had only one message for the giant, "You come against me with sword and spear and javelin, but I come against you in the name of the LORD Almighty, the God of the armies of Israel, whom you have defied. This day the Lord will deliver you into my hands." While his brothers could only look from behind a makeshift barricade, with a suddenness, David whirled his slingshot around overhead and he cut the ugly giant down with his shot to the head. DAVID WON!

Three Hebrew boys had no chance when thrown into a fiery furnace by Nebuchadnezzar, and with the odds of survival at zero, they had a special guest suddenly appear with them, and they WON.

A rag-tag group of soldiers and sailors tackled the premier army and navy of the world. While the world said the colonists would be cut down to size, they had help from the miracle making Father. After the shot heard round the world and seven of hard fighting, they actually won. The war formally ended when the treaty was signed on September 3, 1783.

Our nation which began with a beleaguered disheveled outfit was taken for granted as they stood in opposition to somewhat narcissistic, twenty-two year-old King George III.

Consider John Adams — his reputation was that of being a man of pronounced moral character but also for possessing a gigantic intellect. He also had a reputation for being extremely competitive; one who would fight to the death for a cause. His intellectual vocabulary caused many to call him the "Atlas of Independence." Fellow delegates to the First Continental Congress admired his talk and commitment to high principle, such as his statements of a moral faith, "If "Thou shalt not covet," and "Thou shalt not steal," were not commandments of Heaven, they must be made inviolable precepts in every society, before it can be civilized or made free."[2]

Take Samuel Adams — second cousin to John Adams. It has been said that Peter Oliver, the Massachusetts Tory despised Adams and scathingly characterized him as having "serpentine cunning" ready with a "religious mask" to hide his true nature, revealed by a "cloven hoof."³ He also said that if an artist "wished to draw the Picture of the Devil . . . he would get Sam Adams to sit for him." Oliver wrote such scathing sketches of Adams that historian Pauline Maier called Oliver's work "forty-five pages of contempt" for Adams.⁴ To another historian, Adams possessed "Roman-like firmness," that he "would have made a figure in a conclave."⁵ Despite how he was characterized by his contemporaries, it was Sam, not cousin John, who recognized the need and took the lead in softly persuading those disinclined colonists to embrace the decision for independence.⁶

Reflect on Thomas Jefferson — he became one of the most important political figures in the revolution but he was relatively unknown in America and even in Virginia when he was elected to the Virginia House of Burgesses in September 1774. It's a bit of irony that he did not even attend the First Continental Congress and only attended the Second Continental Congress because he was elected as an alternate, to replace Peyton Randolph, the former President of the Congress, two months after it was assembled.⁷

Look at Thomas Paine — born in Thetford, England, the son of a poor Quaker corset-maker. The first time he was on American soil was disembarking a ship on November 30, 1774. He was known to many as being little more than a bum due to his clothing and demeanor. Becoming an acquaintance of Benjamin Franklin proved providential for him. On September 30, 1774, Franklin wrote a letter of introduction for him to Richard Bache describing the bearer as "an ingenious worthy young man."⁸ Paine was soon employed as a journeymen writer for the Pennsylvania Magazine. As late as January 1776, there was little in his writings to suggest what a colossal role he would assume in the American Revolution. He had little to his credit other than a newly printed pamphlet called "Common Sense." However his tract printed on parchment would be just the medicine needed for the uproar of that day as it stirred Colonists in strengthening their resolve.⁹ It was George Washington, on Christmas Eve, 1776 while bone tired, discouraged, broke, out of supplies, and even his soldiers lacking the shoes necessary to walk in the snow, turned to this contemporary but little known writer, Thomas Paine, for inspiration, whose words turned the tide of the war.

Study the man John Dickinson — He is recognized as the most famous defender of American liberty because of his spirit and intellect. Seated as a delegate in the First Continental Congress in October 1774, Dickinson was still standing on his belief for what he called the "principles of true English constitution." He still thought reconciliation with Great Britain was not only possible, but best for the Colonies, even when King George III would not alter his policies against the Colonies. Though he voted against independence and refused to sign the Declaration of Independence, he remained a steadfastly American and joined the Pennsylvania militia. He wrote against George III's policies stating, "Kings or parliaments could not give the rights essential to happiness. . . . We claim them from a higher source — from the King of kings and Lord of all the earth."¹⁰

CHAPTER THIRTEEN — DEFENDING OUR "SHINING CITY ON THE HILL"

Examine the life of Robert Tate Paine — A native of Massachusetts and expected by family tradition to become a minister, he was known as an outstanding student and school teacher while studying theology. Poor health drove career changes in his life. He worked for many years aboard ships as a merchant marine, doing hard physical lifting trying to build up his body and health in the fresh salt air. He finally studied and practiced law, admitted to the bar of Massachusetts in 1757 and he served his state proudly as associate prosecuting attorney for the state in the trial of British soldiers following the Boston Massacre. Elected to the first and second Continental Congress, "the frail" Paine served in several positions: chairman of the committee charged with procuring gunpowder for the Continental Army, signing the final appeal to King George, known as the Olive Branch Petition, in 1775. He spent much of his life correcting and objecting to people, according to comments made by Founding Father Benjamin Rush, Paine earned the title in Congress of the "Objection Maker," because of his habit of frequent objections to the proposals of others. Eventually attendees must have rolled their eyes when he spoke, for as Rush commented, "He seldom proposed anything, but opposed nearly every measure that was proposed by other people..."[11]

Research more on the life of Benjamin Franklin — Nearly every year of Franklin's life was a book of historical events of tremendous significance. By May 1775, when he joined the Pennsylvania delegation to the Second Continental Congress, he was without doubt the most famous man in America, as well as the most famous American in all of Europe. His life was one of remarkable accomplishments and opportunities. He had a natural impulse toward diplomacy, and that of negotiating, since he also had wrestled with his growing identity of being an American. He had to serve as an intermediary for many, especially John Adams and John Dickinson during the writing of Declaration of Independence building up to the Revolution. He remarked to those in Paris who learned from him the secret of statesmanship: "He who shall introduce into public affairs the principles of primitive Christianity will change the face of the world."[12] Franklin had built his life on a firm foundation as he said in his own writing, "Before I enter upon my public appearance in business, it may be well to let you know the then state of my mind with regard to my principles and morals..."[13]

Remember George Washington — Six foot three inches tall, already possessing a tremendous military record and reputation, already beginning to be the stuff of legend, he was an imposing figure when he arrived in Philadelphia for the First Continental Congress. By the Second Continental Congress he arrived in his full dress uniform as a colonel, nearly arriving late having just left the aftermath of the battles of Lexington and Concord. It was not long until this Congress decided to appoint Washington the commander in chief of the Continental Army, though it was yet unformed. Though he was opposed in this appointment by some from New England, it was a critical step in the decision for independence.

Pay tribute to Roger Sherman — This Connecticut politician is one of my favorite characters from the American Revolution. By the testimony of many of his colleagues and peers, he was "one of the most physically ungainly specimens ever put on God's earth." According to John Adams, his manner was "the reverse of grace," yet at the same time Adams declared him to be "one of the soundest and strongest pillars of the Revolution." Thomas Jefferson would echo his praise, describing Sherman as "a man who never said a foolish thing in his life." Sherman was unlike most of the members of the Continental Congress. He started his career in total poverty. He was the son of a poor shoemaker who died when Sherman was just a young man. But his down-to-earth manner, common-sense approach, and unshakable faith in God through the crisis with England made him a legend along with Jefferson, Franklin, Adams, and Robert Livingston, he was on the committee charged with drafting the Declaration of Independence. Sherman never stood taller when addressing his colleagues saying about his belief of the purpose of our country was, "I believe that there is one only living and true God, existing in three persons, the Father, the Son, and the Holy Ghost . . . that the Scriptures of the Old and New Testaments are a revelation from God . . . that God did send His own Son to become man, die in the room and stead of sinners, and thus to lay a foundation for the offer of pardon and salvation to all mankind so as all may be saved who are willing to accept the Gospel offer."[14]

Keep in mind John Peter Muhlenberg — He is little known by many but certainly one of the characters that "stick out" in the memories from colonial America for those who have heard of him. He is a favorite personality of mine from that period. He was both a member of the Virginia House of Burgesses and a pastor of a local church in 1774. He often preached on Christian responsibility and action, following in the shadow of his father, Henry Muhlenberg, one of the founders of the Lutheran Church in America.

It is documented that in 1775, after preaching a hearty sermon on Ecclesiastes 3:1 which reads, "For everything there is a season and a time for every matter under heaven," Muhlenberg closed his message that day with the following words; "In the language of the Holy Writ, there is a time for all things. There is a time to preach and a time to fight."[15]

Church members reported that when he had spoken those words, he stepped out from behind the pulpit, removed his robe, revealing a Revolutionary Army uniform, immediately announcing that he was ready to fight for the cause of freedom in America. No less than two hundred men followed him from the church and town to join General Washington who named Muhlenberg the Colonel of the Eighth Virginia Regiment. He served America and General Washington throughout the war and achieved the ultimate rank of Major General. Following the war for independence, Muhlenberg held several offices in public service, including being elected to the U. S. Senate in 1801.[16]

This motley crew, rag tag and otherwise, tremendously disadvantaged, all but

Chapter Thirteen — Defending Our "Shining City on the Hill"

counted out by reasonable odds, waged war with the greatest military armada the world had seen, and they WON.

Today Americans from all walks of life: factory workers, students, business owners, clergy, military personnel, public servants, blue-collar and white-collar workers, unemployed, and citizens all of whom love this country and that for which it has stood for nearly 250 years are all being called upon right now to defend our liberty: to awaken and join the good fight against the enemies both foreign and domestic and to defend what remains of our city on a hill, tarnished as she is. In the days, weeks, months, and years to come — they will come from nowhere in particular, many will come from places that do not appear on most maps, they won't have the appearance of thoroughbreds or statesmen, many will have names that do not speak of wealth, pedigree, or royalty. Most of all, they will have long odds against their success. And though the battle promises to be ferocious, requiring all our love, all our strength, all our resources, all our dedication, we are going to WIN. We will win because what is in our hearts is something that no enemy can take from us: faith and freedom. But lest we get lost along the way in the heat of battle against this enemy, we must remember our heritage and that for which we fight, as well as that which is the namesake of this venerated nation. Ask yourself what are we trying to restore and conserve?

First remember what the Progressives have been doing for the past century: attacking anyone who loves freedom, capitalism, or free-enterprise, claiming they are merely clinging to the status quo. They say we are narrow-minded, hidebound, opposed bitterly to progress having attached ourselves to the musty and dusty remains of inappropriate ideas that just do not fit any more. Your actions will determine if their accusations are true, "We are a post Christian nation." In the minutes ahead, you must answer their foregone conclusions: Are we really the derelict group of which they accuse us, opposed to the onslaught in our youth-obsessed and increasingly diverse nation? Are we merely stuck in a time warp that loves freedom when we should be embracing a more defensible Fascism? Have our ideas that a person is created with equal opportunity not worth laboring to protect? We have been branded as those who cling to ancient ways, like quill and parchment and the ideas of some much maligned old dead white guys, who did not even have laptops, IPhones, email, or Facebook. Your choices and subsequent actions will decide if there is truth among these riddles and ultimately, the direction this nation takes. As you make your election, vote from a platform of historical truth.

Progressives, Liberals, Communists, Marxists, Fascists, whatever name they use at the time, all work in the same channels to build a group of disciples. They perpetrate a lie and invent a victim or class of victims. In today's world that floats back and forth between racism, women's rights, poverty, environmentalism, and global warming. Victims are always created in one of those arenas. If there is no victim, the liberals have absolutely nothing to sell. The enemies of their philosophy are self-determination, self-reliance, liberty, freedom, and succeeding in America.

With racism, anyone making some disparaging remark about a person who is black or with a different skin color, gets a person branded as being racist. The problem here is that the biggest elephant in the room are some of the black persons never held accountable for their disparaging remarks. According to Leftists, it is impossible for an African American to make racist remarks, even when they use the "N" word, the "A" word, or the "W" word. This makes an obvious impression that what is going on has not got anything to do with skin color. It has to do with liberals convincing members of society that they are victims based on skin color. Pick women's rights — pick a subject, from child-rearing to equal pay. To gin up support for women voters, abortion was sold as something that would save women and their rights. They had to convince women they are victims of society, and that is how they sold abortion. When equal pay is lauded, even though the evidence presented is built on a false premise, the equal pay is not the issue. The Liberals are creating victims that must be saved by them. If they do not keep those drums beating, they lose their disciples. Liberals create the perception that if you have provided for your family, were self-reliant, were industrious, and worked hard to get ahead, you must have cheated someone to get there. The victim in this case is someone who is poor. There has to be a victim out there and that is usually the poor people. Self-reliance in this case is the enemy of the state, since the state wants to redistribute the wealth. The storyline to support this perception is worked on all the time. The bottom line is that there has to be a victim in order to sell Marxism, Communism, Leftism, and Progressivism. If the victim class would disappear, then that would bring an end to the Progressive movement.

Young Liberals today, as well as other young people know so little of the truth of our world history and the representative government failures of the past. They point accusing fingers at democracy, feeling so upright in their position of defending the so called "social justice" preached by their heroes in universities and high schools. Collectively, they have been taught a lie so long by their Marxist professors, they now believe it, thinking it the fairest, freshest and most innovative idea of how man should be governed. Their belief is a self-constructed reality. In abeyance, we must not forget the old, yet timeless message of our heritage: "we hold these truths to be self-evident, that all men are created equal, that they are endowed by their creator with certain unalienable rights, that among these are life, liberty, and the pursuit of happiness, that to secure these rights, governments are instituted among men, deriving their just powers from the consent of the governed." These words are old, being penned more than 200 years ago in a moment of true inspiration. But that length of time pales in comparison to the eons of time and thousand-year reigns of more customary theories in the organization of human affairs: the despotism, aristocracy, plutocracy, warlordism, tribalism, and empire. The animating principle of these regimes has always been the same: the unfettered exercise of power by force by those who possess it at the time.

Today we have a president wanting to build a centrally controlled government, economy, and society which is managed from their imperial capital for the advertised benefit of his ignorant subjects; this is as old as the hills. It is nothing new. The administrative state presenting its form of social justice is nothing new. It is deeply ancient. Much more ancient than the seemingly old system of ordered liberty our Founding Fathers gave voice to in Philadelphia in 1776, and the constitutional structure they negotiated in that same city in 1787. They were a republic of free men, under God, animated by the spirit of liberty, and secure in their natural rights. A self-governing people with the freedom as well as the right to retain the fruit of their labors was another trademark. They were equal before the law. Conversely what we see now, is a president striving to be a king or dictator, who has eroded the role of Congress. These events are unprecedented.

We are told it is better to give up many of our rights in order to live justly and safely among our fellow neighbors. Should we give up our rights: freedom of speech, freedom of assembly, freedom of the press? After all freedom may be the emptiest of all words if it means only absence from restraint of authority. "Freedom of speech," says Dr. Robert M. Hutchins, "is empty unless we have something to say." What good is free speech if speech is only used to lie? Possibly that is one reason why liberals do not like that rite of passage, the First, because their work and speech has been spent in telling the lies of Marx, Stalin, Castro, Chavez. I believe we have something to say of truth. That is, what a wonderful place America can be if we follow the path laid down by our Framers: to pursue private property, free-enterprise, to make of our lives what we believe we should. Not just to be a cog in some socialist wheel. We are unique; we should pursue our unique dreams.

What is really stale, musty, dusty, and a total failure is what the young liberals and Progressives push: this transformation of America that is nothing but a tired old idea of a larger bureaucracy and control from the top. The same has been a failure through the centuries. The vision of our founders, Jefferson, Franklin, and Madison, continues to smell like fresh picked roses in comparison.

The most popular and advertised diagnosis among the Progressive Left is that freedom has proven too difficult, too unfair, too expensive to follow for equality. It is interpreted as a failure of nerve, a decadence of the spirit, a weakening of the will to be free. As 19th century Russian philosopher Nikolai Berdyaev stated, "Men are slaves because freedom is difficult and slavery is easy." The tendency of the acquiescing human spirit within the masses seems to be proven in history; a spirt that will vote someone in office who promises the easy trough. It is always too late when the voter realizes the trough is never full. History is full of illustrations of people sinking into servitude because they would not face the hard fight to stay free. Someone asked a tramp one time how he decided directions to take and how he made up his mind where he wanted to go. The tramp said that was no problem. When he woke up in the morning, he said he looked to see which way the wind was blowing and he went along with it. That is in large part what made him a tramp; he went along with the wind, which was the way of least resistance. Sometimes people will lose their will to fight and struggle and work against the wind. It seems easier to some just to sell their wretched bodies for bread and soup than to face the hard struggle of the road.

That was the lure of Fascism. Hitler came to people who felt themselves hopeless against the winds of fate. He promised them food, security, the loot of empire, if they would surrender to him their souls, the right to think and venture, and all that made men human. It is the perpetual lure of the totalitarian dream. To the little man who cannot face the wind any longer, this mechanized world seems too vast, too complicated, the struggle too difficult to make. He can lessen his struggle by reducing his freedom by letting other people think for him. Just give him a bit of bread. Just give him a small place to live. We have watched it happen across the world: men and women in a mood of fatigue and frustration, attaching themselves to the strong man who promised bread and protection. They were willing to surrender their rights to throw themselves at the mercy of the mass will, and that took them straight to tyranny. What the Progressive fails to tell is that the remainder of the world has tried this thing called fascism, socialism, or Marxism, and now wished they had not. For when they embraced what they were told was so glorious, they found out it was anything but wonderful. It was nothing but a mirage.

Weird and fantastic are the stories about optical illusions, of which the mirage in one of the many manifestations. Napoleon once crossed a desert on one of his long marches; the hot sun beat down on the long line of soldiers, tired, hungry, burning with fierce thirst, when out there just ahead of them they saw a beautiful lake, green palm trees, sparkling waters — a lovely oasis in the middle of the desert. The men shouted, broke ranks and ran for the water. But as they ran, the lake ran; the faster they went, the faster the lake receded, and then suddenly it wasn't there at all. It was a cheat, an illusion, a mirage.[17]

Many people today are following political mirages: Socialism, Marxism, Communism, Leninism, Progressivism, and Fascism are among the most tempting of illusions to some today since they have been taught that these philosophies promote fairness and social justice. We must continue to teach the truth that each of these 'isms' is not only empty, but very deadly. Hitler and Nazism have maintained a constant presence in America as the evil to withstand, however, few speak of the more ruthless killers, Stalin and the Soviet Communists. They do know not what the Soviets accomplished. The status of ex-communist carries no stigma with it, but use the term ex-Nazi and see what you get! Few in America knew of the Communist death camps because Khrushchev bulldozed them away in his de-Stalinization work in the 1950s. Nazism still has the museums of their former death camps to remind the world of what happened there. Our young people are not aware that between 50 and 65 million people died under Soviet Communism. They only know of Hitler's gas chambers taking the lives of several million.[18] The point is this: the regimes of socialism and communism all promise much, but they never have the bank account to write the check to cover their promises. These regimes always

Chapter Thirteen — Defending Our "Shining City on the Hill"

cheat and never deliver the goods. While a representative republic will never be perfect, it is be better than all mirages.

Patriots must stand with any citizen who has had his rights being taken away. It is imperative. Patriotic resistance usually starts after a period of lassitude and a feeling of hopelessness in the face of overwhelming power. Citizens will spend years, even decades, muttering under their breath, and complaining to each other about the tyranny and abuse of power, yet feel helpless to stop it. Then along comes a rancher, or a business owner, or even students who say, "Enough is enough," and they take a stand. We must stand together or no one will be left to stand with us later, when it is too late.

Dietrich Bonhoeffer famously said, "First they came for the Communists, but I was not a Communist so I did not speak out. Then they came for the Socialists and the Trade Unionists, but I was neither, so I did not speak out. Then they came for the Jews, but I was not a Jew so I did not speak out. And when they came for me, there was no one left to speak out for me."[19]

Standing together, it is imperative we guard what our Forefathers gave to us. That is a step toward atonement for our past failures which allowed our nation to get into the current condition. We must rededicate ourselves to return to and "conserve" the founding heritage of this ordered liberty, which has created the most prosperous and freest society under God, that mankind has ever known. Our Framers laid a strong foundation. Later generations completed the house and gave us the keys for success to preserve and further build; to reject the enemy and his army with their cynicism. I call on you: Mothers, fathers, grandparents, sons, daughters, laborers, professionals, military members, students, and leaders to awaken and see what the enemy is doing in our midst. And then walk together and bear the brunt of our heavy but profoundly joyous national duty: protecting and propagating, what is in the declaration of Reagan, "our shining city on a hill," and in the declaration of Lincoln, "the last best hope of Earth." We must build within our election system, the vetting processes for every candidate, not just certain ones. We must end the cycle of life-time employment of politicians. We must reestablish the fixed moral codes based on solid spiritual rules we find in the Bible.

We must return to a society which gives promise that every individual will be treated not only with dignity and respect, but with demonstrations of love and edification — a Biblical principle. We must return our universities and colleges to places where curricula honor our past heritage. These are teaching the hard sciences, English and math, while booting out the progressive radicals and their dreams of teaching classes on radicalizing the neighborhood. Move the socialism and the Marxism out. Let democracy live. We need to return our primary and secondary schools to curriculums which focus on the "Four R's!" Those are Reading, 'Riting, 'Rithmatic, and Real history. We should teach this real history through many means, involve assemblies for students led by historians, business leaders, war veterans, and elderly people of the community. It is up to us to change these practices and these institutions in our nation. Who better to face the greatest evil of the 21st Century then simple people of faith? If we do not protect our country now, there may not be a tomorrow in which we can protect it. If not us, who? If not now, when? It is time to awaken and start taking back our country by changing the landscape in places like Washington, D.C.

Recall your valor of years gone by, if you must by remembering the inscription in Thomas Paine's "Common Sense," delivered by Gen. Washington to his troops on Dec. 23, 1776, as they faced their government of the day: "THESE are the times that try men's souls. The summer soldier and the sunshine patriot will, in this crisis, shrink from the service of their country; but he that stands by it now, deserves the love and thanks of man and woman. Tyranny, like hell, is not easily conquered; yet we have this consolation with us, that the harder the conflict, the more glorious the triumph. What we obtain too cheap, we esteem too lightly.... This is our situation, and who will may know it. By perseverance and fortitude we have the prospect of a glorious issue; by cowardice and submission, the sad choice of a variety of evils — a ravaged country — a depopulated city — habitations without safety, and slavery without hope. Look on this picture and weep over it! And if there yet remains one thoughtless wretch who believes it not, let him suffer it unlamented."

All of us have a lifetime of successes and a dark closet of failures which have equipped us in a unique way to help lead someone who is younger and less experienced. This would be someone who has been suckered by the secular humanism, Marxism, and the Left into believing that America is a horrible place. You are a treasure trove of experiences wrapped together in a wonderful package. You have the experiential knowledge to help some young person understand great truths about the treasure trove of life this country "has in the past afforded" someone who was willing to work hard. How do you become a completely fulfilled human being? By giving away who you are so that others can have and know the treasures that make up your life. Here is the statement made by a man I greatly respected when he was alive. He said, "You're looking at a completely fulfilled human being. If I died today having produced some of the people God has given me the privilege of shaping, it will have been worth showing up on this planet." Howard Hendricks said that. As your life grows long in the tooth, if you do not figure out how to give away what you are, what you know, and who you are, then when you die what you have comes to an end with you. When they bury you, they bury your life. But you have the opportunity to give what you are to someone who is starved to have the treasure of your knowledge.

Why do I say this? Because we are in a war! This war we are fighting, today, tomorrow and the next day; it is a war against secular humanism and Marxism. Public school teachers have been indoctrinating two generations of young men and women with the tenants of secular humanism and Karl Marx. That comes with the baggage of no set morals, no god, no absolutes. The results are obvious. We know humanism is wrong, you can see the obvious results through their students who listened and believed the doctrines of secular humanists like John Dewey, Harold O. Rugg, Margaret Sanger, Alfred Kinsey, Paul Ehrlich, Peter Singer, Hillary Clinton, Barack Obama, et al, and believed them. There is a standard of behavior that becomes a matter of conscience, and that is not secular humanism. Without conscience and without morals, society falls apart. The secular humanists are a prime example that democracy is a dangerous thing to a people who do not have the moral compasses by which to navigate life. You cannot live in a democracy unless you have the strong "governances" and the "guard rails" of morality provided by Christian beliefs, these morals protect our way of life. But those "governances" and "guard rails" have been removed from our culture, removed by the secular humanist teachers and politicians since the turn of the 20th century. Over time the results have brought devastation, absence of this moral code over just the past generation has removed even the modicum of peace which was enjoyed by our predecessors. Society is in chaos and we are in a war for our family values, our borders, our culture, our way of life!

I have shared the truth with you as I see it. I hope you have seen it too. After seeing the truth, you should want to learn more details of that which makes us who we are, the roads we have traveled, the valleys of darkness through which we have trudged, the mountains we traversed. Witness that truth which made us a special nation in the world for over two centuries. This truth is good. Truth will never hurt our cause. If you lean on it, stand on it, this truth will free you from a prison of secular humanism. This truth needs to be a part your armor. Gird yourself with it, because it is also our weapon of war. God bless you in your stand on truth as you help turn our nation from the brink of disaster. Most of all cling to the first principles that made our nation great. After having learned more truth about those principles, you will be able to find your place in writing the next chapter in the history of our great country. Together we face the challenges ahead armed with this powerful truth. May God bless and restore this great haven we call America.

"The Bible came with them. And it is not to be doubted, that to free and universal reading of the Bible, in that age, men were much indebted for right views of liberty. The Bible is a book of faith, and a book of doctrine, and a book of morals, and a book of religion, of special revelation from God; but it is also a book which teaches his own individual responsibility, his own dignity, and his equality with his fellow man."

— Daniel Webster

Excerpt - *speech at Bunker Hill Monument, regarding the Founding Fathers' regard for the Bible, June 17, 1843*

Appendix 1

Definitions (aka, Glossary of Terms)

To help you understand my use of terms in this volume, please refer to the following definitions, or primer;

Liberalism

There are two kinds of liberals in American history. Early on in American history, "classic liberals" were considered those who believed an individual could do and say what you wanted, without harm to another person. They desired a limited central government, low taxes, and a great many, or "liberal" individual freedoms. Classic liberalism was popular and predominant in America from the beginning of the nation through the 19th Century. Most of the Founding Fathers in America were classic liberals. John Locke and Adam Smith were perfect examples of classic liberals in the Colonial era of America. **Their key belief was securing the freedom of the individual by limiting the power of the government.** It is still popular today with many. The closest political party to hold their views in a platform today is the Libertarian Party.

"Modern liberals" (those described as opponents to freedom in this volume) are in direction opposition to classic liberals. They are focused very heavily on social and economic redistribution of power and wealth, usually done through heavier and heavier taxation. Modern scholars of liberalism will argue that no meaningful distinction between classical and modern liberalism exists. That is not only misleading. It is a lie! You cannot sell the idea of restricting personal freedom without promoting collectivism. (See *Collectivism* below) For example, conservatives will view taxation as a form of slavery; while liberals view it as their much preferred method of redistributing the nation's wealth. Modern liberals tend to live their lives within themselves. While they "believe" many of the same tenants of a Progressive, they differ from Progressives, who want to force liberalism on everyone else.

Socialism

Socialism is an economic concept that advocates public ownership of all resources. The production and distribution of resources with a society are then controlled by members of that society collectively or by the government that represents that society. Goods are produced and distributed based on need rather than on market forces such as profitability, price and consumers' purchasing power. In a socialist economy, workers contribute to society based on their ability and receive according to their needs, rather than being paid wages and using that money to purchase what they want. Private possessions are limited to personal-use items such as clothes, and there is no need or ability for individuals to accumulate wealth, so there is equality among the people. A Socialist believes in collectivism, and working toward eventual control of affairs by the government, which is communism.

Collectivism

The philosophy of viewing the whole rather than the individual unit. Translated for human activities and education, a student would be taught that individualism is wrong. The correct approach is viewed as seeing oneself as just a part of a mass of humanity. Politically, collectivism involves government ownership and run segments of an economy, such as manufacturing or agriculture. The theory of collectivism is prevalent is socialism, Marxism, Communism, and Progressivism. Case in point — A collectivist's Pledge of Allegiance would go something as follows: "I pledge allegiance to the Flag of the Divided States of America, and to the collective state to which we have evolved; one nation under secular humanism which has been divided into factions with level playing fields with justice for all — all those who are politically correct." This would be a more accurate pledge of our country in 2014. (While there are many cultural Americans today who love to say the true Pledge of Allegiance and wave the flag, they do not realize we have abandoned the principles our Founders gave us.)

Marxism

A Marxist Government is one which runs all business, manufacturing, and agriculture. There is no personal property. All income is equal and has an 80% tax paid to the government. This "theory" of economics and politics was taught by Karl Marx in the 19th Century, teaching elimination of private property. Government owns all property, manufacturing, and agriculture, a form of Communism. Marx taught that in following this system, all people would be equal in pay, in wealth, in outcomes.

Communism

Generally with small variations, another name for Marxism.

Progressivism

Simply stated, my use of the word, it means a "patient Communist," willing to wait long periods of time to see government intervention or collectivism, in every area of life. One of the major goals of a progressive is a one world government; such as was the goal of the U.S.S.R. leadership during the reign of the Soviet Union, and that takes time.

Historically in America, the progressive movement was a political reform movement, seen as starting generally between Reconstruction (The time after "The War between the States," aka, Civil War) and the beginning of World War I — or approximately between the 1880s and 1920. This time period is usually referred to as "The Progressive Era" for principally three reasons. 1) The concurrent growth of the industrial revolution; 2) people began lobbying for mass social changes, typically humanistic in nature, or as they called them, "progressive" in thought and design. Among the changes that occurred were renewed focus on the well-being of workers, especially factory workers, the women's suffrage movement, prohibition, and regulation on massive corporate businesses, and; 3) an "elitist" element for the era grew out of academia and major manufacturing. While both were centered in the Northeast at the time, academics put a heavy emphasis on science and reason, pushing for less reliance on religion and God, erroneously thinking a Christian faith would stand in opposition to true reason. Their reasoning? "Look at what we have been able to do on our own for the past 40 years!" Through this time period, all the seeds of secular humanism were sown. A key belief of the Progressive, the Liberal, the Socialist, and to a large degree the Fascist is in having a large, centralized government "leveling the playing field" to make outcomes equal — all by overseeing and regulating the affairs of citizens.

Fascism

Fascism is socialism in bed with bureaucratic 'crony' business, with the federal government picking winners and losers. A Fascist views society and the state through a totally different lens. The simple conventional virtues of commerce, that of producing, trading, and earning profit, working smart and hard, and moving on to the next day to repeat the process, are viewed with hatred and contempt when stacked next to the code of the warrior, which is what the fascist considers himself and what he truly respects. To the fascist, greatness comes not through these ordinary daily pursuits of the market, nor the conviction to perform the duties of your position description, or in the obedience to the duties of one's state in life, but it comes only through the struggle against other performers, who are viewed as ruthless and greedy, for which the fascist needs the watchful eye, the discipline and the help of the government "to level the playground." And therein the cry for social justice is born and raised.

Historically, Fascism is a form of government that was popular between 1919 and 1945, but became taboo after the Holocaust and the defeat of the Axis powers in 1945. Since 1945, few groups have applied the term to themselves, and the term has become a universal epithet for anything bad.

In 2005, scholar Richard Griffiths stated that the word is the most "misused, and over-used term of our times." In particular, fascism is frequently considered synonymous with white power, though many non-white and racially mixed countries have had fascist governments at one time or another, including Brazil, Mexico, Japan, and Zaire.

In contrast to Griffiths' statement and belief, today, fascism has reared its ugly head and is the predominant force within the United States Government.

<u>It is important to note that communism, socialism, progressivism, Marxism take away individual rights. Each of these systems see you no longer as a person but as part of a mass. As such, you are no longer in control of your own destiny. Rather government dictates the rules.</u>

Capitalism

Capitalism is a socio-economic system that allows private owners to profit from the goods and services they provide. One of the cornerstones of this system is the right of the individual to choose what to produce, how to produce it, and what price to sell it for. It is popular in nations that value the freedom of the individual over the stability of the society. Most modern nations use some form of capitalism, such as state, corporate, or social market.

How capitalism works

Also known as the free market system, capitalism requires unregulated supply and demand and little or no government interference in matters of trade. Each individual is free to produce what he or she wants and to sell it at whatever price the market will support. These decisions are typically made by the laws of supply and demand: if there is no demand for a particular product, the producer will not be able to make a profit, but if the demand is high, he or she can sell a lot of goods. Almost everyone benefits because producers create and produce what people want. Consumers will only pay what they think the desired product is worth. The more demand there is for a product, the more goods are produced, and, ideally, the more the price goes down because production is carried on by multiple producers. In this system, competition between businesses is good for consumers because it too drives prices down and usually the competition improves the quality of the products being sold.

Appendix 2

Hearl C. Smith, World War I

Notes

Chapter 1: Our American History Is Being Rewritten for Us

1. W.E. Woodward, *George Washington: The Image and the Man* (Boni and Liverlight, NY), 1926, p. 142.
2. George Washington, *The Writings of George Washington*, Vol. XV (Government Printing Office, Washington, D. C.), 1932, p. 55.
3. *Manuscript Prayer-Book Written by George Washington* (Philadelphia), 1891.
4. Paul Vitz, *Censorship: Evidence of Bias in Our Children's Textbooks* (Servant Books, MI), 1986, p. 3.
5. Ibid, p. 18-19.
6. See *Reporters without Borders*, Press Freedom Index 2011-2012, "Crackdowns on Protests Cause Big Changes to Index Positions,"
7. Ibid
8. My statements are based my understanding of conservative opinion as heard on the Rush Limbaugh program on June 25, 2008. Limbaugh has excerpts from his program under the title of, "The Fairness Doctrine will just be the tip of the iceberg," June 25, 2008, Rushlimbaugh.com.
9. See David French, "*Echoes of the IRS in the FCC Snooping Scandal*," National Review Online, February 20, 2014
10. Ibid
11. Ibid
12. See Investors.com editorial, "*Which Study Has The Right Conclusion On Obama Climate Rule? Environment and Economics*," May 28, 2014
13. Rush Limbaugh, *The Fairness Doctrine*
14. As heard on Rush Limbaugh, February 20, 2014
15. My research for this section comes from the writing of Robert P. Murphy including this section which contain quotes taken from, "*Why Is Unemployment So High?*" Mises Institute, March 21, 2011
16. Ibid
17. See Michael D. Tanner, Stephen Moore, and David Hartman, "*The Work Versus Welfare Trade-Off: An Analysis of the Total Level of Welfare Benefits by State*," CATO Institute, September 19, 1995
18. Ibid
19. Ibid
20. My research came from; George Reisman, "*The Toxicity of Environmentalism*," 1989
21. See George Reisman, *The Toxicity of Environmentalism*, quoting Stephen Schneider from an earlier Discover Magazine article, October 1989
22. See Bill McKibben, *The End of Nature* (Random House, NY), 2006, p. XVII
23. Ibid, p. XV
24. Ibid, p. XX
25. See George Reisman, "*Capitalism: A complete and integrated understanding of the nature and value of human life*," (Jameson Books, IL), 1998, p. 112
26. See Jeffrey Tucker, *It's a Jetson's World: Private Miracles and Public Crimes*, (LvMI Mises Institute, AL), 2011, p. 23
27. See George Reisman, "*The Nature of Environmentalism*," Mises Institute, February 21, 2008
28. Ibid
29. George Reisman, Toxicity of Environmentalism
30. Ibid
31. Ibid
32. Ibid
33. Ibid

34 Ibid
35 Ibid
36 See Alex Newman, "Global Warming Alarmists Stuck in Antarctica Sea Ice," The New American, December 30, 2013

Chapter 2: The Problem with Government Gone Wrong

1   Gordon Tullock, Arthur Seldon, and Gordon L. Brady, *Government Failure: A Primer in Public Choice* (CATO Institute, Washington, D. C.), 2002
2   See Patrick Barron, "*Man's natural rights and the limits of government*," in series on Mises, Kant, and Welfare Spending, Mises Institute, February 21, 2014, http://mises.org/daily/6670/Mises-Kant-and-Welfare-Spending
3   Gordon Tullock, CATO Institute, 2002
4   See T. Hunt Tooley, "*How the Years between the World Wars Created the Modern World*," Mises Institute, January 17, 2014, http://mises.org/daily/6640/How-the-Years-Between-the-World-Wars-Created-the-Modern-World
5   Ibid
6   Ibid
7   Ibid
8   Ibid
9   See Llewellyn H. Rockwell, Jr., "*Mussolini's idea of the state, and its American defenders*," Mises Institute, January 24, 2014, http://mises.org/daily/6645/Mussolinis-Idea-of-the-State-and-Its-American-Defenders
10 Ibid
11 Ibid
12 Ibid
13 Ibid
14 Ibid
15 Ibid
16 See the book which I believe to be a requirement for any student of liberty. This is the finest group of speeches I have seen on the subject and have been compiled by Americans for the Reagan Agenda, Alfred Balitzer, Editor, "*A Time For Choosing*," (Regnery Gateway Press, Chicago), 1983, 359 pages
17 See Ron Paul, "*Warfare, Welfare, and Wonder Woman: How Congress Spends Your Money*," Mises Institute, January, 21, 2014, http://mises.org/daily/6642/Warfare-Welfare-and-Wonder-Woman-How-Congress-Spends-Your-Money
18 Ibid
19 Ibid
20 Ibid
21 See Olajide Damilola, "*Hyperinflation: How can it be Reduced?*" (The African Executive), November 23, 2005. Olajide Damilola, PhD., is Fellow of the Institute of Public Policy Analysis and teaches Economics at Monash University Clayton Melbourne Victoria, Australia.
22 Ron Paul, Warfare
23 See Paul A. Cleveland, "*Obama and the Continuing War on the Poor*," Mises Institute, August 4, 2009
24 See Andreas Marquart, "*The State Causes the Poverty it Claims to Solve*," Mises Institute, December 7, 2013, https://mises.org/daily/6604/The-State-Causes-the-Poverty-It-Later-Claims-to-Solve
25 Ibid
26 Paul A. Cleveland, Obama and the Continuing War
27 Ibid
28 Ibid
29 Ibid
30 See Christopher Westley, "*100 Years Ago: Why Bankers Created the Fed*," Mises Institute, December 23, 2013, https://mises.org/daily/6616/
31 See Richard J. Evans, *The Third Reich in Power*, (Penguin Publishing, NY), 2006
32 Ibid, p. 392
33 Ibid, p. 411

34 See Robert Higgs, "Wartime Prosperity? A Reassessment of the U.S. Economy in the 1940s," http://www.independent.org/newsroom/article.asp?id=138).
35 William L. Anderson, "*Death by Environmentalism*," Mises Institute, July 17, 2003, find at http://mises.org/daily/1269/
36 Ibid
37 Ibid
38 Ibid
39 Ibid
40 Ibid
41 Ibid
42 Ibid
43 Ibid
44 William L. Anderson, "*Earth Day Group Think*," Mises Institute, April, 21, 2000, http://mises.org/daily/415/
45 Thomas J. DeLorenzo, "*Regulatory Sneak Attack*," Mises Institute, September 16, 1999, http://mises.org/daily/297
46 United Nations, "General Assembly proclaims 22 April 'International Mother Earth Day,'" April 22, 2009. See the UN homepage for Mother Earth Day. Also see Ben O'Neill, "*Happy Mother Earth Day, Citizen,*" Mises Institute, April 22, 2011, https://mises.org/daily/5217/Happy-Mother-Earth-Day-Citizen
47 See United Nations, Also see Ben O'Neill
48 Steven Edwards, "UN Resolution Looks to Give 'Mother Earth' Same Rights as Humans," *National Post*, April 11, 2011
49 Ibid
50 See Ben O'Neill
51 Ayn Rand, *Capitalism: The Unknown Ideal* (Signet, NY), 1967, pp. 320–28.
52 Ibid, p. 320
53 See William L. Anderson, "Earth Day Group Think"
54 Ibid
55 See Matthew R. Simmons, An Energy White Paper, "Revisiting the Limits to Growth: Could the Club of Rome Have Been Correct all Along?"; the comments are by Robert C. Townsend, within the white paper.
56 See William L. Anderson
57 Ibid
58 Ibid
59 See Thomas J. DeLorenzo, Regulatory Sneak Attack
60 Ibid
61 Ibid
62 Ibid
63 Ibid
64 Ibid
65 Ibid
66 Ibid
67 Ibid
68 Ibid
69 This excerpt is taken from the National Journal, "Obama: 'Remove Outdated, Unnecessary Regulations,'" February 7, 2011, which is the transcript of Obama's speech earlier that week to the National Chamber of Commerce in February, 2011.
70 Jeffrey A. Tucker, "Obama on Auto-Defrosting Refrigerators,", Mises Institute, February 9, 2011, https://mises.org/daily/5034/Obama-on-AutoDefrosting-Refrigerators
71 Ibid
72 Ibid
73 Jeffrey Tucker, *It's a Jetson's World*, (Ludwig von Mises Institute, Auburn, AL), 2011, p. x
74 Ben Lieberman, "*How the presidency is invading your home,*" Mises Institute, November 9, 2010, http://mises.org/daily/4781/How-the-Presidency-Is-Invading-Your-Home

75 Michael Bastach, *"Happy New Year! Feds list 141 new regulations in only three days,"* The Daily Caller, January 3, 2014
76 Thomas J. DeLorenzo, *"Regulatory Sneak Attack"*
77 See Patrick Barron, "Man's natural rights and the limits of government," Mises Institute, February 21, 2014
78 Frederic Bastiat, The Law (1848 edition reprinted by SoHo Books for Mises Institute, AL), 2007- see Introduction by Thomas J. DiLorinzo, p. vi
79 Wendy Lower, *Hitler's Furies,* (Houghton Mifflin Harcourt, NY) 2013, p 15-16

Chapter 3: Betrayal by the Free Press

1 James T. Patterson, *Grand Expectations: The United States, 1945-1974* (Oxford University Press, NY), 1996
2 Jason Howerton, *There Is an Embarrassing Problem With This ABC 'World News' Report...*(The Blaze Network), Sep. 6, 2013
3 See NBC News, http://usnews.nbcnews.com/_news/2013/08/12/19987718-rodeo-clown-who-mocked-obama...
4 Michelle Malkin, *Russell Simmons, Rape Video Clown* (Townhall.com Column), August 16, 2013
5 See NBC News, http://www.nbcnews.com/id/3131302/ns/msnbc-morning_joe/t/personal-attacks-infect..., December 13, 2003
6 See Tom Tillison, "Bush Rodeo Clown allowed in '94, Obama Clown banned forever," BizPac Review, August 13, 2013, http://www.bizpacreview.com/2013/08/13/bush-rodeo-clown-allowed-in-94-obama-clown-banned-forever-81479
7 See Fox News, "NBC launches internal probe over edited 911 call in Trayvon Martin shooting," April 2, 2012
8 Ibid
9 Bernard Goldberg, *Bias: A CBS Insider Exposes How the Media Distort the News,* (Regnery Publishing, Washington, DC), 2002, see p. 12
10 Ibid
11 Ibid
12 Ibid
13 See Barkgrowlbite blog, "NBC AND MSNBC DELIBERATELY DISTORTED AND FABRICATED THE CONTENT OF THE ZIMMERMAN 911 CALL TAPE IN THE TRAYVON MARTIN CASE," April 4, 2012
14 Audrey Russo, "If it's Muslim lies in the Holyland, it's on PA-TV," Clash Daily.Com, August 14, 2013, http://clashdaily.com/2013/08/if-its-muslim-lies-in-the-holy-land-its-on-pa-tv/
15 Doug Giles, "HEY, SHARPTON: Five Charged With Attacking 77-Year Old Man, But It's Not a Hate Crime," Clash Daily.Com, August 14, 2013, http://clashdaily.com/2013/08/hey-sharpton-five-charged-with-attacking-77-year-old-man-but-its-not-a-hate-crime/
16 Matthew Balan, "CBS's Garrett Hints George W. Bush is A Serial Vacationer Compared to Obama," August 12, 2013, http://newsbusters.org/blogs/matthew-balan/2013/08/12/cbss-garrett-hints-george-w-bush-serial-vacationer-compared-obama
17 See Washington Free Beacon article, "CNN's Piers Morgan Falsely Claims Virginia Had Highest Murder Rate in 2009," http://freebeacon.com/national-security/cnns-piers-morgan-falsely-claims-virginia-had-highest-murder-rate-in-2009/
18 Andrew Lautz, "Obamacare suffers another setback, ABC, NBC Ignore," August 14, 2013, http://newsbusters.org/blogs/andrew-lautz/2013/08/14/obamacare-suffers-another-setback-abc-and-nbc-ignore
19 Ibid, See Newsbusters, August 14, 2013
20 Paul Bremmer, "On MSNBC, USA Today's Page Preemptively Blames Republicans For ObamaCare Failure," Newsbusters.org, August 14, 2013, http://newsbusters.org/blogs/paul-bremmer/2013/08/14/msnbc-usa-todays-page-preemptively-blames-republicans-obamacare-failur
21 Geoffrey Dickens, "Update: Censored! IRS Scandal Being Buried by Big Three Networks," Media Research Center, July 30, 2013, http://www.mrc.org/profiles-bias/update-censored-irs-scandal-being-buried-big-three-networks
22 Tom Blumer, "AP's Nicole Evatt Covers For Oprah Winfrey's Dubious 'Apology'," Newsbusters.

org, August 14, 2013
23. Ken Shepherd, "NBC 'Nightly News' Portrays North Carolina Blacks in 'Fight to Vote' Against GOP," Newsbusters.org, August 14, 2013
24. Jack Coleman, "Ed Schultz Slams Religious Hypocrisy Before Lapsing Into it," Newsbusters.org, August 13, 2013
25. Kyle Drennen, "After Obama Criticism of Reality Show Culture, Kardashian-Obsessed NBC Suddenly Agrees," Newsbusters.org, August 13, 2013
26. Matt Vespa, "NYT Columnist: Pro-Life Legislation Promotes Violence Against Women," Newsbusters.org, August 13, 2013
27. Matt Hadro, "Piers Morgan Still Manages to Praise 'Very Intelligent' Anthony Weiner," Newsbusters.org, August 13, 2013
28. See WND TV, "Vicious: Blacks Pummel White Child on Bus," Worldnetdaily.com, August 5, 2013
29. See Heather McDonald, "Why Cops Stop and Frisk so Many Blacks – Blame high black crime, not police racism," CityJournal.org, February 7, 2007
30. See FBI Uniform Crime Reports, "Crime in the United States-2011,", see at http://www.fbi.gov/about-us/cjis/ucr/crime-in-the-u.s/2011/crime-in-the-u.s.-2011/offenses-known-to-law-enforcement/expanded/expanded-homicide-data
31. See "Federal Statistics of black on white violence, with links and mathematical extrapolation formulas," Examiner.com, August 1, 2009, see at http://www.examiner.com/article/federal-statistics-of-black-on-white-violence-with-links-and-mathematical-extrapolation-formulas
32. See Pat Buchanan, "The Jena 6 Scam," WorldnetDaily.com, February 15, 2008; see at http://www.wnd.com/2008/02/56451/
33. See Noel Shepherd, "Jena Six Members Present Hip Hop Award of Black Entertainment Awards," Newsbusters.org, October 19, 2007
34. See Awr Hawkins, "Media, Political Class Downplay Muslim Brotherhood Killing Christians in Egypt," Breitbart News, August 18, 2013
35. See, "Cairo, Muslim Brotherhood violence targets Church of Virgin Mary in Zaytoun," Asia News.It, November 2, 2013
36. See Tom Gara, "Union Letter: Obamacare Will 'Destroy The Very Health and Wellbeing' of Workers," Wall Street Journal, June 12, 2013
37. As heard on Rush Limbaugh Radio Program and on his website, Rushlimbaugh.com, on January 2, 2014
38. Ibid
39. Ibid
40. Ibid
41. Ibid
42. Rowe Findley, *Great American Deserts* (National Geographic Society, Washington, D.C.), 1972, p. 16; Rowe authored 5 books following his retirement. Each was written for the U.S. Postal Service commemorating the 50th anniversary of World War II. Titled World War Two Remembered, the volumes offered summaries of events of each year of the war from 1941 to 1945.

Chapter 4: Destruction by Bad Barristers and Bad Court Verdicts

1. Adam Freedman, *The Party of the First Part*, (Henry Holt Company, NY), 2007, p. 1-3
2. Ibid, p. 3
3. Ibid, p. 3
4. As reported on *The Kelly File*, Fox News Channel, 9:00 PM EST, Thursday, March 13, 2014
5. See Bob Beauprez blog, "*Lawless in the White House*," A Line of Sight, August 19, 2013. See it at http://alineofsight.com/blogs/lawless-in-the-white-house
6. See Charles Krauthammer, "*Can Obama write his own laws?*" Washington Post, August 15, 2013; Also see Charles Krauthammer, "*Krauthammer: New Obamacare delay is 'stuff you do in a banana republic,'*" Fox News, February 14, 2014
7. See George Will, "*Court orders administration to follow nuclear waste law*," Washington Post, August 21, 1013
8. See Matt Daly, "*Appeals Court: Obama violating law on nuke site*," Associated Press, August 13, 2013

9   Deroy Murdock column, *"Deroy Murdock: The Obama administration has become the Obama regime,"* New Hampshire Union Leader, August 25, 2013
10 Excerpts taken from Harold Thomas Post, "President Obama: Constitution is "charter of negative liberties,"" The Ohio Republic, December 19, 2009. See at http://ohiorepublic.blogspot.com/2009/12/president-obama-constitution-is-charter.html
11 See Roger N. Baldwin, *A New Slavery: Forced Labor; the Communist Betrayal of Human Rights,* (Oceana Publications, NY), 1953, pp. 18-21
12 See Robert C. Cottrell, "Robert Baldwin: Founder, American Civil Liberties Union, 1884-1981," (Notable American Unitarians publisher)

Chapter 5: The Great Pretender

1   See *"Ukraine, Crimea, Russia, Putin, Europe,"* The Guardian.com, March 2, 2014
2   See Michael Curtis, *"Putin vs. Obama: No Contest, No Kidding,"* The Commentator.com, March 4, 2014
3   See The Commentator.com, "The West is led by the weaklings the Left wanted, March 2, 2014
4   Excerpt from The Charlie Rose Show on *PBS*, October 31, 2008, see http://www.freerepublic.com/focus/f-news/2121217/postsj8um
5   Edward Klein, *The Amateur, Barack Obama in the White House* (Regnery Publishing, Washington, D.C.), 2012, p. 62-63
6   Ibid, p. 63
7   Ibid, p. 63-64
8   See Aaron Klein, "Sources: Slain U.S. Ambassador Recruited Jihadists," WorldNet Daily, September 24, 2012
9   Aaron Klein and Brenda J. Elliott, Impeachable Offenses: The Case for Removing Barack Obama from Office (WND Books, Washington, DC), 2013
10 See article, "The Criminal N.S.A.," New York Times, June 27, 2013
11 See Patrick J. Buchanan, Churchill, Hitler and the Unnecessary War (Random House, NY), 2008
12 Ibid
13 See Obama speech, "Text of Obama's Speech," Rocky Mountain News, July 2, 2008
14 See Carlos Caballero Jurado, Ramiro Bujeiro, *The German Freikorps 1918-23* (Osprey Publishing), 2001
15 See Ian Kershaw, *Hitler: A Biography* (W. W. Norton & Company, NY), 2008
16 See John Toland, *Adolf Hitler* (Doubleday & Company, Garden City, NY), 1976
17 See Ian Kershaw, Hitler: 1889-1936 Hubris (W.W. Norton & Co., NY), pps. 456–458 & 731-732
18 See Eberhard Jäckel, *Hitler in History* (Brandeis University Press, Hanover N H), 1984
19 See Eberhard Kolb, *The Weimar Republic* (Routledge, NY), 1988
20 See Peter Longerich, *Holocaust: The Nazi Persecution and Murder of the Jews* (Oxford University Press, NY), 2010
21 See David Dutton, *Neville Chamberlain* (Oxford University Press, NY and by Arnold, London), 2001
22 Patrick J. Buchanan, Churchill
23 Ibid
24 See Drew Zahn article, "Hero General: Obama Following Castro's Plan," World Net Daily, July 2, 2012
25 See Chelsea Schilling, "Obamacare prescription: 'Emergency health army,' Ohio Free Press, March 26, 2010
26 Ibid, Wording of Section 203 of Public Health Service Act before Obamacare amendment
27 Chelsea Schillling
28 Ibid
29 Ibid
30 See Ian Kershaw, *The "Hitler Myth": Image and Reality in the Third Reich* (Oxford University Press, NY), 2001
31 Tacitus, *Annals,* IV.8
32 See Roger Aronoff, "Obama, The Amateur – Interview with Aaron Klein, Accuracy in the Media.com, June 21, 2012
33 Judge Andrew J. Napolitano

34 Paul Bedard, "Be prepared: Wall Street advisor recommends guns, ammo for protection in collapse," Washington Examiner, December 26, 2013
35 Jerome R. Corsi, *America For Sale*
36 Marc Sheppard, "UN Climate Reports: They Lie," American Thinker, December 2, 2009, see at http://www.americanthinker.com/2009/10/un_climate_reports_they_lie.html ; Also See John L. Daly, "The Hockey Stick" A New Low in Climate Science," see at http://www.john-daly.com/hockey/hockey.htm
37 Erica R. Hendry "What We Know From the Icelandic Volcano", *Smithsonian (magazine)*, 22 April 2010
38 Kondrake, Morton, "Pakistan Must be Obama's Leading Foreign Priority," Roll Call, March 13, 2009; Holland, Steve, "Obama Fashions a Government of Many Czars," Reuters, May 29, 2009
39 Office of the Press Secretary, "President Obama Selects Health Policy Expert to Head Office of National AIDS Policy," 'WhiteHouse.Gov,' February 26, 2009; "'The Activists' Wish List, The New AIDS Czar, Jeffrey Crowley," *Advocate*, May 1, 2009.
40 Reported by Gorman, Anna, "Obama Appoints California Physician as AIDS czar," L.A. Times, March 14, 2012
41 Evans and Novak, "U.S. Names Asian Carp Czar," Chicago Tribune, September 8, 2010
42 Thomas, Ken, A.P., "Rattner to advise Treasury on Auto Industry," salon.com, February 23, 2009; King, Neil, Jr., "Auto czar quits post six months into the job," *Wall Street Journal*, July 4, 2009
43 Allen, Mike. "Obama parks 'car czar' plan" Politico, Feb 16, 2009. Brown, Carrie Budoff. "Car czar decision has critics revved up", Politico, Feb 17, 2009
44 Andres, Gary and Griffin, Patrick "Using czars in W.H. to focus on policy", Politico, Apr 27, 2009. Press office. "Herbert M. Allison, Jr. Confirmed as Assistant Secretary for Financial Stability", *U.S. Department of Treasury*, Jun 19, 2009. Thomas LOC Presidential Nominations. PN390-111, confirmed Jun 19, 2009
45 "Secretary Napolitano Appoints Alan Bersin", *U.S. Department of Homeland Security*, Apr 15, 2009; Dibble, Sandra. "Bersin to focus on violence in 2nd tour as border czar", Union-Tribune, Apr 16, 2009; Not a new position, no Senate confirm required. *2008 Plum Book*, p. 79, GPOAccess.gov
46 Franke-Ruta, Garance."Stern Appointed Climate Change Envoy", Washington Post, Jan 26, 2009; Allen, Mike."Secretary Clinton names climate czar", Politico, Jan 26, 2009.
47 American Presidency Project President-Elect Barack Obama Announces Key Members of Energy and Environment Team, December 15, 2008; Dinan, Stephen. Obama climate czar has socialist ties, *Washington Times*, Jan 12, 2009; Romero, Frances. "Energy Czar: Carol Browner", Time, Apr 8, 2009
48 Albanesius, Chloe President Bush Approves 'Copyright Czar' Bill, October 13, 2008; Kravets, David. Obama Appoints Scholar as New Copyright Czar, PC Magazine, September 25, 2009.
49 Jaffee, Matthew "Obama's New Special Master: Don't Call Him 'Pay Czar'", Jun 11, 2009; Press release, "Interim Final Rule on TARP Standards for Compensation", *Treasury.gov* "Gulf claims czar briefing the Hill", July 22, 2010. Politico
50 Cha, Ariana Eunjung, "Elizabeth Warren appointed White House Consumer Czar," Washington Post, September 17, 2010; Lazarus, David, "Consumer Czar needs to get tough with banks," *Los Angeles Times*, October 1, 2010.
51 "Remarks by the President on securing our cyber infrastructure," WhiteHouse.Gov, May 29, 2009; Obama near choosing cyber security chief, Reuters, September 9, 2009.
52 See RTT Staff Writer Column, "Howard Schmidt named White House Cybersecurity Coordinator," RTT News, December 22, 2012; See also Eric Chabrow, "Obama Cybersecurity Coordinator Resigns," GovInfoSecurity.com, May 17, 2012
53 See article, "David Hayes Is Confirmed as Deputy Interior Secretary," <u>Washington Post</u>, May 21, 2009; See also "List of Obama Administration 'Czars,'" Fox News, January 7, 2011
54 "Vice President Biden Announces", *WhiteHouse.gov*, Jun 26, 2009, Works out of the Office of the Vice President; Erbe, Bonnie, "Obama's Endless Czar List Now Includes a Domestic Violence Aide", *U.S. News blogs*, Jun 29, 2009
55 Dave Cook, "New drug czar gets lower rank, promise of higher visibility", *The Christian Science Monitor*, Mar 11, 2009; *Thomas LOC* Presidential Nominations. PN185-111.
56 See article, "Economic Recovery Advisory Board To Be Led By Paul Volcker (SLIDESHOW)," Huffington Post, November 26, 2008

NOTES

57 "Norm Eisen Gets Ambassador Gig Leaving White House 'Ethics Czar' Post Vacant", *The Huffington Post*, June 29, 2010 "Timothy P. Carney: Obama closes curtain on transparency", *The Examiner*, August 12, 2010

58 "Timothy P. Carney: Obama closes curtain on transparency", *The Examiner*, August 12, 2010.

59 Boorstein, Michelle; Shear, Michael D. "DuBois, 26, to Head Faith Office", *Washington Post*, Jan 29, 2009. Goldstein, Laurie. "Leaders Say Obama Has Tapped Pastor for Outreach Office", *The New York Times*, Jan 28, 2009.Mason, Julie. "Obama focuses more on issue czars, less on Cabinet", *San Francisco Examiner*, Apr 21, 2009

60 Weiner, Rachel. "Melissa Rogers promises continuity in faith-based office", *Washington Post*, Mar 22, 2013

61 Flesher, John, A.P. "EPA appoints Great Lakes clean up czar," Jun 4, 2009.

62 Jack Moore, "Obama to Name Zients acting OMB director," Federal News Radio, January 17, 2012

63 Jesse Lee (2009-03-10). "Van Jones to CEQ | The White House". Whitehouse.gov.

64 Rosenberg, Carol, "Fried named as Guantanamo Closure Czar", *The State*, May 13, 2009

65 Office of Press Secretary. *Executive Order, Establishment of the White House Office of Health Reform, WhiteHouse.gov*, Apr 8, 2009; Brown, Carrie Budoff, Obama taps DeParle as health czar, *Politico*, Mar 2, 2009

66 "Obama's Electronic Health Records Czar: HIV Status and Abortions Need Not be Included ", "*CNS News*, July 21, 2010

67 Thomas LOC. E Government Act, 2002, President Obama Names Vivek Kundra,*WhiteHouse.gov*, Mar 9, 2009; Carpenter, Amanda. "Hot Button", *Washington Times*, Jun 15, 2009.

68 Eisler, Peter. "Obama's choice of Blair as intelligence czar covers bases", *USA Today*, Jan 8, 2009; Thomas LOC Presidential Nominations. PN65-01-111, confirmed, Jan 28, 2009

69 Holland, Steve. "*Obama fashions a government of many czars*", Reuters, May 29, 2009.

70 Allen, Mike. "Obama parks 'car czar' plan" *Politico*, Feb 16, 2009; Brown, Carrie Budoff. "Car czar decision has critics revved up", Politico, Feb 17, 2009

71 Bureaus reporting directly to the Secretary. "Special Envoy for Middle East Peace", *State.gov*.; Fletcher, Michael A. and Dennis, Brady.Obama's Many Policy 'Czars' Draw Ire From Conservatives, *Washington Post*, Sep 16, 2009.

72 *Thomas LOC* Presidential Nominations. PN323-111, confirmed Sep 9, 2009; Weisman, Jonathan and Bravin Jess. Obama's Regulatory Czar Likely to Set a New Tone, *Wall Street Journal*, Jan 8, 2009.

73 Brian Fung, "John Holdren, Director, Office of Science and Technology Policy," National Journal, July 17, 2013; Also see Michelle Goldberg, "Holdren's Controversial Population Control Past," The American Prospect, July 21, 2009. In this article, Michelle Goldberg reports on Holdren's view of abortion playing a role in population control. She reports, "White House science czar John Holdren co-authored a textbook in the 1970s that discussed coercive population control. Should this disqualify him as a serious voice on science? At the heart of it is a textbook book that Holdren co-wrote in 1977 with the famous neo-Malthusians Paul and Anne Ehrlich. Quotations from the book about coercive population control have been floating around the Internet for a while, but it's only in the last week or so that they've really broken through. They are indeed shocking, treading a fine line between describing and condoning outrageous proposals to curtail reproductive autonomy. They're a reminder of an ignominious chapter in American intellectual history.... Passages from the textbook, *Ecoscience*. Reading them, it's hard not to conclude that the authors looked kindly on government-mandated limits on fertility. "In today's world, however, the number of children in a family is a matter of profound public concern," they wrote. "For example, no one may lawfully have more than one spouse at a time. Why should the law not be able to prevent people from having more than two children? The authors consider the possibility of adding a sterilant to "drinking water or staple foods." Ultimately, they decide that the risk of side effects "would, in our opinion, militate against the use of any such agent," though there's something disturbing about the equanimity with which they consider it. They also toy with draconian proposals for encouraging "responsible parenthood," including mandating that all "illegitimate" births be put up for adoption and requiring pregnant single women to marry or have abortions."

74 Dschabner, "Obama to Name 'Gumshoe' to Keep Stimulus Honest," ABC News, February 22, 2009

75 See article, "J. Scott Gration: Special Envoy to Sudan," Huffington Post, March 17, 2009

76. Doug Beizer, "Senate Confirms Aneesh Chopra," Washington Technology, May 22, 2009
77. Michael James, "Counterterrorism Czar Brennan Draws Fire for Comments on Gitmo Recidivism," ABC News, February 14, 2010 See also Drew Zahn, "Shock Claim: Obama Picks Muslim for CIA Chief," World Net Daily, February 2, 2010
78. Office of the Press Secretary, "President Barack Obama Announces Key White House Posts," WhiteHouse.Gov, February 19, 2009
79. See Doug Gavel, "Ashton Carter Nominated as Pentagon's Under Secretary of Defense for Acquisition, Technology and Logistics," Harvard Kennedy School, see at http://www.hks.harvard.edu/news-events/news/press-releases/carter-appointment
80. See, "Gary Samore: Special Assistant to the President and White House Coordinator for Arms Control and Weapons of Mass Destruction, Proliferation, and Terrorism (since January 2009)," Washington Post; see at http://www.washingtonpost.com/politics/gary-samore/gIQAf5ZCAP_topic.html
81. See article, "Muslims Appointed to Homeland Security," FactCheck.org, November 10, 2010
82. Brandon Jones, "Homeland security promotes Mohamed Elibiary despite Muslim Brotherhood alleged ties," The Global Dispatch News, September 19, 2013
83. John Rossomando, "Muslim Brotherhood Infiltrates the Obama Administration," Liberty News Online, April 22, 2013, In this article John reports an Egyptian news source, "An Egyptian magazine claims that six American Islamist activists who work with the Obama administration are Muslim Brotherhood operatives who enjoy strong influence over U.S. policy....The Dec. 22 story published in Egypt's Rose El-Youssef magazine (read an IPT translation here) suggests the six turned the White House "from a position hostile to Islamic groups and organizations in the world to the largest and most important supporter of the Muslim Brotherhood. The six named people include: Arif Alikhan, assistant secretary of Homeland Security for policy development; Mohammed Elibiary, a member of the Homeland Security Advisory Council; Rashad Hussain, the U.S. special envoy to the Organization of the Islamic Conference; Salam al-Marayati, co-founder of the Muslim Public Affairs Council (MPAC); Imam Mohamed Magid, president of the Islamic Society of North America (ISNA); and Eboo Patel, a member of President Obama's Advisory Council on Faith-Based Neighborhood Partnerships....Alikhan is a founder of the World Islamic Organization, which the magazine identifies as a Brotherhood "subsidiary." It suggests that Alikhan was responsible for the "file of Islamic states" in the White House and that he provides the direct link between the Obama administration and the Arab Spring revolutions of 2011.... Elibiary, who has endorsed the ideas of radical Muslim Brotherhood luminary Sayyid Qutb, may have leaked secret materials contained in Department of Homeland Security databases, according to the magazine. He, however, denies having any connection with the Brotherhood. Elibiary also played a role in defining the Obama administration's counterterrorism strategy, and the magazine asserts that Elibiary wrote the speech Obama gave when he told former Egyptian President Hosni Mubarak to leave power but offers no source or evidence for the claim. According to Rose El-Youssef, Rashad Hussain maintained close ties with people and groups that it says comprise the Muslim Brotherhood network in America. This includes his participation in the June 2002 annual conference of the American Muslim Council, formerly headed by convicted terrorist financier Abdurahman Alamoudi. He also participated in the organizing committee of the Critical Islamic Reflection along with important figures of the American Muslim Brotherhood such as Jamal Barzinji, Hisham al-Talib and Yaqub Mirza ....Regarding al-Marayati, who has been among the most influential Muslim American leaders in recent years, the magazine draws connections between MPAC in the international Muslim Brotherhood infrastructure.... Magid heads ISNA, which was founded by Brotherhood members, was appointed by Obama in 2011 as an adviser to the DHS. The magazine says that has also given speeches and conferences on American Middle East policy at the State Department and offered advice to the FBI...Rose El-Youssef says Patel maintains a close relationship with Hani Ramadan, the grandson of Brotherhood founder Hasan al-Banna, and is a member of the Muslim Students Association, which it identifies as "a large Brotherhood organization." – Read the article at: http://www.libertynewsonline.com/article_301_33161.php#sthash.CZ4d9dk9.dpuf
84. See Gerald Todd, "The Impeachable Offense (The Muslim Brotherhood in the White House)," Western Center for Journalism, May 28, 2013

Notes

85 See post, "Eboo Patel," The Pluralism Project at Harvard University, at http://www.pluralism.org/pages/events/archives/2003/10/interfaculty/participants/patel
86 See Pradeep Ramamurthy, "Introducing Rashad Hussain," The White House Blog, March 7, 2010
87 This comes in great part from the broadcast of the Rush Limbaugh program, December 9, 2013

Chapter 6: Truth about Discrimination, Prejudice, the New and Old Racists, Slavery and Reparation

1 This excerpt taken from Martin Luther King, Jr. Speech, "I have a Dream," August 28, 1963, See link to the complete speech at http://avalon.law.yale.edu/20th_century/mlk01.asp
2 Ibid
3 See TV acres .com tobac_murielcigar.htm for the story. Also this was partially taken from my personal interview with His Honor, Mayor Paul Lambi, 4-term mayor of Wentzville, MO., January, 2014
4 See history of the Muriel cigar commercial with Edie Adams, at TV acres .com tobac_murielcigar.htm
5 Comments made by Rush Limbaugh as recorded in his transcript from his show; See Rushlimbaugh.com
6 See R.Halliburton, Jr., "Free black owners of slaves," p. 129 of his treatise; Also see John Hope Franklin, "The New Negro History," Journal of Negro History XLIII (April 1957), p. 93.
7 Booker T. Washington Biography Quote; See Halliburton
8 See The Root
9 Look up footnote for first slave owner. 2 sites one is The Root
10 See Conall Ó Fátharta report, "100,000 Irish children sold for slavery in the 1650s," The Irish Examiner, January 29, 2013; Also see John Martin, "The Irish Slave Trade – The Forgotten "White" Slaves," Global Research.Org, April 14, 2008 [Reprinted January 27, 2013]
11 See Abbott Emerson Smith, *Colonists in Bondage: White Servitude and Convict Labor in Amreica, 1607-1776*, (Genealogical Publishing Co., NY) 1947
12 See Warren B. Smith, *White Servitude in Colonial South Carolina*, (University of South Carolina Press, SC), 1961
13 See Foster Rhea Dulles, Labor in America: A History, (Wiley-Blackwell, NJ), 2010 [8th Edition]
14 Joel A. Rogers, 100 Amazing Facts about the Negro with complete proof, 1934
15 See R. Halliburton, Jr..
16 Ibid
17 Ibid
18 Edward Magdol, *Owen Lovejoy, Abolitionist in Congress* (Rutgers University Press, NJ), 1967, p. 273; See also *Abraham Lincoln and Friends* at, http://www.mrlincolnandfriends.org/inside.asp?pageID=101&subjectID=10
19 P. J. Staudenraus, editor, *Mr. Lincoln's Washington: The Civil War Dispatches of Noah Brooks* (March 9, 1864), p. 308.
20 See R.Halliburton, Jr., "Free black owners of slaves," p. 129 of his treatise; Also see John Hope Franklin, "The New Negro History," Journal of Negro History XLIII (April 1957), p. 93.
21 Carl Sandburg, *Abraham Lincoln: The War Years, Volume II*, (Letter from Owen Lovejoy to William Lloyd Garrison, February 22, 1864), p. 600.
22 Francis B. Carpenter, *The Inner Life of Abraham Lincoln: Six Months at the White House*, p. 18.
23 Ibid
24 Justin G. Turner and Linda Levitt Turner, editors, *Mary Todd Lincoln: Her Life and Letters*, (Letter from Mary Todd Lincoln to Charles Sumner, April 5, 1864), p. 174.
25 Roy P. Basler, editor, *The Collected Works of Abraham Lincoln*, Volume VII, p. 366.
26 Nathan William MacChesney, editor, Shelby M. Cullom, *Abraham Lincoln: The Tribute of a Century, 1808-1909*, "Lincoln and His Relations with Congress", p. 504.
27 See news report, "*Elijah Parish Lovejoy: A Martyr on the Altar of American Liberty-1802-1837*,The Alton Observer, " November 7, 1837
28 Ibid
29 See Walter Williams, "*The Legacy of Slavery Hustle*," Capitalism Magazine, July 16, 2001

30 Ibid
31 Ibid

Chapter 7: The History of Unions Is Their Problem

1   Henry George, "The Condition of Labor: An Open Letter to Pope Leo XIII," *The Land Question* (Robert Schalkenbach Foundation, NY), 1982 [1891], p. 77.
2   "Strikes in the United States," *The Columbia Electronic Encyclopedia*, 6th ed. Columbia University Press.
3   United States Bureau of the Census, *Historical Statistics of the United States, Colonial Times to 1970*, Part 1, p. 163.
4   This is a quote by Howard Dickman, *Industrial Democracy in America*, (Open Court, LaSalle, IL), 1987, p. 362.
5   Ludwig von Mises, *Human Action* (New Haven: Yale), 1949, p. 772.
6   Morgan Reynolds, *Power and Privilege: Unions in America*, (Universe Publishing, NY), 1984, p. 101.
7   Murray Rothbard, *A History of Money and Banking in the United States*, (Mises Institute, Auburn, AL), 2002, p. 179.
8   William E. Leuchtenburg, "The New Deal and the Analogue of War," in John Braeman, Robert H. Bremmer, and Everett Walters, eds., *Change and Continuity in Twentieth Century in America*, (Ohio State University Press, Columbus, OH), 1964, p. 87.
9   Murray Rothbard, *America's Great Depression*, (Mises Institute, Auburn, AL), 2000, p. 267. [Punctuation is Rothbard's.]
10 See Robert W. Merry, "This Year's Hot Labor Issue," *The Wall Street Journal*, May 24, 1979, p. 20.
11 Friedrich A. von Hayek, *The Constitution of Liberty*, (University of Chicago Press, IL), 1960, p. 260.
12 Richard A. Epstein, "A Common Law for Labor Relations: A Critique of the New Deal Labor Legislation," *Yale Law Journal* 92 (July 1983): p. 1386.
13 "History of Federal Minimum Wage Rates Under the Fair Labor Standards Act, 1938–2007," United States Department of Labor Employment Standards Administration.
14 Jacob Mincer, "On-the-Job Training: Costs, Returns, and Some Implications," *Journal of Political Economy*, 70 (Part 2, Supplement, October 1962), pp. 50-73; Also see Mincer, "Human capital and the labor market: A review of recent research," *Educational Researcher* 18 (4): 27-34.
15 Milton Friedman, *An Economist's Protest*, Sun Lakes AZ: Horton and Daughters, 1972; for more on the consequences of the minimum wage law cf. Morgan Reynolds, *Economics of Labor*, (Cincinnati OH: Southwestern, 1995), pp. 86-95.
16 This is covered under the 13th amendment to the United States Constitution states, "Neither slavery nor involuntary servitude, except as a punishment for crime whereof the party shall have been duly convicted, shall exist within the United States, or any place subject to their jurisdiction," yet organized labor had no problem with a military draft; instead it hysterically declared the Taft-Hartley Act a "slave-labor bill."
17 For more on the "Taft-Hartley Act," see "National Affairs: Barrel No. 2". *Time* Magazine, June 23, 1947; Also see George R. Fleischli, "DUTY TO BARGAIN UNDER EXECUTIVE ORDER 10988", *Air Force Law Review*, (May-June, 1968)
18 See AR Lee, *Eisenhower and Landrum-Griffin: A Study in Labor-Management Politics* (University Press of Kentucky), 1990 for further study on "Labor Management Reporting and Disclosure Act,"
19 See David Frum, *How We Got Here: The '70s* (Basic Books, NY), 2000, pp. 140–141
20 "H.R. 1409," Government Printing Office
21 S.G. Bronars and D.R. Deere, "Union representation elections and firm profitability," *Industrial Relations*, 29 (Winter Issue): p. 15-37.
22 Ludwig von Mises, *Human Action* (New Haven: Yale, 1949), pp. 764-5.
23 See "A Curriculum of United States Labor History for Teachers," Illinois Labor History Society.

Chapter 8: The Trouble with the Church

1   Ecclesiastes 3:11
2   J. Wallace Hamilton, *Horns and Halos in Human Nature* (Fleming H. Revell Co, NJ), 1954, p. 34
3   Stephen Ertelt, "55,772,015 Abortions in America Since Roe v. Wade in 1973," Life News.com, Jan 18, 2013

4   This and other of the quotes of Ralph Sockman are found in books I used in research, such as: Ralph W. Sockman, How To Believe: The Questions That Challenge Man's Faith Answered In The Light Of The Apostles' Creed (Epworth Press, NY), 1953
5   The New International Translation of the Bible.
6   My research is based on Dietrich Bonhoeffer, *The Cost of Discipleship* (Simon & Schuster, NY), 1995, p. 46
7   See, the Center for the Study of American Culture and Faith, at *culturefaith.com*
8   "Survey Says: Conservative Pastors Don't Always Preach What They Practice," *culturefaith.com*, June 10, 2013.
9   Ibid
10 Ibid
11 Ibid

Chapter 9: Where Do We Start?

1   Keith Feiling, *The Life of Neville Chamberlain* (London: Macmillan), 1946, p. 320; Correlli Barnett, *The Collapse of British Power* (William Morrow, NY), 1972, p.458
2   Nicholas Bethell, *The War Hitler Won; The Fall of Poland, September 1939* (Holt, Rinhart and Winston, NY), 1973, p. 97
3   Martin Gilbert, *Churchill, A Life* (Henry Holt, NY), 1991, p. 410
4   Henry A. Kissinger, *Diplomacy* (Simon & Schuster, NY), 1994, p. 252
5   Patrick J. Buchanan, *Churchill, Hitler and the Unnecessary War* (Crown Publishers, NY), p. 320
6   Edward Klein, *The Amateur, Barack Obama in the White House* (Regnery Publishing, Washington, D.C.), 2012, p. 3-4
7   Andrew P. Napolitano, *The Constitution in Exile* (Nelson Current, NY), 2006, p. 239

Chapter 10: Listen to the Past Speak to the Future

1   See Gettysburg Address by President Abraham Lincoln
2   J. Wallace Hamilton, Horns and Halos in Human Nature (Fleming H. Revell Co., NJ), 1964, p. 52-53
3   John Adams to Thomas Jefferson, June 28, 1813 in Lester J. Cappon, ed., *The Adams-Jefferson Letters*, 2 Vols. (North Carolina Press, Chapel Hill, NC), 1959, 2:339-340; Also see Gary DeMar, *America's Christian History: The Untold Story* (American Vision, GA), 1993, p. 135
4   John Adams to Thomas Jefferson, April 19, 1817 in Thomas Jefferson, *The Writings of Thomas Jefferson* (The Thomas Jefferson Memorial Association, Washington, D.C.), 15:105; Also see Gary DeMar, *America's Christian History*, P. 135

Chapter 11: Servant-Driven Leaders

1   My description of the Dulles brothers was taken partially from my research from the following: Stephen Kinzer, The Brothers: John Foster Dulles, Allen Dulles, and Their Secret World War"
2   Ibid
3   Ibid, Also we should note that John Foster Dulles was a strong personality in American history. Many people have forgotten that even Carol Burnett sang a song about Dulles on the Ed Sullivan Show on August 11, 1957
4   See J. Wallace Hamilton, Horns and Haloes in Human Nature, (Revell), 1954
5   "John Wooden's Pyramid Still Standing," Kristin Edelhauser, *Entrepreneur*, March 26, 2007; http://www.entrepreneur.com/article/176282 ; See also John Wooden, *They Call Me Coach*, (McGraw Hill, NY), 2004
6   Ibid

Chapter 12: Reforming and Starting Over

1   See David Brody, "Brody File Exclusive: Ted Cruz says America Needs a Spiritual Revival," CBN News, July 23, 2013
2   These thoughts came from mainly my research in Bernard Bailyn, The Ideological Origins of the

American Revolution (Harvard, MA.), 1967
3   David Brody

Chapter 13: Defending Our Shining City on a Hill

1   Malcolm Eudaley, *Come Walk the World*
2   Charles Francis Adams, Editor, *The Works of John Adams, Second President of the United States* Vol. 6 (Little, Brown, and Co., Boston, MA.), 1851, p. 9
3   Peter Oliver, *Origins and Progress of the American Revolution*, Editors Douglas Adair and John A Schutz (San Marion, CA), 1961, p. 41
4   Pauline Maier, *Old Revolutionaries: Political Lives in the Time of Samuel Adams* (Alfred A. Knopf, NY), 1980, p. 11
5   Mercy Otis Warren, History of the Rise, Progress, and Termination of the American Revolution (Boston, MA), 1805, p. 211
6   James M. O'Toole, "The Historical Interpretations of Samuel Adams." *New England Quarterly* 49 (March 1976): p. 82–96
7   See *The Thomas Jefferson Papers, The American Revolution: 1774-1783*, Library of Congress; http://memory.loc.gov/ammem/collections/jefferson_papers/mtjtime2a.html
8   See A. H. Smyth, Editor, Writings of Franklin (NY), 1893, Vol. I p. 36
9   See A. Owen Aldridge, "Tom Paine's American Ideology." 1984; See also A.J. Ayer, "Thomas Paine." 1989; David F. Hawke, "Paine." 1974
10 John Dickinson, *The Political Writings of John Dickinson* (Bonsal and Niles, Wilmington, DE), 1801, Vol. I, p. 111
11 See Robert Treat Paine, *The Papers of Robert Treat Paine*, Editors, Stephen Riley and Edward Hanson (Massachusetts Historical Society, Boston), 1992, Vol. I, p. 48, March/April, 1749; Also see Biography of Robert Treat Paine at Colonial Hall.com
12 George Bancroft, *History of the United States, From the Discovery of the American Continent* (Little, Brown and Company, Boston, MA), 1866, Vol. IX, p. 492
13 Benjamin Franklin, Franklin's Autobiography, O. Leon Reid, Editor (American Book Co., NY), 1896, p. 74
14 Lewis Henry Boutell, *The Life of Roger Sherman* (Chicago: A. C. McClurg and Company, 1896), pp. 272-273
15 William Federer, *America's God and Country: Encyclopedia of Quotations*, (Fame Publishing, TX), 1993. P. 460
16 Ibid, p. 460
17 J. Wallace Hamilton, *Horns and Halos in Human Nature* (Fleming H. Revel, NY), 1954, p. 35
18 This was taken mostly from my research from Stephane Courtois, Nocolas Werth, Jean-Louis Panne, Andrezj Paczkowski, Karel Bartosek, and Jean-Louis Margolin, *The Black Book of Communism, Crimes, Terror, Repression* (Harvard University Press, MA), 1999
19 Quote commonly attributed to Pastor Dietrich Bonhoeffer who was imprisoned at Buchenwald Prison Camp. Following a rigged trial within the camp aided by testimony from phony witnesses, he was hung on April 19, 1945, just two weeks before Allied Forces liberated the camp. The quote also is later made by Pastor Martin Niemöller in 1946, most likely emerging from one of his classes in response to a student's question of "Why did the Church not do anything?" In November 1945 Niemöller visited the former Dachau concentration camp, where he had been imprisoned from 1941 to April 1945. His diary entry about that visit and some subsequent speeches he gave imply that that visit triggered his remembrances with the quotation forthcoming.

www.ingramcontent.com/pod-product-compliance
Lightning Source LLC
Chambersburg PA
CBHW031402290426
44110CB00011B/232